In Their Own Write
Adventures In The Music Press

Printed in the United Kingdom by MPG Books Ltd

Published by Sanctuary Publishing Limited, Sanctuary House, 45-53 Sinclair
Road, London W14 0NS, United Kingdom

www.sanctuarypublishing.com

ISBN: 1-86074-341-2

In Their Own Write
Adventures In The Music Press

Paul Gorman

About The Author

Paul Gorman has contributed to and held editorial positions at a bewildering range of periodicals and publications, from *The Meat Trades Journal* to *Mojo* via *The Daily Telegraph*, *Crops Weekly*, *The Grocer*, *The Radio Times*, *Heat*, *The Evening Standard*, *Screen International*, *The Guardian*, *Music Week* and *Music Business International*. His first book, *The Look: Adventures In Pop & Rock Fashion*, was published by Sanctuary in spring 2001. He lives in north London, approximately 400 yards from where he was born.

Reviews for *The Look* by Paul Gorman

"The finest and best-researched book yet about British
post-war fashions" - *Mojo*

"You simply have to get hold of this book" - *The Evening Standard*

"A vital contribution to the style debate - ★★★★" - *Q*

"Paul Gorman's intricately researched book is a must for anyone
interested in the influence of rock and pop icons on style" - *OK!*

"In these well-executed and fascinating 'adventures in pop and rock
fashion' you can judge the importance of pop's stance
over the last 50 years - 8/10" - *Loaded*

"This book is a must for all pop culture fans" - *Marie Claire*

"Gorman covers everything from The Beatles to Bowie,
bringing the styles to life by talking to designers, tailors, stars
and style icons past and present" - *The Face*

Acknowledgements

The journalists covered in this book represent a fraction of those who have laboured within what would loosely be described as the confines of the music press over the last 50-odd years. Some were simply unavailable, some didn't quite make it and there were even some who did but are not represented here for reasons of space, time and narrative flow. Maybe next time!

I am indebted to the following for their assistance, time, participation and patience: Keith Altham, Julie Burchill, Garry Bushell, David Cavanagh, Robert Christgau, Caroline Coon, Richard Cook, Carol Cooper, Ian Cranna, Cameron Crowe, David Dalton, Anthony DeCurtis, Fred Dellar, Paul Du Noyer, Chuck Eddy, Ben Edmonds, Mark Ellen, Mick Farren, Hugh Fielder, Danny Fields, Ben Fong-Torres, Pete Frame, Simon Frith, Jerry Gilbert, Charlie Gillett, Vivien Goldman, Jonathon Green, John Harris, Mary Harron, David Hepworth, Paolo Hewitt, Tom Hibbert, Bill Holdship, Lindsay Hutton, Allan Jones, Dylan Jones, Lenny Kaye, Harvey Kubernik, Nick Logan, Maurice Kinn (RIP), Ian MacDonald, Dave Marsh, Richard Meltzer, Barry Miles, Charles Shaar Murray, Glenn O'Brien, Lucy O'Brien, Tony Parsons, John Peel, Richard Reigel, Simon Reynolds, Ira Robbins, Lisa Robinson, Chris Salewicz, Jon Savage, Greg Shaw, Pete Silverton, Sylvie Simmons, Mat Snow, Neil Spencer, Danny Sugerman, Phil Sutcliffe, Jerry Thackray, David Toop, Steve Turner, Tony Tyler, Jaan Uhelszki, Marc Weingarten, Chris Welch, Chas de Whalley, Mark Williams, Paul S Williams and Richard Williams.

At Sanctuary: Penny Braybrooke, Dan Froude, Alan Heal, Jeff Hudson, Michelle Knight.

Transcription (partial): Lee Coventry.

Special thanks to Charles Shaar Murray for his Jim Dandy intro. Bastard indeed.

In particular, I'd like to thank Barney Hoskyns and his superb website, rocksbackpages.com. Go visit now. Also Scott Woods and rockcritics.com and salon.com.

Dedications

You're my inspiration: The three Ni(c)ks – Cohn, Kent, Tosches.

My crew...their personalities...have changed: Bobby "Blue" Ashton and Paula "Horse" McGinley, Jimmy Brown, Matthew Cang, Tony Farsides, Charlie Fenn, Joe Foster, John Hazelton, Simon Holland, Colleen Ironside, Lloyd and Jill Johnson, Max Karie and Pippa Brooks, Dave Knight, Robert "El Rey" Lopez, Bruce Marcus, Nat, Pat and Eloise Morgan, Nick Pedgrift, Graham "Lunk" Proudlove, Kevin Rowland, Paul Stokes and Debby Raven, Jay Strongman and Julienne Davies, Bruce Marcus, Martin Reboul, James Topham and Babs Weston.

Zhu-zhu-zhu: Mark Donnelly.

Love and thanks to Jen and the Ross clan.

Far hipper than the *NME* – the *Meat Trades Journal*: Derek "Pouvez-vous?" Chapman and Jerry "Mouse" Leese, who taught me about the fine art of hackery and the real meaning of fun; Frosoulla Constantinou; the magnificent Peter Fleming; Peter Graves; Mike "Dad" Hall; Graham Large; Gary Mason; David Mattes. RIP: Tony Pike, Tony Wigston, Tony Williamson.

At Maggie's Bar in eternity: Staff and Tom.

First and last in war: Michael, Anne, Emma, Neil, Louis, Bessie, Alice and Jon, David and Julie, Katherine and Dorathea, Philippa (and Shanghai Tang!), Joanna, Esme, Zoe, Timothy and Tony.

For Caroline Moss: first-class editress and hackette.

Contents

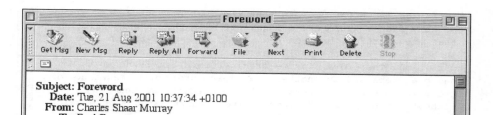
Subject: **Foreword**
   Date: Tue, 21 Aug 2001 10:37:34 +0100
  From: Charles Shaar Murray
     To: Paul Gorman

Dear Paul

Thanks for sending me the book. In the words of Mr Spock, it's
fascinating, Captain, if only because, when you're in the thick
of things and it's a total frenzy, 24/7, you often have no idea
what was going on in another part of the forest or how any of it
seemed to anybody else. Your book will come as a revelation not
only to its readers but, I should imagine, to most of your
interviewees.

You've captured a unique cultural moment. The heyday of the
rock press was an intriguing, and unrepeatable, phenomenon. When
we were crap, we were awful, admittedly; but when we were good,
we were brilliant. So why can't it happen again?

For starters, let me offer a no-names-no-packdrill snapshot of
life in the rock-mag racket circa summer 2001. Not too long ago,
an ambitious and creative New York-based editor talks his
publisher into backing a new magazine which aspires to be as
eclectic and in-depth as 'Mojo' but with a more contemporary and
less retro vibe, as snappy and irreverent as vintage 'Creem',
classic 'NME' or early 'Spin'. The idea was to transgress
arbitrary musical boundaries, toss rock, pop, R&B, hip-hop and
jazz into the same cauldron and heat it until it bubbled into
something neither blandly mainstream nor indie-elitist, something
that provided an indication about how different musics and sub-
cultures can interact with each other. The publisher green-
lights the idea and the editor swings into action.

For the first few issues, everything seems cool. The editor
rounds up name writers and turns them loose on prominent
artists, notching up a few enviable exclusives. Reader response
is enthusiastic, the publisher is happy and the periodical
distribution trade likes it. Sales are pretty good — not
fantastic but highly encouraging.

Eight months in, the whole thing had gone pear-shaped. In
order to survive, the magazine was forced to retool itself as a
specifically hard-rock/heavy-metal product. What went wrong? Very
simply, record company advertising departments didn't like it.
What didn't they like about it? It represented poor bang-for-
the-buck value for ad expenditure, because its eclectic,
holistic approach meant that a label might risk chucking an ad
for a hip-hop album at readers who might prefer heavy metal and
vice versa. What ad execs like are specialist hip-hop mags in
which they can advertise their hip-hop albums, specialist hard-

rock mags in which they can tout the rock product and so forth. So they didn't support the magazine, with the immediate result that the shortfall between news-stand sales and bottom-line income meant that the publisher was losing approximately $60,000 per issue. Therefore, in its original form, it is no more. It has been replaced by another, far less interesting magazine with the same name and produced by the same editorial team but without the open-minded, inquisitive, generalistic stance which made the prototype so attractive.

Never mind, though. The advertisers are happy. And these days, that's what counts.

In a strange way, it's an echo of what happened to 'Musician', another ambitious, eclectic and now defunct American music magazine. A change of editor had meant that the magazine wasn't exactly at one of its all-time peaks of editorial excellence, but this time it was the advertising departments of instrument manufacturers, rather than record companies, that struck the death blow. What was the point, they asked, of advertising guitars to readers who might be keyboard players, saxophonists or drummers? It made considerably better economic sense to advertise guitars in guitarists' mags, drums in drummers' mags, etc. So an excellent magazine went down the tubes, against the wishes of readers and writers, because nowadays neither of these factions wield very much power in the world of periodical publishing. Hipper readers and writers may enjoy generalist magazines, but advertisers like specialist platforms from which they can target specialist markets. Guess who wins?

This is now. The reason that there was ever a rock press vital and vibrant enough for you to want to write a book like this, and for anyone to consider reading it, is that, back in the day, no one knew anything — except, of course, that popular music and the culture that surrounded it was bizarre and fascinating, and that we wanted to write about the music, about the culture and about the subjects that the music and the culture seemed to be about. I'm thinking specifically about the 'NME' of the '70s, because that's where I served my time and it's the magazine environment I know best, but I'm sure it applies equally to other rags. The bottom line is this: You could never have created the 'NME' of the '70s in a marketing meeting, and even if you had, you could never have found the people capable of producing such a monstrosity through any conventional publishing channels.

The rock press evolved the way it did because of a variety of historical accidents, large and small. The end of World War II created an economic boom in the West, which led to the invention of the teenager. This was both economically and socially necessary, socially because kids wanted to enjoy adolescence as a life-stage in its own right, rather than simply an uncomfortable transitionary phase between childhood and adult responsibility, and economically because, once kids had money of their own and distinctive tastes, it made good monetary sense to find things to sell to them. One of those things was rock 'n' roll. Kids dug it because it spoke to them about their lives, while businesses liked it because it gave kids something on which to spend their money.

The ancillary industries which sprang up around rock and pop included printed matter, and as the music gradually broadened its scope — drawing notions of increased musical intricacy from jazz and classical music, a higher degree of emotional authenticity from blues and soul and greater lyrical complexity, depth and political involvement from the world of folk music — it became apparent that writing about this stuff in terms appropriate to the forms that the music was taking represented more and more of a challenge. Initially, this happened outside the mainstream music press (which existed primarily to service the pop industry), in what was known as the underground press. This took the form of vicious satire, incendiary political agitprop, psychedelic fantasising and hardcore sex and drugs. And 'Rolling Stone', of course.

In Britain, the authorities essentially hammered the underground press out of existence with harassment, busts and prosecutions, the most notorious being the 1971 'Oz' trial, which left a bunch of talented and stroppy people with nowhere to go but a music press ripe for revitalisation. It was the transplant of underground elements to the slovenly but basically genteel world of the mainstream pop weeklies that ended up making my old almer mater unique. But that was still only one factor.

The other, and most important, was that, as I said, no one knew anything. There was no MTV, no plethora of 24-hour music radio stations. The national press only paid attention to the uppermost strata of the rock and pop worlds, and pretty cursory attention at that. The music press pretty much had the scene to itself. If a company wanted to break an act, they had no option but to come to us, and we were left alone to do the job however we saw fit. As long as we kept selling papers, making money and not getting sued too often, the management more or less let us get on with it.

And we did. No one was doing marketing surveys every three months and then coming in and telling us which aspects of the paper to play up and which to drop. Obviously, the execs, accountants and bean counters didn't like it if something we wrote lost us advertising or landed us in court, but as long as we kept those papers moving, no one worried too much. It felt as though we were working to our own crowd without outsiders hanging over our collective shoulders and second-guessing us. We, the readers and the musicians were (more or less) on the same side. Most important of all, there was a certain kind of writing — and not always necessarily specifically about music — that, in those days, you literally couldn't do anywhere else. The music press represented an alternative to a stultifying, self-congratulatory and highly privileged junior literary establishment (who are now, of course, the mainstream literary

11

establishment). For people like myself or Jon Savage or Tony Parsons and Julie Burchill or any number of the champs, chumps and charlatans interviewed here, there was literally nowhere else to go — for a while, at least. We eventually became victims of our own success. Everybody wanted a piece of pop, and the number of promotional outlets offered by the media to the music industry dramatically increased. And everybody wanted a piece of the kind of writing offered by the music press at its best, so the number of potential platforms for both established and rising writers increased, also. The specialist music press found itself marginalised, sidelined in the race for writers, access to artists and advertising revenue.

Now there's a glut of pop and of coverage of pop. The music and publishing industries now command marketing and research facilities undreamed of in those more innocent and chaotic days, and they've successfully eliminated most of the random factors that help interesting stuff to happen. Nothing gets released or published by a major corporation without a degree of intensive focus-group activity that would make even New Labour blush. If I was 20 years old today, as opposed to 30 years ago, I very much doubt whether the music press, as currently constituted, would be the focus of my efforts to get into print. Hell, I'm not even sure I'd be reading it, let alone listening to as much rock, pop and related stuff as I did in the late '60s and early '70s. These days, most pop, and most writing about pop, is just toothpaste. Once upon a time, it wasn't. Once upon a time, this shit actually mattered — to a lot of different people and for a lot of different reasons, but it mattered just the same.

Like I said, the whole shebang was the result of a bunch of historical accidents, large and small. Still, I wouldn't have missed it for the world. After all, if I had, I might have ended up as a civil servant or a librarian.

And you've brought it all back. You bastard. You'll be hunted down and strangled like a dog for this.

Charles Shaar Murray
August 2001

12

Introduction

This book tells the story of the golden age of the rock and pop press, which lasted from the late '50s - when teen magazines and Tin Pan Alley journals started to address the emerging musical form properly - until the early to mid '80s. During that period, the standards of critical excellence and sheer good writing in this field were raised in America by an array of periodicals, from the celebratory *Crawdaddy!* and the radical *Creem* to the hilarious *Rock Scene*, the fantastic *16* magazine, the historically aware *Who Put The Bomp?* and, let's face it, the mould-breaking, genre-defining, corporate-cock-sucking but frankly unbeatable-in-its-time *Rolling Stone*.

In the UK, these functions were fulfilled by the inkies (so-called because the publishers cared not a jot for investment in production values and the cheapest of print processes left avid readers with ink-stained fingertips), led by *Melody Maker*, *Sounds* and, of course, the *New Musical Express*. While the UK attempted to emulate the long-view critical stance of the US with overly-earnest titles such as *Let It Rock*, *Cream* and *Street Life*, the Brits were actually best at the rapid-fire weekly turnover thrown up by the ever-spinning action/reaction cycle of pop on this tiny island.

Not for nothing did Johnny Rotten squeal, "I use the *NME*/I use anarcheee!" on The Sex Pistols' epochal debut single, 'Anarchy In The UK', in October 1976. Since its early-'70s overhaul and co-option of the best that the underground press had to offer, the *NME* became a mandatory read for anyone with an eye to popular culture.

There aren't many publications that you can say that about. For a couple of years, every issue had to be read, for fear of missing out on a weekly broadside from the heart of the *zeitgeist*, whether it was Nick Kent providing immediate overviews of pretty much scorned masterpieces by mavericks such as Brian Wilson, Nick Drake, Iggy Pop, Lou Reed, Tim Buckley and Syd Barrett; Pete Erskine tracking the hypnotic Eurogrooves of Can and the rootsiness of Little Feat; Chrissie

Hynde jubilantly reporting from the front line of teen hysteria surrounding the likes of David Cassidy; or Charles Shaar Murray palling it up with Bowie and Bolan.

Tony Parsons (an alumnus who is now Britain's biggest-selling novelist) recalls in these pages how, during a trip around Europe in 1975, he perpetually pestered news-stand operators from Budapest to Paris, such was his zeal, his need for an *NME* infusion. And he wasn't alone; all the while that the *NME* bit the hands of the record companies that advertised and paid for expensive junkets – with manoeuvres such as placing the headline "Is This Man A Prat?" over a photograph of Freddie Mercury – its circulation grew and grew.

Overseen by Nick Logan (a key figure in the development of the music press, along with Jann Wenner), the *NME* was happily under the thrall of Tom Wolfe's New Journalism, striking alliances with such fellow travellers as *Creem*'s Lester Bangs and charging through the mid-'70s doldrums with a manifesto that, with hindsight, created the foundations for punk and every subsequent youth movement. However – and this is the key – it was done with élan, an often drugged-up Dog Days Of Glam sense of style. No one typifies this slightly slurred, unsteady on its bony legs, fuck-you stance better than Nick Kent.

For me, one of Kent's assignments – covering Jethro Tull in the US in 1975 – summed up everything that was great about the paper. He was flown to Los Angeles by the record company and put up in some swanky hotel, into which he immediately installed his hero, friend and fellow drug fiend Iggy Pop. On Chrysalis' tab, they purchased every piece of expensive luggage that they could from the shops in the lobby and sold them for "medication". They then proceeded to have their definition of a real good time. On his return, Kent wrote an absolutely glowing piece about Iggy – whose career had gone into an apparently terminal decline – and slagged Jethro Tull to the ground. For us punters, it was obvious – Ian Anderson was wandering around in a bejewelled codpiece tootling away on a flute and deserved everything coming to him, while Iggy was an incredibly glamorous doomed angel whose day would arrive very soon.

Exactly when the music press ran out of steam is difficult to gauge, even for this writer, who has spent close to 30 years nurturing an unhealthy interest in the subject. According to Charles Shaar Murray (and he should know), the launch of *Smash Hits* and *The Face* did for the hegemony of the inkies. Certainly, these two glossy magazines introduced pop, street fashion and lifestyle as viable commercial prospects into the publishing world.

While the national broadsheets and tabloids filleted the music press for critical insight and spicy titbits in equal measure, the individual elements were broken down to provide seedbeds for entire banks of magazines based solely on different strands of pop, fashion and entertainment, from *Vibe*, *Kerrang!*, *Q*, *The Source*, *Spin*, *Details*, *Select*, *Vox*, *Muzik*, *MixMag*, *Ministry*, *Jockey Slut*, *Sleaze Nation*, *Grand Royal*, *20/20* and *Mojo* to a revivified *GQ*, *Sassy*, *Raygun*, *Arena*, *Maxim*, *Stuff*, *Loaded*, *i-D*, *Blitz*, *Dazed & Confused* - the list goes on. And on. A recent and significant addition is *Blender*, the brainchild of the most astute operator in the field, Felix Dennis, marrying the "New Lad" ethic to broad-church, mainstream music.

As these came (and a lot went), the music press itself fell into petty bickering, careerism, notional empire building and eventual disarray. Wrong-footed and unsure whether to address politics or pop or to dread "youth issues", the seeds were sown for the demise of virtually every title, from *Zigzag* and *Disc And Music Echo* (which were actually not that missed) to the pathetic declines of the once-fine likes of *Creem*, *Sounds*, *Record Mirror* and *Melody Maker*.

In the meantime, *Rolling Stone* continued to reinvent itself anew, most recently for the Britney generation, although a serious slump in ad revenues in 2001 indicates that riding the teen-pop wave may prove perilous.

Of the inkies, the *NME* is last man standing. Just about. Ahead of its 50th anniversary celebrations in 2001, a "radical" redesign was unveiled. Their free-access website, www.nme.com, goes from strength to strength, but the *NME* fiddles with format (should it be A4? a version of *Rolling Stone*?) while circulation figures burn. Sales dropped close to ten per cent in the six months preceding the relaunch announcement. Uh-oh.

This book is also about how the music press proved eventually to be the most potent breeding ground in popular culture.

All these people have one thing in common: movie directors Cameron Crowe, Chris Petit, Michael Winner and Mary Harron; Hollywood screenwriter Joe Eszterhas; Oscar-winning song lyricist Don Black; novelists Mick Farren, Tony Parsons and Miranda Sawyer; cultural commentators Julie Burchill, Caroline Coon, Greil Marcus, PJ O'Rourke, Jon Savage, Cynthia Rose, Stuart Maconie, Barry Miles and Simon Reynolds; leading jazzers Benny Green, Humphrey Lyttelton and Max Jones; television movers and shakers Kurt Loder, Anthony DeCurtis, Stuart Cosgrove and Graham Linehan; writers Lester Bangs, David Cavanagh, Robert Christgau, Nik Cohn, David Dalton, Robert Elms, Danny Fields, Jonathon Green, Vivien Goldman, Barney Hoskyns, Ian MacDonald, Dave Marsh, Richard Meltzer, Paul Morley, Ian Penman, Lisa Robinson, Johnny Rogan, Chris Salewicz, Danny Sugerman, Nick Tosches, Hunter S Thompson, Chris Welch, Timothy White and Tom Wolfe; academics Simon Frith and Dave Laing; pop stars Chrissie Hynde, Bob Geldof, Lenny Kaye, Sandy Pearlman, Patti Smith and Neil Tennant; music business executives Moira Bellas, Dave Dorrell, Danny Goldberg, Jon Landau and Richard Robinson; magazine publishing executives Mark Ellen, David Hepworth, Dylan Jones, Nick Logan, Bill Prince and James Truman; DJs Steve Lamacq, John Peel, Gary Crowley and Kris Needs; television executives Alan Marke, Paul Rambali, Graham K Smith; television personality Danny Baker; Internet mogul Danny Kelly; national newspaper columnists Garry Bushell, Barbara Ellen, Pete Silverton and Neil Spencer; leading publicists Barbara Charone, Alan Edwards, Jerry Gilbert, Rob Partridge, Jonathan Morrish...

I could go on, but you get the idea. They all worked for the music press.

No other media sub-sect could house such a spectrum of tastes and attitudes, from the proto-feminist, forever counter-cultural Caroline Coon and the up-against-the-wall-motherfuckery of Mick Farren to the saturnine Nick Tosches and the tabloid pundit Garry Bushell, whose allegiance to the right-wing Oi! movement rattles cages 20 years down the line; from the bloated tragedy that was Lester Bangs to the elegant Lisa Robinson, who now edits *Vanity Fair*'s annual music issue, one of the best places to read about the state of play in pop and rock these days.

So this is the collective story of many of those who loomed large in the pop and rock press. And it's in their own words, as hack autobiographies have it. But be warned: this is no dust-dry account of publishing launches and circulation fluctuations. Nor is it a chin-stroking debate on "whither the music press in the digital age?" Among these tales lurk death, drugs, drink, divorce, infidelity, jail, sex, celebrity, fame, obsession, jealousy, nervous breakdowns, industrial action, one or two fistfights, some typewriters flying through windows and a hell of a lot of back-biting, bitching and score-settling.

Oh, and Nick Kent's pink underpants.

All of human life, in other words. Well, the best bits, at least.

Paul Gorman
London
October 2001

1 "They Had To Start Writing About It"

"In 1952, Jerry Wexler changed the name of Billboard's *'race music' chart to 'rhythm and blues'. That's where magazine coverage of rock 'n' roll started. Because they had the chart, they had to start writing about it."*
> – Greg Shaw

NME AND MELODY MAKER
"ACTUALLY, I'D LIKE TO HEAR SOME OF THAT"

CHRIS WELCH *Melody Maker* was launched in 1926 and even continued during the London Blitz, when its offices were bombed and newsprint was rationed. At the *Melody Maker*, we used to have a wonderful photograph of one of our reporters, Chris Hayes, working away wearing an air raid warden's tin helmet.

JOHN PEEL In 1976, I was required to produce a radio documentary on the 50th anniversary of the *Melody Maker*. I got to go down and look at the archives, and the cover story of the first *Melody Maker* was "The Banjo In The Modern Dance Orchestra", and that's never left me. I thought that was terrific.

MAURICE KINN One Friday afternoon in January 1953, I got a call from someone on the *Musical & Accordion Express* telling me the paper had lost so much money it was going to close down if they couldn't find a buyer by the following Monday. It had only been launched the year before and wasn't very good, particularly up against *Melody Maker*, which had been going for years and really did the jazz and big-band movements well.

CHRIS WELCH My brother and I were both jazz fans at school around the time rock 'n' roll was just coming in, and we picked up on *Melody Maker* because it was a hipper magazine. The *NME* was very much a pop paper, and we preferred Dizzy Gillespie and Stan Kenton.

MAURICE KINN I was running my booking agency, representing some really popular big-band people like Joe Loss and Cyril Stapleton, so I wasn't really that interested. They were asking £1,000 for the paper, but I went in there to talk to them because they owed me money and got caught up with this idea of running the paper. They were on their knees – within 15 minutes, the receiver was going to be called in.

CHARLIE GILLETT In the '50s and into the early '60s, the distinction between the two was that *Melody Maker* was always orientated towards the live scene, as in proper individual gigs as opposed to package tours, while the *NME* would follow the pop format.

CHRIS WELCH The *Melody Maker* seemed incredibly hip. There was no television to speak of in those days, but it carried weekly coverage of this almost underground music scene, which made you feel like part of a secret society. I used to like Steve Race when he wrote for it. Ironically, he was a presenter on children's TV, but he was also a very good jazz writer. But of course there was Max Jones, who was a great authority in blues and jazz. I discovered later, when I worked for it, that most of the people he wrote about were personal friends.

MAURICE KINN I kept the agency going, which I had to, because the paper – which changed its name – kept on losing money hand over fist. Two months later, I had to borrow money from my mother-in-law to keep the *NME* afloat and I felt like an idiot, like I'd really made a mistake. In that two months, I'd noticed that they had this chart but they weren't doing anything with it. There were these names in there like Johnny Ray or Frank Sinatra or Nat "King" Cole, but they weren't getting the coverage. Instead, it was all about the big-band scene, which was beginning to fade away. So I got hold of the chart and said, "These are the people we should be covering, and the chart should be the reason why people buy the paper." Using my agency, we also promoted big dances with the big-name bandleaders. After a few months, it really started to pick up, and within a year or so the circulation doubled to 36,000.

RICHARD WILLIAMS From when I was about twelve or 13, I read *Melody Maker*, mostly. It wasn't remotely convincing on pop music but it was very good on jazz. I played in bands as well – skiffle groups, folk groups, beat groups and an R&B group – so the *Melody Maker* was the one I liked best. Writers like Bob Dawbarn, Bob Houston, Max Jones – they dealt with music quite intelligently.

JOHN BROVEN I was at Bexhill Grammar School, where one of my classmates was Mike Leadbitter. When rock 'n' roll became popular, he started to dig beneath the surface of Elvis and Little Richard and was buying EPs and 78s by Fats Domino and Chuck Willis. He was a great influence on me, and I can remember finding everything I needed to know about new artists and what records were out in the *NME*. I remember buying my first issue of the *NME* on Brighton station in January 1957 on my way to see Portsmouth play in a first-division match against Burnley.

CHRIS WELCH Apart from anything else, it was a great newspaper as well, done in the style of popular tabloids of the day, *The People* and *The Daily Mirror*. It wasn't a dry-as-dust musicians' magazine but a general paper, with big bold pictures and headlines and shock news. There was a big story about Nat "King" Cole being attacked by racists when he supported The Ted Heath Orchestra on a tour of the Southern states. People say it was all about mouthpieces and classified ads, but it wasn't at all.

MAURICE KINN In 1954, as an extension of the big-band gigs we'd been promoting, I decided to set up the *NME* awards concert at the Albert Hall. Everyone thought I was crazy. They couldn't see why kids would want to come along to see all these acts on the same bill. To me, it seemed obvious, after years of packaging artists. The readers' polls started to help push up the circulation, and a year later we had 100,000 readers and I bought my first Rolls-Royce.

JOHN PEEL The *NME* and *Melody Maker* weren't readily available in the places I went to, so I read things like *Jazz Monthly* and *Jazz Journal*, although I knew nothing about jazz. I liked the kind of fervour of the writing. They used to give a terrible slagging to people like Earl Bostic, and I used to think, "Actually, I'd really like to hear some of that." But the people who wrote for them were all fanatics, really, people who said it couldn't be jazz if it had a saxophone. It was that fanaticism which I found attractive. I just liked the idea of them being so convinced that theirs was the only truth.

JOHN BROVEN My friend Mike Leadbitter caused a bit of a stir in 1960 when he wrote a letter to *Jazz Journal* pointing out that there was a lot of blues music it didn't cover. *Jazz Journal* had no feel for R&B. It had quite an impact; several people wrote in subsequently saying that they were buying Jimmy Reed records, which started to connect all of us up.

MAURICE KINN In 1953, when Frank Sinatra was at the lowest ebb of his career – he'd just broken up with Ava Gardner and come to Britain after a disastrous tour of Italy, where the fans had booed him and called for Ava – we gave him a chance to put his side of the story, and he never forgot our support. A couple of years later, my wife and I visited him in LA, on the set of this movie he was making called *Not As A Stranger*, and he flew us to Las Vegas and paid for our stay at the Sands.

MILES I read *NME* and *Melody Maker* until 1959, then moved on to jazz, reading *Down Beat* – Nat Hentoff and those guys.

HARVEY KUBERNIK Phil Spector told me he wrote a letter to *Down Beat* in 1956 protesting the exclusion of Barney Kessel in an article. A lot of people had letters printed in magazines before they jump-started their careers in music or the press. It was their way of showing their interest in the subject and their only outlet.

MILES I didn't see a copy of *NME* again until 1976, when I started writing for them. And I don't remember any writers from back then. They would have all been Denmark Street hacks, anyway.

MAURICE KINN We had a lot of talented people working for us and a lot of people who went on to work in other spheres. Michael Winner was the film critic for a while. Benny Green wrote for us. Chris Hutchins, who became a leading newspaper reporter. Don Black's first job was as the office boy. This was 1954, when he was 15. One day, I rang a story across from Hollywood and he offered to take it because he said he had shorthand. The following week, the paper arrives and there's nothing there. "What happened to the story, Don?" I asked. "I couldn't read my own shorthand!" he confessed. Every year, when he sends me a Christmas card, he always puts a message in shorthand.

JOHN MAJOR (IN A LETTER TO MAURICE KINN) In my youth, the weekly copy of the *NME* was an absolute must for me.

JOHN BROVEN We didn't realise it at the time, but the music publishers had a tight stranglehold on the *NME*. American rock 'n' roll was always better than British rock 'n' roll, but I can never understand why some of the great American originals never got into the British chart. It transpires that there was collusion between the publishers and the *NME* to ensure that British artists covered the American hits and charted here. A lot of those US originals – particularly on London-American – sold a lot more than you appreciated from the chart position.

CHRIS WELCH At school, we were divided into *Melody Maker* and *NME* readers. They tended to be Elvis and Buddy Holly fans, and there was quite a lot of rivalry.

MAURICE KINN Through the *NME*, I got to know everyone, even people like Elvis and Tom Parker. He used to organise interviews with Elvis for me, always provided front-row tickets and used to take regular adverts in the *NME*. He also organised for Elvis to record a special message for the *NME* pollwinners' concert one year, when he said he was looking forward to coming over and sent his best regards to Jimmy Saville.

MICK FARREN Remember, I'm incredibly old. I was a punter in the late '50s, when, as an eleven-year-old, I'd get the *NME* because it was tougher than the *Melody Maker*, in those days. It ran articles on Gene Vincent and Jerry Lee, while the *Melody Maker* still had that jazzer, snotty attitude. Its pop coverage was Petula Clark interviews.

MAURICE KINN We always championed Sammy Davis Jr, because I'd seen him several times in LA and Vegas, but he was an unknown quantity in Britain until 1960, when he was booked to play the Royal Variety Show, followed by a season at La Pigalle restaurant in the West End. He asked me to throw a party for him so that he could meet some of his fellow performers. Everybody came along to our flat in Upper Grosvenor Street – Lonnie Donegan, Russ Conway, Janet Scott, Connie Francis, Lionel Blair, Alma Cogan, Dickie Valentine...everybody. That night, he put on an impromptu performance. He just got up and sang and danced and told stories. It lasted for 40 minutes, and that was his debut in the UK. Then he persuaded all the other entertainers to each do a turn. It helped launch his career. The entire run at La Pigalle was sold out, and I've never seen this before or since, but when he sang 'The Birth Of The Blues' at the Royal Variety Show, the audience stood up and applauded during the song. While it was going on! They couldn't wait 'til the end.

RICHARD WILLIAMS At that stage, I liked Elvis and The Shadows and bands like that, when I was a kid, but I didn't particularly like the way the *NME* wrote about them, in a superficial kind of way.

CHARLIE GILLETT The *NME* was good because it did actually cover everything. If any new artist came into the chart, it was almost the duty of the paper to cover that artist in some way. I bought the *NME* every week, even at the age of 15. I started cutting the chart out. I've still got all these little charts stapled together from that time. So, when I was researching *Sound Of The City* in the second half of the '60s, I had my own little archive, even then.

JOHN PEEL I used to get highly incensed over the reviews in *Melody Maker* and the *NME*, which were all based on the premise that rock 'n' roll was an embarrassing and transitory thing. They would just fall upon anything that represented an alternative to rock 'n' roll and write things like "Is Calypso The New Rock 'n' Roll?" when Harry Belafonte came along. There was a record by Perez Prado, 'Cherry Pink And Apple Blossom White', and they inevitably asked, "Is Mambo The Next Rock 'n' Roll?"

CHRIS WELCH I was playing drums in a group and we went through all the phases – trad jazz, skiffle, modern jazz – and *Melody Maker* covered all those phases. It was knocked for not covering rock 'n' roll, but it did, even though the jazz critics were very scathing about the likes of Bill Haley.

RICHARD WILLIAMS Jack Good's column in *Disc* was fantastic. He'd take the whole column – probably about 1,000 words – to write about 'Duke Of Earl' by Gene Chandler or 'Hey Baby' by Bruce Chanel. Although they were both hits at the time, they were nonetheless quite extreme in their own way, and he would write, saying, "These are the best things you've ever heard." I really responded to that.

THE US
"GET IT FOR AS LITTLE AS YOU CAN"

PETE SILVERTON I always admired the fact that Jerry Wexler coined the phrase "rhythm and blues" by writing about it for *Billboard*.

GREG SHAW *Hit Parader* really set the tone for the music press in America, because it was written intelligently, taking music away from the teenyboppers and putting it in a more serious context. In the early '60s, when I started reading it, the editorship was taken over by a guy called Jim Delahant. People like Lenny Kaye – all of us who got into the music press were inspired by him because, besides celebrity interviews and so on, he'd have features on unknown, esoteric bands. Weird folk singers, jazz no one cared about – he'd put it in there. He was a great writer, and he had the power to do it. Of course, there were other things like *16* magazine and *Dig*.

HARVEY KUBERNIK Kim Fowley wrote some columns for *Dig* in the late '50s. He used it as an entrée into the record business. He went to Goldstar Studios to interview The Champs when they were recording 'Tequila'. It was his way of getting in. Music journalism has been used a lot as a careerist move to work at a label or get a gig.

RANDI REISFELD AND DANNY FIELDS French-born literary agent Jacques Chambrun wanted to be a magazine publisher, and in 1956 he saw his opportunity. Elvis Presley was a cash cow, and Chambrun wanted to milk it any way he could. He bought a batch of previously published Presley stories and photos from a newspaper editor in Memphis and handed the material over to Desmond Hall, a former actor and one of the founding editors of *Mademoiselle* and at that time an agent in Chambrun's New York office. Hall in turn passed it onto George Waller, who fashioned it into a one-shot *All About Elvis* magazine. Unsurprisingly, sales were excellent, and early in 1957, Waller, who had written all the text and chosen all the photos, suggested to Chambrun he publish a magazine for young girls featuring young male rock 'n' roll singers and young male rock 'n' roll groups.

GEORGE WALLER *17* was very popular at the time and Des Hall proposed that the new magazine be called *16*, the idea being that it would appeal to girls up to 16.

RANDI REISFELD AND DANNY FIELDS None of the founding trio thought a male name on the masthead was a particularly savvy move, so they simply invented a female name.

GEORGE WALLER Georgia was suggested by my own first name and Winters was Des Hall's middle name, so the editor in chief was Georgia Winters.

RANDI REISFELD AND DANNY FIELDS The first issue is dated May 1957, its cover price 15¢. For the next year, the magazine came out quarterly, and while Waller filled its pages with such hot young performers as Elvis, Pat Boone, even James Dean, he did not personally interview any of the subjects but worked from press releases, previously published stories and some commissioned stories. From the get-go, *16* was done on the cheap – Waller, its only staffer, worked from home, and while some funds were spent on photos and stories, Chambrun's iron-clad rule was always "get it for as little as you can". Such was *16* when Gloria Stavers entered in 1958. She gave it life and was its heart and soul.

DAVE MARSH The reasons for Gloria's stature have to do with the way she used every issue of *16*, month after month, from 1958 to 1975, to express her absolute loyalty to a specific vision of teen culture. In *16*, this vivacious, flirtatious, surprisingly wide-eyed and innocent woman created her perfect world where all faces were blemish free and each cute boy was looking for someone like you.

DANNY FIELDS Chambrun was a weird French dirty old man who had sort of lucked into this magazine. Gloria Stavers was a runway model when she first got to New York, and she accompanied rich older European men to places like El Morocco, where she was famous for dancing barefoot, and she was living on her wits when he basically gave her *16* magazine to edit in 1958. It was then just reproductions of press clippings, and she said, "Why don't I go and interview Bobby Darin and do something different?" That's how she built it into this powerful publication, through her intelligence and her charm with boys and understanding of what little girls wanted.

2 "You Can Only Do That For So Long Without Going Mad"

"For most of the '60s, there was no serious journalism about rock, which probably helped build the mystique. What you didn't know you imagined while staring at album covers."
                                                    - Greg Shaw

FOLK
"ROCK WOULD NEVER BE THE SAME AGAIN"

STEVEN WARD In 1961, Paul Nelson and a college buddy started their own Minnesota-based folk music criticism magazine, *The Little Sandy Review*. Nelson and his friend John Pankake wanted to champion music's traditionalists. While Nelson stood in the audience and watched fellow University of Minnesota student Bob Dylan turn his acoustic-strumming folk music into an electric guitar thunderstorm, others in the audiences booed and threw various objects at Dylan. Nelson, on the other hand, was mesmerised and wrote about Dylan's new music like rock would never be the same.

HARVEY KUBERNIK I was buying magazines like *Dig*, which had pictures of Frankie Avalon and Paul Anka, a real pop paper. But, because I was living in southern California, I was buying other stuff - movie magazines like *Photoplay* and sports magazines. It all coalesced when Gloria Stavers got on the beat at *16*. She brought a vibe in and we picked up on music people that way. Some of the first pictures I saw of Dylan were in *16*. You'd think, "Who is this guy?" and then go and find an article about him in *The Saturday Evening Post* or *Time* or *Life*.

CHARLES M YOUNG When I was in junior high and high school, I could go to the supermarket and buy *Tiger Beat* or *16* and read questionnaires filled out by Dino, Desi and Billy, or I could go down to State Street and buy an underground newspaper with passionately propounded opinions about music and very little information. *Time* and *Life* would occasionally run features written by critics with a decidedly non-baby-boom sensibility.

HARVEY KUBERNIK There was *Teen Scene*, published out of Hollywood, and I had a big jones for the stable at Charlton Publications, like *Hit Parader*, because they published song lyrics and I liked the newsprint – it was black and white, gritty. Obviously, I realised it was done on the cheap, but there were really good photos in there of bands in the early to mid '60s. I went for them rather than the trades, like *Cashbox* and *Billboard* – they were expensive, but also they weren't true to the music. I didn't like seeing phrases like "race records" or the black music charts with all these guys with phony smiles holding plaques up. However, I did pick them up occasionally, and that's where I saw names like Jerry Wexler, Ahmet Ertegun, John Hammond, Phil Spector.

PAUL WILLIAMS What I particularly read and was inspired by was a local folk music weekly called *Boston Broadside*. Peter Stampfel's irreverent, enthusiastic column quite pleased me.

PAUL NELSON I first heard Dylan in Minnesota as Bobby Zimmerman. He was doing Harry Belafonte and Josh White songs. He was not writing his own songs yet. He didn't show much promise then. It changed fast. He sought us out at *The Little Sandy Review*.

HARVEY KUBERNIK We were slaves to the AM radio dial. *That's* where you got your information about pop, not necessarily from books or magazines.

ROBERT CHRISTGAU There was no music press to speak of when I was coming up, although I read Ralph Gleason in *The San Francisco Chronicle* when I lived in the Bay area in 1964 and Al Aronowitz in *The New York Post* later and did look at *Down Beat* occasionally.

LISA ROBINSON I was always into jazz, growing up in New York City. I used to sneak out of the house when I was literally about twelve to go see Miles Davis, Horace Silver and Charles Mingus, Thelonious Monk at the Five

Spot. I'd put my hair up and smear make-up on and wear high heels, try and look much older than I was and go and see great jazz.

THE BEATLES
"IT WAS OBVIOUS THEY WERE GOING TO BE HUGE"

KEITH ALTHAM I was an aspiring sports journalist working for *The Surrey Comet*. I had an interview at Fleetway Publications, which was *The Daily Mirror*'s magazine arm at the time. They saw on my CV that I was the school football captain and gave me a job on this magazine called *The Football Library*, but it fell apart after about six months, so the NUJ came up with this job ghosting disc columns for their teen mags *Marilyn*, *Roxy* and *Valentine*. They were teenage love-story comics, but sandwiched in there were articles on pop stars. I was 19 and it was the era of Marty Wilde, Billy Fury, Adam Faith, Cliff Richard, Jess Conrad. Most of them were pale imitations of Elvis, people like Larry Page, "the teenage rage". I ended up ghosting these columns for them.

MAURICE KINN I first met The Beatles at the 1962 Christmas party EMI threw at Abbey Road. They'd just had their first hit, and even then it was obvious they were going to be huge. The *NME*'s was the first chart they'd entered, and we'd done a feature on them right away. I knew Brian Epstein, because he went to school with my brother-in-law. He became a great friend, although he could be shy and reserved. Berenice, my wife, got on very well with him.

BERENICE KINN Brian could be very withdrawn, which you could mistake for sulking, or he was very sunny in his outlook. Either one or the other, nothing in between. I always thought Brian was a sad person, somehow unfulfilled. The gay world was so different then. I mean, we all knew and accepted him, but I think it was very tough for Brian. In 1964, we were staying at the Beverly Hills Hotel and he called up in an awful state. I went to his room and he'd been smoking marijuana and was suicidally depressed. He needed a shoulder to cry on and I sat up with him for four hours, talking and talking.

KEITH ALTHAM I remember seeing The Beatles do 'Please Please Me' in a little tiny room at EMI's at Manchester Square. Then you'd meet all the people who came down from Liverpool in their wake: Bill Harry - who was then the editor of *Merseybeat* and later became a PR in his own right - and Derek Taylor, who became The Beatles' PR.

DEREK TAYLOR I worked for a local paper in West Kirby when I left school and I learned journalism and I loved it very much right up to 1964, when I left to join Brian Epstein as his PA, working for The Beatles. I joined them because I had wanted to work for them, that was all. I'd been working for *The Daily Express*, but you can only do that for so long without going mad.

MAURICE KINN I was in the US when 'Please Please Me' started to really take off and called Percy Dickins and told him to book The Beatles immediately for the *NME* pollwinners' concert. They played every one between 1963 and 1966.

KEITH ALTHAM For the mags like *Valentine*, I usually did a series of six columns over a couple of months and had to interview the stars to get background to make it look like they were writing it. You'd end up with some innocuous copy - "Duane Eddy is a mid-tempo shuffler that I love listening to when I shave in the morning," that kind of crap. Then you'd ring it over to the manager. The first interview I did was with Frank Ifield in a small office off Hyde Park. This was prior to his yodelling fiascos. He had a number called 'Lucky Devil'. His manager was Peter Gordon, who then became Cliff Richard's manager. The thing that's stuck in my mind was that he had these bulging eyeballs, a bit like Tony Blair. [That] kind of threw me while I was doing the interview, but it didn't matter. We weren't even competing with the *NME* and *Melody Maker*. This was kid's stuff.

MAURICE KINN We always used to throw these big parties where everyone in showbiz would come along. Two of The Beatles lived nearby, while Brian was virtually across the road, so they were always around. I remember Ringo brought Michael Crawford - who was then just an aspiring actor - to one, and one of the others was with Richard Burton's first wife. There was one occasion when George Harrison and Pattie Boyd went missing. I found them performing on the bed in my daughter's room. I said, "This is neither the time nor the place," and got my camera.

KEITH ALTHAM Fleetway Magazines put on the pop Proms, which followed the last night of the classical Proms at the Royal Albert Hall. You'd have Kenny Ball, Billy Fury, Cliff Richard, The Dallas Boys, The Vernons Girls. One of them was very exciting, because it was just pre-beat boom. The Beatles closed the show and The Rolling Stones opened it, sandwiching all these people like Adam Faith, Shane Fenton and Billy Fury.

MICK FARREN There was a real crossover point at an *NME* pollwinners' concert I went to. Adam Faith and The Beatles were on the same bill, which showed how things were changing, and that reflected the magazine's coverage.

THE BEAT BOOM
"THEN IT BECAME FUN"

JOHN BROVEN In the early '60s, I re-established contact with Mike Leadbitter, and with another friend – Simon Napier – we used to have these record-playing sessions, and these developed into a network of blues collectors. There was a guy called Dave Williams who knew Brian Jones. In 1962, the first American folk/blues festival in the UK took place in Manchester with people like T-Bone Walker and Muddy Waters. I didn't go, but there was a convoy which went up from London, including Mick Jagger and Brian Jones shoved into the back of this van. If anybody says the Stones haven't got blues credentials, that disproves it. They really were there right at the beginning. But people like us weren't getting the info we need from the *NME*, because it never really progressed. It basically ran publicists' stories, and while it gave you the outline facts, it was, "What's your favourite colour?" and, "What music are you going to follow after rock 'n' roll?" Rock 'n' roll was going to end. They were convinced of that.

KEITH ALTHAM Fleetway, which became IPC, launched *Fabulous*, whose rise was synonymous with The Beatles. The first issue came out in the beginning of 1963 and sold a million copies. They were on the cover and it was just phenomenal. I started working for it as "Fab's Keith". Members of the staff became personalities with picture bylines, and then it became fun. The only person I liked prior to The Beatles was Adam Faith, because he was bright and interesting and witty. When they broke through and all these guys the same age as me emerged – The Animals from Newcastle, whoever – it was like having a large bunch of mates who played guitars. They were all interested in the same things as I was: girls, sport, drinking and having a good time.

JOHN BROVEN In 1962, Mike Leadbitter and Simon Napier formed the Blues Appreciation Society and started issuing newsletters, and the response was good. We found there was a generation who liked the same thing but had been starved. Then they formed *Blues Unlimited* in May 1963 and the British R&B thing was just starting to take off. The first issue was 200 copies done on a stencil machine in the attic of Simon's parents' antiques shop in Bexhill. I wrote an article on Jay Miller and Excello Records. Journalism hadn't entered my mind as a career, but Mike said, "You've got the records. You can write it."

MAURICE KINN Lennon could be a real handful – quite troublesome and rude, sometimes. Also, he didn't really like me, because I revealed the existence of his son in the "Alley Cat" column at a time when it was completely secret.

GEORGE TREMLETT (FROM MUSIC MILLIONAIRES) For John, it had been love at first sight the night he met Alma Cogan at the Knightsbridge home of Maurice Kinn.

MAURICE KINN Then they all got really annoyed when I wrote in "Alley Cat", "Did The Beatles leave their tarts in San Francisco?" Chris Hutchins had been covering their tour for us and told me they were screwing everything in sight. That's why they sent a postcard from the Georges V in Paris one time saying, "Having fun. Have ordered *NME* just to read "Alley Cat", of course!"

SIMON FRITH My first assignment was to interview Andrew Loog Oldham for *Isis*, the Oxford magazine, and that's still the most memorable. I sat in his empty office for a while and then two different people came in [Jagger and

Richards]. "But I don't want to talk to you," I said. "Well, you've got to," they replied.

KEITH ALTHAM It wasn't terribly pressurised in those days. You kind of knew that everybody was winging it. There were PR men like Les Perrin, but it was chummy, not cut-throat. The big money hadn't fully come in yet. It took nearly two years for all these bands to fully break in America, so during that time it was still Amateur Night Out and everybody was having a great time.

MAURICE KINN People used to get their info first hand from the *NME*. Sid Bernstein – who promoted The Beatles in the US and did things like Shea Stadium – saw their potential by reading *NME*. I remember telling my friend Burl Adams, who was vice president of MCA, that he should sign The Beatles in 1963, but he didn't and Capitol finally picked up on them. They were so big that the receptionist used to answer the phone by saying, "This is the Capitol Tower, home of The Beatles." Nat "King" Cole, who earned a hell of a lot of money for Capitol, told me he used to shout, "This is Nat 'King' Cole – fuck The Beatles!"

KEITH ALTHAM We used to have photo sessions down at Fleetway Publications. I rang up Epstein and asked him to get us The Beatles and he had the temerity to demand a taxi. We were all indignant, but I think he got it. They would come down and spend all afternoon doing silly pictures – on the phone, playing pianos, posing. These would be used for the next six months as posters in the teen papers.

MAURICE KINN We flew over for their first US tour, and it was murder when we stayed with them at the Plaza. There were kids everywhere. Then we went down to Miami for their second appearance on *The Ed Sullivan Show* and he was pissing himself with joy because he was a very dull, straight character and it helped his profile enormously.

KEITH ALTHAM When The Beatles cracked America and had five singles at the top, that's when it all began to change. When the realisation hit that there was huge money involved, it became more serious. More accountants, lawyers, press, agents. It became more specialised. Money was available, and you could make a career out of being a music journalist.

1963
"I REALLY THOUGHT IT COULDN'T GO ANY BIGGER"

MAURICE KINN Because we had been there first, championing The Beatles and writing about all these new groups entering the chart, the circulation started to go through the roof, way up beyond 300,000 a week. We were getting all the exclusives, so if you wanted to know anything about what was going on with them or the Stones, you had to read the *NME*.

PETER YORK When I started reading *New Musical Express* in my early teens, it was cobbled together from what I now realise were crude press releases – this group would tour, another would make a movie (they never did), groups' favourite food, they loved their mums – and it suited me fine.

MAURICE KINN In 1963, I was approached by Cecil King, head of the Mirror Group, which wanted to buy the *NME* for its IPC Magazines. I'd been approached a lot of times, but this made sense. It was nearly ten years since I'd taken it over and it was huge now. I really thought that it couldn't go any bigger. So we talked, and eventually I accepted their offer, which was for £500,000 and a position as executive director, which meant that I had my own office and secretary and would continue to write "Alley Cat" and oversee the paper. It also guaranteed me regular trips to New York and LA. I was supposed to stay for two years, but eventually I stayed on for another ten.

KEITH ALTHAM In 1964, I got onto the *NME* largely through my contact with the Stones, The Who and The Animals. Maurice Kinn was associate editor and the editor was this very nice man, Andy Gray, though "golfing correspondent" would have been a more accurate title. There were a few people who were cut and thrust, like Chris Hutchins, who was my news editor and later became the PR for Tom Jones and Gilbert O'Sullivan and went into Fleet Street. Chris was hard-nosed and tough.

CHRIS WELCH Maurice Kinn had tremendous access, but it didn't worry us overly at the *Melody Maker*, because we had better relations with the musicians themselves. He knew the big music publishers, the people who really ran the business.

JOHN BROVEN As the blues boom kicked in, *Blues Unlimited* started to take off, but we just stuck to the authentic American artists. It was a bit elitist, but we knew that Muddy Waters and Howlin' Wolf and those people were the real deal, so we didn't cover the British bands coming up. There was another magazine which Mike Vernon founded - *R&B Monthly* - in 1964 which covered people like Rufus Thomas and Booker T. Between us, we covered that whole spectrum. Then Mike went on to launch Blue Horizon, produce Fleetwood Mac and so on. We were ahead of the game, because The Beatles and The Rolling Stones were buying the same records as us in their teens. Their early releases were literally copies of the great R&B records, but once they started writing their own songs and realised the value of publishing, that's where the streams diverted. They were covered in the pop press while we concentrated on the authentic artists.

MAURICE KINN Early in 1964, after I'd sold the paper, I was having lunch in Iso's with two music publishers, Cyril Simmons and Dick James. Dick said, "If I could get the right offer, I'd sell Northern Songs," The Beatles' publishing company. I asked him if he was serious, and he said yes. He wanted £250,000. I think he really thought the bubble was going to burst. I'd just sold the *NME* and was sodding around and was always interested in getting into music publishing, which, as everyone knows, is where the real money is in the music business. We shook hands on a deal for me to buy it, with Cyril as a witness, and I told Dick I would get my solicitor to draw up an agreement. But the next morning, he called me: "Maurice, when I got home I told my wife, and she's not happy about it. I know that we shook on it, but I've changed my mind." So I had to let it go. Needless to say, when he eventually sold Northern Songs, he got something like £9 million. Then it was sold to EMI, who sold it to Michael Jackson, and it's worth hundreds of millions. But what could I do? We never fell out. In fact, I gave the eulogy at Dick's memorial service.

KEITH ALTHAM Maurice was a distant figure, and I think that was largely due to the fact that he was a shy and retiring man, but because he'd owned it, he was an almost headmaster figure. You didn't see a lot of him, but if you did you were in trouble. I got to like him early on. I made the mistake of calling him Maurice on my third day there and I received a phone call from his secretary telling me that I had to call him Mr Kinn. So I always did, and his response was to call me "M'Lord" the entire four years I was there.

CHRIS WELCH Keith Altham at the *NME* was one of my best friends when I was on *Melody Maker*. We met at *Ready, Steady, Go!*, where he'd be chasing after The Beach Boys and I'd be interviewing Dusty Springfield. That was shot every Friday afternoon, and we'd hop on the tube to the TV studio and have egg and chips with The Lovin' Spoonful or chat to James Brown in his dressing room. Vicki Wickham was running it and the whole thing was like a big youth club. *Ready, Steady, Go!* was very important – you'd interview The Who on Friday and they'd be on your front page the following week.

MAURICE KINN Brian told me in around 1965 that he'd had enough of managing The Beatles and agreed a deal in Paris to sell them to Bernard Delfont. They were getting on top of him, giving him a rough time, and I didn't see any true gratitude because I think they believed they'd done it all themselves. So Brian came back to London and they said they wouldn't allow it. In fact, they said they would never work again: "Our contract is with you, not for you to give us away." We used to talk to Brian, and he wasn't happy after a couple of years because they used to treat him like the office boy, humiliating him.

JOHN BROVEN At *Blues Unlimited*, Simon Napier had a business approach, which he'd got from running his father's antiques business. He realised the value of advertising, which never occurred to us; we were just happy to see the magazine out. That's the reason why it lasted as long as it did, going from a stencil, hand-made job to a professionally printed A4 publication.

KEITH ALTHAM Maurice used to do things like *Juke Box Jury* and get Derek Johnson – who handled reviews at *NME* – to find out what records were going to be played. You weren't supposed to know. Derek would put together a resumé and Maurice would pontificate when he was on: "Of course, this was a song first recorded by The Shirelles in 1961 at Muscle Shoals. I think it was raining at the time..." David Jacobs would say, "Thank you very much, the Memory Man."

MAURICE KINN One night, I was invited by Tito Burns to see Dionne Warwick in cabaret. During the performance, the head waiter came over and said, "Mr Kinn, Brian Epstein is on the telephone." Brian said that he had called the office to find out whether Cilla Black had beaten The Righteous Brothers to Number One with her version of 'You've Lost That Lovin' Feeling.' He was absolutely out of his skin and said to me, "It is very important to me that Cilla isn't outdone by them. What would it cost to ensure that?" I said, "I can't believe you're serious. Let me tell you that you, EMI and The Beatles can put all your money together, but it wouldn't move me. I don't entertain changing chart positions in the *NME* for anybody." In the event, Cilla got to Number Two while The Righteous Brothers were at Number One.

KEITH ALTHAM Maurice could be quite cutting and was none too great a fan of anything that was suggestive. He could be prudish. PJ Proby mortally offended him. He virtually caused PJ Proby's downfall, because he cottoned on to the fact that Proby was accidentally-on-purpose splitting his trousers on stage, and he put that in the "Alley Cat" column. That got into the nationals, and at the time it was not on, so he was carved up. But Proby himself was not a particularly nice chap; he had a sleazy side to him, and Maurice may well have been aware of that and wouldn't have endeared him. There was still something of an old boy's network at the time. I introduced something revolutionary to the *NME*, so I was told later, which was humour. You weren't even supposed to be funny. I think they thought the kids were dumb and wouldn't get it, if you made a crack about somebody. Andy Gray would put in brackets "just joking" for fear of offending anyone.

MELODY MAKER
"THE DAYS BEFORE MUSIC WRITERS BECAME PERSONALITIES"

CHRIS WELCH On *The Kentish Times*, I was covering the local news – bring-and-buy sales and road accidents – but at the same time I was sneaking in articles about The Pretty Things and the Stones and Sounds Incorporated, who were a local band, and people said, "You should work for the music papers if you're so interested in all this stuff." The Beatles were just taking off, so I wrote to the *NME* and they turned me down. I tried *Disc* and then

Melody Maker. To my utter astonishment, they said yes. They needed a young writer to cover the new bands coming up.

NICK LOGAN My main interest was in black music, but it wasn't covered at all well in the music press in the '60s. *Record Mirror* had one section which was an eighth of a page called Great Soul Unknowns, edited by Norman Jopling, and there'd be pieces on Solomon Burke or Otis Redding.

DAVID HEPWORTH I used to watch out for Norman Jopling's stuff. He was very good. His was a name I'd watch out for in the days before music writers became personalities.

NICK LOGAN Luckily, at the same time I was interested – it sounds a bit pretentious to say about an 18-year-old – culturally in the British pop bands, the way they lived, the clothes they wore. So I got that from the others, the *NME* and *Melody Maker*. But black music was completely under-represented.

CHARLES SHAAR MURRAY As a little Beatle kiddie, I read *NME* and *Fabulous*, the latter subsequently dropped in favour of *Disc* and, by the time I was 15 or so, both dropped in favour of *Melody Maker*, which had a more musical and less fannish emphasis, though I was initially puzzled by all the jazz stuff.

CHRIS WELCH They were wonderful people at the *Melody Maker*, sort of the tail end of the trad jazz boom, like George Melly. Bob Dawbarn had been at school with Mick Mulligan – well educated, public school but rebellious. They all had the same Chelsea sense of humour – suave, sophisticated and very dry. There was also a strong Scottish contingent, and they usually make good journalists, because they can be slightly abrasive and to the point. Bob Houston, who was the chief designer, was a Clydeside Glaswegian with a strong Marxist streak.

IAN MACDONALD The *Melody Maker* old guard – respected jazzers like Max Jones and Bob Dawbarn – were still prominent in the mid '60s. I remember Bob Dawbarn's scathing review of 'Like A Rolling Stone'. It was actually quite exciting that he hated it; the controversy turned it into even more of an event.

CHRIS WELCH I felt very nervous about working at the *Melody Maker*, even though I was 22 at the time, because it was my bible at school. The test was to interview Joe Morello, who just happened to be one of my favourite drummers. The main thing he said was, "You don't have to be an idiot to play drums," which they ran as the headline.

TONY TYLER I started reading *Melody Maker* when I left the army in early 1966 and went to work as a guitar salesman for Boosey & Hawkes in the megastore they had in those days underneath Centre Point. I had been running a pop group of sorts within the army for about two years, and my transition from Tidworth Barracks and Chieftain tanks to downtown swinging London was almost uncannily smooth and swift. *Melody Maker* was part of that world – immensely authoritative, smart, well written.

CHRIS WELCH Ray Coleman was the news editor and was very tough, a no-nonsense reporter. He had a strong background in Northern journalism. He once went for a job at *The Daily Telegraph* and the editor said, "So you're working for *Melody Maker*. What made you leave journalism?" My first day was Monday, the news day, and he just fired all this stuff at me: "Phone up Sandie Shaw's management and find out where she's touring. What's Adam Faith up to? Where are The Beatles next week?" And it wasn't easy, because the record companies didn't know what was going on. They were very nice, pleasant people but from a different generation – well schooled, well educated, well spoken. Nothing like the music industry at all! I felt like the oik from the suburbs. And the management people weren't geared to talking to the press, so you had to go around them, calling up theatres to find out who was playing where.

IAN MACDONALD At school, during the '60s, I read *Beat Instrumental* and *Melody Maker*, which was in its heyday then, giving equal prominence to chart acts, club R&B, folk, blues and jazz. You'd find a lead review of Dylan's latest album opposite a review of Ornette Coleman or Albert Ayler, which was exciting if you were one of the groovy kids, the in-crowd who hung out in record shops and went to the London clubs and wanted to keep up with everything that was going on.

CHRIS WELCH On my first day, I went for a drink with some of the guys from the paper and they said, "This pop business is finished, you know. The *Melody Maker*'s on its way out. They're going to close it." I was absolutely exhausted because Ray had been giving me a really hard time chasing up stories and nearly didn't go back in, but I did the next day and the office was empty. They were all at the printers' and my tormentor wasn't there, so I thought, "I'll stay 'til the end of the week." By that time, I'd interviewed The Shangri-Las, Dionne Warwick, Burt Bacharach. It was so exciting, so I stayed and the weeks flashed by. Then the years flashed by. Ray covered The Beatles and the really big groups, whereas I'd be sent out to do The Rockin' Berries, The Hollies, Wayne Fontana. There were so many bands, but it was all very primitive. There'd be the odd press release, but if you wanted to find out about Eric Burdon leaving The Animals or Paul Jones leaving Manfred Mann, you rang them at home. Being single and not having to get into the office until ten, I could spend all night chasing stories around all the clubs and travelling with bands. It was a great laugh.

TONY TYLER I seem to remember the jazz rump of *Melody Maker* was still at that time fighting a strong rearguard action and probably owned about half of the editorial, but no other paper covered what was actually happening in the pop world with such authority. *Melody Maker* was mandatory reading, especially if you worked in a music store and played gigs with a half-assed blues band in the evenings, as I did.

CHRIS WELCH When I joined the *Melody Maker* in October 1963, it was undergoing great upheaval. They were throwing away all these files and photographs from the dance-band era, literally dumping pictures of Ted Heath, Henry Hall, Billy Cotton. They wanted to bury the past. The competition had increased and Jack Hutton had taken over as editor from Pat Brandt. There was a lot of bitterness, actually, and some people were outraged because a lot of people who bought *Melody Maker* were professional musicians and their whole livelihood was disappearing under the onslaught of the guitar groups.

RICHARD WILLIAMS The *Melody Maker* was very much like a traditional newspaper. They recruited pretty strictly from local newspapers, as far as I could see, and that was good. It meant that everybody pitched in on Mondays, doing the news. That's what we all did, the news stories, and people were prepared to go to the printer and read proofs. I came from *The Nottingham Evening Post*, where I was doing the standard four years of indenture – golden weddings, fires, that sort of thing.

HARVEY KUBERNIK I knew that the bands were transitory, and that the producers were the people making the records with 20- or 30-year careers, so I started to get into the English papers, particularly *Melody Maker*, reading about people like Mickey Most and Ivor Raymonde. When I found out Sandie Shaw had the same birthday as me, I went wild.

CHRIS WELCH I had pretty much free rein, and then in '64/65 Ray brought in Nick Jones, who was Max Jones' son and only 16. He was a huge fan of The Who and Eric Clapton and put us at the forefront again with those people. But Nick was very opinionated, like his dad, and eventually fell out with Jack, the editor, over asking for more money and complaining about the groups he had to interview, people like The Honeycombs, who he thought were beneath his dignity. Eventually, he shouted and complained once too often in the office. We were all quite shocked at this 16-year-old berating the editor!

HARVEY KUBERNIK I used to get *Melody Maker* at the news-stand just down the street from my school, Fairfax High. I'd read Chris Welch and Max Jones writing about all manner of music. I was selling papers on the corner of La Cienega and Beverly for a couple of years through school – later I had a job washing out the test tubes at a gynaecologists; think about that! – and I started to spend every penny I made on the English papers – *Jackie*, the *NME*, everything.

IAN MACDONALD The '60s were naturally eclectic – a very '60s word! – more so than at any time than in the last ten or so years, when the mix of musical interests has returned to something like it was then, although at far lower creative pressure. I mean, at that time, The Beatles, the Stones, The Beach Boys, Dylan, The Byrds, James Brown, Hendrix, Clapton, Motown, Otis, Miles, Coltrane and you name it – they were all going on, all very active and present. It was incredibly exciting. I remember being in my back garden one day in the very hot summer of 1966 listening to Radio Caroline. Every single record they were playing was great. I just looked up at the sky in a sort of ecstasy and thought, "This is fantastic. This is the best it's ever been." I think everyone from my generation agrees: 1965-67 were the peak years in pop.

NEW YORK
"IT WAS A VERY SMALL WORLD"

DANNY FIELDS It was a new business. There was very little rock 'n' roll press. *The Village Voice* was the underground press. They had Richard Goldstein writing a rock column, which must have been the first ever, certainly in New York. There was *Crawdaddy!*, later, and *Hit Parader*, but it was a very small world.

LENNY KAYE *Hit Parader* had the words to the songs and a couple of vague articles – mostly biographical – about the bands, but when I started to listen to rock music seriously, around the turn of the '60s, there was really noplace to go and read about it. The first music I got into was New York doowop, and to find out anything about it you had to get it word of mouth from other collectors. The folkies had *Broadside* and *Sing Out!*.

DANNY FIELDS In 1966, I was a proofreader at a small publishing company in New York. I saw an ad in the newspaper: "Pop Magazine Looking For Editor". At that time, I was hanging around Andy Warhol's crowd, and I thought "pop" meant pop art, so I answered the ad with a very extravagant letter describing how fabulous I was, about the people I knew and the parties I went to. Of course, it meant pop music. It was a teenage service magazine with stories about straightening your hair, how to get along with your step-brother, things like that. They had bought the American rights to a series, "On The Road With The Beatles" with Neil Aspinall, which had proved to be much more popular than those articles, and when I went in for the interview I just lied and said, "Sure, I know all about pop music." I had seen The Beatles' first New York concert and liked them because they had long hair.

PAUL NELSON When the whole folk revival took off, *Sing Out!* was the most serious folk music magazine in the world, and all of a sudden they needed a managing editor. They offered me the job, so I took it. I quit *Sing Out!*

because I knew they were going to nail Dylan to the wall for not writing protest songs and I didn't want any part of it. I kept on watching Dylan's shows, like at Forest Hills. One *Sing Out!* critic left after the acoustic section of his show out of protest at the Carnegie Hall show. A lot of people left, except me. It was quite scary. I made it a point to applaud Dylan.

DANNY FIELDS In my first issue, we carried the interview with Paul and John done by Maureen Cleave for *The Evening Standard*. When it originally appeared, it caused no fuss, but we put the headline with John Lennon's quote about being bigger than Jesus and it precipitated the whole anti-Beatles furore on the verge of their American tour in the summer of '66. The KKK rallied outside the stadium in Memphis, there were all those record burnings - they were afraid for their lives. The last public concert at Candlestick Park in San Francisco took place just about two weeks after this. It was wonderful, because it removed them from the public nuisance of performing, but there was still a lot of garbage to be recorded. I thought *Rubber Soul* was sweet, but I was really a Rolling Stones fan. Brian played 'A Day In The Life' in his hotel for me when we were very stoned and it sounded like something we'd never heard, but now all that symphonic stuff I find embarrassing.

LENNY KAYE When Richard Goldstein started writing for *The Village Voice*, that's when it started to come together for me. Previously, rock 'n' roll was considered too immature to merit serious scrutiny, unlike jazz, which had the history.

DANNY FIELDS I didn't know how to be a magazine editor. I got fired after about three months. But I did get my friends - like Lillian Roxon - involved. The photographs we had of the Stones on a boat out in the Bay was Linda Eastman's first published shoot. That resulted because I literally missed the boat. On the way there, my fucking photographer was out of film, so he made the taxi stop in 34th Street and Sixth Avenue - the worst place - to buy film. That took so much time that, when we got there, it was sailing away, and I told the photographer, "Fuck off. Get out of here. You're fired." I was standing there on the banks of the Hudson with Gloria Stavers, who had also missed it. So we're standing there, and some guy with a rowing boat pulled up and said, "I'll take you out to meet the boat for $20." I said,

"Gloria, you want to split it?" She said, "Fuck it, The Rolling Stones aren't worth $10," and got into her limousine and drove off. I waited for two hours for the boat to come back and found that Linda had taken some photographs, so I introduced myself to her and she said she was committed to show them first to a rival magazine, *Hullabaloo*, which I subsequently became the editor of. But she gave them to us, Lillian wrote the story and we became friends. As a result of those pictures, her career as a photographer was launched.

BEN FONG-TORRES Back when I was a kid, there *was* no music press to speak of, or to read. There were only teen mags like *Teen*, *16* and my favourite, *Dig*. The local papers here in the San Francisco Bay area didn't cover music, except for Ralph J Gleason's jazz column in *The Chronicle*.

HARVEY KUBERNIK Distribution wasn't so good, but if I saw a copy of *Cheetah* or *Eye* I would immediately pick them up. They had posters inside them, fantastic colour photos of The Who, articles on whether women should use the pill. There was social information alongside pretty people. They also published pictures of James Cotton and Muddy Waters, unlike at other magazines, where there was almost a policy of "one negro per issue". I wouldn't say they were racist, but lots of great people were overlooked. *Cheetah* and *Eye* would have long articles on Ravi Shankar and George Martin.

DANNY FIELDS I lost my job at *Datebook* when the owner said, "We need a story on Paul Revere And The Raiders," and I said, "I can't run one because I haven't interviewed them." He knew that was not what an editor is about; you get the story even if you cut and paste it, make one up, whatever, to get it in there. That was what *16* was doing.

DEREK TAYLOR I must have written close to 175,000 words on Paul Revere over two and a half years working for him [as Revere's publicist] for the likes of *Flip* magazine and *Teen Life* and *Tiger Beat* and *Teen* and *16*. I took up offers of columns in *Tiger Beat*, *Disc* and *Teen*, well paid, offering snippets of news and forecasts. Clean, honest opinions and views made up the bulk of it, and in this way I was able to drop in the names of clients who weren't making any waves with their music.

DANNY FIELDS I wanted to write about The Byrds, The Mamas And The Papas and *Pet Sounds*, but they just wanted Herman's Hermits or whatever in *Datebook*. The first mention of Jefferson Airplane was in *Datebook* in a picture story. But when I was fired, I went straight to Los Angeles and lived there for the summer. I met Derek Taylor, who had the best publicity roster in town and was a wonderful man who I really wanted to work for. He had The Mamas And The Papas and The Byrds and Paul Revere and was trying to get The Rolling Stones. He had an office at 9,000 Sunset with no furniture. He had a desk surrounded by sacks of unopened fan mail to all those bands.

3 "Don't Try To Out-Hip Me, Be As Hip As Me"

"The music press never was much of a vibrant force, except in the '60s – early Rolling Stone, Creem, Crawdaddy!*."*
    – Miles

SCI-FI GEEKS
"FROM THE POINT OF VIEW OF THE FAN"

GREG SHAW A lot of people in the '60s wave of the rock press had come out of college and had all this kind of theoretical-philosophical framework and intellectual-literary background. I came off the streets; I was just a kid who loved rock 'n' roll. I came out of science-fiction fandom, as did Lenny Kaye and a bunch of others.

LENNY KAYE Science-fiction writing was where fanzines really started. My whole feeling about music writing is that you have to bring to it the same passion and integrity that hopefully the audience has. You know, "Don't try to out-hip me, be as hip as me. And if you don't think I'm that hip, what the hell are you doing talking to me?"

GREG SHAW My idea of it was that it was important to look at it from the point of view of the fan. I was part of the generation that was looking for a more subjective approach, not just talking about the facts and who these people are but understanding the music and why it makes us feel the way we do.

HARVEY KUBERNIK Between 1964 and 1967 in LA, we had free newspapers locally – *The KFWB Newspaper* and *The KRLA Beach*. They were weekly music papers, a bit like *Disc And Music Echo*. Lots of Q&As and Jan And Dean talking about recording at Liberty Studios. That would get me following labels and studios and getting really interested in that stuff.

DAVID DALTON We were in the first ten seconds. Before us, nothing! I suppose Tom Wolfe was the first great pop-cult writer, but my own nutty project early on was to link rock mythology with anthropological mythology – ie seeing Janis [Joplin]'s self-flaying performances as a parallel to the dismantling-their-own-skeleton ceremonies of Igluk shamans.

RICHARD MELTZER I generally read the new mags as they appeared just to check them out as targets for my writing. Some offered me the opportunity to be published and a chance to develop my chops as a writer, occasionally generating a minimal income for me...but I never would've read any of them if it hadn't been with this in mind. With very few exceptions, they were all pretty cheesy. As to other writers...well, we were all always just a bunch of whores.

GREG SHAW I first published myself in fanzines, the same as Paul Williams and any of these guys – A4, run off on some little machine with a crank and stapled together. They had lots of science-fiction names, but they weren't about science fiction at all; they were about talking about what was interesting to you, within this community of people who also liked science fiction.

CRAWDADDY!
"ANYONE COULD BE A PUBLISHER"

WALLY CONGAR At 17, Paul Williams founded *Crawdaddy!* magazine in 1966 and with it rock journalism. By 1969, he had relinquished the editorial reins to others and was living communally in Mendocino, northern California.

RICHARD MELTZER A far cry from *Song Hits*, *Hit Parader* and their pulp-teen hype-sheet ilk, *Crawdaddy!* was the first community of high-falutin' "rock writers" *per se*, and through the spring of '68, when editor/publisher/zealot-in-chief Paul Williams and I had a terminal falling out over who can remember what, they printed virtually everything I gave them.

JON SAVAGE Paul Williams is kind of a forgotten figure now, but he is very important in the scheme of things, and, although we couldn't get

Crawdaddy! at the time in the UK, you look at it now and it was spot on. Of course, he went on to have a great impact at lots of other magazines.

JIM DEROGATIS When it debuted, in February 1966, *Crawdaddy!* was the first publication to bill itself as "a magazine of rock 'n' roll criticisms". Paul Williams, a freshman at Swarthmore College, looked at the home-made magazines produced by science-fiction fans and realised that anyone with a typewriter and a mimeograph machine could become a publisher.

LENNY KAYE For me, *Crawdaddy!* was a revelation, because it was the first time I'd seen writing about this music with some depth. It wasn't just favourite likes/dislikes. The *Crawdaddy!* writers were always my favourites, because they took music writing to a level which matched the creativity of the works they analysed. Sandy Pearlman came up with a genius piece of writing in pieces like "The History Of Los Angeles" in 1968/69. I always enjoyed reading Sandy and Richard Meltzer.

RICHARD MELTZER Well, for starters, I invented this shit, rock writing. I was first. Well, maybe not *literal* first, just one of the first two, three or four. Probably the first to take the ball and actually run with the fucker. Certainly the sole early man-jack you're still reading now. Before Lester Bangs was, I am. And he's dead.

GREG SHAW People were writing their thoughts on various things, from politics to whatever, and music was one of those things. A lot of people who later turned up the rock press started out in this context, so they had this fan-ish approach, being a fan first. This is a uniquely science-fiction concept that's kind of spread out to general culture, just as the word "fanzine" has. To me, being a fan meant something almost like being affiliated to a football team in England.

LENNY KAYE The great thing about the stuff in *Crawdaddy!*, whether it was Paul Williams writing about Brian Wilson or Richard Meltzer writing about anything, was that they weren't trying to be too cool. There was some aspect of the New Journalism at the time, and the music was exploding out of the three-minute single. As soon as I got an inkling from *Crawdaddy!* that writing about music was possible, I started working on the school paper. My first attempt was a review of The Fugs at the Village Theater in 1966.

JIM DEROGATIS Williams wrote about the music he loved in essays that were like letters to his friends, and before long his hand-stapled fanzine began to attract other aspiring rock critics. Jon Landau was a clerk at the Briggs & Briggs record store in Harvard Square, Sandy Pearlman studied at the State University of New York at Stony Brook and Pearlman's pal Richard Meltzer was about to be thrown out of graduate studies in philosophy at Yale.

RICHARD MELTZER Pieces that I wrote with musical content started getting published in '66/67 by early rock sheets like *Crawdaddy!*. Because writing was fairly easy for me then, and the music, it made the most sense to write about what was still rather meaningful and magnificent. I kept doing it. In the process, I – along with two or three others – essentially invented the rock-write genre.

MILES My first regular gig in the music press was in 1970, when I was assistant editor of *Crawdaddy!* in New York, as well as a writer for them. Editorially, it was great – we could write as much as we liked and use any language we liked. The pay was low and the paper was under Mafia control. On a certain day, two heavy-looking torpedoes would come and collect the boards and four days later the magazine was on the streets. I think it was printed at the same place that did *The New York Review Of Sex*, because they shared our space, a sub-basement on Sixth Avenue at 13th Street with a huge iron door leading through to the subway tracks. Some of our writers wrote for them as well.

CHARLES M YOUNG I wrote quite a bit for *Crawdaddy!* in the Peter Knobler regime. I met Timothy White there, and we've been friends ever since. The meticulous effort he puts into his research has always been an inspiration. He really believes in journalism, not just airing out your empty opinions.

MILES On *Crawdaddy!*, people sat around and smoked dope and played records, but most of the writing was freelance. Then, one day, the editor said, "I don't think there's going to be any more money. I'm going out to get a coffee. I sure hope no one rips off the IBM golfball machines while I'm gone." We took the hint. The golfball typewriters were state of the art and worth quite a bit. They were very heavy to carry out, but I certainly got back everything owed to me and a bit more.

RICHARD MELTZER When I started writing for *Crawdaddy!*, The Doors had a residency at this club in Manhattan called Ondine. They were there for three or four months and they played three or four sets a night. We'd go down and see them for free, and I saw them I'd say 40 times. I heard their first album, and it didn't make much of an impression on me, and when I heard The End I thought, "Oh, how theatrical," and then I saw them live, and we looked at each other and we said, "Is this the greatest thing ever, or is this the greatest thing ever?" There was something just mesmerising about it. They seemed to us to be something beyond the Stones.

DANNY FIELDS I got a call from a friend, Ronnie Harron, who worked at the Whisky [A Go Go] in LA and asked me to do some publicity for The Doors when they played this small club uptown, Ondine. The groupies had discovered them by then, because they were a sexy new band, so I went in to their record label, Elektra, and said, "Oh, they did one song about fire last night. You should release it as a single." And they said, "It's seven minutes long. It won't get played on radio." And they put out another single, which bombed.

HULLABALLOO AND JAZZ & POP
"ACTS OF LOVE"

DANNY FIELDS In the summer of 1966, *Hullabaloo* – which was owned by Jerry Rothberg – hired me as editor. The first issue I did was full of The Lovin' Spoonful, The Mamas And The Papas and all the underground stuff I loved, but they hit me in the head with this plan to do an entire issue on Herman's Hermits. I said, "OK, I'll do it. I've learned how to be an editor."

LENNY KAYE I fell in with the *Jazz & Pop* crowd after I was introduced to Patricia Kenneally by her boyfriend, David Whalley. He was toying with rock journalism, working for *The East Village Eye*. The alternative press was growing – every town and city had their own newspaper, which had a music column – so Patricia asked me to write record reviews.

DANNY FIELDS My model magazine was *Copains* from Paris, which had this thing, *"Tout Tout Tout"* – "Everything Everything Everything" – where they spent 24 hours a day with people like Jacques Dutronc and Sylvie Vartan or had seven pictures of them by seven different photographers. It was gorgeous, approaching one artist from so many different angles, but to do it properly at *Hullabaloo* I needed to go hang out with Peter Noone and the guys for a while, but *Hullabaloo* couldn't buy me a plane ticket to LA. In the end they gave me a cheque which someone had given them and I had to endorse that to the airline and they didn't want it. My salary was $110 a month, an act of love, and they couldn't afford a ticket, so that fell apart. It wasn't until they became *Circus* and oriented towards metal and hair bands that it took off.

LENNY KAYE Patricia Kenneally was a really interesting person. There were these stories that she'd had a marriage ceremony performed with Jim Morrison, and there were rumours about her being a white witch, but for me she was really encouraging. Like its title suggested, the magazine had started out as a jazz magazine, but they later spun it into pop. You look at a group like the MC5, who were cover artists, and they were covering songs by Pharaoh Saunders and John Coltrane. It was a style I liked, because I believe in free music. When you get into an improvisational situation, all the genre forms break down. *Jazz & Pop* was a good place to discover that.

DANNY FIELDS After I left *Hullabaloo*, I was Cream's press agent the first time they came here, in 1967. Brian Epstein was partnered with Robert Stigwood in the management of Cream at the time. They hired me for three weeks for $500 to publicise them playing this multi-act show called Murray The K's Easter Pageant, which also had The Who on the bill. I got *Hit Parader* and Lillian Roxon to interview them, but nobody was really interested. I'd say, "You know, in London, Eric Clapton is God," but the only way I could get people to come was...guess what? Meet Brian Epstein. I organised a special press conference at Max's Kansas City. He was getting on a plane at noon and I said, "Brian, I can't get this band arrested, but the press will come if you're going to be there." So he had a few minutes, and of course everyone came. Everyone thought that was very nice, but we still didn't get any coverage.

ERIC CLAPTON All during Cream, I was riding high on the "Clapton is God" myth. Then we got our first kind of bad review, which was in *Rolling Stone*. The magazine ran an interview with us in which we were really praising ourselves, and it was followed by a review that said how boring and repetitious our performance had been. And it was true! I immediately decided that that was the end of the band.

LENNY KAYE My first assignment for *Jazz & Pop* magazine was to review *Ogden's Nut Gone Flake*, and I continued writing for them, reviewing one or two records a month. I reviewed Nico's *The Marble Index* and The Velvet Underground's third record, so I already had a sense of the bands I was gravitating toward. I also wrote my first article for them, which was something I felt only I knew about, the *a cappella*/doowop scene in the tri-state area. When that came out, I was called by someone I peripherally knew from around the New York scene, Patti Smith, who was very moved by that particular article, and we became friends. She asked me to play guitar for a reading she did at St Mark's Church.

RICHARD MELTZER Back in July or August of 1970, Ronnie Finkelstein of *Circus* mag told me there was this dynamite broad working at Scribner's bookstore in New York who was givin' people free books all the time and takin' outta the register, and one of the books she was givin' was my harder-'n-hell-to-read – never read it myself – rock book, which she was even reading. Told me she looked like Keith Richards, so I couldn't miss her.

HARVEY KUBERNIK I liked the things that Patti Smith wrote for *Circus*. You could tell there was a flow from the beat generation, which is what I'd studied at college.

LENNY KAYE I'd moved to New York City and was hanging out at Max's Kansas City and starting to make my way in the New York underground. Although Patti wrote about music occasionally, she wasn't a regular journalist. She wasn't a music writer; she was a Patti writer. She wrote about music the same way she would write about art or literature. If rock writers move from the music outwards, she was out from the start. I like to think that some of our early stuff – where she would do a poem which would segue into a song – was a form of rock writing. We would do 'Hey Joe' and tie it into the Patti Hearst saga, for example. It was commentary using rock music.

MOJO NAVIGATOR
"POPULARITY PUTS YOU OUT OF BUSINESS"

GREG SHAW In 1966, I was living in San Francisco and became very intensely identified with and loyal to the scene that was growing up there, so I wrote about those bands as well as those coming in from the East Coast and The Beach Boys and Phil Spector. I was obsessed with what was going on in my back yard and I was trying to chronicle that in *Mojo Navigator*, which was a commercially distributed fanzine through the underground press syndicate – basically hippies taking hippie magazines and newspapers around to headshops. It was a loose network which Barry Kramer – who later started *Creem* – was part of.

BEN FONG-TORRES I started writing about music at San Francisco State's paper, *The Daily Gater*, covering our folk and blues festivals, which tended to stray all over the music map into gospel, country, jazz and early folk rock. We had bands like Big Brother and Great Society playing for free on campus. Jefferson Airplane played a homecoming ball. You couldn't avoid the stuff.

GREG SHAW I was the managing editor at *Mojo Navigator*. There were twelve issues altogether, and I think we got up to about 2,000 circulation. But the problem you always have with magazines is, as your circulation grows, your printing bill grows, and you're not getting paid by anybody. The popularity of the magazine puts you out of business. In 1967, the third offset issue had advance orders of about 3,000 or 4,000, so it was, "OK, we've got orders for 3,000. We'd better print 5,000 and we can sell the back issues." Then you go to the printer: "I want to print 5,000 magazines." "Great," he says. "That'll be $2,000 cash in advance." *$2,000?* I was living by, you know, selling acid, making, like, $100 a month. My rent was $85 a month. It became impossible to do it.

ROLLING STONE
"HE HAD GOOD TASTE"

JANN WENNER (FROM HIS STATEMENT IN THE FIRST ISSUE OF ROLLING STONE) We have begun a new publication reflecting what we see are the changes in rock 'n' roll and the changes related to rock 'n' roll. Because the trade papers have become so inaccurate and irrelevant, and because the fan magazines are an anachronism, fashioned in the mould of myth and nonsense, we hope that we have something here for the artists and the industry and every person who "believes in the magic that can set you free".

BEN FONG-TORRES Careful to avoid being lumped in with the underground papers of the day, the magazine eschewed psychedelic lettering, emulating instead the classic typefaces and layouts of *The New York Times*, the London *Sunday Times* and *Ramparts*, a magazine where *Rolling Stone*'s founding editor, Jann Wenner, had worked briefly. Wenner, who'd also written for the campus paper at UC Berkeley, set professional copy-editing and proofreading standards from the first.

GREG SHAW I'd known Jann Wenner for a year or so in San Francisco. He used to come over to my flat and sit there and watch me turn the crank and ask me questions: "Why do you do this? How does this work? How do you know to put interviews in the front and record reviews in the back?" I kind of gave him a basic course in putting magazines out. I mean, that's a bit of an exaggeration, but he did hang out and he did ask all those questions.

PAUL WILLIAMS Jann Wenner got together with me and asked a lot of questions before he started *Rolling Stone*. We remained friendly over the years.

BEN FONG-TORRES It was November 1967 when my two college room-mates – buddies who worked on the edges of the rock scene, doing audio, video and lighting work – came across the first issue of *Rolling Stone*. It was a bracing find, a new high, and it jumped around from one set of hands to another in our flat in San Francisco.

DAVID DALTON My theory about Jann is that there are two Wenners, and he ain't ashamed! There's the evangelical Jann, who started the magazine, and Jann the clever businessman, who jointly started the magazine with him.

BEN FONG-TORRES For one thing, it came from San Francisco, but with its correspondents in London, New York and Los Angeles it was clearly out to be a national publication. It didn't appear to be either a newspaper or a magazine but a hybrid. It was printed on newsprint, in black and white, with a single splash of colour on the *Rolling Stone* logo. It didn't even open like a magazine; it was quarter-folded – that is, folded twice. The first issues didn't have covers but a newspaper-styled front page with several stories. Those stories were about rock 'n' roll, written in a style that was knowing, critical, good humoured and hip, neither fawning like teen and fan magazines nor crude and condescending like so much of the mainstream press when it deigned to cover rock 'n' roll.

HARVEY KUBERNIK LA was treated like it was on the margins by *Rolling Stone*, even though they had a bureau here. They never really gave it up for LA or got the right acknowledgment for the music coming out of here. And we had great music on TV. *The Spade Cooley Show*. Johnny Otis had a show. I used to go to episodes of *Shindig!*. It was great here, before what Andrew Oldham describes as "the East Coast infection". There were an eighth as many people here then, and it really was two girls for every boy, but *Rolling Stone* kind of looked down on us from San Francisco.

DANNY SUGERMAN I read every single issue from cover to cover the day that it came out. I lived in Playa del Ray, Westchester, and I'd go buy it at Arons' Records in Inglewood. It was incredibly well put together, the writers were passionate and it gave you an insight into the rock community, which I didn't feel a part of until I saw The Doors in concert and met [Jim] Morrison. You had to be 21 to get into the Whisky. I was twelve or 13 years old and I thought, "This is it."

DAVID WEIR Jann's long, strange trip to the centre of his own conspicuous universe began in a run-down warehouse in the old printers' district in San Francisco's south-of-market area a few short gestational months after the Haight-Ashbury's Summer of Love in 1967. There, *Rolling Stone* magazine – which would become the voice of a generation – was born. Until the moment issue number one launched, Jann had been just a frustrated wannabe, one of the guys jumping around the margins of the action, crashing the performances, handing out fliers, hanging on outside the doors of the stars.

JOHN PEEL When I was a DJ in the States, I used to inevitably read *Cashbox* and *Billboard* but also the early *Rolling Stone*. I've still got all of those. I've got something like the first hundred. They're worth a fortune! It's part of my pension scheme.

DAVID DALTON I saw the first issue in the fall of 1967. I had a payphone in my loft with an open line and started calling up Jann Wenner. In December, I came close to getting busted and thought it a good idea to go back to England for a while. I started sending Jann photos: Yoko's exhibit – the one John saw and fell in love with – Stevie Winwood, etc. "We need stories to go with these pictures," Jann said.

BEN FONG-TORRES (FROM THE INTRODUCTION TO THE ROLLING STONE ROCK 'N' ROLL READER) Our first issue, in November 1967, bore all the signs of the various dichotomies. Was it underground or overground, whatever those terms mean? A trade paper or a consumer paper? A newspaper or a magazine? Rock 'n' roll exclusively or other music and politics and other subterranean/cultural concerns too?

DAVID DALTON The captions to my pictures were getting longer and longer anyway, *viz*, "You'll never guess what happened 30 seconds before I took this picture." I lost my Pentax in an airport and thus began my long, blessed and oft-cursed career as rock writer, first as a journalist and then as a rock-dog-on-the-road anecdotalist – "Ah yes, I well remember the time Janis and I were kidnapped in Kansas City" – then as a rock biographer.

DAVID WEIR The idea was unique for its time. Instead of the puff pieces expected from a trade magazine, *Rolling Stone* would cover rock 'n' roll for what it was: the most powerful cultural and political force in a time of widespread social tumult. The magazine would take risks and run stories no one else was willing to cover. Jann recognised that a new social order was forming, with music as its binding energy. Wenner's mentor in this new world of publishing was an older music critic named Ralph Gleason. Most of the money for the risky venture came from the family of [Jann's] wife, Jane Schindelheim Wenner, a dark-haired, fine-boned beauty who was rarely seen at the magazine but whose presence was always felt in its formative years.

BEN FONG-TORRES The magazine was just across the road from a slaughterhouse. That would explain the increasing popularity of incense around the offices.

DAVE MARSH When 16 magazine ran an early story about *Rolling Stone*, it not only put the new San Francisco rock mag on the map; it also generated enough quarters for sample copies to keep Jann Wenner and his staff eating for a few crucial weeks.

DAVID DALTON When I began writing for *Rolling Stone*, it was as a rock evangelist. This sounds more than a little pretentious - and portentous - even as I write it, sinking it in the past tense of the deep, but, oh my brothers and sisters, that was the way it felt to me then. I was as intent as John the Revelator scribbling his apocalyptic verses on the island of Patmos. Rock was the very plasma that held the counter-culture together. Everything was plugged into it - everything I cared about, anyway. It was the Pentecostal flame that would bring the new Jerusalem into existence. Writing for *Rolling Stone*, I don't think I ever used the word *I*. *We*, maybe. But essentially I saw myself as a chronicler, as a fan who managed to enter this or that sanctum sanctorum and bring back the glad tidings, the revelations, and thus spake very words uttered by our idols.

BEN FONG-TORRES When *Rolling Stone* came along a year or so after I'd graduated, it seemed a natural transition from writing for *The Daily Gater*, and when I heard about a free concert being staged near where I lived to hype a film on the Haight-Ashbury that was produced by Dick Clark I smelled a story and called them. This was around March 1968, four months into the paper's history, and they used my piece as an item in a column called "Flashes".

CHARLES M YOUNG In college, I discovered *Rolling Stone*, which was just coming into its own. It had real information about musicians who had changed my life and it covered the whole counter-culture with exhilarating literary freedom. I wanted to be a *Rolling Stone* writer more than anything, but for some reason it didn't occur to me to write about music. I saw myself more in the tradition of Hunter Thompson and David Felton.

STEVEN WARD In 1970, David Dalton and co-writer David Felton won the prestigious Columbia School of Journalism award for their *Rolling Stone* interview with killer/Godhead/psycho Charles Manson.

DAVID DALTON Like most of my hippie peers – including Jann, who originally wanted to put "Manson Is Innocent" on the cover – I thought Manson was innocent and had been railroaded by the LAPD. It was a scary awakening for me to find out that not every long-haired, dope-smoking freak was a peace-and-love hippie.

BEN FONG-TORRES After assigning me a profile of Dino Valente, Jann called me into his office. "Don't just ask him questions," he said, the certainty in his voice belying his 21 years. He turned to his antique oak desk and grabbed a couple of magazines. They were issues of *The New Yorker*. "Lookit these," he said, handing them over. "This is the kind of detail, description and reporting I want in our profiles."

PAUL NELSON I worked there for nine months or so. I did a big story about the Hell's Angels and the Fillmore East having a big argument once. I worked in New York for *Rolling Stone* as a reporter or something like that when they were all in San Francisco. It did not work out.

LESTER BANGS I started in, like, 1968/69, you know? And there actually used to be a little box in *Rolling Stone* that said, "Do you write, take pictures, draw pictures? Send your stuff to us and maybe we'll publish it." So I actually believed this and I started sending them record reviews and, like, I sent them a pan of the second Grateful Dead album, a pan of the second Steve Miller album and a review that said *White Light/White Heat* was the best album of 1968 and Lou Reed was going to be the Chuck Berry of the '70s, and I raved about *The Marble Index* by Nico, and I couldn't figure out why they didn't print any of this stuff. Then, finally, I sent this review of the

MC5 - I really hated their first album at the time - and they liked that, so they printed that. So that was how I got started.

JON SAVAGE You read that review now and it's interesting because Bangs was right, that album was no good. Because I was brought up in central London, I had easy access to things like *Rolling Stone*. That was the biggest one selling here. *Crawdaddy!* didn't really make it to the UK at all, but through *Rolling Stone* in 1969 I got to know the work of people like Greil Marcus and Ed Ward at their height.

JON MENDELSSOHN I'd originally started writing sheerly out of boredom, loneliness and my hatred of The Doors. *Rolling Stone* ran a little ad that invited people to send things in. I sent something in, my Led Zeppelin *I* review. Next stop, wealth and fame! My review was very sober and boring. It was a miracle that *Rolling Stone* printed it, especially in view of its having already been published in my college newspaper. It was Led Zeppelin *II* that I "destroyed".

"METAL" MIKE SAUNDERS It seemed a conspicuous omission to my mind that *Rolling Stone* - which I got through the mail, because it wasn't available on Arkansas news-stands - had never reviewed John Mayall's *Hard Road* album with Peter Green, so I wrote up a review for the English class assignment, and - what the hell, never mind that the album was a year old - also sent it in to *Rolling Stone*, who didn't have a review editor but instead a back-page box requesting submissions. They actually ran it, rotten grammar and hyperbole and all. No cash payment. The following spring of '69, I sent in a review of some album or other I had in hand, and not only did a small cash payment come back but a note from their first reviews editor ever, Greil Marcus. He was angling for someone to do an interview with [Dylan's producer] Bob Johnston in Nashville and figured Little Rock was a day's drive away on the interstate system. I had to explain that I was a 16-year-old high-school senior and, even though I possessed a 1966 Chevy Nova, had a very tight schedule and a term paper to write, etc. So, you can see, my motivation to be a Cameron Crowe was nil from the git-go.

GREG SHAW Jann Wenner came from a background where his parents had money and he knew people with money, and he got financed and did it properly. I was an amateur from a lower-class background and that kind of thing was not what I had in mind at all. I just wanted to do something cool. He was a writer for the college newspaper. He wrote a music column. He wasn't a music historian – he didn't have a lot of depth. He had enthusiasm, but I don't think he had any penetrating critical insight. But he had good taste. The first thing I thought was, "My goodness, he's certainly borrowed a lot of my ideas," but I guess one would think that; there are only so many ways to lay out a magazine. I mean, we had the *Mojo* letter column, the *Mojo* interview, the *Mojo* review. He had the *Rolling Stone* letter column, the *Rolling Stone* interview, the *Rolling Stone* review.

DAVID WEIR What made Jann and *Rolling Stone* successful was the power of rock 'n' roll, combined with his personal ruthlessness and the opportunism – including kindness – that wealth allows. He was unparalleled in his generation of magazine editors as a spotter of talent, and for creative types of a certain age and temperament Jann will always be considered the magic-maker. He embraced the ideas and generated the excitement. He untapped his writers' best work. He untapped everybody, loosened the words, made the sap flow. That was part of his pure genius as an editor.

BEN FONG-TORRES A strike broke out at the first free-form FM rock station, KMPX, and *Rolling Stone* covered it. As it went on, I told someone there that I had some experience in radio, having majored in radio, TV and film at State and done some all-night work at a "beautiful music" FM station straight out of college and could help cover it. The managing editor said to go down and help the main reporter on the story. Soon enough, that guy split, and I took over the coverage for a few more issues. In terms of music profiles, my first assignment was either Gordon Lightfoot or the producer Eric Jacobsen. I forget which.

DAVID WEIR Wenner was an entrepreneur long before it was cool. And if, as the venture capitalists like to say, entrepreneurs usually have only one good idea, at least his was a doozy. Wenner was, to put it plainly, the star-fucker who always traded up, the ultimate name-dropper who finally became a bigger name in the tabs than many of the stars he worshipped.

JONATHON GREEN I registered the existence of *Rolling Stone* at the beginning of 1968, when they ran "the groupie issue", which I think was *Rolling Stone* 27. Jann Wenner had realised very smartly that if you're going to launch a magazine then you should use something which would get everyone excited, which the groupie issue certainly did. It was amazing – nobody had ever done anything like that. We'd never seen anything like it. Apart from all these gorgeous pouting cuties, we'd never heard of anybody like the plaster casters, for Christ's sake!

MICK FARREN What happened at a number of underground papers was that the music section became ghetto-ised and shuffled into its own section, so Jann Wenner put people like John Lennon on the cover and the major commercial end of things at the underground press was put on a more corporate-friendly basis. That was the start of the collapse of the underground press, because it cut off the commercially viable parts, and then all we were left with was Bobby Seals, John Sinclair and the Angry Brigade, which were not paying the rent. The record companies were happy not to have to do business with us, and that percolated down so that, for bands, getting on the cover of *Rolling Stone* became very, very important.

BEN FONG-TORRES Wenner had created the most unique new magazine, the most effectively targeted new publication since Hugh Hefner founded *Playboy* in 1955. And, being young and full of spunk, we had fun with our notoriety and our perceived power. Before 1969 was over, several *Rolling Stone* staffers and conspirators had issued a hoax album, *The Masked Marauders*. Playing off the mini-trend of superstar jams, the album purported to be a bootleg of outtakes from a super-duper jam with Bob Dylan, Mick Jagger, various Beatles and who knows who else. And so, at year's end, one of my articles was headlined, "Masked Marauders Expose Themselves". Yes, it was self-referential of us, but hey, we'd become news.

DAVID WEIR One of the critical elements in Wenner's success was that he knew not only how to develop and exploit talent but also when and how to dump it. Every *Rolling Stone* writer and editor, photographer and designer has a bucketful of Jann tales – how the outbursts, the abuse, the break-ups, the firings came down. When Jann turned heartless on you, he played that part better than anyone else.

JONATHON GREEN   The journalists on *Rolling Stone* were being paid real money and doing real stories. It was very impressive. And, although it was no more revolutionary than "The Man Can't Bust Our Music", they did some amazing things, like their coverage of Woodstock or carrying Hunter Thompson's original *Fear And Loathing*... They did Tom Wolfe's stories on the space programme, which became *The Right Stuff*. They had the money to hire top people – not necessarily in music, though. The record coverage, I think, was as sycophantic as anybody else's.

BEN FONG-TORRES   Jann Wenner was a great influence, because of his original direction, and he was aggressive and authoritative, but there were lots of others: David Felton was a brilliant writer, a funny guy and a smart editor; Annie Leibovitz used her charm and naked honesty, which resulted in a relaxed subject; John Burks had this casual, jazzy approach and prose; while Dave Marsh has a true fan's passion for the music. Then there's Chet Flippo, Tim Cahill, Charles "Smokestack El Ropo" Perry and Judith Sims, all excellent reporters and natural writers.

DAVID WEIR   The brand names of Jann's once and former stars is impressive: Hunter S Thompson, Lester Bangs, Chet Flippo, Joe Klein, Tim Cahill, Tom Hayden, David Harris, Cameron Crowe, Joe Eszterhas, David Felton, Tim Ferris, Ben Fong-Torres, Howard Kohn, Jon Landau, Dave Marsh, Annie Leibovitz, Greil Marcus, Grover Lewis, Abe Peck, John Morthland, Paul Scanlon, Marianne Partridge, John Burks, Timothy White, Sarah Lazin, Charley Perry, Michael Rogers, Roger Black, Ed Ward, Charles Young, Christine Doudna, Harriet Fier – and that list could go on and on to embrace dozens more.

RICHARD MELTZER   It's debatable whether the *Stone* had ever been a class venue for the writing of rock writers; appearing in its pages was basically always about visibility and money. Well, before there was anything like a rock-write style sheet in the rock/underground/counter-culture press at large, *Rolling Stone* had one in spades. Heavy-handed editors – the meanest in the biz – would routinely, as a matter of policy, alter your text without consulting you, delete entire paragraphs if they contained the itsiest allusion to people or things the "fact checker" of the day was having trouble finding back-up on and try to coerce you out of positions you'd taken on favoured musical celebs.

BEN FONG-TORRES There's no question that *Rolling Stone* was the biggest and, therefore, also the biggest target when the time came to criticise rock critics or to decry hip capitalism. There was envy, jealousy, petty sniping, and – remember this phrase? – bad-rapping. And that was from our side.

GREG SHAW In the beginning, *Rolling Stone* was very hippie and free form, but then you saw all these ads next to interviews, big ads for plastic LA bands. San Francisco is a very colloquial place. It certainly was then. If you didn't have the certain hippie aesthetic, you were considered fake. And by that hippie aesthetic, I thought it was fake, but I liked a lot of things about it. I offered my services to *Rolling Stone* and they said, "You can sell ads for us." I was, like, "I kinda had editorial in mind."

CREEM
"A BUNCH OF WEATHERMEN"

CHARLES SHAAR MURRAY *Creem* was edgy where *Rolling Stone* was mellow, satirical where *Rolling Stone* was sycophantic, fun where *Rolling Stone* was, let's face it, dull with a capital *duh*. *Creem*'s photo captions – many of them written by Lester Bangs, as we later discovered – were either surreal jokes or sardonic digs at their subjects. Where the British pop weeklies of the era treated their readers like besotted teenyboppers and their rockier equivalents addressed their punters as if they were aspiring roadies, *Creem* talked to you as if you were smart, adventurous and passionately committed to the music as a source of both fun and redemption, as we were – or thought we were.

MICK FARREN Barry Kramer started *Creem* to take the opposite position to *Rolling Stone* by becoming corporate-unfriendly almost immediately. They were basically a bunch of weathermen camping out on a farm in Michigan.

JIM DEROGATIS *Creem* came from Detroit and the same milieu which spawned the MC5 and the White Panthers. Englishman Tony Reay worked at a headshop and record store called Mixed Media and he convinced the enterprising young owner that money could be made with an underground music mag. At the age of 25, Barry Kramer launched *Creem* with an investment of $1,200 - $6,300 less than Wenner when he started *Rolling Stone*. The name came from Reay's favourite band, though the spelling was changed, because Cream seemed too obvious. A year after *Creem* started, as a sporadically published tabloid, Reay moved on and a hyperactive 20-year-old named Dave Marsh became the *de facto* editor. In the egalitarian spirit of the times, nobody at the magazine had a formal job title.

JAAN UHELSZKI *Creem* was as close as one could get to a mental care facility. We were all wildly dysfunctional. Who else would work for $22.75 a week just to get published? When Barry Kramer was displeased with someone/thing, he'd hurl a typewriter through the window or slam a phone through a light table. But he wasn't the only one.

LESTER BANGS I edited *Creem* magazine for five years and we had, like, hundreds of thousands of readers who really dug it that we were telling Dylan and the Stones and all these people to go jump in the lake. They weren't idiots that just swallowed any hype that was shovelled to them. I hate that, that everybody thinks that, that fans are just morons that'll just swallow any garbage, 'cause I think the kids are really sharp.

DANNY SUGERMAN Dave Marsh's writing really grabbed me. His column, "Looney Tunes", would pick a theme each month and write about it - Sly Stone's new album or whatever he felt strongly about. He had a lot of heart. I really connected with that. I came from a real dysfunctional family which didn't really express a lot of emotion from the heart, *chakra*, so I really responded to his passion.

MARC WEINGARTEN I thought Billy Altman in *Creem* was one of the best writers on heavy metal and heavy music in general, and I really liked Dave Marsh, Jon Landau, Jon Cott, all those caption writers in *Creem* whose names I didn't know at the time. What I loved about *Creem* was its brilliant irreverence - they just took the piss out of everyone, no matter how exalted or iconic. It was so attuned to the spirit of the music, in a way that no magazine has been since, and *Creem* paid attention to black music in a way that *Rolling Stone* never did – for example, numerous articles about P-Funk. I think *Rolling Stone* wrote about them once, and it was near the end of the '70s.

LISA ROBINSON Dave Marsh gave me my first assignment for *Creem*, which was to interview Jerry Garcia backstage at the East Village Fillmore. That was 1969, when *Creem* was a foldover newspaper, like *Rolling Stone* used to be.

DANNY SUGERMAN With magazines like *Creem* and *Rolling Stone*, there was such a connection between the reader, the writer and the music. Reading *Creem* was a big turn-on for me. I found it on a downtown news-stand when I was working for my father in the garment business. That issue had the review of *Morrison Hotel*. I took it to Jim and said, "You've got to read this, man. This is exactly how I feel. I could have written this."

JAAN UHELSZKI I worked at the Grande Ballroom in Detroit, Michigan, behind the soda fountain dispensing cokes. *Creem* had a stand set up next to the bar where they sold magazines, then a newspaper-type affair in 1969. I used to chat with them regularly and they suggested that I start writing for them, but it wasn't until I met the art director, Charley Auringer, that I really began working there. I offered to sell T-shirts at the boutique I was managing by day without taking a cut, and that got me my foot in the door. They hired me not for my writing prowess, rather my entrepreneurial skills, giving me the job of "subscription kid", then circulation manager. I had to do my writing on the sly during the dead of night.

DANNY SUGERMAN Jim pointed out the little ad they ran in there inviting contributions: "Boy Howdy. Nobody writes for this rag." He called and talked to Ben Edmonds and said he had a friend he thought had the makings of a good writer. He said, "I can't really talk about what happened in Miami, but he can. Is it OK if he sends something to you?" They must have said, "How do we know it's really you?" because he said, "I could sing a few bars of 'Light My Fire', but I'm not going to."

"METAL" MIKE SAUNDERS In the May 1971 *Creem*, reviewing the first Sir Lord

Baltimore album, I threw down the phrase "heavy metal" in its first use in the rock press ever – outside of the Steppenwolf lyric – as a descriptive term. Yep, all blame and shame goes to me. That was also the *Creem* issue where Dave Marsh coined the phrase "punk rock" in the "Looney Tunes" column about seeing a ? And The Mysterians club gig... Something was definitely in America's drinking water that month.

DANNY SUGERMAN I made a lot of mistakes as a writer early on. I sent Lester 20 reviews after they published my first one – of Jo Mama's album – because I got printed so easily. Dave Marsh wrote me a really encouraging letter and they said, "Call these publicists," and I did, writing 20 reviews, which I sent all at once. It became a big joke at *Creem*, because he was expecting one or two.

REX DOANE Nick Tosches emerged from music magazines like *Creem* and *Fusion*, where he placed the fringe figures of rock 'n' roll history in proper perspective, providing a reminder to those at Woodstock that the party started years earlier with R&B giants like Joe Turner. Long before acid, there was bootleg liquor. Long before free love, there was Hank Ballard, who let us know what working with Annie was all about. Along with Lester Bangs, Richard Meltzer and a handful of other noble notables from the era, Tosches elevated rock writing to a new plateau.

NICK TOSCHES We used to take a lot of drugs – you know, beat up hippies and rob them. We were just greasers on drugs.

REX DOANE Picking out records by Stick McGhee or Hardrock Gunter – whom Tosches bills as the "mysterious pig-iron man" – from the morass, dusting them off and placing them in the pantheon of American music was what Tosches did best in his early work. Finding value and merit in what has been cast off by the culture at large may very well be the core initiative to Tosches' research agenda. It has had its personal rewards.

RICHARD MELTZER As '69 gave way to '70, all these mags started calling me. In addition to *Fusion*, I heard from *Rock*, *Changes*, *Creem* and a resurrected, reconstituted *Crawdaddy!*, each of them offering ten bucks and up for rock reviews, features, fillers. The oldest of the bunch and richest, though in many ways least, *Rolling Stone* had once turned down my offer of a boxing piece, but after running two reviews of "The Aesthetics Of Rock" [Meltzer's thesis on '50s and '60s popular music], they now welcomed me. They paid...I don't remember, 25 bucks or even 30 for a 350-word record review. Fat City.

CHARLES M YOUNG At *Rolling Stone*, Paul Nelson and I used to talk about how brilliant and funny Bangs, Meltzer and Tosches were, how they were the rightful successors to the New Journalism thing in the late '60s. I think we were correct in our artistic assessment but naïve about literary politics.

LENNY KAYE Everybody was friendly. There was a big connection between the New York writers and the Detroit writers. I remember going out to Detroit several times and staying at the *Creem* offices on Kent Avenue, hanging out with Dave Marsh, Lester, the gang. There was some sense of mission, and the mission was to get people to recognise how great the Stooges were!

DANNY SUGERMAN Jim [Morrison] was going to do an interview with Dave Marsh, who sent a bunch of questions across, but he wasn't interested. Finally, I got him to write Dave an eight-page letter about what *LA Woman* [The Doors' last album] meant to him, giving snappy answers. Dave asked, "Do you ever see yourself as a leader?" and Jim answered, "No. Well, maybe a cheerleader."

JAAN UHELSZKI We all worked at fever pitch, with little sleep, especially during the monthly deadlines, and confrontations were more the norm than not. Fistfights often broke out among the staff. We would get into it over something as benign as cover headlines. But I think the madness also was channelled into the writing at *Creem*, which was as bombastic and as wild as our behaviour.

DANNY SUGERMAN I got on really well with Dave, so when he was less involved, when he moved to New York, my relationship with *Creem* wasn't so strong Then I put together a six-page story just before Jim [Morrison] went to Paris. To compensate for not really taking the Dave Marsh questions seriously, he compensated by giving me what would become his last official statement to the press. He said, "For me, it was never an act or so-called performances; it was a life and death thing, an attempt to involve many people in a private world of thought. I no longer feel I can do this through concerts. The belief isn't there." At the time, I was in total denial, expecting him to come back from Paris and tour *LA Woman*. *Creem* ended up just using Jim's quote in their Rock 'n' Roll News. That was the last piece I wrote for *Creem*.

LISA ROBINSON Dave Marsh, Lester and Barry Kramer gave me this column in *Creem* which I called "Eleganza", named after a black pimp-like catalogue. I wrote about clothes and style. Some of the guy rock critics were horrified, because this was not serious rock criticism; it was frivolous, more about the way things looked and how that affected pop and vice versa. To my mind, you couldn't separate the two. When I was kid growing up, looking for the next Stones album, I wanted to see what Mick Jagger was wearing or what Thelonious Monk was wearing at the Five Spot. There were a couple of years of tough going, because lots of the critics didn't like it. It was very chatty, name-dropping and, I'm not ashamed to say, gossipy. At that time, I wasn't a feminist *per se* and I was totally comfortable writing about music in a frivolous way. I was determined not to write rock criticism.

JAAN UHELSZKI Dave Marsh dragged me to my first assignment for *Creem*, a press conference with Smokey Robinson, and forced me to cover it when I was so nervous and raw. Lester Bangs always encouraged me. We sat next to each other for most of my six years at *Creem*. He gave me incredible feedback and once wrote one of my papers for journalism class when I was stressed. He got a B-plus.

"METAL" MIKE SAUNDERS I never wrote much for *Creem* because it was disorganised and unprofessional beyond description during Lester Bangs' time there as reviews editor. He chronically assigned things that didn't run and never saw print, ie he solicited far more reviews each month than saw print. It was a big mess. I kinda had the minority opinion that *Creem* was great for about a year, mid 1970 to mid 1971, then had to sell out to commercial considerations when they went to a slick cover in fall 1971. For me as a reader, the magazine pretty much sucked after that point in time.

For instance, they never ran an article on The Dictators in '75, ie *Go Girl Crazy*. I mean, how retarded was that?

PETER BUCK (REM) I read *Creem* magazine. I hadn't discovered the English papers yet, because I don't think they came to Georgia in those days. *Creem* was a big one, because they liked Iggy And The Stooges, so I got turned onto a lot of stuff.

IRA ROBBINS Future Dictator Scott Kempner turned me on to *Creem* in high school, and I found that very inspiring. I was desperate to write for it and sent them a couple of pitch letters/spec submissions which elicited encouraging scrawled notes – in red pen, as I recall – from Lester Bangs. But my classmate Hank Frank was the first to get a record review – of a Sparks LP, I think it was – published. I was green with envy!

LENNY KAYE I wrote a piece for *Creem* on Grand Funk Railroad in 1971. I reviewed their live record by going to see them at Madison Square Garden and interviewing the kids online, so I got three pages of quotes with the tag line, "Grand Funk Is Here If You Want It". They were an example of an extremely popular band who created a critical brouhaha. You could chart the movement of the critical waves from outright abhorrence. Terry Knight, their manager, played the press beautifully, to the point that, when they got a good review in *Rolling Stone*, he put my review in an ad there.

IT
"IT COULD BE ANYTHING"

NEIL SPENCER At university, I got into the underground press. I'd always been an avid consumer of magazines, because my father was a newsagent, and although things like *Oz* were a bit of a squalid mess you always found mad things in there. But it was very parochial, looking back on it, more about who'd been busted down Ladbroke Grove.

MICK FARREN There was a realisation there that there was a market growing exponentially. We'd gone from a couple of hundred at UFO in January 1967 to 12,000 at Ally Pally by April that year. We didn't know what was happening, but this was obviously a youth movement out of control like we'd never seen it before.

JONATHON GREEN Mickey was England's answer to Abbie Hoffman and one of the underground's most outspoken figures as leader of The Deviants, doorman at UFO and editor of *IT*.

MICK FARREN You didn't really read the music press for information at that time. The source was...the grapevine, which was incredibly efficient, because it was based on a different marketing model to corporate distribution. The news came with the dope. Also, I put some bucks together and got a subscription to *Evergreen Review*, which was a magazine put out by Grove Press, who were putting out everything from *The Hell's Angel Book* to the Marquis de Sade. They had excerpts from books and shit and articles by Nat Hentoff about Eric Dolphy. So we got hold of things from America, like *The East Village Other* from Miles at the Indica Gallery, and I had a mate who was a high-church mod who got *Down Beat*.

JONATHON GREEN Miles dropped his given name, Barry, in 1961, about the time he embarked on his role as leading progenitor of the underground. As Britain's leading advocate of US beat culture, he helped found it, and initiated the Albert Hall poetry readings.

MICK FARREN The whole idea of a counter-culture came out first of all at the Poets' Conference at the Albert Hall in June 1965, where everyone was fucking amazed at the amount of people who showed up, and then Dylan in 1966. That's 7,000 people each time. The pirates were going down as the Marine Offences Act was coming in, so we thought, "We've got to put all this in print." There was this instinctive feeling that an underground press was needed, and it was essentially about that. *IT* was very much influenced by what was happening in the States. When *IT* was launched at the Roundhouse, there were basically only a couple of hundred freaks in the city and everybody knew everybody.

NIGEL FOUNTAIN *IT* could be anything – *Intergalactic Times*, like Longhair's Child; *Interracial Times*; *Intravenous Times*; *Interminable Times*.

MILES Other people called it *International Times*, or even "eye tee". We all called it *It*. To the people on the staff, it was always *It*."

JOHN PEEL I was back here by 1967, on a pirate ship for six months or so, and started reading *Melody Maker* and *NME*, which were delivered to the station.

MICK FARREN The English music press has always been in an equation with the lack of radio. The one time we had decent radio was with the pirates, and also Peel's *The Perfumed Garden* was a great lifeline, particularly if you weren't in London. Luckily, I was, but if you were out in the sticks then Peel told you about Captain Beefheart or John's Children. That was very handy information. Plus, he put on 'Sad-Eyed Lady Of The Lowlands' every time he went for a piss.

JOHN PEEL The underground press' coverage of music was a great disappointment to me. It wasn't really covered by the *International Times* and *Oz* because there was no advertising revenue in it for them, so there wasn't enough money to pay for it.

JONATHON GREEN At *Oz*, I don't think Richard Neville was particularly interested in music. He'd come out of this relatively radical student magazine in Australia called *Tharunka* and changed it to *Oz* and gone through a trial because they'd portrayed people urinating, so he'd come over here and started *Oz* again but wasn't any more interested in music than the average punter. Felix Dennis was the person who had more a feel for rock 'n' roll. The *Oz* rock story I remember was the cover story of Germaine Greer and Viv Stanshall, with her with her hand down his trousers, but its music coverage was very patchy. David Widgery would write a piece along the lines of, "Why isn't rock 'n' roll more revolutionary?" And, like all David's pieces, it would be very good until the last paragraph, which would be, "Of course, the solution to all this is that we all join the IS," or SWP, or whatever the hell David was into at the time.

MICK FARREN I was a punter for about three issues of *IT*, then complained to Miles about the lack of Jimi Hendrix and – apart from his Beatles interviews – why weren't we getting more about The Who or The Move?

This is just pre-*Sgt Pepper*. So they made me music editor. I had no journalistic experience, so I was perfectly qualified. I didn't stay music editor for very long, because about two weeks later we were busted and this rift was already in place: the ex-CND/John Coltrane/Bohemian/spot-of-Tony-Hancock thing, with people like Jeff Nuttall against me, growing up on Gene Vincent and Jerry Lee, smoking dope, being down Shebeens in the Grove and generally wanting to talk about Hendrix playing guitar with his teeth. Once we got busted, all those guys took to the hills, so it ended up with me and Mike McKinley - who did the *Tommy* cover - and a couple of other guys. We were also working the door at the UFO club and running the paper *ad hoc*. That fight between the Bohemian/anti-rock people and the ex-rocker/ex-mod/taking-acid contingent went on throughout the life of the paper.

MILES I did a good interview with Mick Jagger about revolution directly after the Grosvenor Square police riot in 1968. Jagger had been at the demo against American involvement in Vietnam. I like talking to people like that about something other than their latest release.

JONATHON GREEN To Miles' credit, he was doing major, in-depth, *Rolling Stone*-style interviews with rock stars long before anyone else, these long, non-adulatory interviews in which they were allowed to wank on, basically.

MICK FARREN There were a few people who caught on very quickly. John Fenton - who was managing Bolan - and Tony Secunda with The Move. Danny Fields was one of them. We got Jim Morrison stories about how he had all the pets in a pet shop from Danny's Monday morning press releases.

DANNY FIELDS The radio stations started playing 'Light My Fire' from the album. Elektra chopped out that dreadful organ solo in the middle, put it out and it became Number One. And in the spring of 1967, I left *Hullabaloo* to start the Elektra press office, because they remembered that I suggested 'Light My Fire' should be a single and thought I had good taste.

MICK FARREN The Beatles were in it, anyway, but the rest - The Herd, or whoever - were very, very wary, because people like Hoppy and Mick

Jagger were going to jail. It got you on Pilcher's shitlist if you were associated with us. To identify with the rebels bought the wrath of the Metropolitan scuffers down on you pretty hard.

MILES One day, I was complaining to Paul McCartney about how little advertising we were getting, and he said, "You should interview me. Then you'll be able to get record company ads." So I did. I just went over to his place and taped a conversation with no questions pre-thought and then ran a Q&A, like Andy Warhol's *Interview* did a little later on, and he was right. EMI took an ad. So I did one with George Harrison next and we got more ads. Then I did Graham Nash, and so on.

MICK FARREN Jann Wenner at *Rolling Stone* presented the safe end of the counter-culture. He might have [had] an Abbie Hoffman interview, but he didn't run covers that said, "Up Against The Wall, Pig, Die!" which we at *IT* did in a 144-point tabloid headline. Miles did his famous series of interviews – The Beatles, Townshend, whatever – but at that point there weren't really that many people who were up for writing about music for the UK underground press. The first one who really came out the woodwork there I think was Charlie Murray.

CHARLES SHAAR MURRAY: In my teens, I discovered the underground press – *Oz*, *IT* and *Rolling Stone*, though these were hard to find in Reading, where I grew up, and scoring copies was always a priority task on trips to London. Then I wrote this appallingly dumb piece for the *Oz Schoolkids* issue, basically pleading for musical tolerance and open-mindedness rather than fashion-following. I've always done my best to prevent it from being reprinted anywhere, because it's embarrassing, even as juvenilia, but at least it led to other stuff. The *Oz* posse invited me to hang out and practise in public and eventually I got better, gradually discarding mannerisms and ideas pilfered wholesale from *Rolling Stone* writers.

MICK FARREN After we'd been at emergency stations for some time, Nigel Samuel came along and put a bunch of money into it. I was on the road with The Deviants, so the Bohemian academics took control again and they started publishing Anais Nin and all kinds of godawful crap. A kind of compromise was reached, because the record-company advertising had started to roll in, which was bizarre. CBS was running ads saying, "The Man Can't Bust Our Music". Yeah, right.

JONATHON GREEN The most important role of the music industry to the underground press was that it provided advertising.

MICK FARREN [The Deviants] broke up at the end of 1969, and then I had three years basically running *IT*. Everything got worse. All the advertising went to *Rolling Stone*, plus we'd been busted for the gay personals, so that was another source of income which vanished. I'd given away the London Listings section to Tony Elliott through complete stupidity. Everybody hated compiling the What's Happening section in it - it always ended up with loads of mistakes and was like punishment detail, being up to your arms in cow gum. So I said, "Tony, if you can make that work, wonderful." I am not a very intelligent businessman.

THE US ROCK PRESS
"THEY WOULDN'T HANG OUT. THEY WEREN'T FRIENDS"

LISA ROBINSON I never read the music press, but I used to listen to the radio and just buy music all the time. When I taught school for a year in Harlem, I used to comb the record stores there. Then, in 1969, I was listening to WNEW FM very late at night, and there was this disc jockey named Richard Robinson who had this great voice and played really weird music. He played The Velvet Underground, The Stooges, Ike And Tina Turner, Otis Redding. He got fired four times, once for playing 'The Star-Spangled Banner' by Jimi Hendrix, which they claimed was unpatriotic. He got fired again for playing "unfamiliar" music, which meant black music. The last time, he was so pissed off he flushed a toilet on the air and walked off. I was just a fan and I thought he was adorable. I knew somebody in the music business who knew him and I called him and asked if he needed his filing done. I worked for him after school each day. Three months later, we were married. He also wrote a weekly column for *Disc And Music Echo* in the UK and was friendly with people like Penny Valentine. He was eventually too busy to do all this stuff, and he turned the *Disc* column over to me. Simultaneously, I started writing this mimeographed gossip sheet about the music industry called *Pop Wire*. We put it out ourselves and I mailed it. Then we started meeting a lot of the other journalists and press agents in New York – Danny Fields, Lenny Kaye, Vince Aletti, Lillian Roxon, Gloria Stavers. At the same time, there were people like Jon Landau, who lived in Boston.

DANNY FIELDS Jon Landau was the eminent rock critic of the time, the word of God. I flew him out to Detroit to see the MC5 and he wrote a 20-page report on them for [Elektra Records boss] Jac Holzman about how the band should be recorded, which songs they should have on the album. It was incredible, so brilliant. When their manager [John Sinclair] went to jail, Jon and I ended up co-managing the band, and he produced their second album long before he got together with Springsteen. Everyone was all over the place, then. It was much more fluid. One way of co-opting the press was getting Jon Landau to write an analysis of this band, and when the rest of them saw that that was happening, their ears pricked up.

"METAL" MIKE SAUNDERS Jon Landau, as review editor at *Rolling Stone*, had to continuously apologise for what their copy-editor back in San Francisco did to his record-review sections he submitted bi-weekly. Writers' copy was hacked and mutilated to the point where it was often unrecognisable.

LISA ROBINSON There was also John Mendelssohn, who was in LA. Lester Bangs was first in San Diego and then Ann Arbor, at *Creem*, as was Dave Marsh. Richard Meltzer was somewhere, I don't know. Danny Fields was really the centre of everything in New York.

DANNY FIELDS I worked at Elektra through '68 and signed Iggy And The Stooges and the MC5 to them, even though I wasn't an A&R man. Jac Holzman liked my taste. In fact, I got him to do a drug album called *Have A Marijuana* by this street singer I found in Washington Square. We recorded him right there and put out the whole album for $2,500. I said, "Put the word *marijuana* big on the album sleeve and every kid will want to bring it home to give their parents a heart attack." It sold 500,000 albums, and although certain conservative elements at Elektra didn't like that, I had a certain begrudging respect. So I flew out to Detroit and Ann Arbor to see The Stooges and MC5, because I'd been getting so much propaganda from them. I'm a sucker for persistence. I thought, "If they care this much, they're going to do a lot of their own work."

I saw them both. The MC5 had sold out the Grande Ballroom and had 2,000 screaming people there. No one had heard of The Stooges, but I thought they were fantastic. They played the student union on a Sunday afternoon and I was mesmerised. This was the rock 'n' roll music I'd been looking for all my life, and the singer wasn't so bad, either.

I waited on the side of the stage and, when they came off, I said, "Hello, I'm from Elektra Records and I think you guys are really good." Iggy said, "Oh yeah? Uh-huh? Talk to the manager." He didn't believe that a record company would travel that far. He said he thought I was some loony janitor.

Anyhow, I called Jac Holzman from the MC5's communal house and had the two managers with me on the Monday morning. I said, "You have to have heard of the MC5–" because they'd played the '68 Democratic Convention and Norman Mailer had written about them in *Harper's* "– while the other is a baby band with a great lead singer who is definitely better than Jim Morrison." Jac said, "I tell you what. Offer the big band $20,000 and the little band $5,000. I'll wait." The managers had never heard about money like that. Are you kidding? They snapped it up. It made history: September 22, 1968.

LISA ROBINSON I was the newlywed wife of this guy who was at the centre of this stuff, and Richard didn't really know any of these other people. He'd see them at concerts, but they wouldn't hang out. They weren't friends. None of them had any money. I thought Richard needed more friends, and I got him together with Lenny Kaye, who was a really cool guy who liked the same music we did and seemed really sweet. I said, "Why don't we have him over to the house?"

LENNY KAYE Knowing the Robinsons was really crucial. Richard especially had a great sense of, "You can do six magazines a month. Don't get precious about your work and have some fun with it."

LISA ROBINSON The president of Buddah Records, Neil Bogart, was very generous, so Richard had this expense account, which meant we could have people over to our house, order up Chinese food and feed them...and basically that's what happened.

LENNY KAYE I don't remember too much about expense accounts. They just seemed to have an incredible amount of energy. He was doing these radio shows six days a week; they were publishing this magazine, that magazine; he was working for record companies.

LISA ROBINSON I started to invite them all over to my house. Some of them didn't have a place to stay in New York, they'd stay with us. Dave Marsh stayed for quite a while, Richard Meltzer was there for a while, too, and Lenny was there to the point that, in August, he asked me, "Are we having a Christmas tree this year?"

LENNY KAYE It was a very incestuous scene. Everybody was writing for everyone else. The pay scales were hardly sustainable, but you were getting free records and places to hang out and you were getting to write constantly. There were a lot of outlets by then – *Crawdaddy!*, *Zooworld*, *Creem* – and that's a good thing, because I got to hone my craft. I don't remember much rivalry. Everybody seemed to be a little bit different. I didn't write like Richard Meltzer, for example. My own particular area might have been a little more as a musical historian. I wasn't as pop as the Robinsons.

DANNY FIELDS Getting these bands press was no problem. MC5 were on the cover of *Rolling Stone* and everyone loved The Stooges, but when the record came out it didn't sell anything and they didn't get airplay. But they were loved by the critics, though, by friends such as Gloria Stavers, Lillian Roxon, Lisa Robinson, Richard Goldstein, Robert Christgau, Jon Landau, Lenny Kaye.

ROBERT CHRISTGAU I got my start replacing *Bonnie And Clyde* co-writer David Newman as an every-three-months "secular music" columnist for *Esquire*, which had been courting me as a reporter after I wrote an award-winning – and, in terms of what became of my career, anomalous – piece for *New York* magazine about a girl who died on a macrobiotic diet. By then, I'd already received and flubbed an assignment from New York to profile Chuck Berry. I'd written my first column before I did a piece about higher education for rock 'n' rollers for *Esquire*'s college issue and then got sent out to cover the Monterey Pop Festival, a life-changing event.

KEITH ALTHAM My first trip to America as a journalist on the *NME* was with Jimi Hendrix to the Monterey Pop Festival. We flew out with Eric Burdon And The New Animals. There were people like Brian Jones wandering around. Keith Richards described him as being like "a ghost leaving a seance". I had the glorious Michelle Phillips driving me around. She'd been detailed to drive me around because I was important, apparently! The whole hippie thing had broken loose and Derek Taylor was doing PR for the festival. He had great style and élan. He spent days issuing passes, and when it opened the press area was bigger than the audience. Derek had to make an announcement over the tannoy: "The day of the purple pass is over. Will all those with purple passes come back to the press tent, where they will be issued with new passes." This huge queue formed and he'd had enough after four hours. He shut the press office and erected this notice, "I cannot relate to your problem," and went home.

LENNY KAYE Danny saw a review I wrote in *Fusion* of the first Stooges record. He's always had a good eye for talent and for someone who's into the avant spectrum, so he called me up and said there was a position just opened up at *Cavalier*. It was one of the men's magazine, a sub-*Penthouse*, but at that time those were a good source of employment for writers – Stephen King was writing stories for them. So it gave me a place to pay my rent, and because I was music editor I was able to get on all the press lists and go to all the parties. All of a sudden, I'm receiving free records and I'm a rock journalist. Within a couple of years, I was writing for just about any magazine. I was the New York columnist for *Disc And Music Echo* in England. I took that over from Lisa.

DANNY FIELDS The reaction to the MC5 and The Stooges was really to the chagrin of the people at Elektra, who didn't like me in the first place. There was some office gossip thing I repeated about one of the bosses' daughters getting knocked up and it got back to him, the executive vice-president, William S Harvey. He was a drunken WASP-y guy who hated me. On January 20, 1969 – I remember it because this was the day Richard Nixon was inaugurated and my mother and father were hijacked on their way to Cuba – he punched me in the head over and over and over in the offices. I was backing out of the room, because I'm not a punching person. Jac Holzman came out of his office and just stood there at the other end of the hall. So I packed up my stuff and I was gone.

LISA ROBINSON When I met Danny, he was so unbelievably flattering to me about writing the *Disc* column. Through him I met everyone else.

LENNY KAYE It was a very tight-knit rock-writer world in a way that it isn't any more, and it was relatively small. There'd be ten or 20 people, but there were three, four, five press parties a week, so you'd go and have dinner at one of those and see whatever they were trying to hustle and do your work. At one point, we even got a group together called the Collective Conscience, people like Lillian Roxon; Jim Fourat, who would go on to be the gadfly of the music establishment; Danny Goldberg, who was one of the editors of *Circus*. It was mostly having meetings up at the Robinsons' and having lots of fun and chuckles over the state of the music business. And we'd meet the rock journalists from all over the US while the British press had their own people here, like Chris Charlesworth of *Melody Maker*, who ended up covering the early CBGB scene.

LISA ROBINSON This whole scene has been so badly reported to the point where it enrages me. In Victor Bockris' book about Lou Reed, he says I had this salon and that Richard and I ruled New York society, which is just utter bullshit. You have to understand, I was just married. It was fun to have all these people hanging out, but after a while it got to be a little bit much. Richard Meltzer was brilliant, you know, but he drank a lot and he has sort of turned on me and says awful things about me these days and I don't know why. I guess he's a bitter guy. I remember when we were still friends. I still think he's brilliant.

RICHARD MELTZER I get an invite to one of her whatsems, I arrive and it turns out there's no party but an "intimate gathering" - me, Lisa and her husband, Richard, Lou and his soon-to-be first wife. I think her name was Betty. I look around. I'm not sure what gives, so Lisa pulls me aside, informs me I'm Lou's entertainment. "He really respects you." Uh, great. What gives is Richard's itching to produce the guy - a feather for his wighat, considering all he's done is Hackamore Brick and The Flamin'

Groovies. Lou, meanwhile, is contemplating a comeback. He's cooling out, working as a bookkeeper or something.

LISA ROBINSON When Richard was working at RCA, they later signed people like Lou Reed, David Bowie and The Kinks. Danny was managing Lou Reed. Richard helped Lou get the solo deal and helped produce the first solo album, so we would have him over to the house and introduce him to the rest of the rock press. Nobody needed any encouragement to meet Lou Reed; he was like a god to them. Richard Meltzer and Lester and whatnot were thrilled to meet him.

RICHARD MELTZER At an opportune moment, Richard hands him an acoustic guitar. He plays, sings rudimentary versions of 'Walk On The Wild Side' and that other one, whatever the title, with "They're taking her children away." Invited, I sing harmony. Lisa videotapes, presumably for posterity, and after songs, jokes. Lou goes first and I've decided by then to spill the ending. I inhale deeply – that's the ending, and Lou is pissed. The Robinsons, too, like maybe I've killed the golden goose... I'm not forgiven, though, when eventually I review the solo album and I don't spout whatever the party line was supposed to be... Time marches on. It's 1973 or 1974 when this interview appears in *Zooworld*, Fort Lauderdale's very own and now very defunct *Rolling Stone*, wherein Lou accuses me of plagiarism. I've done some lyrics for Blue Oyster Cult and it seems to him I couldn't have written diddleyrot without having sat at his feet, basked in his omnipoetic brilliance... Finally, in Thanksgiving 1976, he wants nothing to do with me. Fine, fine. He wants to bear grudges, I can bear 'em too. I will not listen to groove zero by this asshole again, and I ain't.

ROLLING STONE UK, FRIENDS AND FRENDZ
"NONE OF WHICH REALLY TOOK"

RICHARD WILLIAMS There was always this thing, you know: "We'll start a British *Rolling Stone*." Of course, there was a British *Rolling Stone* for a while, which became *Friends* and then *Frendz*, none of which really took.

ALAN MARCUSON I heard that *Rolling Stone* was starting in London and meantime my parents were putting enormous pressure on me to get a job, and I knew a few people on the fringes of rock 'n' roll, so I got this job running advertising for *Rolling Stone*.

JONATHON GREEN I left Oxford in June 1969, just when it was announced that a UK *Rolling Stone* was going to be launched with money from Mick Jagger. A woman called Jane Nicholson was editing it. I think Alan had got her from LSE. Alan had come from South Africa, where his father had made millions in socks, I believe. Alan had done national service and came to study at Leeds University, where he was a contemporary of Jack Straw's, funnily enough.

ALAN MARCUSON There we were for the first month or so bringing editions out of The Rolling Stones' offices. Mick Jagger and Keith Richards used to come in and I used to quake in my boots. These were the gods! I remember spending an afternoon in the offices literally days before Brian Jones died. This sweating figure came in and I spent the afternoon talking to him, not knowing whether to be nice to him because he was a superstar, but he looked very ill and nobody else was talking to him. Finally, we moved to 19 Hanover Square.

JONATHON GREEN On spec, I sent them a review of the second Soft Machine album and a piece on Brian Jones' death. At the same time, I had an interview with *The Sunday Times*. When I went for that, there was a temp secretary there who told me I didn't have an interview, "so fuck off", basically. So I went up to *Rolling Stone* and Marcuson said, "Do you want a job as news editor?" Mark Williams was rather put out at this and left in a huff, saying, "I'm going off to the Speakeasy." Either him or me was wearing a green velvet jacket. I can't remember which, though.

MARK WILLIAMS *Rolling Stone* UK was very much more a rock 'n' roll paper than *IT*. I met Wenner. Wenner was greedy and ultimately brutish and he was also a fucking groupie for Mick Jagger, always was and still is, as far as I'm aware. I was British news editor. It very quickly became apparent to me that it wasn't real. I was hired on the understanding that we were actually going to produce a British edition, and very quickly it changed into just having eight pages in what was essentially an American edition, and it went downhill very quickly.

JONATHON GREEN I was news editor. Great! £20 a week, which I don't believe I ever got paid. I was terribly naïve. The first piece I did was on managers. I remember Steve Marriott refusing to talk about Don Arden because he was so shit-scared of him. I talked to Fat Strat, Tony Stratton-Smith. You'd get all these freebies and write nice things about people. It was incredibly corrupt, in a way. I had this nagging sense that I should be more investigative. I remember being taken by Stratton-Smith to some club full of his sordid mates at 5am with them all talking about "running down niggers on zebra crossings". Huh, huh, huh. I just thought, "I don't want to be involved with these people."

ALAN MARCUSON The problem was that we never got a clear directive. Mick Jagger wanted to start an independent magazine, but US *Rolling Stone* just wanted a subsidiary. US *Rolling Stone* was very independent of the US underground press, but we in London wanted to be part of the British version. Eventually, Jane Nicholson left and I became editor.

JONATHON GREEN There was an element of undergroundiness in it which Wenner disliked. The designer, John Goodchild, had come from *Oz*, and he was always trying to make it weird. He wasn't somebody I particularly got on with. I thought he was someone who was rather too pleased with himself.

JOHN GOODCHILD Here we were, supposedly working for some kind of underground press, and we were in this pretty expensive, plush place, so we tended to abuse it.

JONATHON GREEN It was an amazing office. There was the sofa Mick used to fuck Marianne on, and over there was the sofa he used to fuck Marsha on. All this amazing furniture. Very nice.

JOHN GOODCHILD Jann Wenner would send over these directives all the time, just like the King, so our first reaction was to say, "Who do you think you are?" After a while, we began to take over.

JONATHON GREEN One time, they said, "Here's an ounce of dope. Go and interview Peter Frampton," who had been "The Face Of '68" and was in The Herd at the time. So I produced the dope and it got an incredibly negative response. He just wasn't having any of it. The other thing I remember about that encounter was that Frampton lived in this flat in Hampstead and there was this other guy stumbling drunkenly up the path. It was Cherie Blair's father, Tony Booth, who we all knew from *'Til Death Do Us Part*.

GENE MAHON I was responsible for putting it all together. I was basically labouring, gathering together all the bits and pieces - negs coming in from the States, pages being done in London. It was quite hard work.

JONATHON GREEN The great apotheosis of UK *Rolling Stone* was the party for it at Hanover Square. Bolan took an overdose there. We were spiked with some very bad acid. It wasn't just Bolan; there were a lot of record people completely fucked up.

JEFF DEXTER All the drinks at the party had been spiked. I'd been spiked several times before and had no fear of it. Then my friends began to get sick, fall over, become paranoid. One of them was Marc Bolan. Marc was in a terrible state, flipping out...

ALAN MARCUSON Was it the strychnine LSD or the hash cookies? That was the beginning of the end, the start of the demise of London *Rolling Stone*, when we lost all credibility with the record companies.

JONATHON GREEN I wasn't actually present when this happened, but at the party, Jann Wenner was staying to the staff, "Come on, get out and about and ask questions. We're not here just to drink Mick Jagger's white wine." And Jagger apparently said, "Oh yes you are."

PAT BELL Jann Wenner was very efficient himself and expected things to be done in a far more efficient, professional way. After one of his visits, the rights were withdrawn for us to publish in London.

JONATHON GREEN Perhaps the week after the party, we waltzed into *Rolling Stone* to find the locks had been changed by people from Jagger's office. Alan went around to the Stones' office in Maddox Street and they said, "Wenner told us to shut you down." But we had all the copy - including all sorts of shit like a William Burroughs essay – for the next issue and we decided to call it *Friends Of Rolling Stone*. Alan was already trying to pull it away from pure rock 'n' roll, and I think that was one of the reasons why Wenner didn't like it, that we weren't mimicking *Rolling Stone* 110 per cent. He also no doubt thought that we weren't as good as his guys, which may well have been true.

ALAN MARCUSON Jagger was basically on our side. Then he went off to Altamont, and in the middle of Altamont Jann Wenner struck and demanded we fall under the editorial jurisdiction of San Francisco and do only what they wanted us to do and that we were to submit our material to California and all we were to do was sell advertising. Soon afterward, we were thrown out of the office.

JONATHON GREEN The evening before the lock-out, I had got my friend Pearce Marchbank in as designer to replace Gene Mahon, who designed the apple logo for Apple but had had enough. Pearce was working on *Architectural Design* at the time, and to his enormous credit he hung in there. *Rolling Stone* injuncted us against calling it *Friends Of...* so we ended up just calling it *Friends*, which is how this really soppy name came into existence. Alan got involved with this very dubious American guy called Bobby Steinbrecker, who was the first person who ever gave me coke. He had a flat behind Harrods where we were based for a short time. Alan and I used to cash the advertising cheques and go off to Harrods' food hall on the proceeds. Then we went to 305 Portobello Road, which is where *Friends* hooked up with people like Barney Bubbles and Steve and Eddie, who called themselves Famepushers and backed the magazine.

PEARCE MARCHBANK *Friends* was the smell of feet, the mice that used to run across my drawing board at night. I used to catch them in a little sandwich box I kept some pens in.

CHARLES SHAAR MURRAY When it subdivided into American *Rolling Stone* and *Friends*, I thought that was at least honest – *Friends* was coming at you from Portobello Road, *Rolling Stone* from San Francisco.

JONATHON GREEN It still had a very heavy rock 'n' roll input and was in many ways son of *Rolling Stone* UK. Once again, the ads were all from record companies. Dick Lawson was the rock 'n' roll editor and did a lot of that, while there were also people like John May, who later worked for *NME* and was a real journalist, writing lots of very informed and radical stuff.

ALAN MARCUSON I did *Friends* for 28 issues, 'til the start of 1971. The thing that finished *Friends* for me was that I met Jim McCann, who was an Irish revolutionary and hustler somewhere to the left of the Provos, who'd apparent thrown him out. He dominated the course of my life for the next five or six years.

JONATHON GREEN I was on *Friends* until August 1970. I changed its name to *Frendz* in February/March of the next year, by which time I was living with Rosie Boycott, who had just worked on the special Angry Brigade/ feminist issue. When it became *Frendz*, all these other people started to come on board, including Nick Kent. Kent and I were never pals. I think he saw me as the old guard and I saw him as a jerk-off who wanted to dress like David Bowie. If you're a rock 'n' roll journalist, it doesn't mean you're a rock 'n' roll star, although he obviously thought it did.

MELODY MAKER
"IT GOT BETTER AND BETTER"

TONY TYLER By the mid '60s, *Melody Maker* was beginning to thrash *NME*, which had stuck rigidly to the pop-picking formula of early British entertainment media, whereas *Melody Maker* catered for a more student readership, who didn't want to know what a particular star had for breakfast or what his fave colours were; they wanted his views on Vietnam, Tolkien and the *Bhagavad Gita*.

JERRY GILBERT When I was studying at Highbury Technical College, Bob Houston – who was the production editor of the *Melody Maker* – came down and did a whole thing on page design, and it was so impressive. The whole paper was great in terms of layout and design, like the fact that it had "ethnic" pages – jazz and blues by Max Jones, avant garde by Richard Williams, folk by Tony Wilson and Karl Dallas. I was absolutely in awe.

PETER YORK In a series of cultural spurts from 1967 on, the rock press became increasingly hip, in parallel with the fans' own development.

CHRIS WELCH Lots of younger people started to come on board. Barry Wentzell the photographer joined in 1967 and we went off to cover the Magical Mystery Tour. We weren't invited, so we followed the bus in our car and our presence was tolerated. It was a bit of a scoop.

TONY TYLER *Melody Maker* got better and better through the '60s. Writers I particularly remember were Richard Williams, the Macaulay of rock; Michael Watts, a sharp stylist and natural "star"; and most of all a bloke called Roy Hollingsworth, who for about 18 months was the absolute top of the tree, as far as I and many others were concerned. He was really funny and perceptive. He suddenly vanished and I never heard his name again. We would have been delighted to have him on the *NME* a few years later.

CHRIS WELCH We had people like Tony Wilson, who was a folk writer but was also keen on Led Zeppelin and Yes and having a whale of a time raving it up in London. Then his exploits were written about in *Groupie* as this notorious journalist. He thought everyone recognised the character as him, which they only did when he told them, and was so embarrassed he rushed off to Ireland and was never seen again.

JERRY GILBERT Folk was where I really got off in those days, which is a bit untrendy to say now. The whole singer/songwriter thing and places like Les Cousins with Paul Simon playing there. I did my three years on a local paper, *The Farnham Herald*, and in the last year ran a folk festival with Al Stewart and Ralph McTell. I took my proficiency test and got a job on *Melody Maker* in April 1969, replacing Tony Wilson, who was a legend. He was immortalised in *Groupie* by Jenny Fabian and fled to Ireland, his Kathmandu, were he doused himself in copious amounts of Guinness and worked on the showbiz section of *The Irish Times* or whatever it was, where years later I ran into him. So he left a gap which I filled.

CHARLIE GILLETT The reason why *Melody Maker* got in on Cream and all of those bands that appeared at the Marquee in the late '60s was because it had always been interested in individual live performance rather than the packaged pop format.

ALLAN JONES *Melody Maker* was the first weekly paper that I'd read and at the time seemed to be the one paper dealing with music in some kind of depth and had some personality. It was the first one to build up the journalists with pictures of Chris Welch, who came across as someone you almost knew, with a convivial, chatty style. And, fuck me, he seemed to know everybody from The Beatles to the Stones and Jimi Hendrix. It was incredible. I came from this small town in Wales, Port Talbot, and it opened a new world for me.

CHRIS WELCH What was good was that, when new people came long, like Jerry Gilbert, they discovered new bands for us, so we kept our fingers on the pulse. Jerry was championing Genesis in the early days and everyone had this Monday-morning thing about "I saw this great band at the weekend..."

JERRY GILBERT The folk thing in those days was very political. Socialist. Very Ewan MacColl. I was just a young stripling from Surrey. It was great. Acts would cheerfully come along to meet us in this pub - long since gone - in Red Lion Court, Fleet Street. I'd be interviewing Marc Bolan back to back with Chris, who'd be interviewing Keith Emerson. It was incredibly laid back. No PRs involved - happily - and we all did it in shorthand. It was very old school. The ethos was that a week later it would be wrapping cod and chips.

IRA ROBBINS [Future *Trouser Press* co-founder] Dave Schulps and I discovered that the New York Public Library owned a collection of *Melody Maker*, going back for decades, on microfilm. Dave had this idea of researching British rock using them, so we spent untold hours at the Lincoln Center Library going cross-eyed and seasick as the scratchy old images raced by, writing down every British musician we could find reference to, which bands they had been in and when. Dave came up with a coding system for instrumentation, which I use in note-taking to this day: G, V, K, Y, B, D - guitar, vocals, keyboards, synthesiser, bass, drums, etc. We would write this stuff on sheets of notebook paper, listed vaguely alphabetically by musician's name, and attempt to put their careers in chronological order. Then we would go to the stores that sold cut-outs and look up the names on records' back covers to see what we could add to our knowledge base and our record collections.

JERRY GILBERT I was daunted, working there, because I was so parochial. In the first week, an agent rang me up and said he wanted to take me to lunch. We went next door to the Golden Egg, which is a mark of its time. It was the end of the old jazzers' era. Bob Dawbarn and Jack Hutton had played in Carnaby Street-type places. We were at 161 Fleet Street and Ray Coleman was then editor of *Disc And Music Echo*, which is where Penny Valentine worked and Caroline Boucher, who later became Rocket Records' PR for Elton John.

NICK LOGAN While the *Melody Maker* was doing very well, the *NME* was suffering, post-Monkees. Sales had been higher with them than even with The Beatles – up to around 350,000 to 375,000 copies a week, I think. The *NME* had had this huge success with the beat boom and watched the sales go through the roof and drift down again. And then along came The Monkees and it went up again. I joined when that was coming to an end, and from that point it was all going to go rotten and sour, because there wasn't going to be another thing which the *NME* could understand. I can still see [editor] Andy Gray now. He'd get the page proof of the chart and work down the list of who to cover. It was totally chart based. You might get an eighth or a quarter page on a new group, but they were just waiting for the next big thing, and I don't think they thought it could be progressive music.

MICK FARREN Pink Floyd did quite a serious amount of distancing themselves from the rest of the underground from quite early on. They started doing big *Melody Maker* interviews, denying the drugs. Among many bands, not only was there a hesitation to get down and fuck with the underground papers but the lines were starting to blur between us and the aboveground papers, particularly *Melody Maker*. People like Chris Welch had worked their way in.

CHARLES SHAAR MURRAY: *Melody Maker* had muso-farceur Chris Welch and arch-hippie Nick Jones.

CHAS DE WHALLEY Nick Jones was the son of Max Jones, the *Melody Maker*'s famed jazz correspondent. Nick Jones was the *Melody Maker*'s famed Doors/Incredible String Band correspondent. He later worked for Miles Copeland, doing PR for bands like Squeeze.

CHRIS WELCH In the mid '60s, I had been very much a pop writer, interviewing people like PJ Proby, but I started to follow bands who played live a lot, like The Yardbirds or The Spencer Davis Group, and gradually, when those bands broke up, they formed new groups, like Traffic, Cream or The Jimi Hendrix Experience. Suddenly, all the underground groups had popped up, but most were manned by people who had been in bands I knew previously. So, when Jimmy Page formed Led Zeppelin, he came to see me at the office and showed me how to spell "Led". He liked the fact that I had given a favourable review to a really unknown band he had been in years before. He invited me to the Marquee to see them and I was flabbergasted.

IAN MACDONALD The first young journalist I remember cottoning onto was Nick Jones writing about Hendrix. Then, of course, Richard Williams, who was the model, I think, for many of us who came later – the way he covered all the bases, from Lennon to Nyro to avant-garde jazz. He famously reviewed the test-signal sides of the white labels of *Life With The Lions*, 20 minutes of one electronic tone. I thought that was great. It showed how he was prepared to try anything, which again was absolutely the spirit of the time.

DAVID TOOP I was always an avid reader of the music press, buying glossy titles like *Beat Instrumental* in my early teens, then studying *Melody Maker* from cover to cover every week for the next 20 years or so. Writers like Valerie Wilmer, Tam Fiofori and Richard Williams covered a lot of the music I was listening to at that time – mid- to late-'60s avant-garde jazz, experimental rock.

HARVEY KUBERNIK Richard Williams was a big influence, particularly the pieces he did for *Melody Maker*, when they let him write about Phil Spector, Brian Wilson, Tom Wilson, Lou Adler – the producer stories. Also, Max Jones covering the jazz scene at *Melody Maker* really made me more aware of the instruments and the musicians who played them.

CHRIS WELCH Richard was brilliant and very cool. He impressed everybody because he is very courteous, intelligent and knowledgeable, which is unusual in a journalist. He took on the bands I tended to neglect, who were slightly more cerebral. His tastes divided between, say, Miles Davis and Ornette Coleman and Phil Spector and the origins or rock 'n' roll and blues. Richard has an historical perspective. I was more into going to see bands every night and maybe not seeing the broader picture.

RICHARD WILLIAMS I wrote asking for a job at the *NME* because it wasn't as good as the *Melody Maker*, so I didn't think I stood a chance of getting a job there. But I was turned down, so I sent the *Melody Maker* a review of a West Coast trumpet player in Nottingham, and a few weeks later I got a telegram from Bob Houston saying, "There's a job here. Are you interested?" So I arranged an interview with Jack Hutton and became junior reporter. I was a few months short of my indenture at the local paper, but I said to them, "Sorry, I'm going," which was breaking our deal, but I thought, "I'm never going to get this chance again."

IAN MACDONALD Michael Watts was another excellent writer for *Melody Maker*. It was the top UK paper in the '60s.

CHRIS WELCH One day, Jack called across the office, saying, "We've got this guy Peter Grant on the phone. Led Zeppelin are going to America next week. Do you want to go with them?" This was October 1968. I was the only journalist on the trip. It was the first time I'd been to America, the first time I'd been on a Boeing 707. We went straight to the hotel and then to Carnegie Hall, which they had sold out - there were no tickets left, so I had to stand on the side of the stage with Lord Sutch, of all people. They were just about to go onstage when Robert realised he'd left his harmonicas behind, so I had to rush back to the hotel, make myself useful. Then they really took off. This was a matter of months after Jimmy had wandered into the office saying he had a new band.

NICK LOGAN In 1969, I applied twice to get onto the *Melody Maker*. There seemed to be only one choice. It was highly respected and the *NME* wasn't. I had spent five years on *The West Essex Gazette* and had done the usual thing, run a pop column. I might have interviewed the odd Small Face who lived locally, or the drummer for The Nashville Teens, but it was all minor stuff. So, when I got turned down by Jack Hutton because I couldn't read music – which you had to be able to do to work on the *Melody Maker* then – I thought, "Oh well, fuck you."

RICHARD WILLIAMS I liked Jack very much. He was a nice, old-fashioned gentleman journalist. He played the cornet in a band on Tuesday nights in Crouch End and he was a good boss. *Melody Maker* was on the rise. It was starting to reap the benefit of being a little bit more intelligent, and the musicians were respecting it more. Musicianship was becoming an issue, and the *Melody Maker* was a bit more in tune with the fiddly bits. Mind you, the first story I had to do on my first Monday morning was about BBC banning 'Je T'Aime, Moi Non Plus'.

CHARLIE GILLETT Jack Hutton was very sweet to me. I'd written to every paper there was. This was 1966. I'd come back from America and wrote a kind of thesis about the evolution of pop music out of black music in America. He wrote back saying, "I think your approach is inappropriate for pop music. This is how people write about jazz, and we're not interested in writing about pop music. There isn't a market for it."

CHRIS WELCH Because we'd been covering all those bands when they played the clubs, *Melody Maker* had an entrée into this new wave of bands who were taking over America. Up until 1969, rock was still seen by and large as a small club scene where bands got £100 a night, if they were lucky, sitting in a Transit and playing in front of 250 people. When people like Zeppelin went to America, they established huge audiences and changed it forever. Atlantic started signing British bands like Yes, who were also a Marquee band, and the festivals like Isle Of Wight helped because there were suddenly big sound systems.

RICHARD WILLIAMS Working at *Melody Maker* in those days was very, very, very good fun, I must say. I'm not a big hanger-outer, but there was hanging out to be done, if you wanted, and you did get to go on tour with people. I went to America with The Faces and that kind of thing. You got to go to a lot of gigs; you could go to as many gigs as you could handle. And musicians used to come into the office, in those days. There were PR men around, but they weren't a fence; they were kind of facilitators, more than anything else, and they didn't see it as part of their job to listen in on interviews and censor anybody or any of that kind of stuff.

TOM HIBBERT I had my first letter published in *Melody Maker* in 1970. It was about Crosby, Stills And Nash and how crap Graham Nash was, which I think still stands up today.

THE REST OF THE PRESS
"VERY MUCH SECOND CHOICE"

CHRIS WELCH All of us on the various papers got on very well, sharing the same press trips. There was no violence, like a couple of years later. *Disc* and *Melody Maker* shared the same pub, the Red Lion in Queen Street.

NICK LOGAN For me, the *NME* was very much second choice. The paper where I worked was owned by the group which printed it. I used to see the editor, Andy Gray, on the presses, and I plucked up the courage to ask this grey-haired, distinguished-looking gentleman for a job and, surprisingly, I got one. He had given a job to someone on the same paper as me six months before who was a complete washout. I don't remember his name, but he went mad, I think, and completely blew it, so I thought my chance had gone.

LISA ROBINSON Richard didn't want to do the *Disc* column any more, so he turned it over to me. I'd never written anything, but he said, "You can talk, you can write," so I started writing this column for *Disc And Music Echo*.

NICK LOGAN Maurice Kinn was an absolutely fearsome character, this grand man talking about Frank Sinatra and Sammy Davis Jr. He was still writing the "Alley Cat" column when I joined, and one of my jobs was to handle the corrections when Maurice phoned them through to the printers'. God forbid if you didn't show the right degree of respect and absolutely get it right. I don't remember ever being slaughtered for anything, but you knew it was the worst crime you could commit. He used to put the words ascloseasthis, and if you didn't understand that spacing, there would be trouble.

CHARLIE GILLETT The great thing about *Record Mirror* was that the people who worked for it were interested in reaching their audience. It had Norman Jopling and a guy called James Hamilton, who did the singles reviews. It was absolutely dedicated to the kind of person I felt I was, which was somebody who was interested in records, particularly black music. So it was probably the first to realise that a pop music audience wasn't just into certain music.

JON SAVAGE *Record Mirror* and *Disc* both had very good colour reproduction. *Record Mirror*, in particular, had very thorough record reviews by James Hamilton, which was a big plus, and it also had the charts. Also, the text wasn't utterly patronising.

NICK LOGAN The *NME* at the time was made up of writers who carved up the music acts between them, people like Keith Altham, Norrie Drummond. Alan Smith was there, and Richard Green joined about the time I did.

JONATHON GREEN On *Rolling Stone* UK, we used to refer to Chris Welch and Richard Green as "Boozo and the Beast". That was our way of taking the piss out of the "straight" music papers who were trying to muscle in on the underground scene.

NICK LOGAN Some of the senior guys were very well entrenched at *NME*, and I was very much the new kid on the block. They were incredibly protective of their turf – there was no way I was going to write about the Stones or The Small Faces, because Keith Altham covered them, while Alan Smith was even worse with The Beatles. Norrie Drummond had Herman's Hermits and the dross!

KEITH ALTHAM I had a run-in with Ray Davies about an incident at *Top Of The Pops* when he was completely pissed out of his mind and tried to pull Dave Hill of Slade's wig off, so I wrote it up as a bit of an Enid Blyton story. I got a poison pen letter from him in the post warning me not to take the piss out of him. It was sent anonymously, but I knew exactly who it was from.

CHARLIE GILLETT In 1971, there was an offer to somebody on the staff of all the papers to go to New York to witness the famous gig in New York by

Brinsley Schwarz supporting Van Morrison. Rob Partridge was first choice on *Record Mirror* but didn't want to do it. By some extraordinary process – I think, if there was ranking, I'd have been about 15th on the list – I was the one who went. And that was how I got into Van Morrison. I hadn't really noticed him before.

NICK LOGAN Prog rock became my area because everything else was sewn up, apart from some of the black music, which I was desperate to write about. But the problem was that the artists weren't in the country and you couldn't get the material, even when you did do an interview. Knowing what I know now, I think about the stories I could have got from people like James Brown, but I couldn't get close to him. The high point was interviewing The Showstoppers at the Revolution Club during rehearsals and coming away with nothing. So I ended up with Cream, Fleetwood Mac, Family, Jethro Tull. I liked the lifestyle and I recognised that they were good copy – that was my territory – but the whole culture of the paper was wrong. *Melody Maker* was perfectly poised to cover this stuff because it was serious music.

SOUNDS
"A LEFT-WING MELODY MAKER"

CHRIS WELCH Jack phoned me at home one Saturday in 1970 and said, "Are you standing up?" I said, "Yes." He said, "Well, sit down. I've just resigned." He and the ad manager, Peter Wilkinson, had got together with two directors to launch a new music paper, *Sounds*. At that point, I'd been at *Melody Maker* for about five years, and he asked me whether I wanted to join them.

JERRY GILBERT The divisional directors, John Thompson and Joe Sahl, went off and set up Banner Press with Jack Hutton with a view to launching *Sounds*, so Ray [Coleman] was drafted in from *Disc* to run *Melody Maker*. If I'm honest about it, there was a strange atmosphere there. I don't think everyone was 100 per cent happy about Ray being reinstated as editor. He tried to cross-match journalists with areas outside of their expertise. I was doing a lot of blues at the time, but for some reason he wanted Richard Williams to cover it.

RICHARD WILLIAMS I'd been at *Melody Maker* about six months when Jack Hutton left with two guys to form Spotlight Publications. They took more than half of the staff with them, so immediately there were vacancies at all levels and I went, in two weeks, from being junior reporter to features editor, and the next week I was assistant editor. Ray Coleman had come in and seen that he needed people to do these jobs.

JERRY GILBERT Ray could be very abrasive. It wasn't a comfortable situation. There was an instant personality clash. He'd run into Jane Asher at some party, and Peter Asher was managing James Taylor. There was some spurious reason why he wanted me to write about him, and although I was well into Taylor, I didn't like the manipulation, so I decided to go to *Sounds*. It was drop in salary, I remember.

CHRIS WELCH A lot of people went with them, including Alf Martin, who later became editor of *Sounds*. They even took our tea lady! Maisie was amazing, straight out of *EastEnders*. She used to serve tea to all the visiting musicians, asking Ornette Coleman or Ringo Starr, "Whatcha want, dear?"

JERRY GILBERT *Sounds* was going to have jazz and blues and be modelled very much on the *Melody Maker*. There was this summer in 1970 when we all waited for it to launch. Billy Walker was the chief sub on *Melody Maker* and ready to go, Alan Lewis as well, but the guy who was leading the charge was Richard Williams, who in the event never left. Ask him why. We were all a bit bemused because he was so keen.

RICHARD WILLIAMS Jack said, "It's going to be a left-wing *Melody Maker*." I thought the better thing to do would be to make the *Melody Maker* more left wing. I liked Jack, but it was the *Melody Maker* I'd come to work for, not Jack. I was happy where I was. It was a big shock to me to get promoted.

JERRY GILBERT Penny Valentine was drafted in from *Disc* and Alf Martin crossed over. Billy Walker was the editor. Part of the platform was that there would be a poster in the centre. Just before the first issue came out, Janis Joplin died, so we replated the front cover to feature her. Even though we had the poster in the middle, we felt we could be more serious and take on the *Melody Maker*.

CHRIS WELCH First of all, I said that I would join *Sounds*, but when I got in to *Melody Maker* on Monday morning, Ray Coleman had been promoted to editor, and he offered me a pay rise and said the opportunities would open up for me. Then he said he'd make me features editor and gave me another pay rise. By the end of the day, he'd given me a third pay rise to stay where I was, and I realised I wasn't the dogsbody after all. I was on something ridiculous like £26 a week and it went up to £35.

JERRY GILBERT I was news editor and became features editor. *Sounds*, in its first incarnation, was very much reportage – loads and loads of research and in depth but also designed to be disposable. I was interviewing people like Son House, Bukka White and Keith Christmas and did features on Bert Jansch and John Renbourne.

RICHARD WILLIAMS We viewed *Sounds* as a very serious rival. We didn't think it was as good as us, but it had two or three very good writers. They were kind of doing progressive stuff, but they weren't as broad as we were. What I loved about the *Melody Maker* at that time was that you could write just about anything – if you really liked a daft pop record, you could go and interview a person about that. *Sounds* couldn't do that. *Sounds* had to be very credible. In a way, the *Melody Maker* already was credible, so we could take risks.

CHRIS WELCH After they all left for *Sounds*, we had this week where it was just us, an empty office with wind blowing through it. Then young reporters started to pop up. Laurie Henshaw came in from *Disc*, Chris Charlesworth arrived from a village in Wiltshire to handle news, Michael Watts, Roy Hollingsworth and some others. So, from having no staff, we suddenly had new people arriving every week, all recruited by Ray. My wife, Marilyn, was Ray's secretary, and we were married within a year of her joining. It was a real family.

JERRY GILBERT The early '70s was a period when the record companies sponsored journalists to go the States a hell of a lot. I did the first

American tour with Genesis and Nazareth. I worked my arse off. I said to *Sounds*, "If I'm going to New York, I may as well stay out a bit longer and tap out Warner Brothers and see what acts they've got to build up a fund of interviews." Everyone did this. You didn't take the piss. You arrived in New York and CBS, say, were happy to put you up in a decent hotel for four or five nights and cram you out with interviews. There would be some turkeys, and then they'd roll out Paul Simon. It normally worked out well.

BEAT INSTRUMENTAL
"A SNAKEPIT"

NEIL SPENCER I'd edited my university magazine and knew somebody at *Beat Instrumental* who got me a job there in 1970. *Beat* was this really odd little publication run by Sean O'Mahony, who gets a namecheck in 'Can You Dig It', the Beatles song. He used to publish *Beatles Monthly* and now owns *Record Collector* and was a maverick entrepreneur. He had this constant turnover of people because he didn't pay well, blah blah blah, but he also gave a lot of us a break.

TONY TYLER Around 1970, I went to live in California for about 18 months. When I got back to the UK, in late 1971, I was on the hunt for a job and saw an ad in *The UK Press Gazette* for an assistant editor on *Beat Instrumental*, the forerunner of today's *Sound On Sound*, the musos' monthly. I applied for the job and was turned down for being over-qualified. Then, a month later, I got a call from the publisher saying that the current editor was leaving and would I like his job? In fact, the departing incumbent was Neil Spencer, some years later to become editor of *NME*. He had just completed six months in the job – which, as I soon discovered, was about par for the course. *Beat* was a snakepit.

NEIL SPENCER Beat's office's were great, actually, in Parker Street, in what is now Covent Garden. Sean O'Mahony also had *Construction News*, or something like that, and *Beat* was literally two guys in an attic at the top. Sean was a real stickler – you had to go to work in a collar and tie – but we'd get to interview loads of people: Rod Stewart, Ray Davies, The Byrds. There were favourites they did for the Instrumentalist Of The Month, and

I always steered clear of that, because I didn't know anything about that side of music.

TONY TYLER The most alarming thing about starting at *Beat*, from my point of view, was that I had no idea what magazine editors did. I could write a bit, but like many other writers I had never really considered what needed to happen to a piece of text to make it appear on a magazine page, so I learned on the job. I've no doubt I was pretty incompetent, but I suppose I must have got better. Then, Emerson, Lake And Palmer came along. I make no apologies – though I would, if I thought apology was sufficient – for admiring this band. It was just something that came over me, the way things do. I plastered them all over the cover of *Beat* and did a massive in-depth interview. I toadied like crazy, so naturally they offered me a job as PR, which I accepted, not least because *Beat* was a very unhappy ship for various reasons and, like every other editor, after six months of it I was looking around for an exit. ELP seemed to offer one. ELP was a snakepit, too, of a different kind, but I won't go into that.

NEIL SPENCER My job as the junior was to schlep up and down Charing Cross Road writing advertorials for places like Macari's Musical Exchange, but then they would have a feature and you'd have a chance to get Led Zeppelin on the cover. I did the interview with John Bonham in the Golden Egg on Oxford Street. He ate this huge greasy-spoon meal while we talked and Peter Grant sat there. The music business then was still littered with people like him, who were left over from the showbiz age. But *Beat* wasn't anywhere in the pecking order. I don't think it sold hardly anything. It was actually called *Beat Instrumental And National Recording Studio*, so I spent quite a lot of time interviewing engineers, which made it clear to me that there is nowhere as boring as a recording studio, unless you're making the record, so I left to teach in Tottenham for about a year.

THE US
"A FEW WOMEN ROCK WRITERS"

LISA ROBINSON There were just a few women writing about rock music: Lillian Roxon, who wrote *Lillian Roxon's Rock Encyclopedia* and was an Australian running the US office of *The Sydney Morning Herald* before she went to the *Daily News*, and Gloria Stavers, who was editor of *16* magazine. Then there were two others: Ellen Sander, who wrote for *Life*, and Ellen Willis, who wrote for *The New Yorker*. They were much more intellectual. Ellen Willis was a serious critic – capital S, capital C.

ROBERT CHRISTGAU *The New Yorker* critic Ellen Willis, who I lived with in the '60s, had a tremendous influence on my thoughts.

RICHARD MELTZER *Roxon's Rock Encyclopedia* was the first even half-non-worthless grocery listing of all that shit which, compared to the junk *Rolling Stone* puts out, you'd have to admit reads extremely well.

DANNY FIELDS I first met Lillian at the press conference for Brian Epstein's band The Cyrkle. She asked him in the Australian accent of hers, "Mr Epstein, are you a millionaire?" I thought that was very ballsy.

LISA ROBINSON Lillian Roxon was my best friend, so fabulous. She had been part of this very cool scene in Sydney with a bunch of beatniks which included Richard Neville and was a very beautiful woman who got fat because she was misprescribed cortisone spray to treat her asthma. If you read her *Rock Encyclopedia*, it's infused with her individual take on stuff, full of witticisms. She had a gossip column for *The New York Daily News* while still writing for *The Sydney Morning Herald* and she'd always drag these Australians to Max's Kansas City for us to meet: "This is Australia's leading gynaecologist and this is Australia's leading writer," who would be Germaine Greer, before anyone had heard of her. She was very close to the Warhol set.

RICHARD MELTZER Lillian Roxon, her I remember – her death, if not her dying. The summer of '73, a heart attack brought on by a severe asthma attack, itself brought on by an especially unbreathable two or three days of New York heat and smog. She died alone, and I went up and cried on the Empire State Building. The next six months, every time I got drunk, I'd get all whimpery, 'cause she was, like, the saintliest person I'd ever met. Every day, she'd call up every person she cared about to sincerely encourage every fucking hopeless tangent they were on, like, unconditionally.

16
"GLORIA HAD ALL THE ACCESS"

DAVE MARSH When you tell people that Gloria Stavers and *16* magazine basically invented rock- and pop-culture journalism as we know it today, they think you're just talking about the fact that Gloria was close to Jim Morrison of The Doors, or that she ran the early story that kept *Rolling Stone* afloat, or that she was the first person to take good photographs of teen stars, or that you're being charitable because Gloria had the courage to run an obituary in *16* for her great friend Lenny Bruce. Nope. Gloria was the first real pop journalist, no qualification necessary.

DANNY FIELDS I was first introduced to Gloria when I went to see a friend at *16*'s offices. This friend took me in and said very politely, "Gloria, this is Danny, the editor of *Datebook*," and she started screaming, "Get him the fuck out of here!"

IRA ROBBINS I recall how the late *16* editrix Gloria Stavers – a fascinating and wonderful woman who we later persuaded to write a Doors article for *Trouser Press* – would manage to slip names like John Coltrane and Al Jackson Jr into her pages along with ads for some instrument company that pictured Frank Zappa, and you thought it was all The Monkees and *The Man From UNCLE*!

DANNY FIELDS In the summer of 1966, I'd be surprised if *Datebook* was selling 80,000 copies, but at this time The Monkees were enormous and *16* was up to 1.2 million. It was a very powerful publication. She had a lot of power over these record company bosses and TV stations. She could take a show off the air by instituting a postcard campaign. Each magazine, they figured, got passed around by five or six girls, so that could be seven million letters to CBS. Guys would steal their sisters' copies, because sometimes that was the only place you could read about The Beatles or The Rolling Stones.

DICK CLARK She had her finger on the pulse of what kids were thinking, which impressed me. We both, as adults, could "think young" and see what was interesting and ascertain what the future would bring in the next few months. Gloria helped *American Bandstand* and the show helped *16* – it was a two-way street. We kept track of the kids and who was popular. She would publish stories about them; we would have them on as guests. It was a snowball effect, one augmenting the other. The show grew and so did the magazine.

LISA ROBINSON Gloria was really glamorous. She had been a model who became very spiritual and Buddhist. Gloria had affairs with Lenny Bruce and Jim Morrison and Paul Revere, or whatever his real name was. Gloria did not like serious rock criticism and she, with Lillian, was a huge influence on me.

DANNY FIELDS The *16* style was really personal and intimate and understanding of the fantasies about bands that young teenagers have. No sex, no controversy, stretching the limits of credibility with stories like "The Day He Almost Died!". Sensational headlines, sensational cover-lines, and Gloria took the pictures herself with an old-fashioned flashbulb.

DAVE MARSH She read voraciously and widely, but she didn't dwell on book learning. She was shrewd, as well, and perhaps a little prescient – at least, she always seemed to know what was going to come next, and if she didn't she never let herself show the least bit of surprise. The silly movie *The Idolmaker* made her out to be an opportunist exploiter, and that is what she never was. Bobby Darin might call from the West Coast trying to figure out what shirt to wear, and Gloria might figure it out for him, but she didn't need a commission; she did that because she loved Bobby, because he was smart enough, talented enough, beautiful enough to merit her interest.

DANNY FIELDS Gloria had all the access. At that press conference for The Cyrkle, they got all the press to the CBS building. When the press conference was over, Gloria walked in by herself and was taken to meet the band alone. No press conference for her. So I got a lesson in altitude and pecking order.

DAVE MARSH Gloria Stavers was one of the most beautiful people I have ever known. Her skin was the most beautiful I have ever seen, her jet-black hair could mesmerise almost as much as her piercing eyes and her leggy elegance never wavered.

DANNY FIELDS Gloria was mesmerised by Jim Morrison. Steve Harris, the promotion director of Elektra, who had known her way longer than I had, was convinced that Jim Morrison would play in 16 and sent her roses and champagne, everything to convince her. My part of it was to wangle another trip to California and get a phone call between the two so she could use her extraordinary intelligence and Southern charm and little-girl thing and flatter him. The purpose of the trip was to go to the Elektra office on Sunset Boulevard, him to come there, me to place a call to Gloria in New York and give the phone to him, have him mumble and her do whatever she did, hand the phone back to me and hang up. Then Gloria and Jim became lovers. But that's how I sold my acts. Hey!

DAVE MARSH Of course, she was laughed at in the male-dominated "legitimate" press, even called "the Mother Superior of the inferior" by people who ridiculed girls and women and what was meaningful to them.

DANNY FIELDS Jim was mean to Gloria. They were having an incredible affair – she was giving him incredible blowjobs, fucking all over the place. They would go on mystical adventures and she would tell me he would dematerialise. If only he would! She couldn't wait for him to get to town, and he called her up once and said, "I'm staying at the Chelsea and I really want to see you. Just come up to the room. The door will be open." So she went up there and called, "Jim? Jim?" She was scared, alone in a room in a weird hotel. He wasn't in the bedroom, bathroom, so she's out of there in a taxi and gets home and the phone's ringing as she walked into her apartment. She picked it up and it was Jim, chuckling. She said, "Where. The fuck. Were you? I was just there. I looked all over for you." And he said, "You didn't look under the bed." What a chivalrous guy.

JIM MORRISON
"NASTY DEMON SON-OF-A-BITCH MOTHERFUCKER"

DANNY FIELDS When I flew to LA to fix up the phone interview between Gloria and Jim Morrison, it occurred to me to fix him up with Nico, who I was staying with in a strange haunted house in the Hollywood Hills with Edie Sedgwick, who was a great friend of mine. It was an old house, all overgrown, with a mossy pool high on a hilltop. I went to stay with them along with a friend from San Francisco.

Jim hated me so much, and it was all because of this. I said to him, "Follow me up to the hills in your car." It was tricky, but keeping track of another car in your rear-view mirror, driven by a nasty demon son-of-a-bitch motherfucker who was out to taunt and make miserable everybody in his immediate radius, was another thing. He'd disappear from view, so I'd wait, and then he'd be back behind me. He wanted to make sure that I knew he was in control. I'm from New York, and I didn't drive that much, so it was perplexing and horrible.

We got up to the castle and Nico and Edie fled to their bedrooms to hide, giggling and taking drugs. He started taking drugs as well and just downing quarts of vodka. Nico had stolen all my stash of pills, downers and amphetamines, but somehow I had managed to save the pot and the acid, so Jim and I sat up and he took all that. I thought, "Uh-oh, he's going to get so drunk he's going to get in that car and drive off the cliff and I'm going to get fired," so I snuck down to his car and hid the keys under the floormat. Then he and Nico started to circle each other and he wanted to take her with him, so he was asking for his car keys and trying to search me. He didn't find them.

I went to bed and was woken up by sobbing. She was standing there weeping in this mock-Spanish courtyard. He was completely naked, apart from this crenellated cassock-type of robe and he was leaping from one turret to another. She came flying into my room crying, "He's going to kill me!"

I said, "He's not going to kill anyone. Leave me alone, I'm trying to sleep." There were screams later, and they'd be down in the courtyard and he'd be pulling her around by her hair. It was like the cover of some Gothic bodice-ripper.

So he hated me ever after, because I'd kidnapped him and he wasn't in control of the situation. There was no phone in the house and he was missing for two days. The band finally figured it out. The torture that I've described he inflicted on me was as nothing to what he did to his bandmates. It was this constant game of who's in charge.

We got back to the mansion from an afternoon swimming in someone else's pool and all the dining chairs were on top of the 20-foot table. That was strange, but also on the table was this publicity still of Nico and Andy from Chelsea Girls with this written on the back by the guys in the band and his manager:

> "Jim, your fucking ass is fired.
> Call immediately.
> Grow up!
> OK, you've had it.
> Call Ray, John, Robbie, Sal or Asher tonight or early in the morning."

Jim wanted me fired from that moment on, but Elektra pacified him. There were lots of incidents which I won't even go into. The vomiting – ugh! There was one night they played Flushing and the audience was really crazy. It was one of those nights when you can sense the audience is ready to blow. The Who opened for them, and I spent all my time in the dressing room with them because Pete and I had been having an affair ever since The Who played with Cream in '67. We'd been off-and-on boyfriends. I'd seen The Who's set and said to Jim, "Watch out for this crowd. They're ready to go." He said, "How the fuck do you know?" And they went on, and sure enough, they blew – chairs were flying, the set was disrupted, the police and fire department were called. Luckily, no one was killed.

After I left Elektra, there was this party for The Doors at the entire duplex of the Hilton Hotel and he came down the staircase when he saw me and said to somebody, "What's he doing here?"

4 "I Had Several Masters To Serve, One Of Which Was Me"

"I think everybody's a rock critic to the extent that, when you go into a record store and you decide to buy this one over that one, you're being a rock critic. I don't have any more credentials than anyone else. What I would say for myself is that everybody knows my prejudices."
– Lester Bangs

GREG SHAW The best rock writing was done in the early '70s – Paul Williams, Lester Bangs, John Mendelssohn, Nick Kent...and Nik Cohn. He's got to be number one. He had a way of putting emotion in his writing that would make you feel the same emotion you felt when you listened to the music. The piece he wrote that sticks in my mind was one about girl groups, "Teen Dreams And Baby Love" or something. I remember reading it and being moved to tears, the way a Ronettes record can do that to you. I just thought, "This is what writing should be. It should make you feel the music it's writing about."

NIK COHN Not having been to a place never stopped me from describing it, any more than not meeting someone stopped me from talking about my interview with them.

JOHN MENDELSSOHN Nik Cohn was screamingly funny, with absolute confidence in his own taste. And once he'd dismissed you, you stayed dismissed, boy. My own star began to rise very quickly after I perfected my imitation of him.

ROLLING STONE IN THE '70S
"JANN HIT GOLD"

DAVID DALTON As *Rolling Stone* became more successful, and also as we moved out of the utopian and naïve '60s, cynicism reigned, radicalism was mocked, the more extreme projects of social change became clearly unattainable. We grew older, got married, went into rehab, etc, and rock became part of the entertainment industry again. Of course, it always had been, but the illusion that it functioned as an independent engine of change was a powerful motivator. The Radical Jann was unceremoniously dumped over the stern of the ship one night by the by now hugely successful captain of industry Citizen Jann, who owned the steamship line lock, stock and board of directors.

RICHARD MELTZER *Rolling Stone* in the '70s was, as it remains today, a trade paper, a record industry hype sheet, a promulgator of mass compliance in the consumer sector, a principal factor in the dumbing, maiming and calming down of the public's taste for a rock 'n' roll beast that had once indeed been not only wild and crazy but genuinely anarchic. Like MTV to follow, it has for a looooong time been one of the big things gravely wrong with the world.

PAUL NELSON When I went back to *Rolling Stone* the second time, Jann offered me extra money to be a feature writer and the record reviews editor. I picked just the record reviews editor job, because I was incapable of writing about someone that I didn't like, so he paid me per piece I wrote. Either I had to love them or hate them. He let me pick the articles I wrote.

BEN FONG-TORRES The most intriguing and uncomfortable encounter I had with a pop star was with Dylan in the early days, because he took me by surprise by asking that I not use my tape recorder. He was going through the AJ Weberman-going-through-his-trash and the bootlegging-every-Dylan-utterance craziness of the early '70s. The idea of interviewing him was intimidating enough. Now I'd lose eye contact and would have to be scribbling down his comments while maintaining a conversation, with proper follow-up questions. It was no picnic, but it worked out fine. After that interview, I swore I'd learn shorthand, but I never did.

GREG SHAW I read *Rolling Stone* right up until 1972. They had a number of editors who came and went who were very good. I used to write reviews for Jon Landau, who was good, but there was a point when all the good editors resigned. Maybe it's when they moved to New York and the magazine changed.

CHARLES M YOUNG Just before I graduated from Columbia in 1975, I entered *Rolling Stone*'s first annual college journalism contest. When they got around to judging it a year later, I won, and that got my foot in the door. Chet Flippo gave me an assignment to do a short article on The Ramones, and then I got hired to write Random Notes. Once I was on the staff, I pushed to write features all the time. They put my byline on the cover a lot and my head got a little bloated.

DENISE SULLIVAN On the eve of Mikal Gilmore launching his career as a writer for *Rolling Stone*, he learned that his brother Gary had confessed to the murder of two people in Utah. "There has never been a day since all that stuff happened that I haven't thought about him or, at some point in the day, am still bewildered by what occurred," he explains.

DAVID WEIR By 1977, Jann decided he'd outgrown his home town and he took his whole San Francisco hippie show to New York, the main media stage. Ten years after the Summer of Love, the magazine had survived countless financial and personnel crises that might have sunk it, much as they sank all the other start-up rags from the '60s, but the tyrannical boy-king had stayed atop his throne, always seducing another wave of talent, closing bigger ad accounts, just barely holding it all together. Now he would become rich.

RICHARD REIGEL Lester Bangs said that, when he was writing record reviews for *Rolling Stone*, among the editors he worked for, Jon Landau didn't seem to understand some of Lester's reviews but would publish them anyway; Ed Ward understood them but often disagreed with Lester ("You can't say *that* in *Rolling Stone*!") and edited him heavily; while only Greil Marcus both understood and appreciated Lester's reviews and published them largely as written.

DAVID WEIR In New York, Jann hit gold. Soon he was a regular in the celebrity pages, grinning ear to ear, escorting Jackie and Caroline Kennedy to a party. There he was throwing the party for the Democratic Convention in New York. There he was in a movie, playing himself – *Perfect*, with John Travolta and Jamie Lee Curtis – and he wasn't half bad, though the movie's storyline made a travesty of *Rolling Stone*'s editorial standards. "It must be difficult making the transition from editor to actor," I gently suggested during a visit just before the film launched. "Not really," Jann answered, "not when you have so much natural talent."

CAMERON CROWE
"A GOONY-GOOFY GOSH-OH-GEE KID"

CAMERON CROWE The main effect of my *Rolling Stone* career was that I felt like I had a place in the world. I could write about this thing that I loved so much. And as rough as it was, and caught in the middle as I was, I guess it was my persona back then. I ran into Stephen Stills at a football game a year and a half ago and he introduced me to his wife. Here's how he introduced me: "This is Cameron. He was a fan who always got caught in the middle between wanting to be friends with us and wanting to please *Rolling Stone*, who didn't like us as much as he did." I thought, "Wow, what happened to the power and mystery of journalism and writing?" That was the role I played: the fan who had several masters to serve, one of which was me.

CHARLES SHAAR MURRAY: The teenage Crowe was the very soul of amiability, relaxed and confident beyond his years, as well he might be, considering that he was a top writer for a major publication and made considerably more money than any of us did.

GLENN O'BRIEN I never met Cameron Crowe, but I once got in a fistfight with Elvis Costello's stupid manager in Houston, Texas, because he thought I was Cameron Crowe and started dragging my beautiful female photographer around the dressing room by the hair. I hope he has since gotten what he deserved.

CAMERON CROWE As a die-hard rock fan living in San Diego, I smuggled *Rolling Stone* into my house. My mother, a teacher, was a progressive thinker in so many ways except one: rock 'n' roll was not welcome in our home. It was, she said, a waste of brain cells. My first chosen profession – based on loving the movie *To Kill A Mockingbird* – was to be a lawyer.

RICHARD MELTZER Cameron Crowe was at the first and only mass gathering of the US rockscribble crowd, the Rockwriters Convention in Memphis in 1973. He was for damn sure, in more ways than one, the youngest such being in attendance – 16, maybe only 15, a goony-goofy gosh-oh-gee kid blowing on a goddam kazoo, or maybe an ocarina. Recorder? Something. Playing "name this TV theme song" with anyone who would sit still for 30 seconds. Not really that tough a score on a bus full of stationary writefolk *en route* to a Budweiser brew tour. He was playing *Bewitched*, *The Flintstones*, *Father Knows Best*, *The Jetsons*... Give the boy a bubble-gum cigar!

JERRY GILBERT There was this band called Skin Alley who were signed to Ardent Records in Memphis and managed by this guy called Richard Thomas. He rang me up at *Sounds* and said he wanted to fly me to the Rockwriters Convention, where they were playing. It was also a showcase platform for Big Star, which I guess is how they ended up being the cult band they are among writers. I was exhausted from two trips to the States in the month, with a notebook full of interviews, so I passed it onto this guy called Ray Telford. I really wish I'd been there, because it was obviously an event, with everyone from Lester Bangs to Cameron Crowe.

CHARLES SHAAR MURRAY: Crowe, despite his considerable talents, was essentially a fanboy, a "friend of the stars" who rarely upset the apple cart by expressing a controversial opinion. He had the kind of presence which relaxed his subjects, made them feel protective towards him, encouraged them to open up. This is a considerable asset for an interviewer, make no mistake, and it paid off big-time.

CAMERON CROWE My first exposure to music magazines came via a shop in San Diego where they sold Zap Comix and rock magazines. There was a guy who worked there who would let me look, even though you were supposed to be 18. It was like porno. I thought the guys that wrote for them were the greatest people. They might have trashed the music, but they respected it and lived the rock 'n' roll lifestyle. There was an underground paper in San Diego, *The San Diego Door*, and my sister used to go out with a guy who worked for them. On the condition I wouldn't tell Mom, they took me to a meeting. I wanted to do record reviews for them, and when I asked, of course, they said no. Music was the tool of the corporations. Then they thought, "We need the advertising from the record companies." Next thing, they told me about another guy who sent in record reviews to them, and it was Lester Bangs.

RICHARD MELTZER In the months following the convention, he wrote for *The San Diego Door* and *Creem* – at the time edited by former San Diegan Lester Bangs, who'd also been on the Bud bus – before eventually landing in *Rolling Stone*. By the time Cameron showed up, the paper was little more than a highwater marker for self-effacing, slave-drudge careerism, the most conspicuous place, nationally, to have your copy butchered, your ideas reshaped to fit the moment's market-driven party line.

CAMERON CROWE In 1973, I went into the offices of *Rolling Stone* in San Francisco for the first time. Before this, I had been a freelance journalist working on the end of a phone to music editor Ben Fong-Torres. I'd done my first piece for them in January of that year, an interview with Poco, with Richie Furay. They paid me $350 for it. A few months later, Jann Wenner, *Rolling Stone*'s editor, wrote me, saying, "You may turn out to be the youngest *Rolling Stone* man ever."

RICHARD MELTZER Jimmy Olsen incarnate, the youthsome Mr Crowe accepted the *Rolling Stone* style sheet implicitly. In all likelihood, he worked very hard, but essentially he got and kept the gig when it was discovered that rock stars – such a sensitive lot – were less intimidated by him than by actual, functional grown-ups, who had the disconcerting habit of asking grown-up questions.

CAMERON CROWE There was the Zeppelin tour I went on. That also contributed a lot to *Almost Famous*. As many people probably know, *Rolling Stone* tore into all of their albums, so Jimmy Page said that he'd never talk to *Rolling Stone*, even though *Rolling Stone* always wanted to put them on the cover. The *LA Times* sent me on tour with them and, to convince them to do *Rolling Stone*, I stuck around on the tour with them. And, as in the movie, a couple of days turned into a long, three-week tour. My eyes got blood-red because I didn't get any sleep. One by one, they all said they'd do it, except for Page, who kept saying, "In another city, I'll make the decision."

JAAN UHELSZKI I was on the road with Led Zeppelin for two weeks for *Creem*, and finally, during the last day, Jimmy Page spoke to me, but only through an interpreter. He explained to his publicist that he would not talk to me directly and made me address all my questions to her, and she would in turn just repeat my words to him. He would answer to her, not to me, despite the fact we all spoke English. Afterwards, he told me he was going to have a huge party and not invite any journalists, like I cared at that point.

LISA ROBINSON I was on the same Led Zeppelin US tour that Cameron was on. The one he used a bit for *Almost Famous*. Danny Goldberg, who had been writing for *Circus* magazine and for *Record World*, became Led Zeppelin's press agent in 1972 and he called me up and asked if I would go on the road with them. I said, "Don't be ridiculous. They're a cheesy heavy metal band." But I went, because I'd never been to New Orleans before. And then I interviewed Robert Plant and Jimmy and fell in love with Led Zeppelin. I really thought they were great. No one else could be bothered with them – they thought they were over the top and a joke – but I started writing this good stuff about them in *Disc And Music Echo*. So they got some good press in England. That was how Mick Jagger noticed me. I think he wanted good press from someone associated with the CBGB scene.

JAAN UHELSZKI When the piece came out, Robert Plant was angry because I had revealed that he was seeing a bubble-headed deb type on that tour who had a poodle always in tow which insisted on defecating on the carpets of the Plaza Hotel. SwanSong promised I would never talk to them again. I last spoke to Page in 2000.

DANNY FIELDS I was hired by Atlantic because they were just exploding with people like Led Zeppelin and needed someone who knew rock 'n' roll and had connections with all the rock press. When Jann Wenner came to New York in the Elektra days, he slept on my couch because he couldn't afford to go to a hotel. So two things distanced me from the company. The first was when they said, "We've got this deal with this label for his acts and one of them is playing here. They're not going to make it, but we can at least tell him that we sent someone down to see them." It was The Allman Brothers. Not my kind of music, but it was obvious they were one fucking great band. But they said, "A white guitar band from the South? They'll never make it."

CAMERON CROWE The Allman Brothers Band was my first major assignment for *Rolling Stone*. So much of it became the movie. I was 15. My mom still thinks I'm gonna go to law school. She still says, "You left home when you were 15 and never came back. If I'd known who Led Zeppelin were then, I'd have never let you do it." At the time, I used to say, "Listen to 'Stairway To Heaven'! These are intelligent, committed, enthusiastic gentlemen!"

DANNY FIELDS The other thing about Atlantic was that they begged me to play Emerson, Lake And Palmer to people like Jon Landau and Jann Wenner, but I would not play it for anyone. I couldn't sit there with a straight face and say, "Listen to this." I had no problem with Aretha Franklin, or even the Allman Brothers, but not ELP. So I came in at noon every day, closed the door of my office, did some yoga and managed The Stooges by phone. But there were too many pills and too much destruction. Eventually, I was fired by Atlantic because I went to a big anti-war march in Washington. I claimed that Aretha was playing there, so we needed to go down there. I got a suite at the Howard Johnson's on Virginia Avenue, just across from the Watergate, and it became the hospitality suite for the Chicago Eight – Jerry Rubin was there and Phil Ochs; John Sinclair, who had just got out of jail; Abbie Hoffman. So it was room service, ordering steaks and champagne courtesy of Atlantic Records. There was some rumour that the police were going to round up all the protestors and clear them off the streets, so I decided to go back to New York but left the credit card open on the room for another 24 hours. They managed to get connected to Hanoi through Sweden or something and were on the phone there for 20 hours or something. The bill was $4,000 and I got let go by Atlantic.

RICHARD MELTZER Cameron's write-up of Led Zep demonstrated his ability to fill pages as glibly as the next bozo and a tad more affably to boot, but it offered scarcely a hint of the service with a smile he would provide the singer/songwriter gang in the years ahead as its advocate, mouthpiece, interlocutor, shill, virtual publicist and "man inside" the *Stone*.

CAMERON CROWE The thing is, when I first got out there on the road and was writing about The Allman Brothers and Led Zeppelin and The Who and Lynyrd Skynyrd and Neil Young, it wasn't the version of rock we think of today. It wasn't the penthouse suite, we're so removed from our fans, let's all be rich and happy; the whole fat, rich rock-star thing happened later. '73 was, for me, always the year where it felt like the last moment before rock became a little less personal, a little more global. What I saw was the time before the period that's been captured in the movies in a kitsch way. A lot of that stuff came later. To me, there was a great feeling of "us against the world" in most of these bands. Then, all of rock music sold about the same as one Shania Twain album now, so it was a little more personal. These guys seemed to be in it for the feeling they got onstage and, hopefully, girls and acclaim after that.

RICHARD MELTZER In 1972, after several false starts, Jackson Browne finally had an album out, which seemed a good occasion to bring to light some interesting hokum from his past. I'd known the mutha since '67, so I did the first feature on him for *Rolling Stone* or anywhere else – a rave, for crying out loud – and he freaking hated it. Thought it made him look "too punk". And what might be so wrong with that?... On his first visit to New York, he backed up – and horizontal danced with – the fabulous Nico, had a connection to Lou Reed and the Warhol crowd, blah blah blooey, so I talked all this stuff up. What the hey, it was what I thought would make him most appealing. And he's so upset he gets Asylum Records prez David Geffen to call the *Stone* and have me booted – good riddance, don't come back. Four years later, I was eating at South Town Soul Food in LA when Jackson walked in with gang-sister number one Linda Ronstadt. Not wanting her exposed to my cooties, he motions for her to stay put, struts over, sits down and in less than a minute explains to me how it is: "We singer/songwriters feel we get a better shake from this Cameron kid. He never challenges us. Accepts our side of the story. We don't have to worry what he'll say. No offence, but..."

ROBERT CHRISTGAU To quote myself, *Almost Famous* is "an entertaining fantasy with a cute premise that presented both Lester Bangs and Cameron Crowe as paragons of a j-school integrity few were aware they had anything to do with." Additionally, I'd say that Crowe's Bangs is reasonable as the fantasy of a 15-year-old, except insofar as his Lester is a sweetheart, which, among many other things he was, has nothing to do with the Lester I knew, who has not much to do with the Lester Richard Meltzer says he knew. And so it goes.

LESTER
"EVERYBODY'S A ROCK CRITIC"

JAAN UHELSZKI Lester deserves even more status than he got. He was a funny, humane person who cared deeply about the genre and about elevating those under his care. Young writers, even the girl in the *Creem* office who had romantic problems, would pour their hearts out to him, shopkeepers in the neighbourhood, some local teens he adopted. As well as being an engaging unique voice, he invented an entire style of music writing.

SIMON FRITH Bangs was a rock critic, not a rock writer like Cameron Crowe, and a great critic, too; but what matters is his criticism, not his lifestyle, which is what gets mythologised. Like Julie Burchill's, when she was on *NME*, his criticism mattered because he was primarily a moralist. There are very few critics today for whom music matters so much.

DANNY SUGERMAN I went down to El Cajon to meet him twice before he moved to Detroit to become reviews editor at *Creem*. Lester wrote like music sounded. One of the reasons I wrote *Wonderland Avenue* was because Lester didn't. I really thought he would write the great coming-of-age rock 'n' roll novel.

MARY HARRON Not only was he hilarious and very smart but his writing was the closest thing to the music itself. He had a great appreciation of the moronic brilliance of rock 'n' roll.

GREG SHAW The best thing I read by him was the manuscript for his unpublished novel, *Drug Punk*, which he had when he stayed for a couple of weeks. It was very powerful. It's been a long time since I've seen it, and I don't know why that hasn't been published. It was his dream to write a non-music book, and he proposed about a dozen to publishers which all got turned down. I wonder if he didn't find himself faced with the fact that, actually, he wasn't good enough? The ones he did publish on Blondie just weren't good. He was great in the music press, but would he have been another Kerouac? I don't think so, and I don't rate Kerouac that highly.

GLENN O'BRIEN I was friendly with Lester, but we didn't hang out and we argued about everything from the first time we met, when he tried to turn off the Miss America pageant I was watching on TV at an after-show party in Detroit for Iggy.

LINDSAY HUTTON I'll never forget seeing him put the boot into Emerson, Lake And Palmer on TV. His prominence was down to his non-stop involvement with the scene. There were no barriers then; *all* music was up for grabs. There weren't all these little disenfranchised tribes. Lester rooted for what he considered to be good music, no matter what. His mythic status is deserved, because you can look over his stuff now and still get a kick out of it. You still have to read every word. So much of what is written today is weak, groundless rubbish, PR releases padded out to appease the feeding frenzy of the sorry-ass music business food chain. What would Lester be like if he was still around? What would he make of the constant stream of pish that most record companies want to turn into The Next Big Thing? I'm cautiously optimistic that he wouldn't tolerate Radiohead, at the very least.

LESTER BANGS I'm not God, and just because I write something doesn't make it wrong or right. The impetus for me and a lot of people I knew was just that we really loved rock 'n' roll and wanted to talk about it, you know? And there was this outlet. And what kind of makes me mad is, a lot of times today, it looks like a lot of rock critics that are writing in these magazines...it's like a good way to get a start in a career in journalism or something, you know? You don't sense a real passion for the music.

DANNY SUGERMAN I found it a lot more difficult to be published by *Creem* when Lester was there. I don't think he liked me. When I went out with him in El Cajon, we got drunk and picked up on chicks, and I was the only one that got laid. Lester didn't, and I don't think he ever forgave me.

CHARLES SHAAR MURRAY: Bangs, despite his fearsome reputation, was a genial bear of a man and, on his visits to *NME*, was sufficiently sober to converse perceptively, charmingly and – bogglingly enough – quietly.

RICHARD MELTZER Back in '73, for instance, the soon-to-be-dead Lillian Roxon gushed shameless love for the SOB in New York on *Creem* business, ordering up a Lester button and leaving it in his hotel box. Response to this purest of offerings was, "What's that fat cunt want from me?"

GINA ARNOLD Bangs wrote a few good lines – I liked it when he said that Elvis Presley gave him "an erection of the heart" – but I was more impressed with it when I was younger. Gonzo is kind of dated now, isn't it?

RICHARD MELTZER What's laughable – and downright insidious – is that Cameron Crowe actually believes Lester influenced him. He's said so in a score of interviews. Lots of folks are claiming he influenced them. As far as rock writers go, the whole last 30 years of them – with the exception of "Metal" Mike Saunders – Lester influenced no one. He was the end of a line – believe it! – not the beginning of one.

"METAL" MIKE SAUNDERS I'd agree with Lester Bangs himself that his writing mostly went in the tank after he moved to Michigan and lost his "outsider" perspective. But "Lester Bangs" is one of the great-sounding names of all time, so if they're gonna canonise a rock writer, I can't think of a better suggestion.

LESTER BANGS Critics are the people you love to hate anyway.

CHARLES SHAAR MURRAY: Lester was essentially a critic, ranter and raconteur, a grimy prophet howling in the wilderness. His celebrated interviews with Lou Reed were knockabout classics of the genre (someone, incidentally, should adapt the transcripts of those interviews into a screenplay entitled *Lester And Lou* before anybody here gets significantly older), but his scabrous attacks on the second rate – especially the expensively hyped second rate – and passionate hymns to the transcendent power of loud, filthy noise forever barred him from the first-class lounge, where publishers, performers, record companies and journalists smoothly network and conspire against the public interest.

RICHARD MELTZER Where in the early '70s it was almost cute, once in a while, the way Lester would stumble into classic self-directed drunk jokes – like the time he called me from Detroit Airport to tell me he was headed for an Alice Cooper show in London, presumably England, only he'd got it wrong and was on his way to London, Ontario. There was this half week in '79, for instance, during which he stayed at Michael Ochs' house in Venice with no daily design but to get skid-row-calibre gone and stay there...that was just fucking grim.

MILES Lester was a great writer, not just rock critic. His piece "Everything Above 14th Street Is Gila Bend, Arizona" is one of the greatest, funniest pieces of writing about New York's *The Village Voice* ever published.

LENNY KAYE We all like doomed rock writers, don't we? There's some element of dissolute romanticism, which most rock writers just can't get on – it's a lot easier to be a rock star and dissolute than it is to be a rock writer. This thing about the rock writer as romantic hero is one of the most humorous things I've witnessed over the last couple of years, but if anybody deserves it, it's Lester. He certainly had the passion and the commitment. He was really clever but somewhat self-destructive. My take on that is that you've got to keep writing. I'm not one to let self-destruction get in the way of getting up in the morning and doing a day's work.

IAN MACDONALD There are any number of ways to write about pop music, none of them correct – or, as we used to say in the '70s, definitive. There are writers who pioneer particular styles or schools, and Lester was certainly one of those. We were very keen at *NME* to get reprint rights to stuff he wrote for *Creem*, and rightly so – it was immensely funny and incisive, as he was in person, but it was also extreme and unbalanced, as he was, too, in the long term. He really lived his aesthetic, and it did him in. That sort of living nearly did for Nick Kent, too. It killed Nick's colleague Pete Erskine, another very funny writer.

MILES Lots of young rock critics tried to copy him, of course, Nick Kent and Charlie Murray being the most obvious examples, but the great thing about him was that he wasn't taken in by the rock business. He saw it for what it was and is, a business.

PETE SILVERTON I used to think his stuff was great, but you read it now and it's crap, you know? He is not a good writer. A lot of the links he was making were totally fatuous.

NICK KENT The guy was a poet. It wasn't some bullshit; he had a magic thing with words.

CHARLES SHAAR MURRAY: I really admire Lester for his mad energy, his courage and individuality.

GREG SHAW Lester was in no way a glamorous guy. He was a troubled person. He had tremendous ability to spew out bullshit and to be completely wrong and to change his mind and contradict himself and to go on and on about stuff that was not very interesting. I don't even think he's an important enough writer to justify all this attention.

TONY PARSONS You couldn't avoid Lester if he was around. I'm sorry he died, but he's completely overrated, just a big fat American with a moustache. Cameron Crowe deserves attention, because he has proved himself very well in another field, but Lester never did anything for me. Now he's been turned into this mythical creature, more famous than Lou Reed.

LESTER BANGS The *NME* didn't like [my biography *Blondie*], which I expected coming, because all those Limeys hate us all, 'cause they think we're decadent Americans anyway.

JOHN MENDELSSOHN I find the recent deification of Mr Bangs absolutely incomprehensible. He was capable of being spectacularly funny. Far, far more often, I found him insufferably masturbatory, an infant playing with his own faeces. I'm sorry, but I can't for the life of me see why people prefer him to someone like the all-but-forgotten Rick Johnson, who had a comparably antic style.

MILES His attacks on Lou Reed were great writing, because he was arguing from an impassioned position. Sometimes, if money was short, he would sell out. His three parter – maybe it was less; it felt like a three parter – on The Clash for *NME* was rubbish. He recognised *NME* for what it was, a commercial paper published by Britain's largest magazine publisher, and took them for every cent he could get. The more they fawned over him, the more drivel he wrote. It's one of his worst ever pieces.

IRA ROBBINS I enjoyed reading Lester when I was a kid, thought his Clash trilogy in the *NME* was brilliant, rarely believed anything he said, but often got a laugh out of the superficial silliness. I don't suppose, in retrospect, I really understood what he was raving about. I re-read a lot of it when his book came out and was struck by how much I had missed hidden in the blizzard of bluster. Meltzer was always more my kind of loony.

GREG SHAW The popular image of Lester isn't the full picture of who he was, and the Jim DeRogatis book [*Let It Blurt*] didn't help. It emphasises the sensational. It goes on at length with the anecdotes about him being a fuck-up. It doesn't really paint a fully rounded picture of him. I didn't know him all that well, but I think he relied too heavily on the opinions of people like Meltzer and Morthland.

JIM DEROGATIS (FROM LET IT BLURT) Lester was the last great gonzo journalist, gutter poet and romantic visionary of rock writing – it's Hunter S Thompson, Charles Bukowski and Jack Kerouac all rolled into one. Out of tune with the peace 'n' love ethos of the '60s and the me-generation navel-gazing of the '70s, he agitated for sounds that were harsher, louder, more electric and more alive, charting if not defining the aesthetics of heavy metal and punk.

RICHARD REIGEL I was slightly embarrassed for years, even after Lester died, that I'd always loved the guy so much, but when Rob O'Connor did his special Bangs issue of *Throat Culture* in 1990 I found out that my feelings weren't unique at all. Almost everybody who'd been touched by Lester, either by his writing or by his personality, felt that same intense affection. He had an unusually charismatic soul.

MILES Lester lived for the music. His apartment in New York City was Spartan. The fridge contained nothing but cloudy, months-old bottles of orange juice. The floor was littered with albums – walked over, used to roll joints, review copies stacked up ready to sell; his bed a mattress on the floor. I wouldn't call him a rock critic, though; I'd say he was a writer, as much a writer as Hunter Thompson – where it all comes from, of course.

LESTER BANGS (FROM HIS BIOGRAPHY ROD STEWART) I have always believed that rock 'n' roll comes down to myth. There are no "facts".

RICHARD REIGEL In the summer of 1972, I wrote a review of Leon Russell's *Carney* album and sent it off to Lester at *Creem* with a business-like cover letter, no special commentary. The review came back to me in my SASE a few weeks later. Someone else had already done that review. In the winter of 1972/73, I was in touch with *Who Put The Bomp*'s Greg Shaw, which led to my first paid publication, and I neglected sending anything else to *Creem* for a few months. In the spring of 1973, I sent Lester a very personal fan letter after he had written about *Uncle Scrooge* comic books – also one of my biggest literary influences – in the March *Creem*, and he responded with one of his characteristically exuberant letters, generously inviting me to write for *Creem*.

IAN MACDONALD Lester [became] "mythic" because he was out on the wild frontier, which is what rock 'n' roll myth demands, especially in America. There are plenty of other rock writers equally worth reading who'll never achieve that sort of status because they're more serious, reflective, moderate, introspective, conceptual, ironic, etc, etc. It takes all sorts.

MARY HARRON One of my favourite memories of Lester was in 1980. I was visiting New York, staying at my friend Fran Pelzman's apartment, and it was 3am. We were both up, of course – those were the days – and the phone rang and it was Lester. He said, "I've just been on the phone for eleven hours straight. Can you help me make it to twelve?" He'd just got off the phone with [Voidoids guitarist] Bob Quine and needed someone new to talk to. We took turns on the phone and we actually made it to 13.

RICHARD REIGEL In November 1973, I got a long memo in the mail from Lester laying out this *Screem* parody issue he wanted to do and soliciting my writing for it. The plan was that *Screem* would parody a National Lampoon – which Lester didn't like – parody of *Creem*. Thanks to my intense studies of all the other rock writers of the time, I was more than ready to write parodies of their styles, so I wrote a ton of stuff for *Screem* during the winter of 1973/74.

LESTER BANGS I think this whole thing of being a celebrity and a media personality, it's like...in so many cases it so much tends to eclipse whatever the person might want to do, artistically or creatively. It just about disappears, and I think that's the big trap. Everybody's a media personality now, you know what I mean?

CHARLES SHAAR MURRAY: The world needs a lot more Lesters. It's a dirty job but somebody's got to do it, though comparatively few are prepared to pay the price. Lester paid it in full, dying in 1982 at the age of 33. He died a stupid death after living a stupid life but leaving behind him a body of work which virtually defines its genre. Cameron Crowe, on the other hand, will be remembered primarily for his movies, though possibly not *Almost Famous*.

MICK FARREN I see *Entertainment Weekly* and shit like that and Lester would probably not be able to find work today. I wish there was the courage around that he had. You're not allowed to use "I" in a piece any more. I blame Wenner for it, and the problem is that it produced bad writing. It also condemns people who are coming up now to rewriting press releases, like they were 30 years ago. He was ahead of the pack. If he was occasionally long-winded and indulgent, that comes with the territory.

ROBERT CHRISTGAU
"THE MASTER"

ROBERT CHRISTGAU Now Radiohead is the most important rock band in the world by acclamation. Bull-fucking-shit, you know? They suck.

CHARLES SHAAR MURRAY: Christgau is great, the master of the one-paragraph album review. If I ever have to write one, I always try and put myself in Christgau mode, because he's the best.

ROBERT CHRISTGAU My friend Richard Goldstein had prepared the way for me at *The* [*Village*] *Voice*, an exceptionally permissive place, and they didn't even resist when I unilaterally moved my $40-per-submission column from once a month to twice a month to accommodate the Consumer Guide. But I always felt a front-of-the-book *versus* back-of-the-book – and straight *versus* hip – thing at *Newsday*, where I went later, and Harold Hayes at *Esquire*, where I began, got tired of my shtick real quick, because he was a jazz loyalist. He assigned a death-of-rock piece to me in 1968 which I made why-rock-isn't-dying and which was never published.

BARBARA O'DAIR At Christgau's best, he's fiercely analytical, dispensing dense sentences that twist in on themselves and, sometimes, the reader, rife with allusions, both academic and street, and displaying both a ready conversance with theory and a scathing contempt for puffery.

ROBERT CHRISTGAU I've had many encounters with pop stars, especially early on, most memorably, I guess, the time John and Yoko drove their limo to my apartment off Avenue B and I tried to feed them. They soon took me and my girlfriend to the Cookery instead. Peter Townshend gave me and an earlier girlfriend a lift to Woodstock, too. We'd interviewed him about *Tommy* a few months before. But getting to meet the stars is not why I'm a journalist, and I find it hard to trust the critical judgments of anyone for whom it is. The ability to schmooze and the ability to stand back and weigh meaning and value needn't be mutually exclusive, but they rarely reinforce each other.

MARC WEINGARTEN Christgau was a big critical influence, because he had an easy-to-read Consumer Guide and he was smart, and I bought so many records based on his recommendations. He was the proto-*Entertainment Weekly*.

ROBERT CHRISTGAU I became *Village Voice* music editor in 1974, with the programme of nurturing what I recently dubbed "impolite discourse". I was interested in new ideas and challenging writing that didn't necessarily follow anyone's rules, more cerebral than *Creem* – where I continued to publish the Consumer Guide – and about six times as edgy as *Stone*. As far as I'm concerned, I succeeded, except that finding more Lester Bangses proved an impossible quest, as all too many gonzo pseuds have proved ever since.

JAMES WOOLCOTT When I first got to *The Voice* – Christgau, Richard

Goldstein, people like that – they were going to be the intellectual leaders of a generation. They were going to be *The Partisan Review*. They, in years to come, were gonna take control. The amazing thing is, here they are, all these years later, none of them have done a stand-alone book. All of their books are collections [of articles]. Christgau got a Guggenheim at one point. They were all gonna do these big, original, semi-theoretical works and it never happened. So here's Bob, he's still grading records. Goldstein, I have no idea what he's doing. Ellen Willis is writing as if it's 1973. I mean, she throws in contemporary references, but her whole mode of thinking is, "If we could just get a real sexual revolution, we could tap the energy."

PETER BUCK (REM) I subscribed to *The Village Voice* for a couple of years – luckily enough for me, right when punk started happening, in about '74, '75, '76. I always had access to *The Voice*. So I was reading Robert Christgau and Lester Bangs writing about Blondie – I think he reviewed the first Blondie record. I found out about Television. I was buying those records the day they came out, which for Georgia was pretty different.

MICK FARREN I worked for Christgau at *The Voice*. I think reviewing The Who and The Clash at Shea Stadium for *The Voice* was about the best bit of rock writing I did, because I figured out what stadium rock was about. I said it was more to do with Tchaikovsky than rock 'n' roll and got a nice letter from Pete saying, "That's exactly the problem." It was the one time actually having been on a stage was an advantage.

JAMES WOOLCOTT Jon Pareles was second in command when Bob wasn't around. The weird thing is that the people who were the protégés of Bob started to walk like Bob, talk like him.

RICHARD REIGEL When I wrote for Robert Christgau at *The Voice* in '78/79, that was the first time I'd ever been edited that closely. After he received my manuscript, Bob'd phone me and we'd go over every word, every punctuation mark. It was a bit enervating at first, but I did learn some helpful compression-for-brevity skills that I applied to all of my *Creem* pieces from then on. Bob and I had an absurd but necessary taxonomic tussle one afternoon while editing my Steve Gibbons review over whether British cars have "right-hand drive" – he insisted that cars drive on the left side of the road in the UK, and I said, "They sure do. That's why the steering wheel's on the right side of British cars. In America, both things are just the opposite." We went around and around about that, but Bob finally accepted my explanation. In the blue-collar sweepstakes, his dad was "only" a fireman, after all; mine was an auto mechanic.

LISA ROBINSON Barry Kramer and Dave Marsh loved my style column in *Creem*, "Eleganza", but people like Robert Christgau didn't like it and threatened to quit *Creem* unless they dropped my column. He'll say it never happened, but I've got the letters to prove it.

BARBARA O'DAIR Over the years, Christgau has maintained combative friendships with critics like Ellen Willis, Greil Marcus and Dave Marsh and mentored a generation or two of young critics, notably Ann Powers, now a staff critic for *The New York Times*.

JAMES WOOLCOTT People really thought Christgau was going to be an intellectual broker. They thought Willis was gonna be a...I don't know, Simone de Beauvoir or something. What happened was, all of them became sort of self-styled intellectuals. They were really better when they were journalists.

IRA ROBBINS I have had both fundamental aesthetic and cultural disagreements with his work, as well as enormous respect for it. I suspect that the dean has gone through as much of a growth process as have us mere mortals, though his writing has rarely allowed the possibility of incomplete comprehension or knowledge or insight or foresight, so I can't say for sure whether he would have ever agreed with that assessment, so maybe it's more a matter of a synchronous timing than outlook. I was never part of his club – maybe that's why I didn't get to be *The Village Voice*'s music editor the one time I seriously pursued it, or it could have been because I didn't really want to work with someone who had once called me a white supremacist in print.

ROBERT CHRISTGAU About 15-20 years ago, some academics in Tennessee did a survey and found I was the most respected-by-my-colleagues critic in the US by a margin that I assume would not maintain today. But it would be ridiculous for me to pretend that I don't remain a big fish in my small pond and suicidal for any big fish to believe that there aren't a bunch of minnows and sharks who'd love to see him go belly-up.

MICK FARREN There's an academic school of rock critic in the States – you can fill in the names; certainly led by Robert Christgau and Greil Marcus – that almost has a detachment from the music so they can be academic about it. They have never been under fire themselves. You know, where is Robert Christgau's detective story? The worst facet of the writing is its pomposity. They're never assailed, whereas in England we were all the time, and occasionally assaulted by hooligans. It was Sid Vicious beating Nick Kent with a chain or Paul Weller taking a swing at me. We were all in Dingwalls or the same boozer, whereas with them I think there's something about ivory and towers.

ROBERT CHRISTGAU Once, I was physically attacked by someone I was later told – correctly? I'm not positive – was one of the guys in Suicide, who I'd always put down and still do.

SONIC YOUTH (TITLE OF A 1983 TWELVE-INCH SINGLE) 'I Killed Christgau With My Big Fucking Dick'.

ROBERT CHRISTGAU I've been mentioned by name in a few songs, never positively that I recall. Sonic Youth, a band I came to love after they grew up, suggested my assassination. I wasn't flattered – there are lots of nuts out there in alt-rock land.

MICK FARREN When I came to New York, I was appalled at how scruffy the rock critics were. Then I realised that was because they didn't go out on the town. I always felt like a journalist, that Walter Winchell thing, except the table wasn't at the Stork Club but at the end of the bar at CBGB or the Bells Of Hell on 13th Street. They want the chair for Rock 'n' Roll Studies at Princeton, whereas we were all cartoon characters, and when you're a cartoon character a pie in the face comes with the territory.

GREIL MARCUS
"COMPLETELY OVER-RATED"

CHARLES SHAAR MURRAY Greil has such a unique take on everything, a unique sensibility. I'll always read anything by Greil, even if it's on a subject I'm not interested in, and I'll always be glad I read it, even if I totally disagree with him.

RICHARD REIGEL Lester expressed lasting gratitude for Greil Marcus' editorial style [while contributing to *Rolling Stone*], so I always remembered that, and after Lester's death, when it was announced that Marcus would edit the posthumous Bangs anthology, lots of other writers were alarmed by that seemingly incompatible appointment, but I thought, "Well, presumably this is what Lester would want, based on what he said to me back in 1974."

TONY PARSONS I think Greil Marcus is completely over-rated. I just can't read him.

JON SAVAGE Like Lester Bangs, if he praised something, you could be sure it would be pretty good. I remember Greil wrote a review of *Oar* by Skip Spence which made me go out and buy the record in 1969.

RICHARD REIGEL When I was first reading and loving *Creem* in 1972, I made the mistake of wading into Marcus' "Rock-A-Hula Clarified" magnum opus one day, and after a few pages, I thought, "What *is* this pretentious crap? And how did it get into *Creem*, of all mags?" I was prejudiced against Marcus from that day forward, and while I can see clearly by now that Marcus obviously is a gifted thinker and writer, his icy, anti-flesh tone always puts me off when I try to read him.

JOHN MENDELSSOHN
"CAMPING IT UP IN HIS INIMITABLE FASHION"

STEVEN WARD There was a time when Mendelssohn trashed Led Zeppelin in the pages of *Rolling Stone*, dressed liked Rod Stewart and fronted a band – Christopher Milk – that received as many good reviews as bad ones.

GREG SHAW John Mendelssohn was the most polished writer, possibly the most intelligent of the early-'70s writers. I don't think he was a deep, penetrating analyst the way Greil Marcus is, but his writing was perfect, the way Oscar Wilde's writing was perfect – every word in its right place, a pleasure to read.

RICHARD REIGEL My first favourite rock writer was John Mendelssohn, when I was first subscribing to *Rolling Stone*, in 1969. Lester's reviews were appearing in *Rolling Stone* at the time, so I knew his byline, but his full persona wasn't yet revealed. Mendelssohn was camping it up in his inimitable fashion already.

HARVEY KUBERNIK Mendelssohn was a distinctive writer with a baroque style who could write circles around most people. He could insert the homey with cultural aspects and championed the likes of The Who, The Kinks, The Move and Procol Harum in America before they were fashionable.

PETER BUCK (REM) Mendelssohn wrote for a magazine called *Coast*, which doesn't exist any more, and he wrote articles about Iggy And The Stooges. I went out and bought the Christopher Milk records. This was, like, 1971. So I became a fan of Iggy, The Velvet Underground, The Nazz, Crazy Horse. I'd be the only 13-year-old on the block going, "I think I need to buy this Iggy And The Stooges record." The guys at the counter would be, like, "You'd better wear rubber gloves when you hold this album, kid." So I got turned onto a lot of stuff that was really foreign to me through print.

RICHARD REIGEL Mendelssohn was one of the few *Rolling Stone* writers then who betrayed any sense of humour, who dared to suggest that the whole counter-culture shtick might be a huge joke. That concept was vitally important to me at the time, though John didn't pursue the aesthetic/moral implications of those questions in his writing the way Bangs and Meltzer were to do.

PETER BUCK Mendelssohn was one of the first writers whose byline I learned to recognise. Much later, he said something nice about me in print while disparaging a number of people I know, which only made it better, of course. In real life, we tried to work together a few times, but it didn't really work out. He wrote like what he thought he was, a rock star. I bought the Christopher Milk records when I was 14 and thought they were kind of cool, and they *are* kind of cool, but you can read their influences pretty easily.

JOHN MENDELSSOHN I should never have allowed myself to be talked into being lead singer. The group as a whole – if not the rhythm section – would have been (marginally) better off if I'd remained the (woefully deficient) drummer. I believe that people who love music enough to write about it ought to be forcibly restrained if they try to purchase musical instruments. To cease to be sarcastic, I learned the hard way that you can't really do both simultaneously. I'd ravage somebody in print one week and the next week we'd be opening for them at the Whisky. Their bodyguards would beat me senseless just before I went on stage. My performance would suffer.

RICHARD MELTZER
"GET YOUR OWN TEA, FUCKFACE!"

RICHARD REIGEL I regard Meltzer as an absolute genius, as one of the best writers from my whole generation, but the literary world doesn't seem to have caught up with my ranking of him just yet.

RICHARD MELTZER We'd all be at this party, for instance, for the fabulozoolous Rolling Stones at some fussy French – or was it Italian? – New York eatery after '72, at the Garden. There's this incredible, huge fountain indoors, so who's gonna jump in the thing? I look around. I don't see no candidates – Mick's asleep face-down on a table – so it's gotta be me. Got to, right? 'Cause, if not, if the option's so clear and if nobody does it, rock 'n' roll as we...um...uh...know it will...um...uh...perish, you know? That sort of trip. So I jump and they give me the boot, a big security jerk on each arm.

JOHN MENDELSSOHN Mr Meltzer invited himself over to my home with Mr Tom Nolan, an early writer-about-rock whose work I found breathtaking but whose personality I wouldn't have fucked with your dick. They were both sloppy drunk and suffering from colds or allergies or something. Mr Meltzer made a point of dropping soggy facial tissue all over my apartment. Take that, running dog lackey of The Industry!

RICHARD MELTZER It wasn't only the big stuff I had to flagwave at; the Bitter End banned me for throwing banana skins and, I think, chicken bones at Dr Hook and his band.

PATTI SMITH (AT THE BUFFALO ROCK SYMPOSIUM, 1974) Rock 'n' roll is anything Richard Meltzer does.

RICHARD REIGEL Meltzer's written amazingly great books, like *LA Is The Capital Of Kansas* and *The Night (Alone)*, both "beyond" music, but they didn't sell well enough to give him the leverage to fully escape the rock-write ghetto, as he'd probably call it, and he has to fall back on all kinds of freelance work to keep going. Meltzer is a real inspiration to me in the way that he always demands that the culture comes to him rather than vice versa, no matter how hard that makes it for him to earn steady money.

IRA ROBBINS Richard Meltzer remained a personal hero of mine until his insane and juvenile screed about Jon Tiven's decades-old bathroom activities.

JOHN MENDELSSOHN Mr Meltzer in particular seemed to believe that disrupting record company parties with outrageous drunken displays of infantilism was somehow heroic, the only moral response to The Industry's avarice. Fair enough, but why'd you go to the party in the first place? Call me old fashioned, but I find peeing in the punchbowl after stuffing yourself on free canapés a little hypocritical.

RICHARD MELTZER [It wasn't that] there weren't incentives, and who among us hasn't been a whore? Records, tickets, travel, ten billion horrible parties – the ever-popular "Look, Ma, me in print" in mags that by now were actually read. Some writers – and this always amazed me – even got off on groupie-ing the merchandise, just sitting in a room running a tape – oh boy! – while some wheezer spoke. Me, I always hated interviews. I was willing to transcribe their words and thoughts when they were willing to transcribe mine. They became coddled shmucks. Writers existed solely to write about them, or even just... Well, I was at Island Records, LA, mid '72. Jim Capaldi's there, ex-drummer of Traffic. We're introduced, he hears I write and the first thing he says is, "Get me some tea." Get your own tea, fuckface! And try writing your own reviews.

IRA ROBBINS Dave [Fulchs] and I had met Richard Meltzer and Nick Tosches at Susan Blond's office at UA Records when we were both writing for our respective college papers, before we started the magazine in early 1974. He and Tosches were furiously blagging sealed, unpunched promos they could sell. Richard gave us a crucial bit of advice which I remember to this day. To be honest, I'm completely paraphrasing, since I probably forgot his actual words the next day, that's how awestruck I was. He told us to make sure you put something in everything you write that's just for your own amusement, like ending one word with SH and then starting the next with IT. That beats four years in journalism school – something which I never considered – hands down. Thanks, Dick!

PAUL NELSON
"I DIDN'T HACK IT OUT"

GREIL MARCUS His writing was flinty, elliptical and romantic, an unusual combination. He was drawn to loners and the excluded. There was something seductively hermetic about his work, an invitation to a closed room. His contribution – going back to *The Little Sandy Review* in Minnesota, carried forward in his crucial *Sing Out!* piece on Dylan's electric performance at the Newport Folk Festival in 1965, his *Rolling Stone* pieces on Jackson Browne and The Sex Pistols, etc – was to insist on a moral dimension to pop music, or perhaps one could say pop practice or public speech in the pop arena. Paul saw people making or avoiding choices, striking out in one direction or holding back and fading into the crowd. He was sensitive to the risks and the degree of courage or nerve it takes to make a public choice and to thus stand alone and stand exposed. Paul was a maddeningly slow writer. He suffered writer's block. I think this is because he respected his subjects so much that he was terrified of getting anything wrong.

PAUL NELSON It wasn't that. I just wanted to get the story the way I wanted it. And if it didn't get there, where I wanted it to go, I didn't turn it in. I didn't hack it out. If I didn't like it, I didn't want it published. I wrote them for me. I wasn't really thinking about anyone reading them.

STEVEN WARD Having written feature stories, concert reviews and record reviews for *Sing Out!*, *Circus*, *The Village Voice*, *The Real Paper* and many other publications, Paul Nelson became one of the most influential record reviews editors *Rolling Stone* had ever employed. Nelson even worked for Mercury Records in the first half of the '70s, in publicity and A&R.

RICHARD MELTZER The only publicist who didn't on some level demand or even solicit a return on his generosity – the only major-label guy who, in fact, was generous – was Paul Nelson at Mercury Records. After a typical lunch, he would walk you to the closet. "Take 40 records," that being the max he'd determined could be carried on foot to Sam Goody's so that cab fare wouldn't cut into your monetary score. He was so nice, I felt bad I never wrote up any of his crummy acts.

KURT LODER I first encountered Paul in the flesh in the spring of 1979, when I arrived at *Rolling Stone* as a new Random Notes writer and took up residence in the office next to his. I was instantly impressed by his non-stop consumption of thin, black, Nat Sherman cigarillos and his oceanic knowledge of music, going back to the mustiest folk and ranging up through The Velvet Underground and The New York Dolls, whose albums he had a hand in bringing to the public, via his one-time position as an A&R guy.

PAUL NELSON Ron Oberman at Mercury asked me if I wanted to work for him because I knew all these guys, the rock writers. I thought I would give it a shot. Ron was not a bullshit guy. I was not going to lie to a writer. I was not going to ask a writer to write a good review if the record is bad – that's the worst thing you can do – and Ron told me that was fine. I got a good expense account. I said, "Why not try it?" I got to meet a lot of different writers. I don't think I met Christgau until I took him to lunch. Dave Marsh came in from Detroit at the time and I never met him before, either. We all used to live off selling review copies, in those days. They would come up to the offices for records and I would load them up. It was kind of a game. Nobody at Mercury really knew. I also met Richard Meltzer and knew Lester Bangs from when he wrote reviews for *Circus*. Meltzer was really good for a while, but I didn't know what he was talking about after that. I got along with them. They were all drinkers and I wasn't. We all got to know each other at all the press parties. I also liked Nick Tosches, Jay Cocks, Chet Flippo, Bill Flanagan and Charles M Young. Mikal Gilmore was another younger writer I liked.

KURT LODER Paul was one of the great champions of punk rock at *Rolling Stone* – a difficult position, inasmuch as Jann detested the music – but Paul went to the mat for it, in one case championing, as I recall, a Clash album for the lead review in the face of Jann's insistence on spotlighting a piece of product by The Knack. Jann prevailed, of course, but Paul pretty much put his job on the line duking it out.

JON PARELES In my short time working at *Rolling Stone*, circa 1980, Paul was enigmatic. His office was famously chaotic, filled with albums and thick cigarette smoke – Nat Shermans, I think. He was always friendly but taciturn, keeping to himself and steering clear of the magazine's office politics. I was young and shy about famous bylines, and I regret I didn't get to know him better. Paul is one of the writers who transformed rock criticism in its formative years, making it a discipline fit for adults.

PAUL NELSON I signed The New York Dolls. I was fired because of them. I knew they were going to have to be a big success or I would lose my job, and I did. None of the people at Mercury were really into music. They were all businessmen.

KURT LODER Like Pauline Kael in another field, Paul demonstrated the possibility of bringing all of one's knowledge of art and literature to bear on the more circumscribed musical subjects at hand. He was also a great friend to sometimes difficult writers, such as the late Lester Bangs, whose work he talked up, despite editorial opprobrium from above at *Rolling Stone*. Paul's occasional romantic entanglements were generally of the tragic variety, much in keeping with the *noir* ethos he so prized, and his eventual vanishing from the scene, I think, was tragic, too.

US ROCK MAGS
"COMICAL AND HYSTERICAL"

PAUL NELSON The first time at *Circus*, I was the editor, but at the time it was primarily a teenybopper magazine. He had a special editor for that section. I had to gain some legitimacy for it and line-edit it. I wrote most of the other articles and reviews, but there was still a lot to do, so I did Q&As with rock 'n' rollers. I think Procol Harum was the first one I did. I made a crucial mistake: I interviewed all of them at the same time, so when I played the tape back I didn't know who said what. I didn't know any better.

HARVEY KUBERNIK I couldn't crack *Circus*, *Hit Parader*, *Zooworld*. Then I got tattoo'd by this review I wrote of The Beach Boys' *Endless Summer* for *The LA Times'* Sunday Calendar section in 1972. It wasn't fashionable to be writing about this stuff amid glitter rock and glam. They were out of favour, and it was really square to be affiliated with them. Girls stopped taking my phone calls. I was taunted, mocked, and *The LA Times* got letters. I was grooving to The Beach Boys at Rodney's English Disco and people would boo. It was a comical and also hysterical response. Then Kim Fowley saw me put my dukes up at Rodney's and said, "You're an impact writer." Then Phil Spector later said, "When are you going to wake up to the fact that there are always enemy camps?" He was trying to tell me that, when you do anything, you're going to be loved or hated for it.

RICHARD MELTZER Jon Tiven began publishing the mimeo rag *The New Haven Rock Press* during his sophomore year of high school. All it did was blend the same old shit – "With this album, Elton is performing to his potential...five stars" – with a painful pre-adolescent cuteness. As fate would have it, though, one of the great vanity rock sheets of all time was a contemporary of *The New Haven Rock Press*. The progeny of a core of young hellions from the Bronx and Queens – only slightly older than Tiven himself – who would later morph into the proto-punk band The Dictators, the *Teenage Wasteland Gazette* regarded Tiven as a doofus and made him its designated enemy. "*The New Haven Rock Press* really sucks my noodle. If I see another fuckin' review by Jon Tiven, I will take action," wrote editor Andy Shernoff. "I challenge Tiven to any form of competition he wants. I prefer twelve-ounce gloves, but he may want golf (they have a lotta country clubs in N Haven). Eat five-iron, Limey lover!"

PAUL NELSON I had left *Rolling Stone* and went back to *Circus* for the second time around. Jerry Rothberg was in charge. I liked him a lot. He knew nothing about rock 'n' roll. He once walked by me when I was playing 'Like A Rolling Stone' and said, "Who's that?" But he didn't interfere and he was a sweet guy to work with. He was the nicest guy I ever worked for. I had a lot of fun there. I used to write the letters to the editor there, because it was faster than going through the real stuff. I had fun with that. I had Dick Diver from the Fitzgerald novel write in from upstate New York. Whatever I wanted to get into the magazine, I would write a letter to the magazine and say, "You ought to interview these guys." They never caught on.

LISA ROBINSON In the early '70s, Richard and I co-edited *Hit Parader* magazine, which was owned by Charlton Publications, from Derby, Connecticut. *Hit Parader* was one of a bunch of magazines published by Charlton; *Song Hits* was another, *Rock And Soul*, *Reel Soul*. They had song lyrics and there were a certain number of pages at the front which carried editorial. *Hit Parader* was the main one. It was a chart magazine, but we got a lot of stuff in there – interviews with John Lennon, Lou Reed, David Bowie. Later on, Patti Smith.

RICHARD HELL I felt an immediate affinity with The Ramones. I dug them and didn't have any reservations about them. Lisa Robinson hired me to write about them in *Hit Parader*, the first article that was ever published about them.

GREG SHAW I moved to LA to take a job at United Artists in creative services, and part of it was editing the in-house magazine, called *Phonograph Record Magazine*. It was strange because it was distributed nationally to radio stations but we took ads from other record companies. It had a larger circulation than *Creem*, almost like *Rolling Stone*, but we didn't have to sell a copy, so I could pretty much hire all my friends to write whatever they wanted and get paid well for it.

"METAL" MIKE SAUNDERS Greg Shaw and Marty Cerf at the *PRM* were very good, enthusiastic and didn't mess much with your basic copy or content.

DANNY SUGERMAN Marty asked 22 writers to give a paragraph each on *Exile On Main Street* for the *PRM*. Out of the 22, I was the only one that liked it. They tried to deflect my positive comments by putting, "Danny Sugerman, 16 years old, Westchester High School." Then Lester listened to it again and wrote a letter saying that he and Ed Ward were wrong and at least gave me credit for being right.

RICHARD REIGEL My first paid rock writing was in *PRM*, a sarcastic review of an Allman Brothers/Wet Willie concert in the March 1973 issue. I had another piece or two in *PRM* before I got into the groove at *Creem*. *PRM* at that time had a folded-newspaper format, like *Rolling Stone*, but the writing was far more adventurous – Bangs, Meltzer and other *Creem*sters appeared regularly, ironically enough, in view of the fact that *PRM* was published by United Artists Records as a kind of hippie-run promo tool.

GREG SHAW We could have a ten-page article about Brenda Lee if we wanted to. It was complete freedom. Everybody who was writing in the early '70s was writing for it. It lasted a couple of years, and then the powers that be at UA came to us and said, "Look, guys, you've got to make up your minds. Do you want to be in the record business, or do you want to be in the magazine business?" My partner, Marty Cerf, and I walked away from there with ownership of this magazine worth hundreds of thousands of dollars, subscription lists, basically all of it for nothing. This was 1973. He ran it for another two or three years. I stayed with it for another year and then I split off to do my own magazine on the side, plus I wanted to get into releasing records.

RICHARD REIGEL UA didn't seem to have any problem with hosting all kinds of wild and creative writing, even in praise of their competitors' records, as long as their own product got reviewed somewhere in each issue. A great forum like the early-'70s industry-sponsored *PRM* would be just incomprehensible in today's OUR-brand-or-else corporate culture.

DANNY SUGERMAN
"ROCK 'N' ROLL WAS OUR LIVES"

DANNY SUGERMAN I supported myself with rock-writing from the age of 16 to 18. I lived in this $95-a-month place. I'd go to the Whisky and Jim hooked me up with the PR firm Gibson & Stronberg, who represented everyone in town, which meant I got backstage passes and tickets. I did a lot of interviews with bands I didn't give a shit about, like Head, Hands And Feet or Bloodrock. I almost did the *Playboy* interview with Jagger, but *Playboy* wanted somebody older to do the piece.

RICHARD MELTZER The night I met Danny Sugerman, at an LA party in 1972, the first thing he told me was, "My father works for the Mafia and I'm a heroin addict," uttered with a great deal of teenage pride, like, "Can you top either of these?"

DANNY SUGERMAN There was a camaraderie there. I was really close friends with Jon Tiven and Cameron Crowe. We were all young and rock 'n' roll was our lives.

RICHARD MELTZER He's made great hay of their ten – or was it five? – minute relationship, though others who were there insist that, when The Doors still included Jim, before he took his death cab to Paris, young Danny's bond to the Lizard King was no more, no less, than to lurk about the band office seeking ways to be "useful" – opening fan mail and perhaps going out for doughnuts.

DANNY SUGERMAN *Creem* never paid, but I worked for quite a few others who did, like *Rock* and *Zooworld*, which paid real well. I got to know Arthur Levy, who ran it, and used to stay at his place in Florida.

HARVEY KUBERNIK You'd see magazines like *Zooworld* and think, "How come there are stories on eight bands all represented by the same publicist at Rogers & Cowan?" Kim Fowley would say to me, "Too bad you can't see the movie *Sweet Smell Of Success*."

RICHARD MELTZER *No One Here Gets Out Alive* was a ponderous and despicable piece of celebrity fluff, heavy on the "dark side" – ooh, Jim was such a bad boy – and including a cameo by a kid named "Danny". When it came out, he phoned to beckon me into the night: "Let's celebrate Jim." Uh, thanks but no thanks. I'd rather walk my Schnauzer.

DANNY SUGERMAN I also put out a fanzine called *The Heavy Metal Digest*, which Lester and Richard Meltzer wrote. I did 300 copies and sold it at three different record stores. It was ridiculous – the only ad I could get for the first one was from A&M for Cat Stevens. Not exactly heavy metal! In the third, I did a thing on Iggy, whom I'd met by that time. I'd be getting 100 records a month and tickets I could sell, so I got by. What I was really looking for was someone to take the place of The Doors. They broke up and I hooked up with Ray [Manzarek, The Doors' keyboard player] and Iggy and decided to be a publicist.

RICHARD MELTZER For a glimpse at another of his entrepreneurial *fortes*, rock manager, check out *Please Kill Me*, where Ron Asheton tells a good'un 'bout the time Danny left his "charge" - a fucked-up Iggy Pop wearing a dress - to fend for himself when three surf louts began pounding him outside a David Bowie show, leaving him bloody and minus a couple teeth on the pavement in Hollywood.

LOU AND DAVID AND IGGY
"THE FIRST REAL CONVERGENCE"

LISA ROBINSON Danny Fields and I introduced Bowie to Iggy and Lou. Bowie had been here once, when Rodney Bingenheimer was working at Mercury Records. This was 'The Man Who Sold The World' period; he was still singing like Anthony Newley, with the long hair and the dress and the Mary Janes. Then he came back and he had seen *Pork* in London, which featured that crowd of Tony Zanetta, Leee Black Childers, all those Warhol people. Bowie, obsessed with Andy Warhol, hung out with them and they changed his life. He came here and Richard was at RCA, so we took him and Angela Bowie and this bunch of people to dinner at the Ginger Man. David wanted to meet Iggy, so I called Danny, because Iggy was staying at his house. Danny swears we went to Max's and met him there, but I remember Iggy coming to the Ginger Man. Whatever. Iggy moved into the Warwick Hotel with David the next day. I don't think they were lovers, but I have no idea. But David started to immediately take care of him. That's how they all got involved.

DANNY FIELDS I continued to manage The Stooges after I got fired from Atlantic, but it was a mess. They never had any money and I was deeply in debt. I'd go to the shows and Alice Cooper would all be there getting ready to go on, fixing their eyelashes, all dressed up, getting $1,500 a night, and I'd be looking for Iggy. There'd be blood coming out from under one of the toilet stalls and they'd point over there. I'd go in, pull the needle out, put his head in the toilet bowl to wake him up. Junkies are OK, but not when they have to go to work. It's amazing he's alive, you know? I'm sure that the affiliation with David Bowie saved his life.

LISA ROBINSON They all came to my house two days later. Lenny Kaye was there, a lot of people. This was the first real convergence to my mind of this Warhol/rock-press/glam-rock situation.

LENNY KAYE I always tried to be as faceless as possible in my writing, but sometimes I indulged in "personality journalism" because it was fun. One time, I was flown with a bunch of journalists to see David Bowie right at the start of his Ziggy phase in Aylesbury. At the end of the show, he took his shirt off and ripped it up and threw the pieces into the audience. I caught the sleeve. So, the next day, for the interview I took the sleeve and wrapped it around my arm. He said, "What's that around your arm?" And I was, "Oh, that's just some piece of rag I picked up." That was really as far as I would intervene.

LISA ROBINSON What happened with Lou [Reed] wasn't pretty. Victor Bockris wrote this petty bullshit that I told people not to write a good review of *Transformer*, as if I had that kind of power, which is patently absurd. Nobody told these people what to do, least of all me. What happened was that Richard produced Lou's first album. It was not a good record, and it didn't do well. Richard was supposed to produce his next one. For some reason, 'Walk On The Wild Side' wasn't put on there, even though I have him singing it at my house on videotape with Richard Meltzer.

So we were in London. We had been in the Inn On The Park with Lou every night for over a month, spending a fortune on room service. We just needed to go away on our own together, so we had a vacation in Italy and went back to New York and Lou was furious because Richard didn't go back with him and present the record to RCA. About a year later, when Richard thought he was still hired to produce the next record, we got a call the day before he was due to leave for England that David Bowie was producing the album, which turned out to be *Transformer*. Creatively, it was probably the right thing for Lou to do, but at the time we saw it as a serious betrayal. Richard stopped speaking to him and so, as his wife, did I. And I stopped speaking to Bowie and Iggy and MainMan [Meltzer]. This went on for a year.

PETE SILVERTON When I was on *Sounds*, me, Allan Jones from *Melody Maker* and French and German journalists flew to New York to interview Lou Reed. We saw some gigs and were due to meet him in the bar of the Essex House. He turned up an hour late – during which time his Vietnam vet regaled us with stories of helicopter crashes while we drank – and insisted on us all drinking doubles for another two hours. Then we went up to the room, and he was really out of it, trying to play this new toy, a Roland synthesiser guitar. I did wonder whether Lou Reed could play the guitar at all, at that point. Then Lou made the German journalist personally responsible for the loss of any of Lou's family during the war, and he insisted I read a book which was just out on Delmore Schwartz, the poet who taught him at university. He sent me to the toilet to read one of the stories in there. I passed the test, but Allan didn't – he passed out during his interview. While we were at the Essex House, Donny Hathaway killed himself by jumping out the window of the hotel, so it was quite an eventful stay, all in all.

16 IN THE '70S
"THE STARS WERE CHANGING"

DANNY FIELDS I got a call from Gloria Stavers in 1972 asking me to be her assistant. Then she had one of her huge fights with the publisher and she walked out.

DAVE MARSH Danny, one of my early mentors in the music world, learned his craft from being her competitor at *Datebook*. "Do what they do," his boss told him, and he did so, whether editing *Datebook*, managing Iggy And The Stooges or eventually succeeding Gloria at *16*.

DANNY FIELDS By then, the press had started to multiply and the record business had grown incredibly fast, so by the time I was there there was also *Tigerbeat* in Hollywood, which was very aggressive. It was owned by Walther Publications, which also owned bands which they would push. Gloria left to pursue other interests – she wrote freelance article and a column for a rock magazine. In the fall of 1982, she was diagnosed with lung cancer, though she'd been a two-cigarettes-a-day person all her adult life. The disease spread through that winter, not responding to therapy.

DAVE MARSH Gloria did not live into old age - she died in 1983, which untracked us a bit. Today's rock world could use her example on how to handle that transition past youth with greater dignity and grace. Death from cancer is not a pretty thing, and yet I can remember seeing Gloria in the hospital, right before the end, and she remained glorious, like something Tennessee Williams might have invented in a good mood.

DANNY FIELDS Randi Reisfeld and I were co-editors. The stars were changing – we had Alice Cooper, David Cassidy was a good friend and I'd heard about The Bay City Rollers through the English press, so Lisa Robinson and I went to Glasgow for a weekend and saw them at the Apollo there. It was amazing to see a band close down a city - the streets were roped off, there were girls climbing the walls of the hotel. I went out to stay with the band at some castle without central heating. "That's why you guys have such great complexions, right?" So they came over and broke big-time, and no one had better access than I did. We finally got the cover changed to featuring a single person rather than the old format of multiple heads of stars, and they were on the cover 13 times. They became number one in our mail tallies and Chambrun was pleased but never acknowledged that I had spotted them early on. He was a real bastard.

BOMP AND TROUSER PRESS
FANS AS WRITERS I

GREG SHAW There was a superficial music press in the early '70s. You weren't allowed to go into any depth in *Rolling Stone*, and *Creem* wasn't accurate, from a collector's point of view. My idea was for a magazine where you include something original about an artist, put them in a historical context and include a complete discography and relate it to other aspects of rock history.

IRA ROBBINS Our view of what mainstream rock magazines were overlooking included history as well as obscurity, so *Trouser Press* latched onto the past - namely British Invasion bands - as well as pub rock, prog rock and assorted marginal artists few publications cared about. But we were hardly doctrinaire about it; as you may recall, both Genesis and King Crimson were considered prog bands at the time. In the first two years [ie twelve issues] of what was initially known as *Trans-Oceanic Trouser Press*, we covered The Who, Mott The Hoople, Todd Rundgren, Peter Frampton, Steve Harley, Marc Bolan, Brian Eno, The Rolling Stones, Status Quo and Roxy Music, among others. Confession: As the mid '70s wore on, we found ourselves covering bands we knew we were supposed to care about but actually didn't. Privately, we referred to them – using a bit of borrowed British slang – as "wallies".

RICHARD REIGEL I finally had my first paid writing in *Creem* in the May 1974 issue, a review of Mark Shipper's reissue album of The Sonics, that proto-punk band from the Northwest.

IRA ROBBINS The magazines that really led to our thinking about *Trouser Press* were *Zigzag* (for genealogical history, not an incomprehensible enthusiasm for the wrong kinds of American rock), *Crawdaddy!* (for general excellence), *Bomp* (for record collecting and discographies), *Phonograph Record Magazine* (for serious and entertaining scribing) and Alan Betrock's *Rock Marketplace,* the mail-auction advertising business of which we took over when Alan folded it to launch *New York Rocker*.

GREG SHAW I had *Bomp*. I was into the idea of really digging into what happened in the '60s and trying to develop the fan's point of view to a kind of expertise and become a kind of pressure force to the music industry, to see that reissues were done better – just a general higher level of quality, intelligence and expertise, and maybe use the fans as writers, because there was no such thing at the time.

IRA ROBBINS When we started, in 1974, glam was mostly done and there really was a lull in innovation and novelty, so history made us feel like we were doing something valuable. Anyway, it was how we learned about music, and we were thirsty for info on what had gone before – in the '60s, at least. There wasn't a whole lot of acknowledged pre-Beatles enthusiasm in our house. But once things in the music world got good, history started feeling musty and ass-backwards as a journalistic ideal, so we downplayed it, but we never cut it out completely.

RICHARD REIGEL A rock writer who was as influential upon me as Lester Bangs early on but who's barely known now, since he left the field, was Mark Shipper. His *Flash* fanzine of 1972, which celebrated bargain bins and his beloved Paul Revere And The Raiders and brilliantly ridiculed all sorts of rock-star/rock-crit pretensions, was a major, major inspiration to me that year. Unfortunately, Shipper vanished from the rock-writing scene in the early '80s.

IRA ROBBINS Long before there were skinny-tie bands, I was devoted as a fan and journalist to The Who. When I handed Pete Townshend a copy of *Trans-Oceanic Trouser Press* number three – the second issue of ours to feature his band on the cover – in 1974, he took it to be a Who fanzine rather than a generalist rock magazine.

LISA ROBINSON *Women's Wear Daily* had a column called "Eye" with pictures of these rich women going for lunch, with semi-tongue-in-cheek captions. In 1973, Richard said, "We should do a rock magazine like this," and he convinced one of the guys at Charlton Publications to start this magazine that became *Rock Scene*. We did it ourselves. Lenny and Richard would smoke a lot of grass, look at these pictures of rock stars backstage and at parties and add all these funny, bitchy captions.

LENNY KAYE There was a real feeling of camaraderie. You'd go to your press party at 7pm and have your chicken wings and then you'd go to see gigs. The artists weren't as protected. You'd go into Max's and there'd be Alice Cooper and you'd talk about what was going on. It wasn't completely innocent, because they knew that the nicer they were to the press, the better reception they'd get. And the height of all that incestuousness was *Rock Scene*. It was our *People* magazine, the social life of rock 'n' roll, backstage with the stars. We all had access and it was a fun thing. You did your musicology somewhere else.

LISA ROBINSON Then the scene started to take off – The Ramones, Patti Smith, Television, Blondie – and by the winter of 1974 we were at CBGB every night, so *Rock Scene* became a shameless promotional vehicle for that scene and me as well. There'd be thousands of pictures of me grinning with people backstage.

LENNY KAYE When New York got its own scene, here was the house organ to document these bands, most of which were playing for peanuts. We didn't realise it at the time, but it also spread the word – there'd be Swedish journalists coming over to check us out. It made you realise the press had power.

GREG SHAW Probably more than the others in the music press, I was also a record collector, so I was in touch with other record collectors. There's something about the rigour of historical accuracy that appealed to me, and I wanted to apply this same rigour to obscure records of the '60s, and so I started picking up these unknown records which I called "garage music". At around the same time, Lenny Kaye was discovering this stuff.

LENNY KAYE
"AN OUT-OF-PLACE KID"

LENNY KAYE There was a sense of elevating rock 'n' roll. I'm not sure it was the most objective or the best for the writing, but there was a sense of promoting bands we felt were doing good work. I look at some of the reviews I wrote for *Rolling Stone* – say, of The J Geils Band – and they're not far off being press releases, because you wanted people to pick up on them. That's why writers such as Sandy Pearlman and myself moved into making music, because we knew how we would like to hear it. My feeling was always that it wasn't whether I liked the record or not; it was about placing the record in the context of its own aspirations. I wouldn't apply the same standards to The Bay City Rollers as I would The Sex Pistols. The other end of this kind of promotion of some bands was the rabid promotion, then rabid backlash mentality in the later part of the '70s, particularly in the British press, sometimes not anything to do with the record itself. So you live by the sword, you die by the sword. Some things that were said about The Patti Smith Group were so over the top that we knew that we couldn't meet those expectations. Because I know the critical mind, I could take things with a grain of salt when reviews have gone either way.

DAVID DALTON Lenny really has chops, not only in the godling category – Elvis, Hendrix – but also in the demi-mondes of rock, the garage bands, the glitterati, the bizarre and idiosyncratic demons. Lenny's Mr Nuggets, after all.

LENNY KAYE My approach was to pay tribute to the music that inspired me and moved me as an out-of-place kid approaching adolescence. That's really what *Nuggets* was about. I saw it as rock journalism. Instead of writing an article on garage bands, I got to put 27 of them on the same record and explicate it. It's not that different from *The Best Of A Cappella* I did for *Jazz & Pop* magazine. There was a lot of blurring of the lines then, because people hadn't figured stuff out. It was very natural to move from writing about it to producing it to playing it. I was always close to it all – I fought for The Stooges to stay on the label when I was at Elektra; I was in the studio with The Flamin' Groovies.

IRA ROBBINS Lenny Kaye was certainly a hero of mine. His liner notes are responsible for my ever-since obsession with Eddie Cochran.

LENNY KAYE Generally, when writers take up an instrument, there's some element of self-consciousness, and that's not all bad. The music I've made over the years has some critical relation to the music that I've thought about. And we know that certain people knew I and Patti beforehand for the stuff we wrote about music. But luckily, as a musician, I've had an ability to short-circuit that rationality. I'm not trying to be sarcastic or distance myself; I just jump into the deep end. It's probably a sobering thought for many writers, but in the rehearsal room, or making a record, you're not thinking about the reviews.

ALAN BETROCK There's Lenny K, always appearing from out a doorway, scarf-wrapped and glass-covered, conscious of all – all seeing, all knowing. He is like the bony CBGB canine, for he says nothing, though he obviously knows it all. From fan (didja see The Magicians at the A Go Go?) to chronicler (tonite you're mine, completely) to father figure, Lenny The K, who stands now on the inside looking in. All things to all people, he is none at all, his chameleon personas being shed and reworn again and again. Link could be just as content to play in a New Jersey basement or take some gurls for whirls in his '56 Chevy that only plays pearls like 'Bristol Stomp', 'Get Off Of My Cloud', 'Broadway', and 'Be My Baby' on his perpetual seven-day weekend.

LENNY KAYE Around 1975, I had to quit my job selling records at Village Oldies and stop doing the *Cavalier* column. There came a time when I felt my interests were conflicted – I couldn't write about groups that were alive! My interest is more historical, anyway, but when I started becoming a full-time musician, I stopped writing, except for the very occasional story.

ROCK SCENE AND NEW YORK ROCKER
FANS AS WRITERS II

LISA ROBINSON We thought we could do anything we wanted, because we didn't think anyone saw *Rock Scene*. We would put the editorial and photo package together and send it on a bus once every other month to Derby, Connecticut. It had all these cheesy ads: "Buy this stone and have everything you desire" or "Too skinny on the beach?" Really laughable stuff. The ink came off on your hands. We sent it off and made very little money, not even enough to pay people $10 for a story.

GREG SHAW Everybody was really ecstatic about *Bomp* and it developed into a network of people of the same ilk – Charlie Gillett was a subscriber – and when punk rock happened I knew all the people in punk rock because they subscribed to my magazine. [United Artists UK MD] Andrew Lauder and [Stiff Records founder] Dave Robinson – I knew all these guys. We all had the same vision: "Let's do it ourselves and show how it should be done." The do-it-yourself thing. "The music press will never get it right, so the fans should do it."

LISA ROBINSON In *Rock Scene*, we had a column called "Know Your Rock Writer". We did Lester, Richard Meltzer, Jon Landau. These were very flattering puff pieces on them so people would know who they were. We had Lillian Roxon doing a food column, we had Wayne County with an advice column. I reviewed books, from biographies of Cole Porter to Jacqueline Susann. In the same issue, we had me and David Bowie grinning backstage and Shopping With The Ramones or In The Supermarket With David Byrne or At Home With David And Cyrinda. This was stuff that you couldn't possibly see anywhere else. *Rolling Stone* couldn't give a shit about any of these people, and they were always way after the fact. *Circus* was way too straight and heavy metal oriented. *Rock Scene* was the house magazine for CBGB and Max's.

IRA ROBBINS I was opposed to *Trouser Press* making too much of the New York underground scene we all loved and took part in, because we didn't want to be seen as locally obsessed. It wasn't as if bands like Blondie or Television or Talking Heads would ever escape the Bowery, as I foolishly believed, and be able to be heard by anyone outside the metropolitan New York area. (Bear in mind that most CBGB/Max's groups never released any independent records, and major labels were very slow to come calling.) Then came the deluge, and in retrospect we quickly found out how naïve that view had been.

ANDY SCHWARTZ In the spring of 1975, more than a year before the release of The Ramones' debut album, Alan Betrock founded the magazine *New York Rocker*. In doing so, he changed American popular culture forever. The Queens native was already a leading collector and discographer of '60s rock and former publisher of the mimeographed fanzine *Jamz* and the collector-oriented *Rock Marketplace*, but *New York Rocker* was the visionary move, the product of Betrock's realisation that the music rising from a run-down Bowery bar deserved its own magazine, one with its own style of photography and graphic design, one that would blend a fan's enthusiasm with an educated critical eye.

GREG SHAW In the '70s, the circulation of *Bomp* was 1,500 and growing with every issue. It wasn't a commercial thing; it was only distributed through subscription, and I had a lot of people writing who were just fans, but I also had people like Greil Marcus and Dave Marsh. There was a turning point when Ed Ward – who was a reviews editor at *Rolling Stone* and a neighbour – wrote a piece on rock fanzines. Through that, I got tons of mail and the circulation doubled. Then Warner Brothers started buying ads and financed an issue, paying for 10,000 copies to be sent to their in-house mailing.

LISA ROBINSON Twenty years later, all these people told us how much they loved *Rock Scene* – Billy Corgan, Thurston Moore, Chrissie Hynde, Nick Rhodes, Michael Stipe. It had a very camp sensibility but also a very New York sensibility, and it obviously linked together all these guys who loved to wear make-up: "Oh, God, there are other people out there into the same things! I want to go to New York and hang out with Andy Warhol." We never took it seriously – we thought it was hilarious – but, as it turns out, it influenced a lot of people, so I'm actually quite proud of it.

ANDY SCHWARTZ Through the pages of *New York Rocker*, Betrock defined the new rock 'n' roll. His covers made stars of Patti Smith, Blondie, Television and Talking Heads before they'd even crossed the Hudson. He was a brilliant conceptualist who created board-game centrefolds – "How To Become A New York Rock Star" – and imaginary 45rpm picture sleeves for "singles we'd like to see". He opened *New York Rocker*'s pages to future fashion legends Anna Sui and Steven Meisel, photographers Stephanie Chernikowski and Roberta Bailey and artist Duncan Hannah, among many others.

LENNY KAYE For those of us collectors who cultivate the human-being-ography, Alan Betrock was the rarest and most treasured of collectables.

GREG SHAW Cyril Jordan came to me with a Flamin' Groovies album from Rockfield when I was still at United Artists and doing *Bomp*. He said, "Let's put out a record." So first I put out a couple of singles a year, not a big thing; it was kind of like a hobby. By 1975, Seymour Stein from Sire Records came to Mart and I and said, "I just made a ton of money with this *Hocus Pocus* record [by the Dutch prog rock group Focus] but I want to do a definitive history of British rock." He gave us the rights to all these British Invasion hits from his friends in England and I put together the first one, which was *The History Of British Rock*. Eventually, we expanded it so that we put out a dozen or so albums by people like The Turtles and Paul Revere And The Raiders.

BACK IN THE UK
"GROUND-LEVEL" MAGAZINES BREAK THROUGH

CHARLES SHAAR MURRAY Bob Houston, a big Scottish guy who looked like an unmade bed with a beard, had been assistant editor on *Melody Maker* since the late Palaeolithic era but had struck out on his own with a monthly called *Cream*. I guess, if *Melody Maker*, *NME* and the rest were "overground" and *Oz* and *IT* were "underground", then *Cream* was "ground level", and it drew on writers from both factions.

LESTER BANGS (FROM A LETTER TO CHARLIE GILLETT) How about trading subscriptions, *Creem* for *Cream*? And did the guys that put that mag together have heard (uh, duhh, grammuh...) of *Creem* when they named it? I first saw it when Kim Fowley came up to me in the Whisky A Go Go and threw one at me. Good, literate sheet.

IAN MACDONALD I did some work for *Cream* - just submitted a few reviews, got them printed, then wrote a few articles. Then I did the same with *New Musical Express*.

JON SAVAGE *Cream* and *Let It Rock* were an important bridge between the US and UK music press at this time. Charlie Murray worked well for *Cream* before his take up within the *NME*, while *Let It Rock* showcased Simon Frith, Richard Williams, Charlie Gillett - those who wrote for the *Melody Maker* and Fleet Street later on.

CHARLIE GILLETT In 1973, I went over to the States to interview loads of people for *The Story Of Pop*, a 26-part series for Radio 1. John Lennon was living in Lou Adler's house in LA around the lost weekend time and we drove up this grand drive in Beverly Hills and rang the bell, expecting a butler or whatever, and it was himself. He said, "Ah, the famous Charlie Gillett!" In 1973, I didn't think I was very famous, so it took me most of the interview to get over that.

LET IT ROCK
"A BIT RIGOROUS"

CHRIS SALEWICZ I liked the people, but *Let It Rock* was a bit rigorous in its manifesto. Basically, it was a lot of people from Sussex University, International Socialist members, that lot. Then there was Charlie Gillett, who at the time was known as the man who'd walked out of a Velvet Underground gig.

CHARLIE GILLETT I was at one of the first ever Velvet Underground gigs, in 1966 at the Dome in New York, but I didn't walk out. I was hypnotised and fascinated and sort of appalled, but I remember I definitely stayed until the end.

BARNEY HOSKYNS *Let It Rock* made an impact on me because it had intelligent discussion of pop, rock and other genres. It was the first time I'd come across that. I remember buying an issue in 1973 which impressed me because it wasn't just about Jagger and T Rex; it showed that country, soul and all types of American music could be hip.

DAVID HEPWORTH *Let It Rock* was hugely influential, with writers like Simon Frith. That was probably the biggest influence on *Q*, and also on *Mojo*. Interestingly enough, *Mojo* covers a lot of the music they championed in the early '70s - obscure American funk and old country records that have never gone away, the likes of Bobby Charles. You think to yourself, "These records can't have sold more than 50 copies ever," and, "How come I know all 50 people that bought them?"

JOHN BROVEN *Blues Unlimited* was being published by *Private Eye*'s company, Pressdram, and in the early '70s Mike [Leadbitter] moved to London and got swept up in the whole London thing, having his *Blues Records* published by Hanover Books. That was run by Peter and Derek Shephard, who launched *Let It Rock*, and Mike started to write for it, meeting other rock 'n' roll writers, like Phil Hardy and Dave Laing. But he kept *Blues Unlimited* going, and at its peak it had around 2,000 readers. Mike died in 1974 at the age of 32 - he contracted TB but missed doctor's appointments and it developed into meningitis. They didn't spot it until it was too late. He was a very important figure in the blues movement and really an excellent writer, inspirational.

BARNEY HOSKYNS *Let It Rock* also had American writers like Lester Bangs, but I really liked the Top Ten lists that readers submitted. There was such eclecticism - you'd have Todd Rundgren and Curtis Mayfield in them - so it broadened my horizons in a big way. You'd read about Tamla Motown and go and buy records on the label.

CHAS DE WHALLEY My first printed piece of journalism was a review of Ducks Deluxe's last gig at the 100 Club which appeared in *Let It Rock* after Jonathan Morrish - who was one of the editorial team before moving onto PR at CBS and Sony - cut it right back from a glowing lengthy piece to about one paragraph.

JOHN PEEL I read *Let It Rock*, but everyone talks about this period like it was the golden age of music journalism. Ultimately, what the reviewers were doing was reviewing themselves, and although it may have been terrifically interesting from a sociological point of view, if you wanted to know what the records were like, you had to go somewhere else.

CHARLES SHAAR MURRAY: Having failed to gain any academic placement, I ended up on a one-year training course under the auspices of the National Council for the Training of Journalists at Harlow Tech, so I basically spent the college year of '70/71 in Essex, DJ'ing one night a week in a local club for way less money than I was spending on records and writing as much as I could for *Oz* and *IT* and then *Cream*.

CREAM AND ZIGZAG
"THE POOR GUY WAS A HERO, REALLY"

CHARLIE GILLETT Bob Houston was a sub-editor in the sports section of *The Observer*. When he started *Cream* magazine, he got in touch with me and various other people who he thought would be interested to contribute. It was around the same time I started my radio show. Many of the staff at *Cream* were frustrated at not having any influence over Bob. I always remember this ridiculous moment when everyone was in his house and he had a colour TV and we were thinking, "How can he afford a colour TV and we're still all stuck with black-and-white sets?" It was that kind of mentality. I'm sure there was no money to be made. The poor guy was a hero, really.

CHARLES SHAAR MURRAY: *Oz* had this offshoot mag called *Ink*, a fortnightly tabloid which aspired to a much harder, grittier political edge, edited by John Lloyd. He writes for the *New Statesman* from a stern Gordon Brownish position these days, but back then he was a full-on, long-haired lefty. The music editor there was Charlie Gillett, but he quit early on and marked my card with Bob Houston.

CHARLIE GILLETT At *Cream*, I think there was an understanding that there was this difference between rock and pop. All the music papers were dealing with pop as a whole, even the *Melody Maker*, which had this orientation towards rock. People could write these long, detailed articles. But then I think Bob ran out of funds.

CHARLES SHAAR MURRAY: It was through *Cream* that I first encountered Neil Spencer and Ian MacDonald. Bob commissioned long pieces from me, 5,000-worders, and sent me out to do things I would never have dreamed of doing, like interviewing Tony Blackburn. He was the first really rigorous editor I'd ever had. In fact, I saw him a few weeks back for the first time in ages and he said, "You've done all right for yourself, Murray, considering you haven't had an editor for 30 years."

CHARLIE GILLETT The biggest problem was *Cream* couldn't get advertising outside the music industry, and the music industry wanted to advertise Genesis or Yes or whatever were their big-selling records, but there wasn't anybody on the staff of either of *Cream* – or *Let It Rock*, for that matter – that genuinely liked that stuff. They liked The Byrds, Gram Parsons, which is now perceived as a major important stream of music, and was already slightly covered in *Zigzag*, but in a real, absolutely intense fanzine kind of way. My impression is that nearly all of these kinds of magazines get to a circulation of 15,000 to 20,000, enough to show that there's a market there but not quite enough to support an infrastructure.

BARNEY HOSKYNS *Zigzag* was much more purist than the other magazines about the music it covered at the time – "Laurel Canyon dogshit", as Denny Bruce put it. I did have a foot in that camp, because I did have a big West Coast phase, so I bought *Zigzag*.

PETE FRAME *Zigzag*, which I founded in March 1969, was the first "serious" independent UK music magazine, the template for *Mojo*, etc, etc.

BARNEY HOSKYNS I was looking through some back issues of *Zigzag* the other day and Adam Mars-Jones submitted a Beefheart Top Ten. Obviously, I didn't know who the fuck he was then, even though I was at school with the Mars-Jones brothers.

JERRY GILBERT For a time, *Zigzag* was owned by Charisma, Tony Stratton-Smith's company, who I worked for. Pete Frame had set up *Zigzag* after working as a draughtsman for the Aylesbury Beer Company. It never made money and bumped around until it was picked up by Strat, who was a dandy, in the true Oscar Wilde sense. His big thing was horse racing with Steve O'Rourke, the manager of Pink Floyd. I think he really just fancied the stable boys down in Lambourne. He set up a book-publishing company, Spicebox Books, and then he bought *Zigzag*. Pete Frame was the A&R manager and a guy called Andy Childs came in as the editor. Once they needed some space to fill, so they rang me up asking for an interviews. "Anything you can do quick!" I'd interviewed Bruce Springsteen and had his home number. He answered the phone. We did this off-the-cuff interview. It was about the time he had to split The E Street Band because they weren't earning enough money and some of them had alimony problems. He just spilled his guts over the phone. By five o'clock that night, I'd delivered an exclusive on Springsteen. That was the way things were done then.

SOUNDS
"I THOUGHT I'D DIED AND GONE TO HEAVEN"

JERRY GILBERT In 1973, I did the only interview Nick Drake ever gave, but the problem I seem to have is that David Sanderson – who worked for Drake's management company, Witchseason – insists that it took place in a coffee house in Charlotte Street, close to their offices. I was convinced it was done in the house of a PR lady in Swiss Cottage. He says he remembers it vividly because, to his shame, he had no money, so I had to pick up the coffees, but I can remember walking up the stairs in the house in Swiss Cottage. At the time, of course, I had no idea it would turn out to be an historic interview, but I do remember being nervous. I knew he wasn't up for it. I think he'd only performed about four times, and I'd seen two of them on the South Bank. I loved his music and kind of respected his privacy and knew it would be difficult to extract anything from him. True to form, he shambled in in his greatcoat and we never made eye contact once.

CHRIS SALEWICZ When I was on *Let It Rock*, I did a couple of reviews for *Sounds*, but to be honest it really didn't seem to be happening. I remember filing this copy and the person who was taking the copy told me to stop halfway through because the ribbon ran out on the typewriter, which seemed to sum it up.

HARVEY KUBERNIK In late 1974, I had an interview with Roger McGuinn published in *Sounds*, but I didn't get paid for it. I called them up but didn't get anywhere, which made me feel really bad. Three years later, they rang me and asked for a piece on Mike Love from The Beach Boys. I said, "OK, I probably haven't paid some people, either." I got paid.

JERRY GILBERT CBS paid for me to attend one of their legendary conventions during the time when Walter Yetnikoff ruled the roost. That's where I met Bruce Springsteen, who had just released *Greetings From Asbury Park*. I was supposed to go on tour with him, but when I got to New York CBS rang and said he had a throat infection, so they asked me to hang on and put me up in a hotel on their tab. So I was holed up at the Plaza and they set up some interviews, including one with Paul Simon. The first interview was with Johnny Winter, just after he got over his massive heroin addiction. He had a spiral staircase walkdown in his place and he was an albino guy with about 20 per cent vision. *I* couldn't walk down it, so how he managed it, I don't know. He offered me a drink, but all he had was Harvey's Bristol Cream, so we sat and killed the afternoon drinking sherry. I had the mother of all hangovers. Then the Springsteen tour resumed at Georgetown University in Washington. He came off at three or four in the morning and we disappeared off into an all-night burger joint, finishing up at 6am.

JOHN PEEL I can't write about music, to be honest. The more you like something, the harder it is to write about it. When *Sounds* asked me to do a column, I tried to avoid writing about music. I'd just write a load of bollocks about where I lived in the country. I used to write that we had a gatehouse and about me and my showbiz mates, even though I never had any. We used to go and stand on the battlements and we had a refrigerator full of frozen dog turds that we used to pelt at peasants as they went by. Clearly complete bollocks.

VIVIEN GOLDMAN At Island Records, I was working as a PR. This guy at *Time Out* refused to do anything on Marley because he thought he was some ghetto youth, so I went over his head to [owner] Tony Elliott and got him on the cover to coincide with the Lyceum gigs in July 1975. Straight after that, I was poached by *Sounds*.

JERRY GILBERT I think those trips were the record companies' way of expunging their guilt over the dodgy dealings and bad contracts of the '60s. On the first trip I ever did to the States, Nazareth's management paid for half of it with CBS. They booked me into the St Moritz. There were a lot American groupies heavily into English acts at the time, and as long as you had the accent they were all over you like a rash. I arrived with Nazareth and within half an hour of being in New York City I'd been pulled by some groupie who was waiting for Brinsley Schwarz to arrive. It was all so matter of fact. She had taken it upon herself to move in with me for the week I was there. We got to my room and there was a record player and speakers set up, a pile of biographies and LPs and a note from CBS saying, "Welcome to New York. Give us a call when you wake up. PS: Open the top right drawer of your dressing table." In there was a bloody great lid of grass. I thought I'd died and gone to heaven. I was 22, there was this girl, drugs, records, a record player and an open ticket to put anything on room service.

VIVIEN GOLDMAN Alan Lewis knew me because I had written for him at *Black Music*. He knew me from a piece I did on the Philly Sound. It was an interesting moment for *Sounds*, because this was all immediately pre-punk. There wasn't much interesting going on – still Genesis and Rod Stewart – and people like Barbara Charone were firmly of the old school, unreconstructed. She worshipped these people. She elevated them as gods.

JERRY GILBERT Penny Valentine was the first to leave. She did the early interviews with Elton John and went to work for him at Rocket. One thing about the '70s was that the pay was very poor. When I left *Sounds*, in 1974, I was earning £2,500 a year, so I went into PR. It's not something I want to boast about, but I went to this company called WWA, WorldWide Artists. They said they would double my salary, and like a fool I took it. They were a management company who had Black Sabbath, Yes, Medicine Head, Gentle Giant and The Groundhogs and wanted to start a label, also called WWA, so I was supposed to be the PR. One of the managers at WWA was Wilf Pine, who was from the Don Arden school of management – you know, if you couldn't get a band legitimately, you stole them using strongarm tactics. He was extremely pleasant to those he liked but basically crushed the bones of those he didn't. I wrote some sleeve notes for The Groundhogs and they sent 'round a crate of champagne - well over the top in those days - and then offered to fly me out to Madison Square Garden to the Ali-Frazier fight to discuss a proposition. I was terrified so invented a reason not to go, but eventually I took the gig with them because *Sounds* was stagnating. I'd done four years there. I was only at WWA for ten months. Even though I was writing for *Zigzag*, it was an unsavoury existence. I brought the PA from *Sounds*, who was in therapy within six months. We were based in these offices in Mayfair, but we had to be out by 6pm because they wanted to shoot blue movies in the evening. Every manager had so much cocaine. It was rife. They were owned by the film group Helmdale, and eventually the whole thing collapsed in a blur of cocaine. I know one day I got back from lunch to find Wilf had threatened a *Melody Maker* journalist called Steve Lake, who had written something in their light-hearted singles review that week taking the piss out of a Groundhogs single. Wilf had threatened to break the guy's legs. I was firefighting all the while - *Private Eye* were on the phone trying to dig the considerable dirt on the two people who ran WorldWide, Patrick Meehan Sr and Patrick Meehan Jr. Pretty scary times. They closed down after ten months and I was made redundant, so I went to Charisma as press officer and then A&R manager.

MELODY MAKER
THE PROG ROCK YEARS

CHARLIE GILLETT When I was managing Kilburn And The High Roads in the early '70s, if you ever thought about taking an ad for musicians looking to put a band together or looking for a drummer or for a gig, you would only think of the *Melody Maker*. The *NME* wouldn't even cross your mind. The people who were buying *NME* were buying records. They weren't going to gigs; they weren't themselves musicians.

KEITH ALTHAM I freelanced for a while at *Melody Maker*. Bob Dawbarn, the news editor, came up with the pseudonym Sammy Glick, the PR played by Tony Curtis in *The Sweet Smell Of Success*. There was a certain irony to that.

IRA ROBBINS By 1971, I was buying *Melody Maker* and subscribing to the *New Musical Express*, which came months late, via sea mail, rolled into a baton-like tube. In twelfth grade, future *Trouser Press* co-founder Dave Schulps and I would read it furtively behind the large fume-gathering hoods on our desks in an elective chemistry course at Bronx Science that year.

RICHARD WILLIAMS The writer who had the most potential on *Melody Maker* was Mick Watts. He was a terrific writer and could write about anything he wanted. His writing had a kind of maturity that none of the rest of us had at that time, apart from the fact that he wrote those really big scoops, like Bowie declaring he was bisexual.

CHRIS WELCH Before Mick Watts' story, I had interviewed Bowie in the Red Lion pub when he was wearing the dress for 'The Man Who Sold The World'. I think David was trying to get through to me that I should be writing about his new look and attitude – he was sort of coming out – but I wasn't taking the bait, so rather foolishly I tried to cover up in the piece by pretending he wasn't being camp and gay. "Don't be silly, David – put that dress away!" I didn't take it seriously, because I'd known David from the Marquee days when he was in The Buzz. I rather missed the point. Then Mick fell in and actually reported it as David wanted it.

KRIS NEEDS Bowie had appeared in *Melody Maker* saying he was bisexual. The photos showed he'd had his hair chopped short and spiky and dyed orange, while his clothes were space-age jumpsuits. He'd gone androgynous-alien. Forget that old folkie; Ziggy Stardust was now among us.

RICHARD WILLIAMS Mick Watts was a grown-up. I was always stunned that he'd wanted to be an editor, because I thought he was the man who should have done the David Bowie biography, a really good one, about five years into Bowie's big-time career.

CAROLINE COON By the early '70s, we at the vanguard of the underground movement were being targeted by the authorities: *Oz* had been busted for the *Schoolkids* issue, free festivals were being banned and rock 'n' roll had become corporate. Because I was by then quite well known through founding Release and had written about social issues in the underground press, Ray Coleman, the editor of *Melody Maker*, asked me to start writing for him.

ALLAN JONES I joined *Melody Maker* in June 1974. The previous summer, I'd left art school in Newport, Wales, and had been working at Hatchards in Piccadilly in the horrible, Dickensian mail-order department. A friend of mine saw this ad for a writer. You had to be under 21, opinionated and no previous journalistic experience was necessary. I wrote a long, long, rambling letter which said that *Melody Maker* had gone a bit stale and wasn't exciting and should cover The Stooges and Velvet Underground and groups I really loved. I ended it by saying, *"Melody Maker* needs a bullet up the arse. I'm the gun. Pull the trigger." It fucking worked! Ray invited me along for an interview, which didn't appear profitable – I suspect he didn't like my attitude, because I told him I preferred *NME* – but I got the job as junior reporter, the lowest of the low, which was great because I had no experience. The first interview I did was with Ken Hensley from Uriah Heep. I researched it and sat up all night writing it, as though it was with Don DeLillo.

RICHARD WILLIAMS Ray gave everybody lots of scope and could see what needed to be done. For a couple of years, *Melody Maker* was really on the button. He wasn't dictatorial; he had firm ideas of what he thought journalism should be, and the further away I get from that, the better it is. I see that now. Sometimes we used to laugh behind his back, because he seemed rather strict, but he knew the value of a good story and he wanted to broaden things out. He didn't want Pete Townshend talking about chord changes; he wanted Pete Townshend talking about Vietnam. At the time, we were a little bit sceptical. To give him credit, Ray saw what *Rolling Stone* were doing. While we read the record review pages of *Rolling Stone*, he read the more political stuff.

ALLAN JONES I decided to do everything that was offered me. It encompassed everybody. In the first few weeks, I interviewed Showaddywaddy, Leonard Cohen, Mud, Bryan Ferry, The Bay City Rollers. I discovered what a good scam it was – the more you did, the more meals you got. Free drinks. I was on an absolute pittance as a salary, something like £12 a week. At the end of the first month, I was going to hand in my notice to Mick Watts, the assistant editor, because I was spending more money on getting to gigs than I was earning. They hadn't told me about expenses. He explained the arcane business of claiming expenses and introduced me to Max Jones, who gave me a crash course in creative accounting.

HARVEY KUBERNIK I couldn't get it going in LA, even though Brian [Wilson] would be calling to say, "Let's go to Canter's," or I'd be hanging out at recording sessions by Barry White, Bob Dylan, Leonard Cohen. I realised people are taken for granted, locally, so I sent a letter to Ray Coleman and then went to England in August 1975. I'd met him at a Wailers gig at the Roxy there and had covered a George Harrison press conference, and he said, "Call me when you get to England." So I traded in my barmitzvah bonds and got some bread from my parents and went. When I got there, I was picked up in a car and taken to see Led Zeppelin in Earls Court. Then [super publicist] Tony Brainsby's on the phone: "Freddie Mercury wants to talk to you. Steve Harley's manager wants to meet you in Knightsbridge. Paul McCartney wants to say hello." I said, "Hey, they like writers in this town."

ALLAN JONES Ray was old school. He wasn't dictatorial in a table-thumping manner, but he did have a heavy, brooding presence and used to sulk around a lot. He liked everything ship-shape. His model for the *Melody Maker* was *The Daily Telegraph*, in the way it should look, read and be regarded. This was a bit of a shock to me, thinking it was going to be a rock 'n' roll paper. He didn't like people staggering around drunk after lunch. The office wasn't as relaxed as I thought it might be, not terribly informal. A definite sense of hierarchy. The one thing which struck me was how self-regarding everyone was. They really felt that *Melody Maker* was very important to the world at large, the music fan's bible.

CHRIS SALEWICZ In the late '60s and early '70s, *Melody Maker* had been quite interesting, but it took itself very seriously. You realised that when you met the people.

ALLAN JONES There wasn't a lot of intrinsic humour in people's writing, so I kind of stuck out like a sore thumb there. I think there was some suspicion because I didn't have any qualifications, while most of them had journalistic schooling of one kind or another, but I hung in there.

CAROLINE COON There was a very funny period when I tried to become one of the lads at *Melody Maker*, going out drinking beer, all that. I thought that, if you go out drinking and partying, part of it is to surveil the scene and get laid. I always imagined, when the guys came into the office with dreadful hangovers, that they were having a good time, but when I went out with them, I was the only one who got laid. The more drunk they got, the less attractive they became and the less likely they were going to get laid! So I couldn't become one of the lads. By three o'clock in the morning, if you haven't seen somebody pretty, you go home, don't you? What's the point in being out? Then the double standards about women who got laid kicked in. I could have cared a shit. If it had been a guy, it would have been, "Well done, mate," but with me it was shock-horror and jealousy.

CHRIS WELCH I really regret something rude about Paul McCartney I wrote in a Wings review which upset Linda, who I really liked. I wrote something about Paul singing 'Yesterday' forever and she wasn't happy, because they had been very friendly to me, and it must have come across as me stabbing them in the back.

RICHARD WILLIAMS Ray wasn't dictatorial. If I wanted to go off and do a long interview with Lou Adler, a producer, a background person, I could get a spread for that. Or, if I wanted to write about Laura Nyro before anyone had heard of her, I'd get a page. He trusted people's instincts. When I think back to all those people who were there – Mick Watts, Roy Hollingsworth, Chris Welch, Colin Irwin – everybody was allowed to write about what they were enthusiastic about.

HARVEY KUBERNIK When I called Ray, he took me to San Lorenzo. I thought it was great that a Fleet Street/IPC guy like him would give me two hours. Michael Ochs had written stuff for them in the early '70s, but they needed someone in LA to cover rock. He wasn't exactly a mentor, but he was an extremely supportive person.

RICHARD WILLIAMS He was good at picking people and trusting them. The overall direction of the paper in the end suffered a bit because it wasn't quite as flexible as it needed to be, but you can't blame somebody for not changing their character. That was Ray's character; that was Ray's paper. In the early '70s, it was terrific, no doubt about that.

CHARLIE GILLETT The best writer of my era has been Richard Williams. He had the ability to listen to music and hear things that nobody else hears and to articulate what he's heard very, very well, so he can describe the song, the way a lyric works, the way a guitar part that you hadn't even realised was in there came through. He could do it in a lot of different genres – country music and jazz, as well as pop music. As the editor of *Melody Maker*, he was responsible for putting Bob Marley and Roxy Music on the cover when it mattered. Subsequently, it wasn't any kind of badge of honour to be on the front page of the *Melody Maker*.

HARVEY KUBERNIK I wrote 250 columns for *Melody Maker* over five years, covering everything from disco people to meeting Tammy Wynette, reviewing Elvis Costello at the Whisky A Go Go and hanging out at Deep Purple rehearsals. Because I started pre-punk, I think I was less than myopic, and for a lot of the visiting English groups, I was their only link to LA.

CAROLINE COON I thought a lot of the journalists at *Melody Maker* were great. I liked what Chris Charlesworth was doing and Roy Hollingsworth. I would have loved to have been a colleague and a comrade, but their perception and fear of women excluded that. It's to do with the fact that, if a man can't have something, he can be very hostile.

JOHN PEEL As I said at the time, the one distinguishing feature of progressive rock was that it didn't progress, because progression was regarded with a great deal of suspicion.

CAROLINE COON There were plenty of female artists at the time, but they were hidden, not given the same status as male musicians because of misogyny, and the same applied to black artists. All of the journalists loved black music, but could you get a black band on the cover of *Melody Maker* or *NME*? No, because of the specious belief that to have a black musician on the cover meant that it wouldn't sell. It would be overt. In meetings, they would say, "We've had a black artist on the cover this month. That means we can't have another one for at least three months."

CHRIS WELCH One of my regrets is a foolish article I wrote about reggae, which was reprinted in the *Melody Maker Yearbook*, which was awful because I wanted it to be dead and buried. I wrote it as joke, but it wasn't at all funny. It was meant to be a spoof, but it was rubbish. I got letters from reggae fans slagging it off, and I agreed with them.

NEIL SPENCER It's true, they didn't like black people on the cover. "Too much ink" – that was the euphemism they used. I never gave a fuck when I later became editor of *NME*. The second cover I did was a Dennis Morris picture of Culture.

RICHARD WILLIAMS One of the things I loved about the *Melody Maker* was that it kept this guy called Chris Hayes doing a thing called "Any Questions?". He was even then in his '60s and sat at home answering readers' questions on absolutely anything. He made no value judgements about anything – you know, a query about Victor Sylvester was the same as one about Marc Bolan – and he was brilliant. He got answers to these incredible questions from extremely famous, busy people, and I liked that. He also did this thing called Radio Jazz, which was where you could find jazz on obscure radio stations, which was a hangover from the days when there was nothing on the radio, and I just loved that.

CAROLINE COON The music papers were pretty much a male-dominated culture, and there was an incredible amount of disparagement about women musicians, as well as an absolute contempt for pop and dance music. I didn't want to write about the big bands like Yes or The Rolling Stones; I wanted to write about women in music, and I loved the camp kind of pop of Mud and Showaddywaddy and Suzi Quatro. I told Ray that that was the area I wanted to cover. It's the same now. Today is not the time to interview Madonna. I would have loved to have done that 15 years ago.

SYLVIE SIMMONS I got this job writing the bubble captions on photo stories in this now-defunct teen magazine, *Mirabelle*. About a week after I started, the girl who wrote the pop column left, so I pitched in, interviewing people like Slade, Mud and The Bay City Rollers. So I went and asked them where they got their clothes and what their favourite food was under the pseudonym Sylvie King, which sounded like a shampoo.

RICHARD WILLIAMS The Roxy Music thing happened because Bryan [Ferry] dropped a demo tape around to my flat, I think. I listened to it and rang him up and got a piece in the paper and they got signed on the back of that. You could do that. You didn't have to ask anybody. We had a page called something like Arising, and it was devoted to absolutely new people. Nobody had done that before. You could cover bands before they were part of a process, and nowadays I guess they've already sorted out their market at that stage. And one could possibly blame Bryan Ferry for that.

LISA ROBINSON Richard Williams turned me on to Roxy Music because he had brought them to Island Records. I knew he was a big Lou Reed fan, so when we went over to London for Richard [Robinson] to produce Lou's album, we introduced them.

CAROLINE COON Was there resentment from the male journalists when I joined? I think you would call it blatant misogyny. The minute I walked into the *Melody Maker* office, there would be howls, catcalls, jeers, so it needed a tremendous amount of bottle and courage when I wanted to put forward ideas and participate in editorial meetings.

CHRIS WELCH It was a very male environment, very much a boys' club, and the environment wasn't great, when you compare [it to] what life is like now. The world was never going to change - you had a job for life; people tended to pick you up in a limo to take you to a gig or fly you to Japan. It was a rarefied existence, unreal.

CAROLINE COON I twigged as a result of leading Release that my class protected me. Although I was a woman, my manner and my Queen's English stopped the bucketsful of macho bullshit being aimed my way. One would put on one's Princess Margaret hauteur to get it to back off. And it worked.

RICHARD WILLIAMS Somebody like the photographer Barry Wentzell was as significant at the *Melody Maker* as Pennie Smith was at the *NME*. His pictures set a tone for the paper. He would have taken the picture of Viv Stanshall and Keith Moon in Nazi uniforms, which is pretty grotesque and horrible, but nevertheless, if you look at them now, they're still good pictures. They don't have that edge and hardness that they used to, but they have something else that was completely appropriate to its time.

CAROLINE COON I was quite up-front about being a feminist, but it was quite confusing, because I wore lipstick and was determined to be decorative for its own sake. I loved beauty, I loved champagne, I loved fucking, but I knew you could write about pop, because I had read Penny Valentine, and you need enabling images - "OK, it can be done" - people like her, Chrissie Hynde, Viv Goldman, Moira Bellas and fantastic Barbara Charone, who is a tough woman and had a different style to me but was great.

CHRIS WELCH To a certain extent, Caroline was recruited by Ray as a response to what happened at the *NME* when they got people who had worked for the underground press. She was really into pop and then came into her own when punk happened a few years later.

CAROLINE COON I always wanted to write the real story about Barry Manilow, get under the skin and talk about what his sexuality really was, his days playing in the bath-houses, so I went to review his show in Amsterdam and the PR - who was a very powerful man at the time - came into my room to take me to the show. He closed the hotel door behind him and said, "You're not leaving here until I've fucked you." I knew immediately that the man didn't fancy me. This was a rape scenario. In fact, he was gay. He was one of a whole group of men on that pop scene who were closet gays. So I became Princess Anne and talked myself out of it and covered the gig. But when I got back, I just couldn't write the story. So I told Ray what happened and he said, "Oh my God, don't worry. Just drop it." There would have been a view then: "Of course, what do you expect when you send a bird on a story? PRs behave like that." We weren't socially advanced enough to handle it. So, to a certain extent, there was a lot of stuff you couldn't write about.

CHRIS WELCH By 1970/71, there was this appetite for live music, and Britain was producing all the bands. Elton John, Jethro Tull, Yes, ELP, Deep Purple - they were all very big, especially in America, and then in Japan as well as here. We were so spoilt. Then, within a year or two, I was flying to Japan with bands like ELP and they were hiring their own jets. These were guys I'd seen play in pubs in East London and now we were flying to Tokyo in their own jumbo! It helped *Melody Maker*. We were streets ahead of the *NME*. [We] knew all the bands.

CAROLINE COON There was one story I really wanted to write, but they wouldn't have allowed it. I loved this band and its music at the time. This was between Queen getting really big and punk. I went to interview the artist and – snigger snigger – the PR and the artist had decided I was to do the interview in a Rolls-Royce driven to Stonehenge with champagne in the back of the car. I love champagne, I love Rolls-Royces, I love driving through the countryside, but it was such a set-up. That artist spent the whole drive trying it on in between answering questions. But I could never have written about it; there was this double standard that, to maintain your professional standing, you didn't fuck or look pretty. Look at Val Wilmer – she is a brilliant and a wonderfully attractive woman, but she wasn't seen by the men on *Melody Maker* to be stereotypically pretty, so she could just get on and write her stuff.

5 "We Wanted To Sin Mightily"

"Nick Logan was tea-boy at the NME *and knew exactly what was going on. I have a lot of admiration for Nick because he saw* Creem *very early on and fought his way up through the ranks, attempting to bring that to fruition."*
                              - Mick Farren

NME
"WE KNEW WHAT WAS WRONG"

NICK LOGAN Percy Dickins was instrumental in recognising that the *NME* wasn't going anywhere. IPC had been very much in the background, and we were out of sight, out of mind in this office above the Strand. We knew what was wrong: it was not a good-looking magazine, not well written, not pertinent and completely outclassed by rivals.

CHRIS WELCH There was a period when we at the *Melody Maker* used to laugh at the *NME*. They had these terrible front pages with headlines like, "Controversy! Beach Boys Never To Tour England Again!", really weak stories, whereas we had powerful stuff, interviews with John Lennon or Led Zeppelin. The *Melody Maker*'s circulation was racing up to 200,000 a week and we'd look at the *NME* in disbelief. I remember one week we cut out an entire issue and stuck it up on the wall as an example of poor layout and terrible coverage.

TONY TYLER Sales had slumped so badly that the management sacked the entire top echelon of the paper and pulled Alan Smith out of the staffroom to handle what might well prove to be *NME*'s last stand.

KEITH ALTHAM I was doing stuff for *Rave* under the name Mike Grant, had a double-page spread there every month. I wasn't allowed to say I was doing that, because I was on the *NME*. I was also freelancing for a BBC radio programme called *Scene And Heard*, interviewing people and doing news stories with Johnny Moran.

NICK LOGAN We kind of half wanted it to go down, because that was the only way it was going to change. It was very demoralising for us. But then Collin Shephard was brought in as publisher, and there was a point when he got the staff together and said, "If we don't turn this around, the magazine will close." Alan Smith was made editor and I think he was given six months.

KEITH ALTHAM I left around that time to go into PR. Alan was a contemporary of mine, a Liverpudlian, tough, shrewd and easy to underestimate. He liked to play at being this Woody Allen/Mr Magoo character. With Nick Logan as his right-hand man, they took on a whole bunch of people who were much more serious than us, writing about a culture, not just bands. I wasn't into that because a) I was older and b) I never did – and don't, to this day – think that pop music is that important.

CHRIS WELCH Years later, I met Alan Smith at a party and he told me that they decided to copy the *Melody Maker* by recruiting individual reporters to each cover one type of music or artists. They started doing strong lead stories, and overnight it was transformed. Within a few weeks, they started to become a threat to us.

FRED DELLAR I had been working in a book warehouse and contributed to the magazine of the union SOGAT. Then I got made redundant and saw this ad for a young, single reporter living in London to work for the *NME*, and since I was none of those things, I went for it. Alan Smith interviewed me in what turned out to be the week before he was made editor. He asked me if I had any ideas for the *NME*, and off the top of my head I said, "What you have to do is get ahead of the opposition. Instead of waiting for records to come out over here, you should review the imports," because at that time there was a bit of a gap. I also said they should get into studios and interview musicians before records were finished. I also said they should cover cassettes – which were really big then – to get extra advertising. I'd made it all up as I went along, but he said, "Oh, great. You can do three columns on imports, cassettes and studios." So I never got the job I was after, but I remained a freelance ever after.

TONY TYLER The happy outcome of my time with ELP was that I got to know many of the music press staffers. Nick Logan was always particularly helpful, even though I don't think he liked ELP all that much. He introduced me to Alan Smith and, to my amazement, Alan offered me a job. Of course, I jumped at it. He was in hiring mode and, as I was the first semi-literate hack to come his way, he hired me.

FRED DELLAR The whole thing changed in February 1972. As I gradually worked there more and more, I got to know the new writers coming in, as well as the regular staffers like Fiona Foulger, who did the behind-the-scenes things like the charts. It was pretty hectic in those days, in a ramshackle office down near the old Covent Garden.

CHRIS SALEWICZ By the time I started working for them, Alan Smith was overhauling the *NME*. The story I'd heard was that he was given twelve weeks to up the *NME*'s circulation or it would be dumped, so they raped what was left of the underground press for writers.

NICK LOGAN I had applied for a job at *Sounds* but didn't take it. Alan [Smith] and I had talked endlessly about what we would do to change things, and when he got the job he told me he only wanted to do it for 18 months and then he would pass it on to me. He was one of the first people to get into the property market, in that way of painting artisans' cottages up in Fulham and selling them on. Him and his wife had two or three on the go even then. Alan always had paint on his knuckles.

CHARLES SHAAR MURRAY: At *Cream*, Bob Houston commissioned this massive 8,000-word piece about T Rex, and Tony Tyler – who was *NME*'s features editor at the time – spotted it and dug it and head-hunted me for the new-look *NME*. They wanted to keep reinventing the paper, so they got me in.

TONY TYLER Charles was, and remains, totally professional, hugely knowledgeable and completely reliable.

CHARLES SHAAR MURRAY: I was a bit undergroundy about it, at first – "Oh, no, man! Selling out to the corporate pigs, man! Really uncool, man!" – and all this, but I'd had a pair of pants at the dry-cleaners' for six weeks and a pair of boots at the menders' for five because I couldn't afford to get them out, so I signed up.

NICK LOGAN Alan used to introduce Charles as his new acquisition. "Like a piece of furniture," as Charles said good-humouredly.

TONY TYLER Under Alan, things could get tense from time to time. He was a merciless critic, and Wednesday post-mortems were often rather cruel affairs for the week's offenders.

FRED DELLAR Alan caught me out once on a review of a Dory Previn album which was rather bizarre and nightmarish, so I reviewed it in pretty much the same way. He said, "We don't do those sorts of reviews here." I felt quite proud, being called outlandish compared to all the other writers.

TONY TYLER At the same time, our morale was boosted by the knowledge that this was a new approach. We still hadn't got the look and feel, but the articles were beginning to set the trend of things to come, plus a lot of expensive promotions, like stick-on 45s, were bringing sales back from the grave at an encouraging rate. Even before Alan left, we were neck and neck with *Melody Maker*. The other papers, like *Disc* and *Record Mirror*, were nowhere.

CHARLES SHAAR MURRAY: I brought along Joe "Captain Snaps" Stevens, an American lefty photographer I'd met via the underground connection – we did an MC5 piece together for *Cream* – and Nick Kent, my buddy who wrote for *Frendz*. Nick brought in his photographer, Pennie Smith, and then Ian [MacDonald] and Neil [Spencer] showed up, and the new-model *NME* was well and truly up and running.

IAN MACDONALD Alan hired me as a freelance. He was looking for young blood and had just hired Charles Shaar Murray and Nick Kent.

TONY TYLER The first important piece I wrote for them was a review of T Rex at Wembley. Alan praised the piece to the skies, completely rewrote it and plastered it all over the front cover. With the advent of Charles, Ian and Nick Kent, I rather fell into the second rank of featured writers and concentrated more on production, which I liked far more, since you didn't have to meet rock stars.

PETER YORK *NME*'s class of '72 introduced the rock-writer superstar – rock writers who were personalities, musicians who wrote, who were obviously part of the culture.

CHARLES SHAAR MURRAY: By this time, Jimi Hendrix, Janis Joplin and Jim Morrison were dead, The Beatles had broken up, The Rolling Stones were wearing their cynicism on their (album) sleeves, Bob Dylan was off somewhere being gnomic and incomprehensible, Sly Stone was sinking into hard-drug decline and radical idealism was sprawled bleeding outside Kent State University or locked up with the Black Panthers. In America, nevertheless, it was still possible to pretend that the '60s were still alive; in Britain, it wasn't.

NICK LOGAN By the time the changes had started to happen, we moved offices to Long Acre and added people. Ian MacDonald was very important, and, obviously, Kent. I was more responsible for getting Nick. He came with Pennie Smith. They arrived as a double act from *Frendz*. Pennie might have come first and introduced us to Nick.

RICHARD WILLIAMS Pennie Smith was a wonderful photographer who I thought was very important to the *NME*, as much as Nick and Charlie. The texture of the pictures and what they said about the world meant so much.

CHARLES SHAAR MURRAY: In fact, Kent came on board because, when I arrived, they asked me to do an Iggy piece, and I said, "Well, I'm happy to do it if you want me to, but I know this guy who's *really* into him." So I called Nick and said, "Hey, I think we're on to a good thing here. I mean, they *pay!*", because we were from the underground press, and getting paid was a pretty high concept to us.

PETER YORK Kent was so right for 1972 it was dazzling. He was late-hippie *fleur du mal* to the power of *n* and he looked like he'd crawled out of a Lou Reed song. Talk about decadent. Charles Shaar Murray was complementary to Kent, being altogether less of an aesthete. He was a stocky Jewish guy from Reading with a *Time Out* afro. He'd come out of the underground press with a lot of ideas, this very vigorous, logic-chopping style and this new vocabulary, which was at a premium on the *NME* then. Between them, *NME* was quite unbeatable.

NICK LOGAN Alan's version of the *NME* was laudable, and he did a fantastic job. It was really hard for him to take over from the previous generation, and he took on a lot of conservative forces. And, with the help of Collin Shephard, he overcame them. He cleared a lot of the deadwood for me to take over.

TONY TYLER Alan wasn't always easy to work for, and he was probably right to leave when he did, but he doesn't get enough credit for the work he did. Under Nick Logan's editorship, the *NME* became something very special, but it was Alan who saved it from extinction.

CHARLES SHAAR MURRAY There was a weird transition phase. There were a few old guys in blazers left over from not even the early '60s but the bleeding dance-band era. They soon vanished. Roy Carr was there from the *ancien régime*; Logan, obviously; Tony Stewart; Julie Webb; Derek Johnson, the seriously old-school – no, seriously old – news editor.

FRED DELLAR Along the way, I became assistant news editor, covering for Derek Johnson when he was on holiday. Derek was the best news editor anyone worked with. He was always the one who got the stories no one else could get.

CHARLES SHAAR MURRAY There was also a louche public schoolboy called James Johnson and this bearded, pony-tailed American hippie called Danny Holloway, who always did the singles.

TONY TYLER Perhaps the hardest job in rock writing is the interview, and the best interviewer on the *NME* in my day was Tony Stewart, later editor of *Sounds*. He was so quiet and unforthcoming in interviews that his subjects would babble their heads off out of sheer nervousness, giving him great material to work on.

FRED DELLAR Because I was doing imports, it gave me a chance to champion people whose music wasn't easily available in Britain at the time. More by luck than judgement, I sometimes got ahead of the game. People like Joe Ely, or Tom Waits, whose first albums weren't realised here. I think I was the first person to interview Tom Waits when he came over, and did live reviews of his shows. At that time, they'd only issued one album, even though he had three out by then. He lies all the time in interviews and came up with these wonderful quotes during that first one. He was talking about how he worked at a jeweller's once and said, "When I left, I took a gold watch, because I figured they weren't going to give me one for long service."

CHRIS SALEWICZ The route into the music press was live gigs no one else wanted to go to. Tony Tyler rang me up with the baptism of fire of reviewing Camel at Wandsworth Prison. Then it would be the features no one else wanted to do, so Tyler was quickly on the phone, asking me if I wanted to interview Uriah Heep. Actually, that sort of thing was quite good fun, because there was plenty of opportunity for jokes.

CHARLES SHAAR MURRAY I remember I did this piece about Stone The Crows, a Scottish soul rock band with Maggie Bell as lead singer and Alex Harvey's kid brother, Les, on guitar, and James came ambling up to say, "Awfully sorry, old man, but Stone The Crows are one of my bands." I was, like, "What? Are you fucking joking?" The old system was like that, where one writer staked out special turf and monopolised coverage of specific acts. Well, we broke *that* shit down.

TONY TYLER Early on in my *NME* career, I subbed a piece of Charles' – a review of a book by Ray Connolly – in which he referred to Connolly as a hack. Not knowing any better, I left it in and used the same word in the headline. In those days, "hack" was a *prima facie* libel [not so today], and Connolly collected £900. Not my finest hour.

LISA ROBINSON In 1973, Nick Logan contacted me and asked whether I'd do a New York column for the *NME*, so I jumped from *Disc And Music Echo*. I was on tour with Led Zeppelin and would file all these glowing reports about them in England, which they were thrilled about, because their parents read it and it was their only good press at the time. I remember Jimmy pissing and moaning about Chris Welch's review of them in *Melody Maker*, but I never had a problem with Led Zeppelin. I went on five tours with them, and they were total gentleman to me, lit my cigarettes, opened my car door – just stars. But I could see what they were like. Richard Cole, Peter Grant – they reminded me of Espresso Bongo. All those guys were heavy, dark, that East End music scene.

NICK LOGAN When Alan left, in 1973, he carried through his promise that I would be editor, but I didn't know he'd been talking to IPC about launching a rival weekly as the antithesis of the *NME*. Four months later, he launched *National Rockstar*. It was a bit of a sour thing, because he'd never mentioned it to me. It lasted for about nine months. I think Mark Williams was among the people who worked there.

FRED DELLAR My recollection is that Alan went to Spain and then returned to launch *National Rockstar* about 18 months after he left.

IAN MACDONALD Nick needed a new assistant editor. To my astonishment, Alan and Nick asked me to do the job. I was still a freelance then and had never done any editing or layout. There were several on the paper who were better qualified than me, though I never felt any resentment from anyone. I guess it'd been decided that *NME* was going to take *Melody Maker* on and they wanted someone from outside the immediate scene. I continued to write and do interviews, but my main job after that became helping Nick reconceptualise and redesign the paper.

CHARLES SHAAR MURRAY Somewhere along the line, we had another underground press invasion, with Miles and Mickey [Farren] transferring over from *IT*, along with John May from *Frendz*.

MICK FARREN Me and Edward Barker had been busted for *Nasty Tales*, which was the comic book supporting *IT*. We spent 18 months waiting to go to trial, nine days at the Old Bailey and were acquitted, so me and Edward quit *IT* and he got his cartoon in *The Observer* while I was writing for *Fiesta* magazine.

CHRIS SALEWICZ John May was very good as Dick Tracey. He started the film coverage with what was called Silver Screen, and he was quite instrumental in changing the paper.

CHARLES SHAAR MURRAY By this time, *NME* was pretty much an underground rock weekly published by a major corporation. A bloodless coup, you might say. Well, almost bloodless.

THE STRIKE OF '73
"IT REALLY DID GEL"

MAURICE KINN On 1 March 1973, I retired from the *NME* and they gave me a fantastic farewell. Sir Hugh Cudlipp, who was then head of IPC, made the speech, and there were all these people there - Noddy Holder, Vera Lynn, Max Bygraves and John Entwistle. My old friend Tony Bennett was in the country at the time, so even he came along.

NICK LOGAN When I became editor, I was 25, incredibly young. I thought I could do it, but it was an onerous thing to take on - there was still the remnants of the Maurice Kinn era around, and I was working closely with Percy Dickins, who was 30 years my senior.

TONY TYLER Almost immediately Nick Logan took over, our printers went on strike against their own management for, as it turned out, nine weeks. We couldn't shift the job to another printer, because that would have meant sympathy strikes - this was 1973 - and the dispute wouldn't resolve itself, so for nine weeks we had to get an issue together every week as normal, hoping to be able to print it the following Tuesday.

NICK LOGAN Although copy was being spiked and frustration built up, the staff really gelled together. The chief sub was Jack Scott, an unsung hero. So we sat and waited. The strike wasn't our fault. There was this great music going around and it really did gel.

TONY TYLER It could have been intensely frustrating and demoralising - we were just hitting our stride - but in fact it did nothing but good. We accumulated a huge stockpile of quality articles ready for The Day, and at the same time the atmosphere was almost carnival-like. An intensely enjoyable nine weeks, in terms of personal relationships. A lot of friendships were formed in that period.

NICK LOGAN The first issue after the strike had a front-cover shot of Bryan Ferry walking along a beach and the headline "We're Back!" or something. There was such a rush of energy in that issue, it was exhilarating. If it hadn't been for the interruption of the strike, I don't think it would have quite happened in the way it did. After the strike, it was a different magazine.

TONY TYLER When we came back, we did so with such a rush that no one was ever able to catch us up again. I remain convinced that the strike of '73 was the making of the *NME*.

NME
"IT SEEMS LIKE A FUCKING GOLDEN AGE"

TONY TYLER For me, the golden age starts here. We were reinventing the idea of the music weekly as we went along, and not only was it working, it was tremendous fun. We went to work in the mornings with a sense of pleased anticipation. I've never had a job like it before or since. We were flying.

CHARLES SHAAR MURRAY For us, 1973 was about the science-fiction glam rock of David Bowie and Roxy Music and the hypnotic new groove filtering over from Jamaica. Our taste in Americans ran more to proto-punks like Iggy Pop and the late, lamented MC5 than to hayseed millionaire hippies like Crosby, Stills And Nash, and our midnight turntables were more likely to be spinning Bob Marley's *Burnin'* or Iggy's *Raw Power* than any Mellow Mafia mumblings from LA.

CHRIS SALEWICZ The *NME* was really funny, and its assessment of things was pretty spot on. It very much hit the *zeitgeist*, and you began to see *Melody Maker* was quite uptight.

RICHARD WILLIAMS I left the *Melody Maker* in early '73 to be head of A&R at Island Records, and I guess I was already feeling that the *Melody Maker* was losing its edge. The *NME*, by that time, was beginning to make strides, and we had too much faith in the traditional journalistic approach. The *NME* obviously picked up pace.

CHRIS WELCH The *NME* really became a threat when Bowie came on the scene. I think they covered Bowie really well. I remember suggesting that we cover his return from Japan on the Trans-Siberian Express by going to Paris to interview him, but when we got there Charles Shaar Murray was already there. Mercifully, he went and sat in the same carriage as our chaps, so we got a good interview.

TONY TYLER We had no rivals, though I hope we were friendly enough. I have personal memories of *Melody Maker* staffers big-timing just a little when the tables had been the other way around, so I suppose we were the same. Individuals handle these things differently.

CHRIS WELCH I realise it now that we at *Melody Maker* were writing too much – we had become victims of our success, because there were powerful advertisers booking large amounts of ads, which meant we had a lot of space to fill. And it wasn't very well laid out. We had these acres and acres of verbiage which made the paper look dull. We were struggling with headlines like "Bob Dylan May Tour Next Week", and the '60s suddenly looked stale.

ALLAN JONES When I joined *Melody Maker* in mid 1974, it was going off the boil. The *NME* had undergone its incredible transformation. It was cynical, funny and a lot less reverential than *Melody Maker*, which never really shook that off. Reverence seemed to cling to every page.

TONY TYLER At the *NME*, we can't have been that exclusive, since it was in this period that we hired Andrew Tyler from *Disc* and Pete Erskine from *Sounds*. We also opened excellent relations with *Creem* magazine in Detroit. But we were by now top of the tree, and under those circumstances you keep your distance just a little.

ALLAN JONES I think I was hired at *Melody Maker* to be the equivalent of a Charlie Murray or a Nick Kent. Unfortunately, they were much better writers with much better contacts. So I'd been hired with this vague notion of, "Do the same sort of thing." I heard that Nick Kent hated me, because I'd been taken on in his image, and rather than being flattered he got a bit cranky, so I never met him for years. Charlie I knew quite well, because he always covered the same stories I would, so we'd go on trips together.

NEIL SPENCER There was huge hostility towards all the other publications, but we got on with most of the people who worked on them. Everyone knew each other, because we were all on the same junkets.

IAN MACDONALD My first tries at layout were a bit stumbling, but then I got the hang of it and started to introduce elements of things that made me laugh. I was a fan of *MAD* magazine, so I stole a lot of that style and speed. We gradually loosened the paper up, introducing new ideas and formats, playing with headlines and captions and speech bubbles. I wanted *NME* to reflect the life of the staff, which was so funny and energetic.

TONY TYLER Nick invented how the *NME* should look and feel - headlines in Century Bold; large-sized, grainy photographs; generally sharp, austere appearance - and Ian invented what it should read like.

TONY PARSONS I was a big *NME* reader. It started when I was going to see people like Rod Stewart, The Who and David Bowie, especially, because you felt you weren't sharing that with anyone - Bowie was for people coming of age in the '70s. The first thing I read was a Nick Kent review of Bowie at Earls Court. I'd been to the concert but I really didn't like it and couldn't work out why. I'd gone with my first girlfriend, a big night out for us. I was 17 or something. It was really unpleasant. There were guys getting drunk, throwing up, taking their clothes off, people chucking stuff at the stage. It all seemed a long way away, physically distant. And Nick Kent wrote this piece, tearing it to pieces, being quiet snide in a "get you, ducky" kind of way. It was unlike any journalism I'd read before, like a direct line of communication to me.

NICK KENT (FROM NME REVIEW, 19 MAY 1973) And there he was, the little man in the red spaceman suit, exhorting his aficionados to "give me your hands". It was beautifully symbolic, in a way, because this gig was a formidable bunch of nails set in the potential coffin for which the whole

Bowie mystique will soon be placed and solemnly laid to rest. And all the costume changes and mime poses in the world won't compensate for that, sweetheart.

PAOLO HEWITT I was 14, at St John the Baptist School in Woking, obsessed with music and books. Somebody brought the *NME* to school and I was stunned. It was so amazing, and the lifestyles of the writers were fascinating. I used to imagine them rolling at twelve o'clock, going on the road with The Faces. It just seemed so glamorous. I had a careers interview at school and told them I wanted to work for the *NME*, which they just couldn't handle.

IAN MACDONALD I had a soft time as a sub-editor on *NME*. I had Charlie Murray and Andrew Tyler and Mickey Farren and Max Bell and God knows how many others turning in pieces that required nothing doing to them except marking up for printing, headlining, blurbing and laying out. Those guys were run as they wrote, so you can judge how good they were.

CHAS DE WHALLEY When I freelanced for the *NME*, they invited me in to the editorial meetings. Because I wasn't an *NME* reader and a bit naïve, I didn't realise the reverence with which the likes of Nick Kent or Charles Shaar Murray were supposed to be treated. I mean, I went to boarding school in Reading, which is where Charlie Murray is from. There was one epic evening when he was the opening act at a local pub and introduced a blues number by saying, "I got a letter today from Newcastle University today turning down my application to study there, so I went up to my room and wrote this song." Cue lots of harmonica wailing.

CHARLES SHAAR MURRAY My heroes were Hunter S Thompson, Tom Wolfe, that whole New Journalism trip. My favourite critics outside pop were Pauline Kael and George Orwell. I love Raymond Chandler and Norman Mailer's political journalism. That was what I was essentially drawing on. I was reading an awful lot, writing an awful lot and doing terrifying amounts of speed, biker sulph, like snorting razor blades off a toilet floor. Cheap, but it worked.

TONY TYLER Andrew Tyler was the most human of all our writers, the most grown-up - thoughtful and quiet, more interested in people than music. He later became more interested in animals than people and is now CEO of Animal Aid.

CHRIS SALEWICZ The chemistry of the people there was quite good. There were some very interesting, intelligent people there – Ian MacDonald, for example.

TONY TYLER Ian specialised in definitive, intensely erudite mega-articles, the kind of last-word-on-the-subject stuff we saw in his recent *Revolution In The Head*.

CHRIS SALEWICZ There were quite a lot of drugs around, and that probably unhinged certain fragile personalities. I don't think it helped these highly sensitive, out-there people who were actually working very hard. The work rate was quite impressive. We'd be bashing out pieces of more than 2,000 words every week on those old typewriters. I really fucked my back up.

IAN MACDONALD Nick was – as he continued to be after *NME* – the classic mag editor: very stylish, very sharp, very much in control of the overall operation. I was the mad ideas man, always pushing the – ahem – envelope. Tony Tyler, who was nominally features editor, was very much with me. We had the same sense of humour, and we'd compete to make each other laugh with layouts and headlines.

TONY TYLER There was actually a lot of scope even for production people like myself and Ian to make a big contribution to the look and feel. People don't realise how much of this is due to headlining, blurb writing, caption writing and sundry other bits and pieces. Ian was by far the best at this, too, but I had moments of my own.

VIVIEN GOLDMAN When I left university, I went for a job as a secretary on the magazine *Cassettes & Cartridges*, which was part of *Gramophone* magazine and had offices above that strip joint Sunset Strip in Soho. I ended up writing it all, and then they brought this guy in who fired me. He said, "Horses for courses. What I really want is somebody in a miniskirt to bring me tea." So I said, "Well, I don't know who's going to write the magazine, but bye!" Then I got a job as a PR at Transatlantic Records and ran into this guy, Tony Tyler, at some lunch-time lig. He told me to come by the *NME* and gave me this job to interview this truly dire French pop group at Biba's Rainbow Room. They were awful, really naff, so I wrote a very scathing review, not realising that I was playing into their hands, because they liked people to rip things to shreds.

DAVID TOOP I liked Penny Reel in the *NME*, modelled on Damon Runyon but transposed to the London reggae scene of the mid '70s, and Brian Case was applying a very fluid, funny and hip prose style to cutting-edge jazz. On the whole, I [used to] read articles for the content rather than the style. These days, it's the opposite.

FRED DELLAR Brian wrote in a very jazzy way – he'd come from a jazz background – but when he started writing about rock, he was different and very funny. He had the ability to produce absolutely pristine copy. He'd bring it in on deadline and it would be absolutely perfect. You didn't want to edit it. It was flawless, down to the last comma, but very human.

IAN MACDONALD I wrote the jazz coverage for a while, but I was reaching the limit of my knowledge and needed a specialist. When I hired Brian Case, that, too, was sewn up. He was encyclopaedic on jazz and wrote beautifully, having already had a couple of novels published. Tony Parsons was another published novelist when he joined, as, of course, was Mickey Farren, who came in and sold himself to me one afternoon in 1974. There was a lot of depth to the team. We were totally unbeatable by 1975.

MICK FARREN I was at Edward Barker's birthday party when Charlie said, "You know, you really ought to come to the *NME*, because making a living is fun. Come down and see Ian MacDonald. You're a fool to yourself." I said I didn't want to work for IPC, and he said, "What else are you going to do? You going to be Bruce Springsteen next week?" And I said, "No, that doesn't seem to be on the cards." So I went down and saw I Mac and said I didn't want to write about music at all, going into my rant, which was repeated all the way down the line: "Why bother to write about the new ELO album on the day *The Godfather* comes out?" I turned in a piece of copy about *Star Trek* and the Trekkie cult and I wrote about Evel Knievel. Then I discovered record companies, trips to America and free coke, and I *did* start writing about music. They were totally unscrupulous in the '70s, so our attitude was, "Yeah, why the fuck not?"

MILES Mick Farren, Charlie, Nick Kent and various others came from the underground press but put up with this terrible censorship – self-censorship, most of it – because we were trying to pay the rent. You could no more investigate payola then than you could now.

JULIE BURCHILL I started reading the *NME* at the age of twelve, due to its coverage of the career of Marc Bolan, and stayed with it even after he grew fat and my love grew lean. I had never heard most of the music they talked about. Obviously, they had made The New York Dolls up. Come on!

TONY PARSONS My mum bought me a New York Dolls record in Basildon town centre because I asked her to, after reading about them in the *NME*. I felt I had access to the cultural heart of other cities and music I'd never have got hold of, otherwise.

MARK PERRY I used to read the music papers every week and hung on every word of writers like Nick Kent and Mick Farren. That paper was so hip at the time it was frightening.

PETE SILVERTON The rock-critic-as-star thing got so big that there was this occasion – I can't remember whether it was Charlie Murray or Nick Kent – that one of them was signing autographs on the way to his seat at the Hammersmith Odeon.

LISA ROBINSON The CBGB thing was just about starting, and I knew all about it because Lenny Kaye was Richard's best friend, and I found out about the music he was doing with Patti before anybody else, so I would write about it in my *NME* column.

CHARLES SHAAR MURRAY One of the things about *NME* at that time was that we were considered to be in the cultural doldrums, so we did our best to liven things up. But, looking back, it seems like a fucking golden age.

IAN MACDONALD It wasn't all mucking around, though. I shared Nick Logan's concern for style and tried to make sure there was a serious backbone to the paper. I remember egging him on week by week to get the "cover story" off the front page and go with a full-page photo. He made the cover story smaller and smaller and then finally did away with it by putting a huge photo of a Pink Floyd concert on the whole page and reversing white headlines out of black. That was the most obvious break with '60s music-paper design, moving to something between a newspaper and a magazine. All the other papers copied that.

CHRIS SALEWICZ Actually, the *NME* editorial meetings were quite serious and business-like. People would be given a hard time about things they'd done. Logan was quite a hard taskmaster, and he had a lot of other stuff going on – people smoking spliffs in the record-review room. He obviously disapproved, and was rather nervous about it all. It was a culture he didn't understand, although he was reasonably cool about it.

MICK FARREN It was a wonderful time to be a music journalist. Record companies treated you like God. Everything was on offer but cash money and hookers. Unfortunately, you couldn't get anything to wear from the waist down; T-shirts, jackets, hats – nobody ever sent you a pair of Johnny Cash cowboy boots or some tour jeans.

NICK LOGAN I did get the headline "Must We Throw This Pop Filth At Our Kids?" in *The Sunday People* over Cliff Richard saying that he wouldn't have *NME* in the house. I was really pleased with that.

NEIL SPENCER I was contacted by Tony Tyler because they needed to do something about black music. Nobody on the *NME* was interested. They had the soul correspondent Roger St Pierre, who knew everything about the subject, but he was not a writer in the same way that the *NME* had writers. That was my entrée to write about soul – Johnny Bristol, the Philadelphia Sound, TK Records, George McCrae. I did pieces on Smokey, Stevie, Curtis, Al Green. There was a lot of derision. Tony Benyon, who did "Th' Lone Groover" cartoon, was always taking the piss out of The Chi-Lites and people like that because they wore the wrong clothes – Dralon flares.

BARNEY HOSKYNS The *NME* didn't really cover soul that well until Cliff White got there. He talked about the subject in an inspiring way. But they weren't really interested in that or country music.

VIVIEN GOLDMAN In these days of fax and email, it's all changed, but then freelancers used to go into offices all the time. A lot of stuff used to go on. We'd smoke a joint in the listening room. The impression I got from Julie [Burchill]'s book [*I Knew I Was Right*] was that it was joyless, but I seem to remember everyone being very nice. There weren't many women – Caroline Coon at *Melody Maker*; there was Kate Simon, the photographer; Kate Phillips, who was sweet; and Cynthia Rose – that just about completed our merry band.

TONY TYLER One day, we got a call from a girl called Kate Phillips who was working on one of the IPC women's mags at the time and was just crazy to join the *NME*. She sounded nice and clever, so I said, "Come in for a chat." She came in and not only did I like her, everybody liked her. Everybody. She did a few freelance pieces and did them really well, so Nick Logan said, "Take her out to lunch and offer her a job." I don't think we actually had a job vacant, but we made one for her, she was that good. So I took her to Chez Solange down the road, had a splendid lunch and I said "You've got the job if you want it." She then said a curious thing: "Thank you very much, but perhaps I should now tell you who my father is." Her father? Who could that be? Gandhi? And what difference did it make? So I sort of yawned and said, "OK, who is he?" She said, "Your boss." Ron Phillips! MD of IPC Magazines! We all really respected the way she'd kept that dark until she'd been offered the gig on her own merits. She wasn't at the *NME* long, but during that time she was the first to review the Pistols. She also managed to upset Bryan Ferry, which was no bad thing. By this time, I was hopelessly in love with her, so we got together and, soon afterwards, took off. We're still together and happier than ever.

MICK FARREN I think I sort of scared Nick Logan as this combination of a Yeti and Dracula hanging around the office, but we all scared him a bit. His major weakness was that he was a working-class moddy geezer who'd come up the hard way and us flash cunts didn't go to college, or, if we did, we'd got thrown out. He'd take an awful lot of Valium some days, but he had a hard job, you know? The management [were] breathing down his neck all the time over the language, because we were playing Howard Stern to a certain degree. We'd have meetings about headlines such as "Bryan Ferry Screws Up", because we'd already rejected "Fucks Up".

CHRIS SALEWICZ They were pretty contemptuous of PRs. I remember Bryan Ferry had all the advertising for Roxy Music pulled in the *NME* over the headline "How Gauche Can A Gaucho Get?" when he adopted the gaucho look.

CHARLES SHAAR MURRAY We despised the record industry, gave not even two hoots for the sensitivities of our publisher or the profits of their shareholders and relentlessly satirised even favourite musicians like Bryan Ferry, whose ludicrous clothes and fragile ego inspired us to seek endlessly for new ways to misspell his name. The most memorable included Brain Fury, Biriyani Ferret, Byron Ferrari, Brown Furry and Brawn Fairy.

MICK FARREN The arrogant swine were Kent, Murray and Chris Salewicz, the Rasta Pole. He was hilarious.

CHRIS SALEWICZ I really liked reggae. I'd been to the first Wailers gigs at the Speakeasy and done the first interview with Burning Spear. Much later, I did this big two-part piece on Jamaica. I'd been working on [Lech Kowalski's punk movie] *DOA*, and he said, "Go down there and see if you can film an interview with Rotten." I very quickly saw that it was out of the question. That sort of stuff is...you know, life-changing stuff, basically. You're pretending that everything's cool and it's as fucking dodgy as hell.

NEIL SPENCER I always felt like an outsider, not only because our musical interests were different but also because of the lifestyles which went with the musical interest. I thought the music and the people Nick Kent was interested in were completely dull. I thought Lou Reed was a complete twat. I was a bit bemused by the *NME* staffers, because they were impractical as people. They had no social skills that I could see. Nobody drove a car. I'm from the Midlands; you learn to drive a car when you're 18. Nobody danced, and anybody who couldn't dance was a bit beyond the pale for me at that time, because I was a dancing fool then, going down soul clubs, and I'd started to hang around the reggae scene as well.

MICK FARREN Maybe Pete Erskine was a member of the arrogant swine as well. He was a sort of negative of Kent, blond where Nick had dark hair. Very nervous, tenuous, ghostly. Kent and him were leaving one day and I was heard to remark, "There's Verlaine and Rimbaud clocking out."

IAN MACDONALD A characteristic moment? I remember Kate Phillips reviewing the singles in this black-draped gothic cubicle we maintained for the purpose. We were chatting while some dumb record was playing when the door opened and Pete Erskine leant in with an air gun, said, "What's that ridiculous crap?" and shot the stylus off the record. Perfect aim. I'd say that was pretty characteristic.

ALLAN JONES Shortly before he died, Pete Erskine was going to write some stuff for us at *Melody Maker*. He called me up just after he got out of prison and he'd been getting it while he was inside, and by then I was editor. Rather than go back to *NME* – who I don't think were very keen on taking him back, because he still had numerous personal problems – he came along to us and took away a pile of records. Within a week, he was dead.

MICK FARREN Pete Erskine was a good writer, but I think he was too androgynously cute for anyone to take him seriously. Lester really did look like Pablo Escobar and was one of the scruffiest geezers you ever met. Kent had the same power, but in an epicene way.

NICK KENT
"THESE LITTLE PINK UNDERPANTS"

NICK KENT Loud music by self-destructive white boys was what I wanted to write about – The Stones, The Stooges, The New York Dolls – so I wasn't interested in temperance. I was devoured by rock 'n' roll.

PETER YORK Kent was the thinnest man on Wardour Street. You'd see Kent walking down Piccadilly at night with a girl as fabulously thin and pale as himself in a white, wet-look miniskirt and black stockings. Kent looked the part but better still. In 1972, everyone knew he was doing a lot of drugs.

DANNY SUGERMAN God, I remember Nick Kent. He OD'd at Wonderland

Avenue when he came over with Iggy one time. He collapsed in the bathroom and we found him in there in these little pink underpants, so we had to rush him to hospital just wearing those.

JON SAVAGE I really liked Charlie Murray's writing, because he had then – and still does – humanity, and I thought some of Kent's stuff was terrific; but when I became a rock journalist, I discovered that I really disliked Kent's MO, which was to hang around groups and then print stuff which was off the record.

TOM HIBBERT I remember reading his review of the first Television album and going out and buying it because the writing was so potent. I played the record and thought, "He's got it absolutely spot on."

TONY PARSONS I don't think anyone on the paper wrote anything as good as Nick Kent. He was really the man. He wiped the floor with anything I did. It is such a shame you can't buy his anthology, *The Dark Stuff*, on Amazon. If this was America, people like him and Charles Shaar Murray would be lionised, national figures, well known. They're worth a hundred Greil Marcuses, either one of them. They never got the recognition they deserve.

MORRISSEY I could tell you stories about Nick Kent which would uncurl the hair in your afro.

IAN MACDONALD Nick Kent was the wild card on the paper. I never had to change a word of his copy, but he had this neurotic compulsion to get insanely close to deadlines before he started writing, which he did in spidery longhand and enormous sentences that went on over sheets and sheets and sheets of paper, usually sitting in the office with me standing over him, telling him through gritted teeth that he'd only got minutes left. He almost always managed to finish the last sentence about ten seconds before copy was collected for the printers.

TONY TYLER Nick was pure fireworks, though his deadline-busting habits were so awful that we "sacked" him for a week or two as a way of saying, "Shape up." I don't think he ever really forgave me for that.

NICK LOGAN Kent never dressed for the weather. If it was minus 23, Nick would have the arse hanging out the back of his trousers. In summer, he'd have a leather coat with the collar up. But none of that mattered; he wrote fantastically. There was a series of articles in '73/74 about then-forgotten geniuses – Syd Barrett, Nick Drake, Brian Wilson – which forced us all to reappraise where music had got to. I'm so proud I was editor when they came out. They're among the best pieces of journalism in any genre, I think.

BARNEY HOSKYNS I was very inspired by Nick Kent's three-part Beach Boys opus, which was absolutely magnificent. Things like that really played a part in my appreciation of the major American figures. The whole Velvets/Stooges axis was much more alluring and mysterious than fucking Pink Floyd or even Led Zeppelin at that point.

JULIE BURCHILL He habitually looked like a six-foot three-inch lizard standing up on its two back legs and dressed head to toe in leather. He is one of those naturally weird-looking people who have decided at some point it would be pathetic and pointless to try to pass as normal and so have made themselves even weirder. He can literally stop traffic.

JONATHON GREEN I do remember once seeing him and Cynthia Rose. I was on a bus going down Edgware Road and spied these two stick figures in black clothes walking along, and all the people on the bus got up and stared at them, they looked so weird.

IGGY POP An unlikely, ungainly figure, well over six feet tall, unsteadily negotiating the sidewalks of London and LA like a great palsied mantis, dressed in the same tattered black-leather and velvet guitar-slinger garb, regardless of season or the passing of time, hospital thin, with a perpetually dripping bright-red nose caused by an equally perpetual drug shortage, all brought to life by a wrist-waving, head-flung-back Keith Richards effect and an abiding interest in all dirt. That's Nick Kent for you in the '70s and '80s. In short, a true rock 'n' roller. Someone who cared.

TONY PARSONS Nick Kent is a fucking god. I hero-worship him. And he was the perfect man for those subjects like Lou Reed or Iggy. Without him and

Charlie Murray, I would have continued writing obscure novels in the gin distillery where I worked.

IAN MACDONALD Chrissie Hynde was Nick's girl at the time, and she was so obviously full of talent that I got her to write some stuff for us. She was never comfortable with it and believed she was no good, but we all thought a lot of her. I wasn't surprised that she made it big-time a few years later. I remember her as she was when she used to hang out at *NME* – really funny, warm, great company.

CHARLES SHAAR MURRAY One of the constituents of the Nick Kent legend was that he never learned to type. He would sit there scrawling all this stuff, and he's left-handed, so he'd be, like, [hunches over uncomfortably] really crabbed and weird. One day, he brought in this immaculately typed copy, saying, "Hey I've been practising". Then we found out that Chrissie [Hynde] had typed it. I remember Ian [MacDonald] saying to Nick, "Well, what do we need you for? She's got plenty of attitude and she can type." So Chris did some freelancing, but she was never a staffer. She was a good writer. Even if she couldn't write songs, sing or play the guitar, she'd have had a future.

CAROLINE COON Chrissie Hynde was absolutely wonderful as a writer, but I knew that, although she was writing about rock 'n' roll, she actually wanted to be a musician.

JULIE BURCHILL I thought Kent was a middle-class wanker and a junkie and a freak to boot. Rumour has it that Keith Richards was once copiously sick on his jacket after a prolonged smack binge and Kent never washed it again. Later, his cred would sink to an all-time low when he repeatedly brought an unknown, 19-year-old Paula Yates up to the office because he and Richard Hell were reportedly sleeping with her.

CHAS DE WHALLEY When I was at *Record Mirror* in 1981, Paula Yates used to come tripping in to write her column. John Shearlaw, who was assistant editor, used to say that the only reason they employed her was because she used to put her feet up on the desk and she wasn't wearing any knickers.

TONY PARSONS When I worked there, Kent would be walking around with his bollocks hanging out. He had ripped clothes and these trousers, which were literally hanging off him, and his family jewels were swinging in the breeze. Physically, he's strange, very tall with a long body. You add heroin to that equation and you get something really weird looking.

DYLAN JONES The best story about Nick Kent is the one about the waitress who approached him, Iggy and Bowie in a Chinese restaurant. She asked him for an autograph because he looked more of a rock star than the others.

NME
"I JUST CARRIED ON"

MICK FARREN There were the geezers who came out of the mail room, people like Steve Clarke and Roy Carr, circulating the whole thing like a planet unknown to man.

FRED DELLAR Roy has this habit of knowing what is entertaining for the reader. He and I are probably far from being the greatest writers in the world, but we do try and entertain.

MICK FARREN Steve Clarke rewrote press releases until we all arrived. I'm being unkind, but that's the truth. Kent wanted to write about more than music, people like Harry Dean Stanton, and I was doing Kenneth Anger and all kinds of shit. Logan would say, "Fine," but it terrified the hell out of Steve Clarke, because he didn't know fuck all about Harry Dean or Evel Knievel or Kenneth Anger. Julie Webb we kept quiet by making her our own Lisa Robinson and doing the gossip. Overseeing all this was Logan, taking Valium.

CHAS DE WHALLEY The story I heard was that the A&M press office started at Steve Clarke's desk. He was a very nice guy, into Gallagher And Lyle, but he got thumped by Jake Riviera because of a bad *NME* review of Dr Feelgood at Dingwalls and he didn't write it. He was that kind of guy. I was with him when we were trying to get into a gig by The Jam in Newcastle. These Geordies got heavy, and who got punched out? Steve Clarke.

NICK LOGAN Ron Phillips, the MD of IPC, had his secretary go through the paper every week counting the obscenities, but I just carried on. You couldn't have the magazine without swear words. Later, his daughter Kate came to work for us and married Tony Tyler.

MICK FARREN The big battle at the *NME* was, did we put out a kind of high-school magazine about everything which might be interesting to a bunch of people pulled together by their liking for music, or did we put out purely a music magazine? I mean, how could we write about Bob Marley without at least giving an insight into colonialism or the politics of Trenchtown? Nick Logan kind of sat on the fence, leaning slightly to our side.

NEIL SPENCER The chances of getting anything about reggae in the *NME* at that stage were very remote. The first time I wrote about Bob Marley was when he did *Natty Dread*, 1974, and I had to fight tooth and nail to get that piece in. Trojan had reissued a Bob Marley album, and I remember Pete Erskine holding it up and making some remark or other and throwing it in the bin. I walked across the office and hauled it out, thinking, "I'm having that." It was beyond the pale.

IAN MACDONALD I think all the other papers knew by 1974 that *NME* (we began to use the abbreviation as a logo that year) had become the best music paper in Britain. We had most of the best writers and photographers, the best layouts, that sense of style and humour and a feeling of real adventure. We also set out to beat *Melody Maker* on its strong suit: being the serious, responsible journal of record. We did Looking Back and Consumer Guide features that beat the competition out of sight, and we did this not just to surpass our rivals but because we reckoned that rock had finished its first wind around 1969/70 and deserved to start being treated as history, as a canon of work. We wanted to see where we'd got to, sort out this huge amount of stuff that had poured out since the mid '60s. Everyone on the paper was into this.

MICK FARREN We were very aware of the audience. The *NME* had an incredible pass-on rate – we could claim 900,000 readers at its peak. It was a massive attraction, but a bit like the thing about starting out as Che Guevara but ending up as a mercenary, which is probably why I drank so much. The pride was in getting really good at it, also not running with the worst scumbags. It was the Mirror Group with a certain socialist tradition. At least we weren't presented with Emap at the time!

CHARLES SHAAR MURRAY There was an 18-month period in '75/76 when I only slept three nights a week because my sleep cycles were geared to *NME*'s production schedule. I would start doing speed Friday night, go straight through the weekend and Monday night, when I'd take the big sheets of graph paper and the photos home and either write or lay out. There was one emergency when a centre spread feature fell out on Monday and I actually wrote and laid out a new one overnight. Then I would go to the printers' on Tuesday, collapse and sleepwalk through Wednesday and Thursday before starting the cycle again. Needless to say, after a year and a half of this, I crashed and burned and had to stay home for a couple of months to recover. Then punk kicked off and I came back to work, full of dire warnings concerning the hideous consequences of amphetamine abuse, and of course Tony [Parsons] and Julie [Burchill] were saying, "Fuck off, Grandad. It's not our problem if you can't handle your drugs."

TONY PARSONS That period before I joined was when the paper was creatively at its strongest. I don't think the writers who came after – including me – were anywhere near as good as Nick Kent, Charles Shaar Murray or Ian MacDonald. People like me and, to a large extent, Julie always felt we were passing through. When I joined, I didn't feel the same way about the *NME* at 22/23 as I did when I was out there in Readerland. I did love it but wasn't starry eyed any more.

IAN MACDONALD We felt like pioneers, in a sense, pioneers of the first era of post-modernism in pop music, the era defined by Bowie, Roxy, T Rex, and so on, the era when the music started to be conscious of itself and look back and begin to make syntheses and style references and be ironic. Pop lost its innocence with glam rock, which was the period of the rise of *NME* as the major force in pop/rock journalism in the '70s. We were lucky to have smart people like them to write about and poke fun at. We helped to make them shine, and vice versa. Tony Benyon's cartoon strip, "Th' Lone Groover", was part of that. The music scene lost a lot of its solemnity because of us.

CHARLES SHAAR MURRAY In those days, record companies seemed to have unlimited amounts of money to blow on dumb stunts to promote dumber records, and we considered it our revolutionary duty to make sure that they spent as much of it as possible on entertaining us. Coaches would be chartered to schlep several dozen lurching, reeling hacks to see risibly useless bands at Bristol's Colston Hall. Beer, wine and non-vintage champagne would flow as press officers – prettily accoutred in the latest company T-shirts – sauntered down the aisles dropping large chunks of hash and fresh packs of Rizla papers into passengers' waiting hands. No conceivable album was so inconsequential a cultural event that it didn't arrive bundled with T-shirts and badges or wasn't marked by a launch party. Sometimes, the bands would actually perform, which was irritating but often unavoidable.

PETER YORK These new writers wished to shape the world; the biz merely wished them to interview the product favourably and spell their name right. Thus, by the mid '70s, you had something nearing open war between the commercial departments and the editorial bloods. Many old-style business hands were empurpled at reviews that described their artists as "Tory rockers", "cretins" and "bozos" and the product – product advertised in those very pages – as dross.

NICK LOGAN Yes, there were complaints from advertisers, and Percy [Dickins] and I used to spend a lot of time discussing them. I just used to try and be nice to people and tell them that this was the way things were. Ads were pulled, but Percy was very supportive. He knew what we'd been through, so he knew there was no future in that old approach. It got increasingly...not anarchic, but Jack Scott and myself were holding it together and doing the donkey work, which is the way with papers, isn't it? The editor and the chief sub and one or two other people hold things together.

CHARLES SHAAR MURRAY Look, we were the awkward squad. We set out to be. We did it on purpose, and we really enjoyed it. We were a bunch of fucking troublemakers and loved every minute of it. I miss that spirit of collective transgression. We wanted to sin mightily. I used to write 2,000- or 3,000-word features on an acoustic typewriter at a desk in the middle of a crowded room with people taking drugs all over the place, fights, screams, three different records playing. Now I have to sit in a quiet office, completely isolated, just me and my Macintosh, and almost anything can blow my concentration. Then, I would almost do it as a party piece, writing in the midst of chaos. After the *NME*, I could never work in another office again. Anywhere else would just be an office. It wasn't; it was this stoned playpen full of loonies.

IAN MACDONALD I'd just come down from Cambridge, so I was used to a more elevated style of banter. To be honest, when I first walked into *NME*, it seemed like a loony kindergarten. Everyone was mucking around and laughing and sprawling on each other's desks like delinquent kids. It took me about ten minutes to adjust. After that, I became one of the silliest members of the team. Being on that paper was a riot. And we never stopped. Come lunchtime, we'd straggle off through the West End to find some lunch, preferably somewhere with a jukebox so we could keep the soundtrack going. Early in the evening, we'd reluctantly knock off and collect in the pub next door. Then it was all back to Tony's place in Highbury or Charlie's eyrie in Islington or Mickey's flat in Notting Hill or the shabby communal house Andrew, Kent and I shared in Maida Vale. In the early hours, we'd crash...then reassemble in the office next morning to take up where we'd left off. And we carried on through the weekends, one long party. You'd think we'd have got sick of the sight of each other, but we even had a post-modern office outing to Margate, the entire crew, about 30 of us, whirling stonedly around on Dodgems in silly hats, howling with laughter, and then back to town for yet another evening party. It was a complete world of its own. I can't imagine anyone who was there not looking back on that time with great fondness and nostalgia. I've known nothing remotely like it since.

MICK FARREN The relationship with the record companies was they'd bribe us and we'd tell them to go fuck themselves. They didn't like us slagging their bands off, but they got used to it.

CHARLES SHAAR MURRAY Indicate that you might, under certain circumstances, be prepared to write a 400-word concert review of some dodgy combo and the next thing you knew a press officer would be flying you to Amsterdam, buying you a stupefyingly expensive dinner, taking you on a tour of the red-light district and uncomplainingly parting with corporate wedge to buy you a wrap of over-priced cocaine. Then you'd get home, slide behind the typewriter for 15 minutes and slag the band off. Oh, how we laughed!

LESTER BANGS In Britain, they have a tradition of adversary journalism. It's *expected* that, if you put out a record, the critics are gonna lambast it, or that the writers or the press are gonna kill you.

CHRIS SALEWICZ I remember it being quite revolutionary when you'd go to a newsagent in the mid '70s and you'd see Rod Stewart or Mick Jagger or, later, Bob Marley in a national newspaper. Basically, none of those papers had a clue about youth culture - it really was another world out there - and I think that was probably part of the fun of the *NME*. You were saying, "Fuck you," and doing it with a sense of humour. Certain people didn't have a sense of humour, but Tony Tyler, Charlie, I think my stuff, Kent - who was always a bit sneery - Farren and Ian MacDonald were all very, very funny writers.

NEIL SPENCER I found that whole fixation on Mott The Hoople or 10cc laughable. Nothing could interest me less. And the dress sense! The leather trousers and promotional T-shirts and satin bomber jackets from Warner Brothers. For their part, they were bemused by me, because I used to come to the office in DMs and barathea trousers.

IAN MACDONALD I soon found out that I was no good at interviewing. Most people in the music business aren't very interesting, to tell the truth, or not interesting in terms of original ideas and developed points of view. I enjoyed talking to Eno, because he had a lot going on in his mind - more than I did. Eno gave me my best interview. He had lots to say, about two solid days' worth.

MILES I did this intriguing interview with Brian Eno for *NME* then sent him a copy of Tom Wolfe's *From Bauhaus To Our House*, which had just come out in *Harper's* or some such magazine. Eno called to say that the Wolfe piece had caused him to rethink all of his ideas, and could we do the interview again? We did and it made a cover story on *NME*, so it was worth it.

TONY TYLER For some reason, I took against Brian Eno soon after he left Roxy and consistently sniped at him in various sneaky ways, via captions and so forth. I have no idea why I disliked him so much. He'd never done anything to me. Pretty soon, word got back that he loathed me equally, and so Ian MacDonald – who was friendly with both of us – well-meaningly but disastrously tried to organise a reconciliation. Eno and I stood in a room and glared at each other for about ten seconds before one of us – I think him – walked away. It was like Sharon and Arafat. But in the long term, it was I who was in the wrong. These things happen.

IAN MACDONALD Too many of my other attempted interviews consisted of me asking inordinately complicated questions to which the answer was, "Not really, no," or, "Fancy a pint?" I gave up interviewing altogether after getting a terrific interview out of Bill Bruford only to find, when we'd finished, that I hadn't turned the tape recorder on.

MILES I did an interview with Rush and purposely encouraged them to air their ultra-right libertarian views. The band was outraged, even though they promoted Ayn Rand's books from the stage. It was supposed to have lost them gigs or something. There were angry phone calls to *NME* from the record label and management. Lots of congratulatory letters to me, though, many of them from other bands.

PETER YORK The rock press – particularly *NME*, under Nick Logan's editorship – was not boring. Running off at the mouth, it was self-important, bigoted, self-indulgent. It gave a lurid perspective on the whole world. It was irresistible, the liveliest writing going.

NICK LOGAN The record companies didn't take too kindly to some of the treatment of their artists. We were picking up on Monty Python and that style of humour, which Ian MacDonald was so good at – the headline "Is This Man A Prat?" over Freddie Mercury's picture.

IAN MACDONALD My main memory of interaction with pop stars is a phone interview I did with a couple of The Osmonds, not because of anything outrageous about them but because they were nice guys and I felt compelled to *NME*-ise what had been a perfectly respectable interview after I put the phone down. In effect, I stitched them up. I'm glad to confess that I felt very guilty about it and never did that again. That sort of compulsion seems to have gone now.

CHRIS SALEWICZ On press day one Monday, Steve Clarke had been to interview Steve Marriott for the cover and Joe Stevens came in with the pictures. One of the things they were talking about was how broke Marriott was, and Marriott had pulled out this picture and said, "Look, there's my horse. We're so poor we had to eat it!" Tyler was insisting we put it on the cover with the headline "The Horse That Steve Marriott Ate". Eventually, they put a picture of Marriott on the cover sharpening his knives with a tiny little snap of the horse at the bottom.

IAN MACDONALD I was mainly a backstage-hand at *NME*, helping to arrange the scenery and organise the production. I never had Dr John nod out on me in the middle of an interview, as happened to Pete Erskine - though, come to think of it, Viv Stanshall did tip over face-first into a plate of biriyani while I was with him in a restaurant. I left him there, snoozing gently...

TONY PARSONS I grew up in Essex and used to travel up to Oxford Circus to buy my copy of the *NME* a day early from the little newsagent that's still there. Later, I found out loads of us were doing that, people like Jonathan Ross, because it mattered that much.

NICK LOGAN The music we could get behind - and there was enough - we would really throw ourselves behind, whether it was Little Feat or Roxy Music. There was no doubt what our thoughts were. I was always prepared to give lots of space to things we were positive about. At the same time, there was a lot of stuff which was complete garbage. I don't know how we got away with it, but we still did those readers' polls in those days, and all the people who figured in those polls we were slagging off.

MICK FARREN I was travelling all the time, courtesy of Warners, CBS or whoever. It got to the point where I'd call Ellie Smith at CBS and Susan Blond or some other lunatic at Warner Brothers and say, "What I want to do really is spend two weeks in Nashville, 'cause I've just seen the movie." They'd buy the ticket, pay for the Holiday Inn and up comes a car to go to

Johnny Cash's roadside attraction, write a bit about Steve Earle, who was coming through then, or someone else. Basically, it was "Mick Gets Drunk In Nashville". You'd hear about what's happening in Austin and that Willie Nelson was poised for a comeback and then see if you could stop off in New York on the way back on the premise of covering Mahogany Rush at the Academy. But fuck Mahogany Rush; you'd be straight down CBGB and somebody says, "You've gotta see this band..."

MILES There were always lots of drug-crazed ego problems during interviews from the years I covered the CBGB beat for *NME*.

LISA ROBINSON In 1975, Mick Jagger was preparing for another big tour and he'd gone through that very jet-setty 1972 tour with Andy Warhol, Truman Capote, Lee Radzwill and Bianca. Mick was beginning to feel like a dinosaur. He was no fool – he'd been reading the *NME* and seeing all this stuff about the CBGB scene, which I was covering there. I'd never met him before, but I was standing at the side of the stage at an Eric Clapton concert and he came sidling over to me and starts to do an imitation – in this high, campy voice, as he is wont to do – of my column: "Ohhh, Jimmy Page was wearing a pink-satin jacket..." And I just looked at him, and all I could think about was that he was wearing the worst shoes, these rhinestone-encrusted shoes. I said, "Those are the tackiest shoes I have ever seen," and we just got along from that moment on. Ultimately, Jane Rose – who is Keith's manager now – suggested to Mick that he hire me as a consultant liaison on tour. Annie Liebowitz was taking photographs, and I'm sure it was a terrible conflict of interest but I got paid for being a consultant and still wrote about them. I didn't give a shit. Initially, Mick was supposed to approve everything I wrote. Once, I showed him my copy and he laughed uproariously and said, "Oh, you have a much harder job than I do, dear," and never asked to see anything again. I was also plugging him in to the current scene that he wanted to know about. I mean, he had Patti Smith open for them in Atlanta, on that tour. They didn't know who she was, but she was beside herself about playing alongside them.

TONY PARSONS In 1975, when I was 20, I travelled around Europe, and the one thing I missed about home was the *NME*. I tried desperately to get it in Vienna, Belgrade, Athens. For my generation, which grew up as kids when

The Beatles were around, music really mattered, was important, so I felt like I had a stake in the paper long before I joined it. The writing and attitude was brilliant, and it told me about things I'd never have heard of.

CHARLES SHAAR MURRAY The encounter with the Stones in Frankfurt [when Murray was physically ejected from the band's dressing room after giving the album *Black And Blue* a poor review] was quite high on the weirdometer. For legal reasons, I wrote up a section as a dream, but that was exactly how it happened. I wish I still had Keith's note [guitarist Keith Richards pinned a message to Murray's hotel door], but I did bring it back and transcribed what he wrote. There was also a reference to one of the other writers on the junket, and I'll decline to name him because he's dead now and his activities in other spheres entitled him to a lot of respect.

KEITH RICHARDS (IN HIS NOTE TO CHARLES SHAAR MURRAY) Dear Charles (the disappointed man). Just to say that we hoped you got yourself and your critical faculties safely back to Tin Pan Alley. How come you don't get high? You sure work at it hard enough. That's what London does for you. Enthusiasm = unhip (an equation from the Smoke). Did you ever write a review of *Exile*? If you did, and still have a copy, I'd like to see it! Anyway, thanks for the number at the door! Come see us in London and we'll get you mighty high (you deserve it, hanging out with neurotic queens from the provinces is gloom by the bucket). I'd love to see a review of your visit to Ronnie's room, now we understand it all. Death to Eddie And The Hot Rods! Stones.

MILES I remember one meeting in which Charlie Murray was trying to reveal that Keith Richards had passed him a joint in the course of an interview. Eventually, Nick Logan allowed him to include it, but only as a dream sequence! This was a straight paper, with none of the freedom of the underground press.

NICK LOGAN IPC were happy to let me get on with it, because *NME* has always been such a huge earner - it was very cheap to produce, the staff weren't paid very much and it was often their second- or third-biggest money-maker, alongside things like *Titbits* or *Country Life*. I was much more aware of the risks in hiring this new staff than they were.

NEIL SPENCER Nick was always remote. The big joke in the paper was always about "the steely glint behind the steel-rimmed spectacles". It was that vibe. But he was always all right to me, as a freelancer, and he gave me a job.

NICK LOGAN We were really isolated, separate from the rest of the company. The offices had quite a grand frontage on Long Acre, but we were up flights of stairs, past the rooftop where Julie [Burchill] and Tony [Parsons] had their famous picture taken, on the third floor, right at the back. I would go and see Percy Dickins or Collin Shephard, but the people from the business side never came to us. I was very naïve about it – I'd kind of hear about circulation figures and what they paid to print the paper, but I took minimal interest. All of that cost me dearly, later.

CHARLES SHAAR MURRAY There was another influence, when it came to presenting the writers: Marvel Comics. Not the comics themselves, but the cool way Stan Lee would answer the letters on the letters page – half self-deprecatory and half self-aggrandising – or the way writers, artists, letterers would have nicknames. And there would be a page of plugs for forthcoming comics and little items about themselves. Frank Zappa did the same for himself and his musicians in his packaging, creating a little mythology. It was a way of involving the readers more. This wasn't totally an innovation – there had been byline pictures in *Melody Maker* in the '60s – but at *NME* there was a very permeable membrane between our private jokes in the office and what was in the paper. We all wrote Teasers And Thrills, and then Ian MacDonald came up with the personalised letters page and the totally surreal and out-of-order Next Week box.

IAN MACDONALD Every Tuesday, down at the printers, Tony Tyler and I'd be cackling all day over things we were adding to the pages. The Next Week box became a sort of competition between us, each trying to outdo the other with loonier ideas.

TONY TYLER About 1974, Ian burned out with the tension of it all and left the staff. I took his job as deputy editor and Neil Spencer became features editor.

NEIL SPENCER I got the job because they knew I could sub-edit. The connection I had with people like Nick Kent was that they liked the way I subbed their copy. His was always delivered on sheets of A4, written left handed in longhand in a large, sloping script with amendments and crossings out and erratic punctuation. But I enjoyed working on his stuff, because he's such a good writer. There would be references to John Donne and other people I liked.

TONY TYLER After 18 months, I too had had enough. I was a bit older than most of them, and the downside of the heavyweight rock era - self-importance in rock stars - was getting to me, so I too left to get it together in the country. Still here after 26 years, folks.

NICK LOGAN Increasingly, *NME* was this maverick organisation which we felt was ours, and I really encouraged that feeling, but it was a bit scary, because you know that things like that are going to come off the rails, eventually.

JON SAVAGE Not having been part of that *NME* myth-making process, I was always suspicious of it at the time - you know, was it such a great thing to be a star music writer so early in your working life? A conflation of the idea of being a POP writer with being a POP star with all the attendant problems - burnout, premature fixing of style, pseudo-celebrity behaviour - which have all but submerged many of my contemporaries.

CHARLES SHAAR MURRAY I think Jon Savage is the best rock writer of my generation who never worked for the *NME*. In fact, I'd say that, of the whole generation, he and Ian Mac are the *absolute* best. He has a great eye and a great ear and a very broad range of knowledge and interest.

IAN MACDONALD *Melody Maker* was our main rival, with *Sounds* the junior interloper. We knew we had to beat *Melody Maker*. We wanted to be for the '70s what *Melody Maker* had been for the '60s. They were our enemy - notionally, at least - so there was reason to keep some distance. *NME* was in Long Acre, then, a long way away from *Melody Maker*, so we didn't fraternise much.

MICK FARREN The real rivalry wasn't with the *Melody Maker* or the other papers but creatively, between ourselves. We were pushing each other all the time: "Will my piece this week be as good at Kent's last week?" The people at *Melody Maker* were beyond all hope. I liked meeting Chris Welch in the Marquee – he's fine, we'd have a few beers – but it was all a bit like a work outing.

CHRIS WELCH It was fine at that time – we all seemed to get along. Not like later, when it all turned horrible and the violence kicked in.

RICHARD WILLIAMS In one of my *Melody Maker* columns, I wrote about an imaginary Elvis Presley recording studio session, about a year before he died, because I sat down one day and thought, "If you were producing Elvis, what would you do? Which musicians would you get? Which songs would you use, and who would produce it?" So I figured it would make a nice piece of fiction. At the end, I put something like, "Fans are eagerly awaiting the release of an album called *Elvis: The Way It Should Have Been*." The next week, the *NME* printed the whole thing as a news story. They took the personnel, they took the song titles, they took it completely literally. It was a small victory.

CHARLES SHAAR MURRAY I always felt like I had a quarter of a million people sitting on my shoulders and I wanted to take them with me. I have to say that *NME*'s first loyalty was to its readers. It was a little bit of that "power to the people, the truth will set you free". Sometimes you had to go up against the prejudices of the readers, but it was all in the common interest: "This is how it is; this is what is behind the façades." Of course, you can't do that shit now, because it soon got into that copy-approval crap.

6 "Oh No, Here We Go"

"During the period when I was working for the music press, there was a standard of excellence up there with any contemporary writing. It may have sometimes been crude and naïve, but it was very often staggeringly good."
— Pete Silverton

PUB ROCK
"THE FIRST FORESHOCKS OF PUNK"

CHAS DE WHALLEY Progressive rock had ossified into the likes of Yes, and the only really exciting stuff was the return-to-mono, back-to-the-roots movement, which meant a return to beat groups, the stuff that Charlie Gillett was playing on his *Honky Tonk* radio show – R&B from Chicago and New Orleans. And there was a new generation of bands who were playing it live in the pubs and were much more entertaining than what you would see down the Marquee or at your average college gig. Pub rock then wasn't yer bad blues but an attempt to look at the roots of rock. You had bands like Kilburn And The High Roads packing 400 people into the cellar of the Hope and Anchor. It was a French disco conflagration waiting to happen.

CHARLIE GILLETT It was really difficult to get anyone from the press to come to Kilburn And The High Roads' gigs when I was managing them. Nick Kent – bless him – came and really liked it and was very supportive, but hardly anyone else wrote anything about them. The people that were writing about pub rock liked the kind of rehashed R&B thing. Dr Feelgood, Eddie And The Hot Rods, Ducks Deluxe – they just got a lot more coverage than we did. We were seen as far too musical and diverse and inexplicable by any of the criteria that people had. To me, it was exciting and different and unexpected. I mean, not every gig was great from start to finish, but in every gig one song would...just take off and be completely sublime.

CHAS DE WHALLEY I wanted to get into the music business and went around to see Charlie Gillett at his place in Clapham. He gave me the names of a couple of people who might have jobs going, including Vivien Goldman, who was PR at Island Records, and Clive Selwood, who was running UK Records for Jonathan King. When I went to see Clive, in walked The Kursaal Flyers, who were my favourite act at the time, which I thought was a good omen. I was going to see two or three pub bands a week, and Vivien suggested I should write about them.

VIVIEN GOLDMAN I was poached from Transatlantic to work at Island Records and was freelancing for the *NME* and *Black Music* all the while, writing the prototypical bios of Bob Marley and Aswad. In the summer of 1975, I worked with Bob Marley on the Lyceum shows. It was amazing because, up until then, he was only known by West Indians and hip students.

CHAS DE WHALLEY I sent in about six weeks' worth of reviews to Chris Welch at *Melody Maker*. He didn't print them, and when I said, "You're being scooped by the *NME* every week," he said, "Go and write for them, then!" So I did. I sent them to Bob Woffinden, and within two weeks I was in print with a review of Joe Strummer's band The 101ers at the Hope and Anchor.

PETE SILVERTON Basically, Joe Strummer got me my job in the music press. I'd known him since we were teenagers – he went to school with a friend of mine. In late 1975, I was looking around to break into journalism and I went to see The 101ers at the Hope and Anchor. It was such a revelation, and I wanted to write about them. I'd written a piece about Ducks Deluxe for *Trans-Oceanic Trouser Press*, so then I wrote a bit about The 101ers for them.

ALLAN JONES I couldn't get the space in *Melody Maker*, at the time. I went to see The 101ers every week for four or five months at the Elgin in Notting Hill, and they wouldn't let me write about it. Instead, the issue would be filled with Steve Harley and huge amounts of coverage of Yes, ELP and Genesis, all those groups people my age were disgusted by.

PETER YORK In '74/75, Charlie Murray starts in heavy with the next big little scene, which is pub rock or real rock 'n' roll, and he makes new sightings in the quest for the authentic in bands like Dr Feelgood.

CHAS DE WHALLEY I saw a very early review by Charles Shaar Murray of Ducks Deluxe at the Hope and Anchor, a seminal act of the pub rock scene at a seminal venue. He said things like, "I don't know what I'm doing in this smoky cellar in Islington. This band are so crude I'm out of here." And that was how those bands got treated. Rock was Art, and therefore you needed multiple chord changes. The existing rock journalist fraternity were stuck in this idea that any act had to have a record deal or an album out before they could be considered worthy of attention.

MICK FARREN Bit by bit, all these things started happening. Pub rock was around, the first foreshocks of punk.

CHAS DE WHALLEY I was slightly too young to write about Ducks Deluxe and Bees Make Honey and those bands, but I was covering the second raft who got signed to big record labels – Kursaal Flyers, Eddie And The Hot Rods, Graham Parker And The Rumour – all of whom were drawing on a pre-prog rock tradition. There was a year to 18-month gap when they started chopping away at all the excess and laid the foundations for punk. I was the first to cover it systematically, and then some others followed – there was a guy called Gary Herman who wrote about it, and Giovanni Dadomo on *Sounds* was nosing around. It wasn't until the punk thing that there were a bunch of younger journalists writing about young acts.

CHRIS SALEWICZ The second review I wrote for the *NME* was Dr Feelgood, and I always used to go and see them. Most pub rock I really hated – it was so boring – but Dr Feelgood were really a forerunner of punk. Their role isn't quite appreciated, the first group at that time to play two- or three-minute songs wearing black suits with short hair.

GREG SHAW By working with The Flamin' Groovies, I ended up going to London and saw what was happening there. We're talking 1975. I was seeing bands like Dr Feelgood. You could see the beginnings. You could just see what the next stage was going to be. I just thought, "I'd like to be a part of this." There was a whole generation in the '70s talking about what was great in the past, what was wrong with the present and how the future could be better, and we all felt that people like us could create a kind of music that wouldn't be determined by commercial interests but promoted with a fan's love of rock 'n' roll.

CHAS DE WHALLEY I reckon I was the first of a new breed of rock journalist actively seeking out unsigned bands. When I first started writing – in August 1975, first at *NME* and then at *Sounds* – I was working the London pub circuit – venues like the Hope and Anchor, the Kensington, the Newlands Tavern – and writing about unsigned bands, something which I know nobody else was doing to anywhere near to the same extent. Two years later, of course, everybody was doing it, but I was there first. In a very bad-tempered interview with Nick Kent in *NME* sometime in 1978, after I'd left *Sounds* to serve in the CBS A&R department, Elvis Costello was complaining about being ignored by the press in his early years with Flip City and said, "Of course, there were no Chas de Whalleys around then."

DAVID HEPWORTH In 1976, I was working at HMV in Oxford Street, where Fred Dellar used to come and buy imports for his *NME* column. I pestered him until he said, "Have a go," so I wrote a couple of spec things and Fred, bless him, looked at them and said, "These are quite good. I'll show them to Bob Woffinden," the reviews editor. I used to hassle him, like you always do, and they gave me crumbs from the grand table. I was reviewing things like The Amazing Rhythm Aces, tiny little pieces, and after a while they rang me up on a Friday morning and said, "Can you go to Hamburg tomorrow with The Little River Band?" And I was just thrilled. I was beside myself.

CHAS DE WHALLEY In November 1975, I discovered The Stranglers in the Hope and Anchor. A mate of mine who booked bands had seen them at a lunch-time gig in Redhill when the bass-player's amp had broken down, so Jean-Jacques Burnel had sung his bass lines through the microphone for the whole set. I saw them and thought they were good, but it was the first time that a group didn't fall over themselves to get into the pages of the *NME*, which I thought was impressive. I wrote the review, but the *NME* refused to run it. Neil Spencer said, "Max Bell's our resident punk man, and he doesn't think The Stranglers are any good, so we're not running it."

STREET LIFE
"WHO KNOWS WHY IT DIDN'T TAKE?"

RICHARD WILLIAMS While I was head of A&R at Island Records, I wrote a few things for *Street Life*. I liked it. It could have been really good, so who knows why it didn't take? Maybe the people in this country who wanted to read that kind of thing were already getting what they wanted from *Rolling Stone*. One of the main people there was Bill Walker, who was chief sub of *Melody Maker* when I went there, before he went to *Sounds*.

JERRY GILBERT Penny Valentine went to *Street Life* after working for Elton John, joining Billy Walker. She had moved in with a guy who also worked for it, Mike Flood-Page. Simon Frith was also involved at *Street Life*. It wasn't a bad magazine.

JON SAVAGE *Street Life* was very good and tried to cover everything. Like *Let It Rock*, it lasted until the end of 1975, just before punk.

THE SINKING OF THE TITANIC
"THE FULL HORROR WAS REALISED..."

CHARLES SHAAR MURRAY The piece I wrote about the New York scene in November 1975 turned out to be very influential. Jon Savage said people formed groups based on my descriptions of The Ramones and the others. They hadn't heard the music yet, because it hadn't been released.

MARK PERRY Early in 1976, I started reading in the *NME* about a new "punk scene" which had been developing in New York. Like London's pub rock, it revolved around small venues, such as CBGB and Max's Kansas City. The writers made it sound exciting and vibrant, and I could sense this was no R&B scene.

CHARLES SHAAR MURRAY In stories like that and Mickey's "The *Titanic* Sails At Dawn" piece a few months later, we were predicting what would happen with punk but were still taken completely by surprise by the form in which it eventually appeared.

CAROLINE COON All the journalists that ran the music scene at that time were like men in aspic. They had spent years hanging out and socialising with the people they championed, so they'd lost a journalistic distance. They weren't about to betray the great Keith Moon by championing Rat Scabies.

MICK FARREN The "*Titanic*" piece wasn't just me; it was the old lags from the underground press wanting to get their kicks. It was an open goal, and I looked like a hero. It was prompted by the fact that we got the biggest fucking mailbag ever, after The Who played Charlton and the Stones were on tour. The readers were just horrified. Stadium rock had arrived in England and the full horror was realised: "What the fuck are we doing here?" Reading was a bit manageable, but being stuck in these football grounds or Earls Court was awful.

NEIL SPENCER There were incidents like Eric Clapton saying that Enoch Powell was right, onstage in Birmingham. He's standing there, playing the music of Muddy Waters, and you just thought, "This man has lost his fucking mind."

TONY PARSONS In the early '70s, there were a lot of people like me who thought, "Wow! Earls Court is really big, and this is so distant. How do I find a way back to the thing that I love?" Punk was finding our way back to things which were exciting, relevant and important. To me, it's a shame that Mick Jagger is a millionaire several times over and Joe Strummer isn't, and I don't quite understand how that could be.

MICK FARREN I started to be Peter Finch in *Network*. It's very easy to say, "I'm mad and I'm not going to take it any more" when you know that there are thousands of punters out there who feel the same. To be truthful, The 101ers had already convinced me that something was going to happen. I think it was the very last thing I did in the Black Panther school of rhetoric, applied as calculated propaganda. It stirred up the readers, but it also meant that CBS took The Clash's phone calls, know what I mean?

PETE SILVERTON The "*Titanic*" piece was a *cri du couer* for punk to happen, but when it came along it wasn't what he dreamed of; it was a Frankenstein's monster. On *Sounds*, Giovanni Dadomo had written similar pieces, and he felt the same way. Those guys were precursors to punk, in terms of their attitude, but they always felt uneasy about it. Like Frankenstein, the monster wasn't under their control.

PUNK
"ALL THESE MANIACS WITH SHORT HAIR GOING MENTAL"

CHAS DE WHALLEY Up until punk, the writers in the music press loved music. Afterwards, there was another generation of writers who couldn't care a fuck about music. They were into writing about the politics of hatred, envy, situationism, whatever was going around, and that grew into the situation where everything was there to be knocked. The function of the rock critic was to knock. Music played a secondary role to fashion and political ideologies.

MILES When I was freelance in London, there was an artificial antagonism between *NME* and *Melody Maker* which I couldn't understand. They were all working for IPC, for God's sake! *Melody Maker* sometimes had some good stuff and *NME* sometimes had some good stuff. *Sounds* even had some good articles, sometimes. They were in on punk long before *NME* was, that's for sure.

CAROLINE COON In 1976, I'd reached 30 and was very interested in what was going to be the next youth movement. I was living at the Portobello Hotel and Alan "leather and chains" Jones, who worked behind the bar there, said to me, "Have you heard of The Sex Pistols?" All the names of bands at that time were organic, sort of hippie and passive. I thought that, whatever the music was like, this name was right at the cutting edge, symbolic of what's to come.

TONY PARSONS I was working in Gordon's gin distillery in City Road on this horrible night shift. Me and this lovely hippie guy called Ray used to sabotage the equipment so we could flee into the night with free gin. We used to go down to the 100 Club and watch bands. To be honest, I don't know who I saw, but I remember The Damned and I saw lots of people like Siouxsie Sioux walking about in stockings and suspenders and swastikas, that early shock wave of the Bromley Contingent. I wasn't any kind of expert but knew this was the music for me. Suddenly, in this tiny little club, all these maniacs with short hair were going mental.

GREG SHAW I had been saying for years there has to be a revival of the '60s do-it-yourself spirit, using the term punk rock – a lot of us had since 1971 – and then suddenly it all came together and it caught me by surprise. I mean, I was really excited about Eddie And The Hot Rods. I thought they were a great garage band.

PETE SILVERTON Paul Rambali was also writing for *Trouser Press* and I was hanging out with Joe a lot through 1976. Paul says that we reached an agreement that I would cover The Clash while he would cover the Pistols, and – though I don't remember it – that's the way it happened. So we did a big punk piece for *Trouser Press* together.

CAROLINE COON Mary Harron and I were at the Marquee reviewing Eddie And The Hot Rods, who could have been incorporated into punk rock because they were young, sparse, fast, pared down. Stupidly, at the point it was taking off, they said it was dead. Anyway, both of us went backstage, and we were literally pounced on by the band. They physically attacked us and ripped our clothes off. We were standing there with our notebooks in our hands and our T-shirts around our waists. We just got our quotes and walked off.

MILES I always liked Legs McNeill, particularly when he was at *Punk*. He had some of the old Lester Bangs energy and commitment. But he is a friend of mine.

PUNK MAGAZINE
MEANWHILE, BACK IN NEW YORK...

LEGS MCNEILL How did *Punk* magazine start? [*High Times* publisher] John Holmstrom and I were friends. I was friends with these two guys, John and Ged, who were older than me, and we moved to New York City and John wanted to do a magazine. I don't think we knew exactly what it was yet. John said he wanted to start a magazine, and I said, "Gee, I think that's a stupid idea," you know, and he said, "No, no, I think it would be great! People will invite us to parties." I said, "No one is going to invite us to parties. No one invites us anywhere. Everybody hates us," 'cause we weren't hippies, you know. We were really lousy. And then John said, "We're going to call it *Teenage News*," which, I found out years later, was an unreleased New York Dolls song. I was, like, "That's stupid, John! Why don't we call it *Punk*?" And then they started laughing and they thought it was a brilliant idea. John said he'd be the editor, and this other guy, Ged Dunn, said he'd be the publisher, and they said, "What are you going to do?" So John said, "You can be the resident punk." That's how that started.

DEBBIE HARRY John Holmstrom and his living cartoon creature, Legs McNeill, were two maniacs running around town putting up signs that said, "*Punk* is coming! *Punk* is coming!" We thought, "Here comes another shitty group with an even shittier name."

MARY HARRON The *Punk* magazine office was known as the Punk Dump. The editor lived there when they first started, and for a while Legs did, too. Fran Pelzman and I used to deposit Legs on the doorstep when he got too drunk to make it home alone. For a while, John Holmstrom put Roberta Bayley – the staff photographer – and me on salary, literally $25 a week, and we would hang out and do filing, but then John couldn't pay us any more. It was a fun place to hang out. It had a loose, underground feel.

LINDSAY HUTTON John Holmstrom at *Punk* pointed the way toward the drafted nature of my writing. When things are handwritten, they're more direct. I think it's that personal nature of my scribbling that seems to hit the spot with people. It would be nice to translate that vibe to this Internet lark.

MARY HARRON In the fall of 1975, I was living in New York after leaving college, working as the cook in this crazy film commune in exchange for room and board. I met Legs McNeill there and told him I wanted to be a writer. He said his friend John Holmstrom was starting a magazine called *Punk* and I should write for it. I thought it was a brilliant title, but I had no idea what kind of magazine it was going to be. Legs and John dragged me to CBGB's to see The Ramones. I'd never heard of them, but then neither had the rest of the world. That night, we met Lou Reed, whom I *had* heard of, and they asked me to interview The Ramones.

LEGS MCNEILL What's interesting about *Punk* is that it was distributed at 7-11s. It had a circulation of 30,000 immediately – I think it went from 5,000 to 10,000 to 30,000 – so we were actually out there. People were just so shocked when they saw it. You see, the 7-11s didn't know whether to sell it as a comic book or a rock 'n' roll magazine. And if we kept our production schedule, we actually made lots of money, instead of having all the fun in the world. We did 18, [and then] I went into detox – my first detox, in '77. Already, I needed one. I left the magazine, and then it shortly folded. I think we all hated each other by then. They certainly hated me.

MARY HARRON For the second issue, they decided to have a letters page. John just put in all the letters that came into the office, including one from his mother complaining about his dad, a letter from the gas company, a jealous letter from a girlfriend, a rejection letter from a distributor, an offer of life insurance. I thought that was very punk.

THE SEX PISTOLS
"THERE WAS AN IMMEDIATE RECOGNITION"

GREG SHAW I loved the Pistols. I really did think they were revolutionary, because of the attitude. I spent a lot of time with the Pistols, even though I was never a mate to them. I was obviously from a different world. They were probably calling me a hippie behind my back. But I had long talks with Rotten, at least. From the beginning, his agenda was that he hated rock stars, he hated the whole rock culture, which is what I hated. We had that in common.

CAROLINE COON Allan Jones took me to the Pistols' second gig, and there was an immediate recognition, seeing these 19-year-olds deconstruct pub rock and take rock 'n' roll back to its basics, but with a genuine anger. Standing at the back – as you do, as a journalist – you could see the pub audience turning their noses up, but the kids in the crowd knew what was going on. I couldn't go to any gig at that point without the manager of the band wetting his knickers. So afterwards, Malcolm McLaren introduced himself, and I thought, "Interesting." I think that, at the next gig, Bernie Rhodes came up and said, "I've got a band, too," because The Clash were in rehearsal, and within about three weeks I'd seen The Damned and pretty much knew by then what was going to happen.

CHRIS SALEWICZ I was asked to go and check out this gig at Fulham Town Hall – Roogalator, supported by The Vibrators and The Clash, who were absolutely great. The Vibrators were obviously crap, and by the time Roogalator came on their career had evaporated.

GREG SHAW Seymour Stein said he'd sign The Flamin' Groovies, but only on the basis that I was the manager, so I was roped into that. We were touring England in early 1976 and it was such a transitional time. Our opening band on the tour was The Damned, but they started getting more response than we did, so we kicked them off and got The Vibrators. I knew people like Kris Needs at *Zigzag*, which had been a fanzine in the early days, when Pete Frame and John Tobler were doing it with complete discographies and family trees and The Byrds and Love on the cover. Then, suddenly, punk came along and Needs was in there.

KRIS NEEDS In early 1976, I was still cooped up in a Milton Keynes shoebox, commuting to Aylesbury and *The Buckinghamshire Advertiser*. Lunchtime usually involved hooking up with Pete Frame, of *Rock Family Trees* fame, who was then still editor of *Zigzag*, the pioneering fanzine he'd started in 1969. Frame let me write a few album reviews and was propagating an unjust image of me as a pissed maniac in his editorials. As I turned 22 on 2 July 1976, he took me to do my first rock interview. The victims were The Flamin' Groovies. I was a major fan, but once the tapes started rolling I completely dried up from nerves, especially when the Thai sticks appeared.

GREG SHAW In London, when the Groovies played Dingwalls, The Sex Pistols – well the guys who were going to be The Sex Pistols; they weren't yet – were hanging out backstage with us, and they nicked our bags, which had our plane tickets and everything in them. I had to go to Malcolm and get the stuff back, and I ended up being pals with him.

MICK FARREN I'm sorry that Malcolm McLaren was in charge of so much of it, because it went rather quickly, and I'd seen "rather quickly" once already and I wanted a bit of entrenchment, a bit of digging in. But it was Bill Grundy and, oh no, here we go, and the same mistakes are happening all over again but at 15 times the speed. Them guys didn't have time to look around.

CAROLINE COON I went into *Melody Maker*'s next editorial meeting and said, "I want to do a story on what's happening on the streets. There's this band called The Sex Pistols who are part of a new movement." All I got was sneer, sneer, sneer from Mick Watts, Allan Jones, all of them. Had I been a male journalist, they would have said, "Really? OK, go and find out more."

ALLAN JONES Looking back on it, I'd been infected by this complacent, patrician attitude about the young punks: "It'll all blow over and we'll be fine." The first time I saw The Sex Pistols supporting The 101ers at the Nashville, I thought they were a fucking joke. Then I went to an all-nighter at the Lyceum to see The Pretty Things, and the Pistols were on the bill, and by then the penny dropped with a very loud clang and I thought, "Fuck, this is brilliant."

VIVIEN GOLDMAN Me and Caroline really hit it off. There wasn't a sisterhood of us women writers as such, but she was really important. I think she is a really brilliant woman, and she made me aware of some of the pitfalls which could occur, working for the music press. We were very tight, and Jonh Ingham of *Sounds* was close to both of us.

GREG SHAW The whole backlash mentality is part of the culture of England. American music culture is not edgy and not oriented towards that flavour-of-the-week syndrome. It takes so long for things to percolate here. Look at punk rock. The big year in England was '77, right? America didn't really accept it until 1991.

CHRIS WELCH I didn't like punk at all, although the whole idea of new bands coming along was hopefully good. I remember Allan Jones saw The Sex Pistols and said, "Let's hope we never hear from this group again" in a review of their first gig, at St Martin's College of Art.

ALLAN JONES I think I reviewed them when they were supporting The 101ers and I hadn't liked them, but soon I felt I had to redress this.

GREG SHAW Punk gave me a lot of stuff to write about, and *Bomp* changed completely. I'd go to London, I'd come back, I'd file a whole report on what was happening in London and a whole discography of every punk record that had been released in England. I believe I was the first American to interview The Sex Pistols, because I'd seen their third gig or something. It was an early, early gig at the 100 Club. There was only about a dozen people there, and I wrote a review of it a year before anyone in America really knew about The Sex Pistols.

NEIL SPENCER Tony Tyler and his girlfriend, Kate Phillips, had encountered the Pistols at some strange event. He and I went down to the Marquee to see them supporting Eddie And The Hot Rods, and the doorman said, "You'd better get in there quick. They're busting the place up." I opened the door and a chair sailed across the room and crash landed. There were only about 20 people there, but it was immediately obvious that something fantastic was going on. They didn't look like anyone I'd ever seen. So I wrote the *NME* review, which was the first.

CAROLINE COON Since *Melody Maker* weren't interested and wouldn't give me a photographer, I bought myself a camera and followed its development, taking photos, asking the bands to give me their lyrics, interviewing them, even though none of them had contracts. They were quite thrilled, because here was this big-shot journalist coming to their gigs. Any moment, they expected a review to appear.

GREG SHAW Through managing the Groovies, I got to know a lot of people on the British punk scene, which is kind of a strange thing, because all of the people who were in that scene had come out of the earlier scene – they'd been in punk rock or they'd been fans. It wasn't an abrupt change. It wasn't like a rejection of everything from the past; it was a rejection of all the obvious stuff from the past. But the Groovies were a hard band to work with. Cyril Jordan had kind of a career death wish.

CAROLINE COON Barry Plummer took a picture of the Pistols fighting with the audience and *Melody Maker* finally woke up. The editor said, "Caroline, you've been following this," so I wrote that definitive first piece about the reasons why kids liked this, because rock 'n' roll had betrayed its audience. That became the cover story, with the picture of the fight.

ALLAN JONES By that time, I thought the Pistols were brilliant, but I got put in an awful position where Caroline did a pro-punk piece and I wrote a piece which was really mucked about and came out anti-punk. The connection I was trying to make was the link to the people I'd been writing about, like Kevin Coyne, but it was a huge stitch-up. So, after that, I was determined to write about them as much as possible and ended up getting along very well with Rotten and did the cover story the week that 'God Save The Queen' went to Number One.

GREG SHAW I got to know Malcolm when we went out for lunch, and we talked and compared notes, because I was having a lot of problems with the Groovies and they were having problems with their record company, and we stayed in touch. He was trying to get the band across in America and I hooked him up with a lawyer.

CAROLINE COON The only other journalist who was following what was going on was Jonh Ingham at *Sounds*. I was absolutely determined to get *Melody Maker* to run a story first. I'd see him every week at a gig and think, "Shit, is *Sounds* going to get in before us?"

PETER YORK Ingham and Coon are, without a doubt, the best-dressed, most socially clued writers there have ever been in the rock press. Both came out of the hippie stream, but Notting Hill, not red-brick up-market. You can't fault Coon's timing. In the '60s, she set up Release and then, in the '70s, you see her modelling at the neo-decadent benefits. They say she's been Ferry's girl. She mixes high with the Performance Playpower rich hippie world. Ingham is a pale, thin, sandy New Zealander, a son of the manse who's run this little conceptual sci-fi magazine and has exactly the right pleats in his trousers, the right art on his T-shirt.

CAROLINE COON To begin with, Jonh and I were fiercely competitive, although both *Melody Maker* and *Sounds* were blindly refusing to cover it. Then it started to develop really quickly and there were maybe two bands playing on the same night. I couldn't cover it all myself, and neither could he, so we began to collaborate. I would tell him what was happening in Croydon and he would tell me what happened in Manchester. Although my story came out before his, we were in fact collaborating by that stage.

JON SAVAGE I had a real urge to start writing, but I didn't have a great urge to write something "literary", because of the kind of people I'd been educated with, who I realised I despised. After putting out a couple of issues of my fanzine *London's Outrage*, I'd met people from *Sounds* like Dave Fudger and was picked up to write for them in April 1977. My first task was to work pretty much all night with Vivien Goldman, Giovanni Dadomo and Dave on something called "Images Of The New Wave". That became the cover story, with a picture of Shane MacGowan rolling around on the floor.

VIVIEN GOLDMAN I was writing good solid stuff about The Crusaders and Gladys Knight And The Pips, and all of a sudden all these weird things started to arrive through the post from new record labels like Stiff and weird people started to crop up at the office, lively people. There were midnight gigs and an active scene. All these people who had previously been cut off from society.

GREG SHAW The Flamin' Groovies headlined at the Fourth Of July show at the Roundhouse, but when people saw The Ramones lightbulbs went off in people's heads, kind of like, "Ahhhh, this is how you do it." Everyone respected the Groovies, but we were obviously out of place there.

KRIS NEEDS I undertook my first solo interview on a brick wall outside Dingwalls with The Ramones. It went fine with the New York cretin ambassadors and resulted in another friendship, which took me around the country until the end of the '70s. They were my first encounter with the sonic-guitar *Blitzkrieg* which had inspired the erupting UK scene. By now, I was *Zigzag*'s token punk and the butt of much uneasy piss-taking from the Eagles contingent. The more tolerant Frame – who might have hated the music but enjoyed the apple-cart-upsetting attitude – gave me my own supplement called *Over The Top*. On the cover, I was shown tucking into an Eagles album in spike-top, safety-pinned jacket and paint-splattered shirt.

VIVIEN GOLDMAN At The Sex Pistols' press conference to announce the signing to A&M at a West End hotel, nobody was saying anything, so I decided to enliven things and lob a verbal grenade by asking Sid Vicious,

"Has joining The Sex Pistols improved your sex life?" Of course it had, but they were shouting at me, "How can you ask this question?"

GREG SHAW With the Groovies, I began to notice the treacherous side of the British press – they would praise you over the top one day and slag you off the next. The competition between *Melody Maker*, *NME* and *Sounds* made it worse, because if one paper liked the band then the other had to hate them.

LINDSAY HUTTON Joey Ramone told me that he wanted to put a version of 'See My Baby Jive' on the album, which vindicated him completely, but John just wouldn't let it lie. One of the most outright cool things that happened to me during my many years in these rock 'n' roll trenches was being able to call Joey Ramone a friend. His recent passing devastated me, because this guy was the equivalent of what Elvis and John Lennon were to previous generations. If it hadn't been for Joe then I wouldn't be doing this, pure and simple.

MARK PERRY Nick Kent reviewed The Ramones' first album for the *NME*, and from the minute I digested his description I was hooked and couldn't wait to hear it.

SNIFFIN' GLUE AND BEYOND
"A MYTHIC START"

PETER YORK *Sniffin' Glue* had a mythic start. Mark Perry, 19-year-old bank clerk from Deptford, bright, bored with job, long hair, flares, hears an album by The Ramones, then sees them, thinks its so great he writes a review, copies eight pages on a Xerox at his girlfriend's office and dishes it out, cuts his hair, buys tight trousers and Day-Glo socks, leaves Williams & Glyn's and becomes Mark P.

MARK PERRY After The Ramones' gig, I asked the guy at *Rock On* whether there were any British magazines covering this new music, because, apart from the New York magazine *Punk*, I had seen nothing. He suggested I start one up myself, and I think it was said as more of a joke than anything else. I obviously took his idea seriously, because I went straight home and

216

typed the first words of my fanzine *Sniffin' Glue And Other Rock 'n' Roll Habits*. I pinched the title straight from The Ramones' 'Now I Wanna Sniff Some Glue'.

PETER YORK With the media overkill in the new wave, it grew and had to take on, by default, the role of spokesmagazine. This was a strain, and it showed! By issue ten, it had a flavour almost of self-parody.

MARK PERRY I was starting to see Caroline, knocking around with her. She took me to see The Sex Pistols and I saw one of their late July shows at the 100 Club. I didn't know there was stuff like this going on. It was just mad!

LINDSAY HUTTON I started *Next Big Thing* to holler for what I figured to be real punk rock, with a heavy emphasis on US acts. The staple in the corner of *Sniffin' Glue* heralded the age of folding and collating not being necessary any more. Praise the Lord and pass me that wee stapler! There was a pilot issue with Eddie And The Hot Rods in September 1976, and the first proper issue came out on 1 April 1977, the day The Damned came to Stirling University.

PETER YORK I met Danny Baker at the *Sniffin' Glue* office. I couldn't get a word in, and there didn't seem to be much to say then. Most of it was the sharpest line of chat I've heard in years, and I thought Baker – he was 19 then – was going to move it.

MARK PERRY Another friend was Danny Baker. He left school a year earlier than us and went to work for a record shop in South Molton Street – which we thought was a pretty cool thing to be doing – and was the nearest thing to the music business we could imagine. He was always showing off the latest imports he'd gotten hold of.

DANNY BAKER Caroline and Jonh, because they were so steeped in understanding what brought about the first wave of riots in Grosvenor Square, knew about "situations". They seemed older and more worldly wise, very art school. They knew about anarchy. We didn't fucking know what anarchy was. I think they invested in us a lot more credibility than we certainly had. For example, if you were talking to Joe Strummer or Johnny Rotten, you would talk about nothing, in case you said the wrong thing. It would be, like, "All right?" "All right, yeah." "So what's going on?" "Same old shit." You couldn't actually open up and say, "What's next?", 'cause you didn't know! At the time, it was thrilling. We found out a bit later that Joe Strummer came from a privileged background. He was a diplomat's son. Nobody in their right mind would come right out and say, "You're a diplomat's son." It was accepted, but nobody would have said it.

JON SAVAGE I'd self-published a fanzine called *London's Outrage* in December 1976. It was one of the first ones and very much stimulated by *Sniffin' Glue*, but then Mark had been inspired by much the same sources, things *Like Who Put The Bomp*, which was a great magazine, and Brian Hogg's *Bam Balam*. The whole fanzine idea, as Mark would freely admit, came from those two magazines, funny little magazines that wrote about pop history.

LINDSAY HUTTON I really liked *Bam Balam* and *Hot Wacks*. My fanzine, *Next Big Thing*, was mostly handwritten, and I never figured myself as much of a writer, and still don't, but something about *Next Big Thing* struck a (power) chord in people. From there, I ended up running The Cramps' fan club, the Legion Of The Cramped, initially with the soon-to-become pop star himself Steven Morrissey. The Legion Of The Cramped generated a lot of goodwill, despite the way it all ended with the band pulling the plug and I had to come down on the side of the membership. When that ended, Edwin Pouncey got me on board at *Sounds*, and I kept on doing *Next Big Thing* and also turned the Legion Of The Cramped mag, *Rockin' Bones*, into a more open-ended garage-rock/punk thing.

PETER YORK Later, Danny Baker started writing for the frightful *Zigzag* and I registered his name again because his stuff was so good, and – this was the point – he seemed to be picking up on all the little things I liked myself. A bigmouth, but he couldn't be all bad. He'd say a record was good and I'd know it was worth buying, not just something to talk about. Later still, he joined the *NME*. Now he's on TV and everything.
SLASH

"IT HAD STYLE"

GREG SHAW Slash was the brainchild of Steve Samiof and Claude Bessy. Claude was really the heart and soul of things. Steve was the business guy.

CLAUDE BESSY Steve always wanted to do a little publication, and he'd read a couple of papers about the punk explosion in England. He'd heard a couple of singles, so he said, "Let's start a paper. We'll get into a couple of outrageous numbers. We might even get an ad from A&M, based on pure luck, from some group they've got called Eddie And The Hot Rods." So we got this one ad from A&M and another from I don't know where, which totally financed the first issue, which came out on May Day 1977. And by luck we ran into The Damned, who were doing their first concert here, for an interview in that issue. For the first two or three issues, we pretended there was an LA scene when there was absolutely nothing.

GREG SHAW *Slash* was punk, but it was nothing like *Sniffin' Glue*; it was literary – not in a polished sense, but it had style. Mark Perry, bless his heart, he's not a writer; he was a participant in the scene, and he was just kind of chronicling what was going on. I think *Slash* had an aesthetic with what they were trying to capture of the LA punk scene, or maybe a bit wider.

CLAUDE BESSY Before we knew it, the paper started interesting some kids, some bands started forming because of the paper and, before we knew it, we had a scene to report on. It started snowballing.

RICHARD MELTZER More than anything else, what finally set me straight was reading *Slash*, especially the rantings of its editor, Claude Bessy, aka "Kickboy Face", the greatest rock-writer you never heard of. In matters of punk versus not-punk, I defer to Claude.

CLAUDE BESSY The media and the artist became very connected. We featured The Screamers on looks alone – we let them play the very first *Slash* concert before we had heard one note of their music – and it worked. Suddenly, *Slash* was indispensable!
GREG SHAW To me, *Slash* was uniquely the LA vision, because it was nothing

like the New York vision or the London vision, but it was a very clear vision and they had a good staff of writers. I wrote for it.

CLAUDE BESSY Suddenly, we got all these lame middle-of-the-road publications calling up all the time, wanting to know what the truth was, like we were holding some secret and everybody wanted to pry us open like an oyster to get the pearl.

JON SAVAGE Claude Bessy was great. I met him a year before his death in Barcelona in 1999. He was very ill, but he checked me out. He put on 'Forming' by The Germs VERY LOUD and we started headbanging like Beavis and Butthead. When the record finished, he turned to me and said, "Well, you still like the same old shit, then," and laughed his head off.

WHO WAS FIRST?
"THERE'S BEEN A BIT OF REWRITING OF HISTORY"

CAROLINE COON Actually, the *NME* was ignoring punk rock. It didn't come on board until after my pieces appeared, and first of all they knocked it. Neil Spencer had come across the Pistols in April, but there was nothing after that for a long time. There's been a bit of rewriting of history.

JON SAVAGE The *NME* wasn't as on the case as *Sounds* and *Melody Maker*, but it was the brand leader, which was very important. I have a lot of affection for *Sounds*, though, because we didn't have to hang back, and in a way we were luckier working there, because the older writers – people like Vivien Goldman, Giovanni Dadomo and Jonh Ingham – were very helpful and very nice to the new people they got on board, such as myself, Sandy Robertson and Jane Suck. They were supportive, and I don't think they would have been, on the *NME*.

PETER YORK (FROM STYLE WARS) Coon and Ingham are something very strange. It looks as though they've copped a sub-culture. They've got some spreads on some really weird-looking kids in the summer of '76 and the little gangs/contingents who follow the Pistols around. And it really stands out, this stuff. Ingham's quoting Sid Vicious saying, "In the Summer Of Love, I was playing with my Action Man." Sid Vicious especially sets

Ingham grinning – he's so frightful, the best cartoon character ever. Coon's interviewing Johnny Rotten, who is on about throwing bricks down from the top of the council block.

NICK LOGAN I wouldn't argue about who was first with punk – I think we were there just as much as the rest of the music press, though obviously some people were more enthusiastic than others on the staff. To my mind, we picked up on the news value of it. It was really exciting to actually have real news stories. It was icing on the cake.

NEIL SPENCER The pace of events was crazy – there'd be a riot at a Pistols gig, a new band would emerge every week, the Jubilee thing was bonkers – but there were some people on the *NME*, like Steve Clarke, who just wanted to review the new Jackson Browne album. I don't think someone like Max Bell had time for punk rock, because he would have thought they couldn't play.

CHRIS SALEWICZ A lot of people at the *NME* didn't like punk. I remember Kent having a go at me for writing about "this punk stuff". I was bit surprised, because this was the man who had been hanging out in CBGB and jammed with The Sex Pistols.

TONY PARSONS I realised that the *NME* was having difficulty covering this stuff. The other papers had stolen the march, because the passion for the music wasn't there. Although he could have ended up in the Pistols, I don't think Nick Kent ever liked them as much as he did The New York Dolls. Also, I thought it was a class thing. Those concerts could be quite violent, but no more than going to football with unsegregated fans. I was used to dodging bottles. That didn't bother me too much.

CHRIS SALEWICZ There was this attitude at the *NME* that was, like, only people who were articulate and literate and could do proper joined-up writing were intelligent. I remember Nick Kent's attitude to [Sex Pistols guitarist] Steve Jones. I'm very fond of Kent, but there's a side to him that always had big blinkers on. He was really dissing Steve Jones, but in fact the guy's fucking dyslexic. It doesn't stop him being a genius guitar player.
NICK LOGAN We needed some new blood. This was after the "*Titanic*" pieces,

221

and we knew some new music was needed and some new writers to go with it.

PETER YORK In the autumn of 1976, the overground rock press – that curious rag-bag of magazines from *Melody Maker* and *NME* to *Record Mirror* – started going bananas about punk rock.

ALLAN JONES By this stage, Ray Coleman had realised that punk wasn't going to go away, so what did we do? "Put Tom Robinson on the cover as 'the most talented young punk'." No, Ray! He was handed a stick and he got hold of the wrong end of it and wouldn't let go. Or they'd go big on The Stranglers when it should have been The Clash. It seemed so false. I'd be tearing my hair out at editorial meetings, so what they liked to do was keep me on the road.

HIP YOUNG GUNSLINGERS
"EWWW, MACHO COWBOY IMAGERY"

JULIE BURCHILL About a week after I heard Patti Smith's *Horses*, I spied an advert in the back of my *NME* for a hip young gunslinger. I thought, "Ewww, macho cowboy imagery. They must be really sexually inadequate up there."

CHARLES SHAAR MURRAY I actually composed the ad using that phrase, "hip young gunslingers", and even while I was writing it I was very conscious of the fact that this was almost five years, like an echo of the ad that I had answered in *Schoolkids Oz*.

PETE SILVERTON I was one of the hundreds who applied for it, along with Nick Hornby, who has now come full circle and now writes about pop music in *The New Yorker*.

TONY PARSONS People like Charles Shaar Murray and Nick Kent had been there for a few years and done fantastic work, but they had done their time, and when I joined there was a sense of a torch being passed.

JULIE BURCHILL I thought, "I can do that. I am singularly thin and pale and profoundly, lividly young. My youth stands out on me like welts, stinging, and I wear my zits like medals. I am young, young, young, and I'm going to milk the cash cow for all it's - all *I'm* - worth." I wrote my *Horses* review by hand on bad school notepaper, torn and jagged, just like me, a word or two deliberately misspelled.

TONY PARSONS I don't know why it never occurred to me earlier that I could write for the *NME*. It never crossed my mind, yet I had written a novel, got an agent and a publisher. It wasn't a very good book - juvenilia, really. It's amazing to me that I did all that but it never crossed my mind to review Dr Feelgood in Canvey Island. I'd already seen a lot of the bands I knew they'd want covered.

JULIE BURCHILL The *NME* - which had been the feather boa'd, eager-Biba'd belle of the bisexual ball during glam - found itself hungover and wearing too much of last night's make-up when the harsh light of punk broke at last upon the suede-brained '70s. They reached out, like drowning men, for the nearest possible lifebuoy, and in doing so put their arms around a pair of crocodiles who could shed no tears for them at all.

TONY PARSONS I'd made £700 out of my novel *The Kids* and I sent them a copy. Of course they didn't read it; you didn't expect them to. Then I got a call to go in and was on a list of 15 people interviewed by Tony Tyler. I really wanted the job. Then it was whittled down to five: me, Julie, Paul Morley, Ian Cranna and some other guy I never heard of again. I think he was at Cambridge.

NICK LOGAN I remember thinking that Paul Morley could be a good stringer, but he had this annoying habit of putting three spaces between every word on his typewriter. Very strange. I remember that Ian Cranna was interesting and a few years later made him editor at *Smash Hits*.

TONY PARSONS It wasn't really a job interview, more an audition. You had to look right, and I think that's why the standard of writing in the paper went down, because it became more about, "What do these kids look like?" I think they were impressed because I was really young to have had a novel out, even if it was crap. At the second interview, Nick Logan said, "You've got one of the jobs. The other one will go to either a girl from Bristol or a boy from Manchester."

TONY TYLER About six months after I'd officially left, Neil Spencer told me they were advertising for two new writers and would I sift through the applications and produce a shortlist of twelve for interview? Kate and I were living together by that time, so we took the job on together. There were, as I recall, over 1,200 applications for these two jobs. Kate and I went through the lot. It was me who turned up Tony Parsons and Ian Cranna and Kate who discovered Julie Burchill's application. I interviewed all twelve hopefuls up in King's Reach and was really impressed with these three, less so with the others. Tony and Julie got the two jobs and Ian Cranna obviously went "on file", because later on, after Nick left and founded *Smash Hits*, Ian was his first choice for editor.

JULIE BURCHILL I had done so well in the first [interview] because, on some level, Tony Tyler smelled like my dad: calm; sexually confident; sexually *verboten*; kind, for want of a better word; tall. Nick Logan, God help him, probably smelled like me: skinny, rattled, scum surfing. He stood up and shook my sweaty hand with his sweaty hand. He was no taller than me. He looked like someone half a year ahead of me at school, with cropped hair and an Ace T-shirt. Later, of course, I learned he'd been a big mod. They all looked like that in later life, scared stiff because they'd glimpsed Nirvana and settled for Neasden – or, in Logan's case, Wanstead.

CAROLINE COON As a matter of fact, Julie Burchill was hired by *NME* as a kind of antidote to the posh Coon. She could be "a real writer", because she was working class. Even though I had built up all the contacts on the punk scene, there was immense prejudice in the music press because of my status. I was deemed to be posh – not what you were meant to be, if you were writing about rock 'n' roll.

PETE SILVERTON I always liked Julie's writing. She would never let facts stand in the way of an opinion.

JULIE BURCHILL I liked Tony Parsons a whole lot, more than I'd liked anyone in my life. He was, it must be said, immaculately working class, like me. I should never have married him – good God, no one should have married either of us! – but Tony was just so impressive. He impressed everyone. The staff of the *NME* pretended they weren't, at least for a while. Nick Kent was the only one with enough of his own spotlight to fall like a trembling leather leaf, at first glance. The punk bands, on the other hand, hung around slack- jawed and starry-eyed. He was the boy who'd beat them up at school, but he was smart. Smarter than them.

PAOLO HEWITT Tony Parsons was incredibly important, an inspiration. He would spell things like Sta-Prest correctly and was obviously not part of that middle-class hippie stuff.

TONY PARSONS The day Julie and I started, our desks were full of unopened applications. They got something like 5,000, and I don't know how many they opened, because they didn't have the manpower to handle it. I don't know about Julie, but that cut me down to size. I realised the competition had been stiffer than they presented. Over the years, I've met tons of people who went for it, like Neil Tennant.

CAROLINE COON Julie was 16 when she started writing. The first time I saw her, I wanted to go up and hug her and say hello, but she virtually spat at me. It was almost heartbreaking, but maybe I shouldn't take it so personally. She *had* been set up. The male journalists spent 99 per cent of their time absolutely knocking me and other women writers, using the most vicious sexist language. She was getting a lot of male approval, and I think it ruined her writing.

PETER YORK One evening at Hammersmith Odeon, I was with this clutch of Modern Girls – Caroline Coon, Judy Nylon, Kate Simon and Vivien Goldman, who was then doing the features on *Sounds* – and Vivien had overheard Julie somewhere in the interval. That Julie Burchill had said, "People aren't really very interesting. There's not much to be said for individuals." You could see it worried the girls. Individuals not very interesting? What did she like, then?

VIVIEN GOLDMAN At the time, Julie was quiet as a mouse. We didn't really register her as a presence in a room. I wasn't that friendly with her.

JULIE BURCHILL Sebastian Faulks was one of the 15,000 applicants for the job. Excuse me, in which solar system was Sebastian Faulks a gunslinger, hip or otherwise? I thank God – and so should Mr Faulks – that he didn't get it. With a name like that, he'd have been catmeat within a week.

NICK HORNBY There was a time in British music writing where the journalists were bigger than the artists themselves. People like Nick Kent and Julie Burchill, they were really scary people. The idea of walking into this office at the age of 19 and having to deal with these people... I thought, "Well, I'm not even going to try."

PAUL DU NOYER I'd just left the LSE and I sent in a review of Kilburn And The High Roads' album written out in biro. They sent me a telegram telling me to come in for an interview. Tony Tyler said that, even if I didn't get the staff job, they would like me as a contributor, so I started doing freelance reviews and then went on staff finally in 1980. Initially, I got the stories no one else wanted to do – Bram Tchaikovsky in Sweden.

JON SAVAGE I always find it funny that Hornby *et al* would have killed to work on the music press in the late '70s but they weren't good enough, or they refused to enter – in any way, small or great – into the maelstrom. Because that's what it was – to me, at least: a risk.

DAVID HEPWORTH I was radio promotions man at the UK office of Beserkley Records for 18 months, and when I jacked that in I rang up the *NME* and said, "I'm back on the market again. " They said, "Sorry, we're not interested." They were a very unsympathetic bunch, very tough to work for.

JOOLS AND TONE
"COMPLETE PAINS IN THE ARSE"

PETER YORK The main thing about them is the class thing. In rock press terms, they were 100 per cent unreconstructed, inner-urban prole, which in late 1976 was just about the most exotic, lurid, transcendental thing you could get. They also look the part, which is important for editorial atmosphere.

CHARLES SHAAR MURRAY They arrived absolutely right on time. They wanted to kick over the statues, which is a totally healthy impulse, but I was a bit mortified to find that I'd become a statue, because that's never been how I think of myself. For fuck's sake, Parsons was only four years younger than me!

PETER YORK As it turns out, within a couple of months, three things are apparent, namely they can write, they are a team and they are totally uncontrollable.

GARRY BUSHELL Parsons and Burchill were my big favourites. Even though *The Boy Looked At Johnny* was spectacularly wrong, the book was more punk in spirit than Paul Morley's self-indulgent doodling.

JULIE BURCHILL The *NME* staff were generally very nice to me to start with, even if Tony and I had put their coke-ridden noses out of joint a little, especially the class of '73 *enfants terribles* - translation: pain in the arse under 40 - who had been flavour of the month before punk came along, and rendered their afros, boas and satin 'n' tat somewhat redundant.

PETER YORK Julie said Bryan Ferry was a worthless person - think of it, a worthless person; I hadn't heard that kind of language in years - because of the social climbing and because he'd deserted the kids who made him. Bowie was "a toothless piece of old burnt meat...a dead man's brain floundering around the stage" because he'd gone so esoteric.

NEIL SPENCER There wasn't any real issue over Tony and Julie until punk kicked in, because punk divided people. You either went with it or you didn't.

CHARLES SHAAR MURRAY I don't recall ever having cigarette butts flipped into my hair by them. If it had happened, it would have set fire to it, because I didn't get my first punk crop for another couple of months. I was still with the 'fro at that point. I had Mickey's old hairdo. Then I got mine cut, but Farren kept his. It was his trademark. I remember Mick saying, "I've been listening to arseholes telling me to get my hair cut for years. There's nothing new about this."

JULIE BURCHILL They did tend to call each other "man", which grates, if you're a girlie, and one's working-class credentials did tend to make them a little chippy. "Stop flexing your roots, man!", one of them said to me when I innocently cracked open a tasty tin of Tizer one day.

CHRIS SALEWICZ I remember her being this quite sad little girl, frightened. Miles, who was a good guy, took her to this press conference given by her idol, Patti Smith. People like Mick Watts from the *Melody Maker* were there, taking the piss out of Patti Smith for taking herself so seriously and Burchill burst into tears! I don't remember her being this switchblade-wielding girl, but I also feel that certain people there didn't treat her terribly well.

NICK LOGAN They were great writers and fantastic people, but they could be complete pains in the arse. And there's grown up this myth about "the kinderbunker" they built in the office. I don't remember any barbed wire. They took a little space in the middle of the office which no one else wanted. It had little privacy. It was basically just a walkthrough so they put up an incongruous curtain of plastic strips, like you find in shops' back doorways to make people go the other way around. It wasn't quite the kinderbunker. There were certain people who wouldn't walk through it, probably those from the album department who were less impressed by them. I ran the risk of walking through it.

JULIE BURCHILL Two lively minds with more dash than cash soon tumbled that the door jambs could be lined with barbed wire and have attractive multicoloured plastic stripping hung from their tops. The barbed-wire motif was cheap and cheerful and broken glass made a shiny, optimistic contrast when alternated with it. Finally, a charming noose, hung high slap bang in the middle of the room, provided an interesting conversation piece. "The kinderbunker was worth a couple of thousand a year in itself," wrote Peter York in *Style Wars*.

TONY PARSONS We were told off sometimes for fighting in the office and taking drugs too obviously. They were quite frightened, because it was a different pace – speed, mostly. Smoking dope wasn't considered drugs there. Bob Marley did it, so it must be all right.

CHARLES SHAAR MURRAY It was funny because Tony Parsons arrived, and in the standard welcoming gesture I passed him a spliff. He practically turned into a puddle and slipped down the wall. He obviously wasn't quite used to the level of spliffication that was our standard.

TONY PARSONS They weren't a bad bunch, but they were a bit frightened, and I can understand it, being presented with a movement of amphetamine-crazed young people running amok through the city. But I always felt that I got on well with the people I worked with. Charlie was a young man – what, 25 at the time? – and he was very young to have been involved in all that hippie stuff with the *Schoolkids Oz*. I admired Charles Shaar Murray and Nick Kent, but I'm not sure if they were aware they were heroes to me. I didn't like it that I was that much in awe of them, so I wanted to surpass them. We were very young and probably took everything much more seriously than it deserved. There was a lot of confused thinking. We didn't know whether we should take drugs or save the world.

PETE SILVERTON Tony's cover story on The Clash in April 1977, which was used on their giveaway single, was a masterstroke because it just placed them in a different league. But there's no doubt that there was some canny PR going on there, probably handled by Ellie Smith in the CBS press office.

IAN MACDONALD I laid out Tony's Clash story, calling it "Sten Guns In Knightsbridge". I was out of touch by then, but I got the gist from the way Tony and Julie talked about them, so I used big pictures of all the band members on the basis that they were about to be famous. Considering there were only four years between our lot from the early '70s and the punks, the generation gap was fairly explosive. Mick Jones and Paul Simonon came into the office looking moody in leather and were a bit touchy about the reaction they got, like they expected to be sneered at and meant to get their retaliation in first. Nice blokes, actually, rock 'n' roll business as usual but with a good grasp of image and how to come on. UK punk was sharp in that visual conceptual way, which was more to the point than the music. Punk was very art school and designerish, arriving equipped with a fully specified sub-culture of its own – McLaren and Westwood's input. The job of people of my vintage was pretty obvious: stand aside and let it come through.

PUNK GOES MAINSTREAM

"IT WASN'T ALL POSING"

TONY PARSONS Nick Logan offered me direction. Often after an editorial meeting he'd make suggestions about how to improve a story. Maybe in practical terms it was because I was a little goldmine, because of my access. If the Pistols got kicked off a label, I could ask them about it later that night when we were sharing a line of sulphate and a couple of lagers. Nick Logan would always say to me, "Stop and think about it. You have got incredible access." It was true. Other people – like Caroline Coon and Jonh Ingham – had written about it, but I was considered to be one of their peers.

PETE SILVERTON It was a time when the record companies couldn't control the journalists, because we were so close. The artists would be calling us up, saying, "Do you want to go for a drink?" I was really good friends with James Honeyman-Scott of The Pretenders, and it became a joke at the office because he'd be pitching up every lunch-time asking me to come out and play. The office changed their attitude when The Pretenders became very big, but he'd still pitch up and drag me to the White Lion.

TONY PARSONS One of the reasons I did well there was because these were the guys I was drinking with. I'd see The Sex Pistols every night of the week. You'd only see Rotten when Johnny Thunders and The Heartbreakers were around, but I'd see the rest, always be bumping into The Stranglers. The Buzzcocks were in London, Paul Weller most nights. It was a very small world. Weller was a bit of a Noel Gallagher type – real raw intelligence; a bright, working-class kid – but you'd get some Linda Ronstadt fan on the *NME* and they couldn't tell the difference between Weller and Ronnie Kray.

NEIL SPENCER I always thought The Jam were good, particularly since they had "Fire And Skill" emblazoned on their amps. I thought that was a good slogan.

TONY PARSONS On the Anarchy Tour, what stood out was that nobody had stayed in a hotel before. We were all saying to each other, "There's this little cupboard in the corner with drinks in it," or, "If you call up, they'll bring you a sandwich!"

PETE SILVERTON I covered the Manchester date on that tour for *Sounds*. Jonh

Ingham had gone back to America for a bit and there weren't that many punk writers. Jon Savage couldn't go on the tour, because he was training to be a solicitor, and Jane Suck was there.

JON SAVAGE Actually, I *was* training to be a solicitor but didn't go, because I didn't start writing for the music press until April 1977.

TONY PARSONS On the first night of the Anarchy Tour, I was introduced to this little guy from New York backstage in Leeds. Meeting Johnny Thunders was a big deal, because of The New York Dolls. They were a real test on where you stood, after Bob Harris called them "mock rock" on *The Old Grey Whistle Test*. People like Morrissey and Mick Jones and the Pistols absolutely loved The New York Dolls. To a lot of us, it was the best music we'd heard since we were ten years old, with groups like The Beatles.

LISA ROBINSON I taped everything in those days. I got The Sex Pistols and The Clash at the Electric Circus in Manchester in 1976 and I ran back to the Montcalm Hotel and called every record company executive I knew and told them to sign those bands. [CBS chief] Walter Yetnikoff was the only one who said, "OK."

CHRIS SALEWICZ One thing which has never been pointed out is that they fixed the fucking annual readers' polls in the *NME* at that time. In 1976, Genesis, Brand X and Led Zeppelin were all still really big, but the polls at Christmas featured all the new bands. Logan basically saw that a paper's success is linked to a tribal movement.

TONY PARSONS Respect to Led Zeppelin, though. The only people I ever saw with long hair in the Roxy were Robert Plant and Jimmy Page, who turned up separately to check it out. I had a chat with Robert Plant, and it turned into a really nice little piece. There was an embarrassment of riches at that time. You'd be sitting at dinner and Marc Bolan would be at the other end of the table and you wouldn't bother going to talk to him.

CHARLES SHAAR MURRAY I went to Stockholm with The Sex Pistols in the summer of 1977 and it was fascinating. What stood out was how much effort John Lydon put into being a curmudgeon. It wasn't him being him;

it was a persona thing, and he was working on it really hard.

TONY PARSONS It wasn't all posing. The worst beating I've ever seen was what the police did to Malcolm McLaren when he came down the gangplank off the boat on Jubilee Day. OK, he was asking for it, calling them fascist pigs and Nazi stormtroopers, all this Kevin the teenager stuff, but what they did to him was shocking. There were ten coppers kicking the shit out of him. I'm not saying you took your life in your hands, but you were provoking a lot of people just by wearing a Sex Pistols T-shirt that summer. It didn't make for an easy life, as you wended your way home past north London pubs after another hard day taking amphetamine sulphate in the *NME* offices.

CHAS DE WHALLEY When The Stranglers got their record deal and their first single, 'Grip', came out in early 1977, there was a chart error at *Music Week* and it was missed off the chart, so we planned one of those photo-montages like you get in teen mags, with the band kidnapping me, pretending to be an employee from *Music Week*. So they tied me up and carried me down Carnaby Street, and then they turned on me, stripped me naked and poured ice-cold water over my genitals, the bastards.

JON SAVAGE In retrospect, we were exploited terribly, but of course at the time we were very eager to get into print. There was the lack of unionisation [and] proper payment, the lack of any kind of regulation, and this became clear when I was attacked – not at all severely – by one of The Stranglers and I got absolutely no support.

CHAS DE WHALLEY I was sitting at the bar with Jean-Jacques Burnel and Jon walked in. I think at this distance I did it innocently, though maybe at the time my motives weren't all that pure. So I pointed him out to Jean-Jacques.

JON SAVAGE I wrote a very bad review of their second album, which I still stand by, and the word was out that Jean-Jacques Burnel was looking for me. Chas de Whalley pointed me out in the Red Cow. It wasn't a big beating or anything, but the idea of that kind of violence was revolting to me. I remember he hit me three or four times, I slapped him on the face and that was that. I didn't really think a great deal of it. It didn't stop me doing what

I was doing. In fact, it made me more determined.

CHAS DE WHALLEY I felt absolutely dreadful afterwards. In fact, I wrote Jon a letter, apologising for the part I played in it. I also had a go at Jean-Jacques, who is a very bright guy but sometimes a bit too handy.

JON SAVAGE Chas was not very happy with me, because I was striving ahead with new musick at the time while he was trying to promote power pop, which I thought was shit, and I also hated The Jam, who he was also thick with.

CHAS DE WHALLEY Another thing about punk was that it created an explosion of independent labels, which meant there was far too much product for the public to get their heads around. So then began this championing by writers of the next big thing. These were taste-making journalists who couldn't differentiate staying power from a flash in the pan. If the band were pretty enough or ugly enough and were playing in the right place and the right two or three taste-makers from down the King's Road were saying, "They're fantastic," then they'd get huge coverage in the music press.

ROBERT CHRISTGAU I have in my files a telegram from someone associated with The Stranglers threatening to "slip your wife a bit of British beef" if I ever criticised them again. I replied that, under the circumstances – threaten me, not my wife; she's not me – I had no choice but to make sure they weren't mentioned at all. A few years later, someone from their organisation called to apologise, blaming it on some terminated underling, but declined to put the apology in writing.

LINDSAY HUTTON I had my own long-running problem with The Stranglers which was both absurd and intriguing. I loathed them – still do – and had written a negative review. Anyway, following that, their manager stopped me from meeting The Dictators when they played together. That was Dick O'Dell's revenge. At a gig in Falkirk, Burnel allegedly wasn't going to play until I was ejected from the hall, but the promoter talked him around. There went my public-service award. The only reason I was there was because The Rezillos were supporting. Sometimes a perspective needs to be retained

233

and people need to be warned about bollocks like The Stranglers.

CHARLES SHAAR MURRAY Sid Vicious struck me as a good-natured goofball. He was so unscary, and that's how I wrote about them. It's always a pleasure to do that, whether it's to say that somebody portrayed as nice is a shit or somebody who is supposed to be a tough guy is actually very nice.

MILES The most absurd interview I ever did was trying to interview Sid Vicious at Max's Kansas City after he stabbed Nancy, when he was totally out of it on heroin and could barely stand up. He died the following week.

CHRIS WELCH I didn't like the horror that went on at the gigs, having to wade ankle-deep through urine, like at the Vortex, that club on Wardour Street. It was horrible.

TONY PARSONS In early 1977, I remember going down the Speakeasy with Joe Strummer and Mick Jones to have a drink and try and chase a few birds. They wouldn't let us in, even when we dropped the *NME*'s name or said that the band had just signed to CBS. This was the big industry hangout and we couldn't even get in, never mind a blowjob. In a year, that was completely turned around.

PETE SILVERTON The piece I am most proud of from my time at *Sounds* is probably the most naïve I ever wrote, the review of the first Clash album. It was such an over-the-top clarion call of a review it should have gone straight into Pseud's Corner without stopping, but it was heartfelt and, more importantly, it did strike a chord with lots of people. The line was something like, "If you don't like this, you don't like rock 'n' roll."

CHARLES SHAAR MURRAY (FROM NME, 11 SEPTEMBER 1976) They are the kind of garage band who should be speedily returned to their garage, preferably with the motor running, which would undoubtedly be more of a loss to their friends and family than to either rock or roll.

NEIL SPENCER In terms of the *NME* office, a lot of people were affronted by punk. A big issue was their musicianship. At the gig I reviewed at the Marquee, a lot of people were shouting, "You can't play," and John Lydon was saying, "So fucking what?" Charlie's review of The Clash in their really early days, telling them to get back in the garage, was a bit of a mistake. I thought it was a good gig.

TONY PARSONS Often, there was a form of punishment to cut me down to size by being sent on the road with bands who weren't punks, like Thin Lizzy or Lynyrd Skynyrd, but I think that is where my best writing came out. I'd never seen a woman peeing until I'd been on the road with Lynyrd Skynyrd, just like in *Almost Famous*.

RICHARD WILLIAMS I had this column in the *Melody Maker* for about 18 months, and one week I wrote a piece projecting what would happen to punks 20 years into the future. What I did was take a template of Rod and Britt and imagined where Johnny Rotten would be. Nobody could imagine at that time that he would be sitting by the pool in Hollywood with a German film star. And someone told me he was really pissed off with it. "He's written my bleedin' obituary" is what he said, apparently.

TONY PARSONS A lot of the stuff I wrote was actually worked out beforehand with the band. I remember I got IPC to pay for a cab to take me and Julie and The Jam on Paul Weller's 18th birthday to go and see Pete Townshend at his house in Twickenham. It was a good little story, even though he wasn't in so we went around to his Meher Baba temple and talked to some of the monks there.

PETE SILVERTON Because of the smallness of the circuit, we all used to hang out together. Joe introduced me to Glen Matlock and we're still friends. There was a closeness between the musicians and the writers, but it wasn't corrupt. I'd see people all the time. They'd play me demos. You got a lot of access. I did get phoned up in the middle of the night and attacked and had beer poured over me because of bad reviews, but that came with the territory. John Foxx of Ultravox used to ring me up so often I had to go ex-directory. Bob Geldof hates me still, I think, for a bad review of The Boomtown Rats. I was meant to interview him for the cover of *The Radio Times* for Live Aid and he cancelled it when he found out it was me.

PAUL DU NOYER Maybe I'm romanticising it a bit, but the *NME*'s offices in

Carnaby Street were pretty funky. You've got to pine for the days when papers could be holed up in their own shabby little premises and Paul Weller, Joe Strummer or Elvis Costello might call in at any time. They were in Soho, which is where the record company offices used to be, in any case. They'd call up to either hang out or settle some grudge.

VIVIEN GOLDMAN There's this Yiddish word *maches*, which is where you are proud of people close to you, and that's how I felt about people like Johnny Rotten or Bob Marley. These were my friends. Not that I was conscious of it at the time; it was part of day-to-day life.

MICK FARREN Paul Weller threatened to hit me one night at Dingwalls after my review of the third album by The Jam pointed out the stage The Who were at by their third album. I wandered in and he's going, "You didn't do me no fucking favours, did you?" and pulled his fist back. So I shook his hand.

PAOLO HEWITT The Jam did a surprise gig at the Marquee under the name John's Boys. Because I knew Paul from Woking, I got in and reviewed it for *Melody Maker*. They didn't know about my relationship with Paul and so thought I was some kind of boy genius. Then I reviewed Setting Sons and they sent me up to interview The Jam in Manchester. I never thought to tell them about me and Paul. I didn't think it was an issue, really.

ALLAN JONES I remember going to see Elvis Costello's first gig and raving about it in the *Melody Maker* office, saying we should put him on the cover, and they just laughed at his name. Every time he phoned me up at the office to arrange an interview, which kept getting blown out, the receptionist would say, "It's that bloke Elvis Costello for you," and everyone would fall about as though it was the funniest fucking thing they'd ever heard.

CHAS DE WHALLEY I knew all about Elvis Costello, because my band Dust On The Needle had supported his first band, Flip City, at some pub in Putney. Then, at the beginning of 1977, I got a call from this guy called Ken Smith who said he was managing a folk singer called DP Costello. When his first single came out on Stiff, it was slated in *Sounds*, so I raved about it the following week, and I wrote the first feature on him, when he gave me the whole spiel about the hate-list of all the people in the music industry who had turned him down. Then I got a copy of the first album and I reviewed it for *Sounds*, and it was all going swimmingly until I reviewed it for *Record Mirror* under the pseudonym Ronnie Wheely. I revealed that the backing band was the great but distinctly unhip country rockers Clover, which was supposed to be a secret, mainly because they didn't have work permits. About a week later, the phone rang at home and Jake said, "Are you Ronnie Wheely?" I said, "Yeah." He said, "Right, next time I see you, I'm going to break every fucking bone in your body." I was genuinely frightened. For the next two or three weeks, when I went out, I made sure I had a couple of mates with me.

CHRIS SALEWICZ The musicians who did well in the music press really were people who were very articulate and knew a few big words – Sting, Lydon – although with Lydon you'd cut out the stuff he was getting completely fucking wrong. Neil Spencer and I were talking about the number of times you've made someone seem really quite intelligent because you warm to them. You really quite like them, and you just cut out all the shit that they're coming out with. And it's really not very good for them, because you're just making them more arrogant.

MARY HARRON The article I wrote on English punk for *The Village Voice* that came out in early '77 was the first long series piece in an American publication about English punk, and it had a huge reaction, the biggest to anything I've ever done. It was a defence of the movement, and it just caught a wave.

TONY PARSONS I was sent to Denmark to interview Iggy when he was coming over here in '77, and I spent days and nights with him, but I still don't think I delivered a good interview. What I see now is that he was very afraid about coming here, because he was lionised and actually he was this shaky, middle-aged junkie. As someone said, he looks like a recently exhumed body-builder, and my first thought was, "God, he's so old," but I left that out, because I felt the readers wouldn't want to hear that. He'd made some great records and would make some more – *Lust For Life* was coming out, so creatively he was at a high point – but I see now he was afraid of not living up to expectations. Iggy is very combative, so he said, "I'll race you back to the hotel." I'd always played a lot of sport, so I was still reasonably fit. We ran through the streets until he saw I could keep up, and then he said, "We won't do that any more." So we were strolling along and then we stopped at some traffic lights. There was this little Beetle waiting at the red lights and Iggy's chatting away when he suddenly pulls his enormous great schlong out and starts to piss over the car. The guy in the car was, like, "Fuck! Iggy Pop's pissing on my Beetle!"

JULIE BURCHILL When Tony saw Iggy Pop make a slipshod, automatic pass at me, he saw red. After this incident, just before his final foregone-conclusion capital-city triumph at the Hammersmith Odeon, Iggy came around looking for drugs to speed him up. Straight-faced, Tony slipped him a handful of dramatic-looking capsules. Well, of course, they were laxatives. Iggy Pop, idol of Babylon, godfather of punk, untouchable, had been reduced to using – frequently – a bucket in the wings of the mighty Hammersmith Odeon on his triumphant final date.

TONY PARSONS In Stockholm, he was on all the time. I had flown across with some pop writer from *The Mirror*, and he was really nasty to her, reducing her to tears, the kind of gratuitous unpleasantness which I wouldn't tolerate now. He was quite an unpleasant character, old Iggy, going on about Jew bitches all the time. There was a lot of that game-playing in the '70s, with people fucking around with everything from the Devil to fascism. The punks were far from innocent – stupid, moronic stuff like Siouxsie Sioux and Sid wearing swastikas – but theirs was an art school, misplaced thing, and I'm sure you wouldn't hear Siouxsie going on about Jews. Iggy, however, was much worse. It was a real sign of self-loathing.

NEIL SPENCER One problem was that every time you went to a gig there was a punch up. Another issue was that punk was quite ambiguous about fascism – flirting with swastikas, that stuff. If it hadn't been for the fact that John Lydon was Irish and The Clash had lots of black mates and liked reggae, it could have gone far more in that direction.
SOUNDS

"IT JUST GOT THE VIBE"

PETE SILVERTON I was at the Roundhouse bar with Joe Strummer, who was having a drink with Giovanni Dadomo. He said to Gio, "You need some better writers at *Sounds*. You should hire him." So I went down there and they got me to write some stuff for them. Vivien was there, Pete Makowski, and Jonh Ingham had started to disappear.

CHAS DE WHALLEY I jumped to *Sounds* from the *NME* in April 1976. There was Alan Lewis, Vivien Goldman and Barbara Charone. My enduring memory of Barbara is of her sitting at her desk writing a feature and blagging records at the same time. I was very impressed.

PETE SILVERTON From when I arrived at *Sounds*, I didn't get on with Barbara Charone, although we only overlapped by a couple of months. She's not a very nice person and got more abrasive as she took more coke and I spurned her advances. She was the features editor and hanging out with Keith a lot. As a journalist, I always thought Barbara was an embarrassment to the trade – all that slavish stuff she wrote about American acts, and she wrote really positive stuff about the Stones in a period when they were making the worst music of their career. There were no critical faculties at work.

VIVIEN GOLDMAN When Barbara Charone left *Sounds*, Alan Lewis made me acting features editor for three months, which I felt was ridiculous, like I was acting my role, so I talked about it to Caroline Coon, who was something of a mentor to me, and she said, "Darling, you've just got to stand up to him and tell him." So what I wound up doing was grabbing him and pinning him against the wall and saying, "Look around this office. Who is going to be a better features editor than me?" So I got it, and probably wouldn't have if Caroline hadn't had given me the guts to do it.

PETE SILVERTON We'd moved from a warehouse in Holloway to Covent Garden which was like a bombsite then and kind of echoed what was going on in punk. We were just down the road from the Roxy, and I remember Alan Edwards [the punk PR/manager who now handles the likes of The Spice Girls] had an office which was so decrepit you could only get to it by ladders.

VIVIEN GOLDMAN Alan Lewis and I talked, and the general feeling was that *Sounds* was not the front runner, so the best thing to do would be to go out there. "We're the underdog, so let's ally ourselves with the underdog music." And that's what we did. It was punk-a-go-go from then on, plus reggae.

CHAS DE WHALLEY Alan Lewis, who I rate extremely highly, had this policy of recruiting young writers and giving them their head. He wanted to make sure that everything turning up in the Gig Lists supplement was being reviewed. Through The Stranglers, I got to know the Albion Agency, which owned two major pub venues, the Red Cow and the Nashville, and I'd be off to see the bands that played there and elsewhere, riding in the van with Eddie And The Hot Rods and The Stranglers.

VIVIEN GOLDMAN Reggae was really my beat, and when I started I don't think anyone else was really covering it, not Neil Spencer or Chris Salewicz on the *NME*. Maybe Penny Reel was there first. He's a real character.

NICK LOGAN Punk gave us a lot of opportunities for presentation and design. It was hugely invigorating. I always thought it was funny how *Sounds* went too far in trying to make their magazine look like it had been produced in a back room. That's not what you do. You take some things which have been done in fanzines but find other ways. We used the technology which we had and they didn't, which is where I think they were getting it wrong.

CHAS DE WHALLEY *Sounds* didn't attempt to be highbrow. It wasn't catering for readers looking for a cultural assessment.

SYLVIE SIMMONS After my stint working on *Mirabelle*, I packed up everything I owned and went to LA. I scored a couple of interviews, one with Steely Dan – who just had *Aja* out – and the other with Mink DeVille, so I called *NME*, who said, "Fuck Steely Dan." *Melody Maker* were OK but not interested, but Alan Lewis at *Sounds* was really nice and said he would look at the Steely Dan piece. They liked it and ran it as a cover story and then did the same with Willy DeVille. So I became their LA correspondent with a column, "Hollywood Highs".

PETE SILVERTON The *NME* were very snotty about us, calling us *Snouds* and things like that, but once we learned the playground thing of giving it straight back to them it took the wind out of their sails. I got on with people like Tony Stewart, who was an awkward bastard at the best of times, but Charlie Murray was the snottiest one, in a way. To your face, he is never snotty to anyone. If he ignored you, it's because he was out of his skull. At *Melody Maker*, I used to get on well with Caroline Coon and Allan Jones, because he knew Joe Strummer from Newport, but his attitude to Joe was one of anger, because Joe hadn't turned out to be what he envisaged punk to be. His dream was for a more successful 101ers.

JON SAVAGE I thought the graphics were excellent at *Sounds*. Dave Fudger was a very creative designer who used things like typewriter fonts really well, whereas the *NME* had that rigid format and the *Melody Maker* was hamstrung because it had to fight with all the other stuff – folk, jazz, etc. *Record Mirror* I didn't really rate, even though it did have one or two quite good journalists.

VIVIEN GOLDMAN We stayed up all night taking speed and turning the magazine into a fanzine, because Jon had come out of fanzines and that was the look of punk.

PETE SILVERTON Dave Fudger's design work shouldn't be underestimated. *Sounds* looked punk in a way that the *NME* never quite did. It just got the vibe and had that for a couple of years, and the sales really did increase during that period.

JON SAVAGE The person doing all the work and overseeing *Sounds* was really Dave Fudger. Alan Lewis would just smile and say, "Yes, go ahead." Geoff Barton was the reviews editor and into heavy metal and probably regarded us benignly. And then there were the others Jane and I used to call "the furniture" because they had been there forever. They hated us because we questioned their use of Debbie Harry photographs at every turn. Jane and I would be the *enfant terribles* and were wound up to be so by Vivien Goldman and Dave Fudger.

VIVIEN GOLDMAN They were always putting these pictures of girls all over the gig guide, so I went, "OK, how about getting some guys in there with their kit off?" They were shocked. Sometimes I would make them uncomfortable and they couldn't be as rampant as they wanted to be. I was the killjoy who would get on their tits about the tits.

PETE SILVERTON The music press was very boy-heavy, but at least on *Sounds* we employed a lot of women writers, from Barbara Charone to Jane Suck, Vivien Goldman, a woman called Donna MacAllister and the secretary, Beverly Glick, who went on to call herself Betty Page as a writer.

VIVIEN GOLDMAN There were all these connections between punk and reggae, and I think me and [Roxy DJ, film-maker and Big Audio Dynamite member] Don Letts were the main bridges.

CHAS DE WHALLEY At *Sounds*, Alan developed this idea of the journalist being in cahoots with the bands and filing regular stories. Jonh Ingham and Jon Savage were doing it with the Pistols, Pete Silverton with The Clash, Vivien Goldman with Bob Marley. Pete Makowski and Geoff Barton – who started *Kerrang!* – had the whole heavy metal market sorted out.

SYLVIE SIMMONS I was doing stuff for *Kerrang!* under the pseudonym Laura Canyon and was photographed in a blond wig for that.

PETE SILVERTON I was on *Sounds* for only three years, but it seemed like a decade. It was a very exciting time, particularly to be living in London. It was good to have that at an early stage in my career, because I did so much work. I lived for my work, travelling the world the whole time. People didn't work the long hours they do now. If there was anybody there after 6pm, it would be because they were taking drugs or drinking or fucking somebody in the toilet.

VIVIEN GOLDMAN There wasn't the barrier between press and artists; everyone was stealing each other's drugs, so we shared our enthusiasm for reggae as well.

PETE SILVERTON The punk years were an incredibly important point in people's lives. I've worked on Fleet Street for 20 years, but if anybody recognises my name, it'll be from my time at *Sounds*. It's got me an in at really senior companies I'm writing about. The financial director will turn out to have read my stuff at school.

FARREN AND PARSONS
"IT WAS KIND OF WEIRD"

MICK FARREN The coming of punk meant that I was allowed to make some records again, and I don't think it's ethical or smart to be writing about music when you're actually doing it, so I didn't and jacked it in about 1977.

CHARLES SHAAR MURRAY The atmosphere in the office was variable. It all had to do with how much speed individuals were taking. I always got on pretty well with Parsons, you know. I never had a fistfight with him.

PETER YORK There were even some real argy-bargies in the classroom, like the time Monty Smith, who was long-term staff, was lecturing Julie – "Now look here, young lady" – and Tony grabs him around the neck and...you've really done it now, Tony.

MICK FARREN Parsons and Burchill were a pain in the ass to have around, most of the time. They produced a lot of attention we didn't really need. And, of course, their mates came around, the Jane Sucks of this world, and it became a bit chaotic.

ALAN LEWIS She was totally out there. One day, I came in and she had destroyed the women's toilets. The windows, wash-bowls, mirrors, everything was smashed to bits. She was so talented that I rehired her the following week under a pseudonym.

JULIE BURCHILL Jane had read my adolescent ramblings, been teased by my Sapphic posturing, and boy did she like what she read. She chucked in her education – she was 18, a year old than me – and came to London to be the new Julie Burchill. *Sounds* – which was a music paper quite like the *NME*, only crap – decided they wanted one just like me, and Jane was there, on their doorstep, teenage, alienated and boasting a stupid, sexually provocative name to boot.

JON SAVAGE Jane, I thought, was the best of all of us at that point.

MICK FARREN The whole influx of punks was very exciting, but sometimes you didn't want to be excited. A lot of life was conducted in the pub, and I just drank my way through it, basically.

JULIE BURCHILL Mickey seemed both dangerous and attractive because he appeared genuinely to despair in life while never, ever whining about it. I really, really admired the way he abused his big old burned-out body, and I wanted to be the same. When somebody told me that, as well as being a radical hero, he was a sexual sadist, there was no stopping me. Well, obviously.

MICK FARREN I was deteriorating rapidly within the context of...oh, I don't know. It was kind of weird. In many respects, I was running interference for Logan a lot of the time because a) he was off the scene and b) I was metaphorically handling Burchill continuously by giving her things to do.

CHRIS SALEWICZ They had this room where albums could be reviewed and I went in there one Monday to bag it and there was Steve Clarke looking absolutely shocked and Farren had blood pouring out of his mouth. Parsons had come and whacked him a few times.

JULIE BURCHILL A scream and a crash from the hippie enclosure next door gave tongue to my childish fears and I ran in to see my beloved Mickey sprawled inelegantly on the floor, a bin on his Isro and blood on his mouth. Charlie was doing his best to hold a raging El Tone back and Jah Spence was making a real meal of this little crisis/drama.

NEIL SPENCER Julie had put herself between Tony and Mick and instigated this thing between two competing men, which females have been doing forever.

CHARLES SHAAR MURRAY I remember getting a call on the office internal phone system and it was Mickey saying, "'Ere, Charlie, come in 'ere and roll me a joint. I just had the shit beat out of me."
TONY PARSONS That was a personal thing. All my life, the only time I've got

into fights has been over women. I've never thought of myself as a tough guy. That was the case before the *NME*, and ever since, even in the last year, that's the only thing worth fighting about.

LINDSAY HUTTON Tony Parsons threatened to kick my head in after I sent him a note about his feature on The Ramones, when he gave them a drubbing. A prized possession, scrawled on IPC letterhead.

CHARLES SHAAR MURRAY Julie is an unreliable narrator, let's put it that way, and that's apart from the fact that, in her book, she said I was two years older than I really am.

NICK LOGAN I suppose I must have carpeted Tony for hitting Mick Farren, but I can't remember any of the details. There was a lot of stuff going on at that time, but overriding all this was the place we were in, Kings Reach Tower. It was miserable. It wasn't Julie and Tony in isolation; we were all unhappy.

NME MOVES TO KINGS REACH
"ALL HELL BROKE LOOSE"

NEIL SPENCER Part of the problem I had in all my years working for *NME* was that people could kid themselves they didn't work for a multinational called Reed International, one of whose branches was IPC Magazines. I was never under any illusions about that. I'd seen *The Sunday Times* article which exposed Reed as a great polluter of the North American wilderness via its paper mills. But if you're secure in a little office in Long Acre or, later, Carnaby Street, going off on record company junkets and writing about your favourite groups, you can pretend that none of this has anything to do with you whatsoever.

MICK FARREN Nick had a horrible life. Then they fucked us when we moved to Kings Reach Tower and all hell broke loose.

NICK LOGAN In retrospect, it was a mistake to put so much distance between the two. I should have made everyone aware: "These are the people you work for. We can make it work within this."

CHRIS SALEWICZ Before the move, some people on the paper were saying,

"They wouldn't move us there. They wouldn't dare!" And I thought, "Well, why not?" There was a bit of naïveté around, a bit of, "Oh, we're a maverick organisation." IPC weren't going to understand that at all. They were just interested in the profits. It's a big corporation, and that's how they think.

NICK LOGAN There was conflict going on with IPC, and it came to a head when we were uprooted and put in Kings Reach Tower. That was when it all came home to roost. I'd kept the two cultures apart, and here we were in this awful monstrosity of a building. It was open plan, and we were on the same floor as *Titbits* and *Horse And Hounds*. It became impossible to control the situation. At least, I wasn't up to the job. These people I'd kept apart were confronted with each other. Nick Kent was bumping into Ron Phillips in the lift. I couldn't cope and cracked under the strain of it.

CHRIS SALEWICZ It was a difficult time, anyway. The paper seemed in a period of transition. IPC, with colossal sensitivity, had not allocated enough space at Kings Reach. I remember going in once and Logan was freaked out. The editor of this very successful music paper was in his office with Steve Clarke crammed in a corner reviewing an album with headphones on. You could feel the tension coming off them both. There was a lot of speed around at that time, and I'm sure it was to do with the stress of the situation.

RICHARD WILLIAMS Nick Logan's problems were probably more creative than mine, in the sense that his staff probably created a certain amount of problems which, generally speaking, mine didn't. Maybe they should have done. We did some really good things on *Melody Maker*, and we got some really good writers, like James Truman and others, but in a sense I had too much faith in really good writing, instead of being on the edge. I think the *NME* had more of a commitment to that.

PAOLO HEWITT I went to Camden tube station one week to buy my *NME* and they'd sold out. I was gutted, so I bought *Melody Maker*, which I never did, because it was naff. I get it home, open it up and there it is: an ad. "Young writer required." This was on the Tuesday, and I sent off all my cuttings from the college newspaper, and on Thursday I got a call to go in and see them and went in to see Richard Williams. I walk in, nervous as shit, and look up and see this poster of the 1970 Italian football team above his desk.

We got on really well, and he gave me things like The Helicopters at Tufnell Park Tavern, that sort of thing.

CHRIS WELCH I felt quite sad that we were portrayed as unhip, because for me the *Melody Maker* had always been the hippest paper, whether it was The Beatles or Led Zeppelin. We were there first with the news about these great new bands.

IAN MACDONALD I spent some time as a freelance sub at King's Reach, 23 floors up in the air in this open-plan nightmare which was driving everyone round the bend. Nobody settled in that place. It was just endless chafing and kicking at the walls and anarchic unrest. During one of the negotiations with the management, a crowd of us decided our representatives had been gone too long and it was time for a peasants' revolt. We all waded upstairs with torches and pitchforks and were about to smash the door down and lynch the IPC negotiating team when one of our guys emerged, pale-faced, to cool us out. Nothing happened, though, and I'd long gone by the time the bosses admitted stupidity and shipped the paper out to Carnaby Street.

CHRIS SALEWICZ Logan got us out. He basically spelled out the case as to why it was impossible to operate there. But he was ill - you could see he was in a state of deep depression. They sent him to America on a trip, acknowledging that they had fucked up. Logan was someone who didn't really like talking, basically, but I think he had to go out on a limb to get us out of there.

NEIL SPENCER Tony Tyler fought very hard to get us out of there, because his girlfriend, Kate, was the daughter of the MD, but I don't think Nick did. He wasn't in a state to do very much. He had a nervous breakdown instigated by the move, which was why Tony was handling the representation. Nick got a sick note and was on and off for months. The way I remember it was that Tony came back in while Nick was off and came to me and said, "Fuck off home. We're going to miss an issue, so make up something. You're suffering from vertigo." There was a week when we didn't put a paper out, and then they let us move.

NICK LOGAN I was off work...only two or three weeks, but I won the argument and got the magazine moved out to Carnaby Street. There was another strike as well during the early Pistols stuff which meant I had to produce the paper single-handedly at the printers' for seven or eight weeks. I think there was one issue we missed. But it wasn't, like, "We're on strike. We're not putting out the paper until we get what we want." They were pretty supportive when they realised how serious it was. They said, "OK, we'll deal with it as best we can."

NEW MUSICK
"SPACE AND FREEDOM"

JON SAVAGE I was very excited at that point, going around the UK - not quite with a Baedeker, but nearly - and unearthing all these weirdos and bedroom cases. And when I met Cabaret Voltaire, I played them The Seeds' *No Escape* and discovered that they loved two-chord '60s nonsense as much as I did. I was on a mission at that point. Between November 1977 and summer 1978, I had a very definite program about the groups that I wanted to feature - the Banshees, The Slits, Subway Sect, Devo, Pere Ubu, The Residents, *et al* - and I had become a big writer on *Sounds*, so I could do what I wanted. Don't forget how awful the urban landscape was at that point. Sheffield seemed like the end of the Earth, still a bombsite 30 years after war's end.

PETER YORK When the editors started looking to the original punk centres and fanzines, recruitment didn't always go quite like they'd planned. A lot of these kids turned out to be pale boys in grey conceptual macintoshes and berets who were a bit on the arty side. *Sounds* had this Jon Savage, who was Cambridge, would you believe, and stylised in a big way.

JON SAVAGE I reviewed *Never Mind The Bollocks* for *Sounds* and remember being very puzzled. It sounded like a tombstone. Airless. No spaces in the music. Jane [Suck], Sandy [Robertson], Viv [Goldman] and I were all habitués of Rough Trade, so this failure and the attendant issues were discussed when we went in there to get the latest obscurity to fill our articles. Don't forget that the need to fill space quickly was paramount. This move was interpreted as a *putsch* by our competitors. We completely wrong-footed the *NME*. I remember Paul Morley - who I stayed with that winter – exclaiming with envy about the space and freedom we had.

VIVIEN GOLDMAN The first time I met Johnny Rotten was when he was on the verge of reverting to John Lydon and forming PiL. He was, like, "I know you. You're the one that reviews the reggae. Why do you always pick such terrible records?" And then we became fast friends, and as a result of our friendship we made [the twelve-inch single] 'Laundrette' together. Julie Burchill paid me the greatest compliment when she compared me to Joni Mitchell. I ended up writing a lot of stuff on the band, which was incredibly easy because he was doing a lot of brilliant music which still stands now, like *Metal Box*. I also went on the Jamaican trip when he'd left the Pistols and Don Letts came along with [photographer] Kate Simon. That wound up being a bit of a caravan or circus.

PETER YORK Later, *Sounds* got Garry Bushell, who was leather-jacketed and cropped-haired and off the White City estate and, so it seemed, could cover the Tony Parsons number.

GARRY BUSHELL I had my own 'zine in 1977. I interviewed Jimmy Sham and Poly Styrene. Before that, I'd done what would now be a comedy 'zine called *Pink Tent* at school. I did my journalist training on *Socialist Worker* and wrote the first piece in the left-wing press about The Clash in it – in 1976, I think – and then I landed the *Sounds* job in July 1978. Alan Lewis was the editor. I showed him a Sham interview I'd done, and I think he liked my tattoos. He asked me to show him what I could do, so I went out every night, saw bands like UK Subs and stuck the reviews through the *Sounds* office door the next day. After a week, he called up and said, "You've got the job." Wallop! Straight onto the staff.

JON SAVAGE One of the reason's I'd left *Sounds* was because Alan Lewis was championing Garry Bushell and Dave McCullough. I didn't particularly like either of them, and I thought, "If this is the kind of person Alan Lewis is going to hire, there's no real place for me here." Also, Dave Fudger and Vivien had left and Jane had been sacked.

GARRY BUSHELL I was in awe of it all. I was so naïve I actually thought Jon Savage made sense. After a few years, some of the *Sounds* staff resented me because rowdy bands would always roll back from the pub with me. I mean, there were nine or ten people in Bad Manners, most of the time.

PETE SILVERTON Giovanni Dadomo took up heroin instead of writing. He was a talented writer and moved to *Time Out*. I knew he took a lot of drugs, but I didn't know he was a heroin addict back then. He became very unreliable even when he was at *Sounds*. It was the same thing with Pete Makowski, but he's still alive.

CHAS DE WHALLEY Giovanni had taste and latched onto things as they cropped up. He went to New York with Eddie And The Hot Rods. They were all out of their heads on black bombers and he filed this copy which was just about being up for four days in New York with a proto-punk band.

JON SAVAGE I can't remember whether Jane had taken too much amphetamines or whether it was part of the amphetamine-abuse scenario, but she'd interviewed Suzi Quatro and she'd threatened her, I think, in some rhetorical way. Suzi didn't mind, but the publicist did, and they got Alan Lewis to sack her. I thought that was shoddy, because Alan Lewis had exploited her talents but hadn't taken any care to look after her. That's what I mean about the fact that we weren't looked after.

GARRY BUSHELL Alan Lewis was very encouraging, had great vision and was always drunk.

PETE SILVERTON I suspect that young journalists now are a lot happier people than a lot of the people I worked with on *Sounds*, a lot of whom were quite disturbed, myself included.

JON SAVAGE We were very young and there were a lot of drugs around. By the end of 1978, hard drugs like cocaine and heroin started to replace speed and a few people in the music press, including one or two on *Sounds*, got messed up.

PETE SILVERTON Giovanni died from liver cancer three years ago. Maybe he was one of those Lou Reed fans who should never have heard 'I'm Waiting For The Man'. Some time later, I was working for *20/20* and we used Giovanni for a piece. The thing about his copy wasn't that it was bad or good; it was just frozen. Nothing had changed. That's what heroin does to you – it freezes you. But the record business was ruled by drugs then, and all of us partook. Don't forget that the Zanzibar club opened with grooves cut into the bar for people to snort from. Nobody ever did, but that was the joke.

JON SAVAGE Alan Lewis called a meeting with Viv, Jane, Sandy, Dave [Fudger] and myself and said, "We've got these great pictures and we're going to run Images Of The New Wave Part Three." *Sounds* had already done two of these things, which basically meant cheap content – you know, one photo one page. This was October 1977. We all went, "Bleeeaurgh! We hate new wave and we even hate punk." The music industry had long got involved and turned it all into dreadful 30-year-old pub rockers with bleached hair or, even worse, the endless refried mod of The Jam. For all of us in varying degrees, the thing we'd loved about groups like Subway Sect, the Banshees and The Slits was that they were new. Punk had become a cliché, and we wanted to continue that sense of newness, of discovery and of course – it *was* 1977 – total science-fiction alienation.

PETE SILVERTON The other thing is we did take it all quite seriously. That's probably why the general quality of the writing was so high. They may have taken a lot of drugs, drunk a lot, come in late, chucked typewriters around the office in fits of anger, but these people really applied themselves. Someone like Tony Stewart, who was viewed as an arch-cynic, was actually passionate about music. People cared.

JON SAVAGE The great advantage that *Sounds* had was that it did not hang back like the *NME* to give its imprimatur; it would just jump in willy-nilly and cover anything that moved. This would later cause problems under the ghastly Garry Bushell reich. So Alan Lewis gave us our heads and we all put in our twopenny-worth over two successive issues at the end of November and the first week of December. Viv did a great piece on dub and a great interview with Siouxsie, Stephen Lavers wrote about Kraftwerk, Sandy did Throbbing Gristle, I did Devo and The Residents, purely from a couple of singles and the articles in *Search And Destroy*, at that point the best magazine in the world. Jane got to explore all this in a great keynote editorial, which I remember as being among the best writing done by any of us.

VIVIEN GOLDMAN Hopefully, I played my part in making Bob Marley a star, because I was writing about him long before that. Then I wrote a book about him – the first biography of him, I believe. I based it on interviewing him and socialising with him. I remember I was once in Jamaica and my hotel room was cancelled and it looked like I had to go home and he invited me to stay at Hope Road. In the evenings, he liked to just play his acoustic guitar, and one of my most poignant memories is listening to him work out that song 'Guiltiness'. This was in the days immediately before he was shot. I got back and heard about it on the *Sounds* radio. I was, like, "Fuckin' hell! I was there 30 hours ago!"

JON SAVAGE I got into trouble with members of the social-realist cadre, many of whom wrote for *Zigzag*, who hated me writing about Devo, which I did at length, later. These arguments nearly came to blows. But, you know, we were *totally right*, not least in linking white electronica with dub.

GREG SHAW There was a time when I'd get these calls in the middle of the night from England. One time, Jonathan King called me and said, "I want this band Devo." Nobody had signed them yet, so I went to Devo and said, "Jonathan King wants to sign you to UK Records," but it didn't happen.

DISCO
"THE MUSIC PRESS NEVER DEALS WITH BLACK MUSIC PROPERLY"

PETER YORK Early in 1978, Danny Baker – who'd joined *NME* as the New Model receptionist and went on to write – did the singles review and made a disco number his single of the week. If he'd gone for The Eagles or Des O'Connor, he couldn't have been more obviously spoiling for a fight, because right then disco was just about the most unfashionable thing out.

JON SAVAGE Davitt Sigerson [later Ze act, producer and music industry person] did a piece about disco in one of *Sounds'* two New Musick issues, which squares the futuristic circle, I think.
BARNEY HOSKYNS I met Davitt Sigerson in New York through a friend from

Oxford. Davitt was writing for *Melody Maker*, *The Village Voice*, *Black Music*, all these magazines. He was a really good writer who loved disco, writing all this intelligent stuff about Chic and Michael Jackson. Not enough people were paying it attention, but Davitt was at the forefront. He gave me all these records and I was buying twelve-inches on Salsoul and really getting into it. I was also really pissed off with the snobbery towards disco in the music press. Richard Williams at *Melody Maker* was another person who sometimes wrote about it, but Danny Baker was virtually on his own in championing it. Whenever Danny did the singles column in the *NME* and said, "These are the best twelve-inches around," I would go straight out and buy them. I still remember his review of 'Good Times' as being a classic piece which opened my ears.

PETER YORK In his review, Danny said how all the pale boys were knocking disco as mindless, consumer fodder, all these theory boys, and how they were contemptuous of the real people's music. He meant it perfectly straight, though of course he was paying off a few scores, since here was somebody who really had worked up a sweat to Johnny Bristol and the Philadelphia Sound in the mid '70s and who knew the whole white-suited world. It was one of those pieces that makes you want to send a telegram. Within a month, however, there was the theory of disco and the pale boys were writing about Donna Summer and Abba and The Bee Gees as if they'd been keeping tabs all along.

CHARLIE GILLETT I've always had a problem with the British music press, because it never deals with black music properly. It's always incredibly white. In 1972, there was a poll of the *NME* writers' top 100 albums, at a time when *What's Goin' On* by Marvin Gaye would have seemed to be eligible, and it wasn't there. Just about ten years later, it was something like Number Five. Curtis Mayfield, at the time of his success, was not as big an artist as he's seen to be now. I'd do the singles review for *NME* quite regularly, and I remember picking out George McCrea's 'Rock Your Baby' and making that record of the week, saying, "This is going to be a Number One." At the time, they were really impressed, because it did go in at Number One.

PETER YORK From 1974, the most effective way of manipulating a single's success was to get it played in the right discos. The highbrow music papers never really cottoned onto this. It was left to *Record Mirror* and the real kids' papers to chart the progress of disco, who was getting what down where.

PUNK
"ASSIMILATED AND SUPERSEDED"

JON SAVAGE July/August 1977 was exactly the point when UK punk became over-exposed, assimilated and superseded in real time, so the New Musick issue was an important step in our recognition, at least, of that fact. Don't forget that Jane and Sandy and I were brought in as punk writers. The end of the Electric Circus was also indicative of this mood. Plus, we had begun listening to Bowie and Eno. The Lewisham Riot and the rise of Sham 69 drove a wedge into the split between the arties and the social realists, whom punk had once incorporated side by side.

PETE SILVERTON I was with Thin Lizzy in New York and The Clash were recording *Give 'Em Enough Rope* there. Phil Lynott and I went to the studio and tried to persuade Mick and Joe to come with us to see Sid Vicious, who was playing at Max's Kansas City. They said that they'd already seen him and it was too sad for them to go again, so we felt we had to go, and we did, and they were right. We were pretty fucked up ourselves, but it was awful. In fact, it was after a week in New York with Phil that I cleaned up my act.

JON SAVAGE I was starting to develop a relationship with Vale at *Search And Destroy* and Claude Bessy at *Slash* and realised, incredibly, that there were like minds several thousand miles away, on the other side of the world, and that seemed far more interesting that England trying to claim punk for itself as a kind of negative version of Swinging London. Punk had also become very blokeish, which was not what I and Jane and Viv and Sandy were interested in, not at all at all at all, which is why we loved the campness of 'Orgasm Addict'.

PETER YORK The other big post-punk opportunity was for girl writers, and there was quite a little post-hippie, counter-sexism number mixed in with the class politics. Caroline Coon wrote about these delinquent girl types like The Slits – actually very much the Holland Park types – who she said were upending all the old stereotypes, and Vivien Goldman on *Sounds* cornered the dreadlock market in reggae features and Jamaican round-ups. And this was really radical, because rock had always been boys' stuff.

PETE SILVERTON I knew The Wailers because I would see them around at Vivien's place, but I'd never met Bob Marley before, so when I interviewed him he talked at me in this thick patois – even though he could have used clearer English, I'm sure – and I had no idea what he was saying. We found no area of common ground in which to engage, so I was fairly horrible to him in the resultant piece. I don't regret it, not because he was an incredible talent, but because he was deliberately Mau Mau-ing me.

CAROLINE COON One of the reasons I left *Melody Maker* in 1977/78 was because they wanted me – having done the job, real journalism – to write the gossip column, which they wanted to call "Bitch". I said, "Sorry, guys. Fuck off. Fuck you. Goodbye." In other words, as a woman, if you were going to be a writer, there was incredible pressure on you to be "the bitch". Julie Burchill, as a 16-/17-/18-year-old, played that role and was absolutely lauded and salivated over by a côterie of male journalists. So off I went.

LISA ROBINSON I stopped my column in the *NME* around the time Nick Logan went off for a year. A lot of people were furious about the tongue-in-cheek stuff I wrote. Unless you're kissing their ass and flattering them, what musician wants to read one bad thing about themselves? They are always telling you that they want "constructive criticism". I defy you to tell me what that is.

CAROLINE COON Another reason why I left *Melody Maker* was because Paul Simonon told me The Clash were breaking up on the verge of their first American tour. The thing is that bands get to a certain level and you have to start talking hundreds of thousands of dollars to record companies, and if you're a male manager then you have to deal in quite a confident way with men who have more authority than you. Neither Bernie Rhodes nor Malcolm McLaren feel very comfortable with men who they perceive to have more authority. Rather than nurture them to the next level, they broke their bands up. It's very easy to do; you just have to set the band members against each other. By 1978, The Sex Pistols had broken up, and

Alan Edwards – who's now a very famous public relations man – was the manager of The Damned and had stupidly told them to break up because punk rock was over. When The Clash told me they were breaking up, I said, "You can't do it."

JON SAVAGE I didn't have much sense of my gay identity at the time, nor did Jane, but it dictated our response to the increased laddism of punk, which we abhorred. There were endless arguments in *Sounds* editorial meetings about their objectification of Debbie Harry. I hated – and still do – the bully-boy aspect of punk which began to emerge in later 1977. The Clash fell victim to it in a big way with awful mates like Kris Needs and Robin Crocker, who was Robin Banks, the object of the mawkish *Stay Free*. Hence everyone goes on about The Clash and The Jam in our degraded lad culture. Being a lad was not what punk was initially about.

PETE SILVERTON I did two big early pieces on The Tom Robinson Band which definitely made them successful, no doubt. He talked about being gay and, although it was pushing at an open door, it made the difference, and that was largely due to the canniness of their PR, who was also their manager, Colin Bell, who went on to run London Records.

CAROLINE COON I had put myself on the line as a journalist to say, "This movement is going to be the defining music for the next decade." Having said that in the press, I was bloody well not going to stand by and see the bands at the vanguard of the movement be broken up by incompetent managers, so I said to The Clash, "I'll do it." I knew them very well – I'd seen them before they did their first gig, and having been onstage myself I knew what you needed – but, despite the other political advances they may have had, The Clash were still very orthodox, and the idea of a woman managing them seemed to be very sissy. So they said, "Absolutely. Do the job. But you can't call yourself the manager."

PETE SILVERTON I went on the Clash tour of America for *London Calling* and had to use my credit card to pay the hotel bill because they were so broke.
MARK WILLIAMS

"HE WAS VERY CHARMING"

NICK LOGAN The Kings Reach experience was hard to shake off completely, and I eventually left because I could see 30 looming and was fighting the same battles.

NEIL SPENCER Midway through 1978, they short-listed Mark Williams and myself for the job and gave it to Mark. I remember him coming around and being introduced to everybody, and at that point I thought, "I'm going now."

CHRIS SALEWICZ The job went to this guy Mark Williams, a friend of Farren's. He'd started *Bike* magazine and he'd also edited *The Observer* colour supplement. He was just about to take over from Logan and he was busted for quite a lot of coke. He thought he was going to be sent down, so he went to IPC and said, "I can't actually take the job." I liked him. He was very charming.

NEIL SPENCER Mark was caught in Camden High Street with 16 deals of cocaine on him. So there was about a two-week gap when they passed me over and then came back to me and told me I'd got the job. They were pretty shame-faced about it.

NICK LOGAN I wasn't involved in that whole business regarding Mark Williams. Would I say if I was? I didn't even know him. I recommended Neil and was really pissed off that they didn't take him up at first and viewed with some amusement what happened.

JONATHON GREEN Mark's a friend of mine. I've known him since we were both at UK *Rolling Stone*. In fact, when he stumbled again more recently and had to serve time here in Britain and in New York, me, Felix Dennis and Tony Elliot put up bail for him.

CHRIS SALEWICZ The job went to Neil, who was the right person for it. It always seemed very unfair and off the wall that Williams was given it in the first place.

NICK LOGAN One thing that really pissed me off - not because it was Neil, but because of their attitude - was that I was on a ludicrous salary, £4,250 a year for all that strain. It was also a fantastically successful magazine, remember. Neil immediately got 20 per cent more.

NEIL SPENCER The paper looked completely different when I got hold of it because I got Barney Bubbles to redesign it, and they're still using Barney's logo to this day. I also shook down staff – I had to get rid of Tony and Julie because they were holed up in the 'burbs with speed habits and had stopped coming into the office. They hadn't come in for six months and nothing had been done about it.

TONY PARSONS With Neil Spencer, Julie and I caused a lot of trouble. We were quite disruptive and really full of ourselves. We must have been quite unbearable. In some ways, we were friendly, and there were people we liked, and they would be amazed how charming we could be – a couple of well-mannered working-class kids – but other times we were incredibly cocky.

NEIL SPENCER I just gave them an ultimatum: "You're on the staff and getting paid for doing fuck all so either you go or I fire you. Do you want it to be messy? We'll get the union involved and go through the procedure?" What I did say was that I would continue to use them after they left and that I would pay them above the going rate.

JULIE BURCHILL Neil Spencer was as Rasta as you can be when you're as bald as Friar Tuck on top, have a grating Nottinghamshire accent and quite resemble Bugs Bunny in the mush department.

CAROLINE COON I asked Neil Spencer whether I could write for the *NME* in 1977 and he sneered, "No." These days, I don't think he would admit to his level of sexism and classism and prejudice, but if you read his review of my book *1988: The Punk Rock Explosion* he said, "Why does this chick think she can write about rock 'n' roll, since she was born with a silver spoon in her mouth?"

TONY PARSONS At that point, our careers had gone up and up and up, and nobody's careers do that. You think its going to go on for ever, and I know now that it just doesn't. But we were shielded from the management. The only contact I had with anybody at IPC outside of our editorial office was a woman from *Horse And Hounds* who used to come in and turn our music down.

NEIL SPENCER I replaced them with Max Bell and Paul Rambali and started to refurbish the staff.

PETER YORK By the end of 1978, Tony and Julie had brought out a book, *The Boy Looked At Johnny: An Obituary Of Rock 'n' Roll*, and they moved off the staffers list. Two years off and out by 1978.

TONY PARSONS It was exhausting because it was really full on and quite a rough ride in many ways. Staying up three nights in a row would be nothing, but you're in a very strange place, quite a frazzled position, if you're ingesting that much drugs with that little sleep. And the two guys I liked most in the industry – Johnny Thunders and Phil Lynott – later died.

GARRY BUSHELL A lot of the people I befriended ended up dying – Phil Lynott, Malcolm Owen from The Ruts, Randy Rhodes, Steamin' Steve Clarke from Def Leppard. I'm not saying I was a jinx; that was the lifestyle we were leading.

TONY PARSONS Thin Lizzy was the first band I went on the road with, and Phil Lynott really took care of me. He was a beautiful guy at the same time as being Mr Rock 'n' Roll. He did have a girl in every town, and when we would go out on the town it was like going for a jog with Linford Christie. You had to struggle to keep up with this guy. Johnny Thunders was a complete maniac, but he had so much charm and charisma, more than anyone I've ever met. I've never seen anybody have the effect on women that he had. They loved him. But if you're that much of an addict, you're not interested in anything apart from heroin. One time, we were on the road and he said to me, "You know, I prefer drugs to women." What can you do? Keep on that and, unless you're Keith Richards, you've got big trouble. By the end, I was struggling to get him in the paper. I'd arrange to meet him and he wouldn't turn up, and then I had to tell him that they really didn't want him any more.

7 "Now The Music Press Is A Thing Of The Past"

"In the 1970s, it was the music press who made acts. Now the music press is a thing of the past. Only Smash Hits *counts now."*
– Connie Fillipello

POST-PUNK FALL-OUT
"I'D DONE MY TIME"

JULIE BURCHILL By 1979, pop was lying fallow and through its teeth again. All around me, men of 30 were still looking for The Word in a spinning plastic platter. "Is there life after *NME*?" they'd ask after they'd had one too many lemonade shandies before doddering off to addle their brains even further with help from the demon weed.

TONY PARSONS I felt that I'd done my time. When stuff came up like two-tone, I could relate to it and see they were essentially provincial punks from Coventry and Birmingham, away from the epicentres like London, but I'd already covered it.

GARRY BUSHELL It's hard to beat memories like the early two-tone tours. I drove through the southern states of the USA with Selecter. The bus had bullet holes in it where the KKK had driven it out of town.

TONY PARSONS The *NME* was still saying, "Do you want to go to America with Ian Dury?" and I said, "No." And I didn't want to talk to The Specials, either, because I thought that I'd kind of done it. It was time for someone else to have a go. There was also a fear of getting stuck and not being able to cut it in the big wide world, so Julie and I set fire to the bandwagon.

GARRY BUSHELL I interviewed Tony Parsons for *Sounds* after he left *NME*. I think it was to plug his book *Platinum Logic*. I didn't meet Julie Burchill until a Newman and Baddiel gig party years later. I wrote some stuff for her *Modern Review*.

GREG SHAW Punk wasn't sustained. Everybody was too quick to grab the money. A few people got some money and everyone else was left with nothing. I got really fed up and folded *Bomp* magazine. This was 1979. The magazine had grown to the point that we had a national distributor. We had to publish 20,000-30,000 copies at a time, and it's really hard to meet a release date when a magazine is just put together in your spare time. A year later, I folded the label. I wanted music that came from the heart, and none of that new wave music really came from the heart.

JULIE BURCHILL During my three years at the *NME*, I was flash, amateurish, out of my box on sulphate, unable to hold the most basic conversation with record company personnel – in fact, I could barely function as a grown-up – but I also brought a degree of innocence and integrity to the paper that was unheard of. I wasn't interested in ligs or freebies or expenses or all those other things that ruin writers.

PETER YORK By 1979, the rock press was right off the boil again. Danny Baker said it was hard to see which side you were on – as if sides meant anything in the great rock 'n' roll Phoney War. Rock 'n' roll was, after all, "just a Western luxury" and rock writing was just a job. If they were honest, said Danny, they'd have packed it in two years ago, when it meant something – died before they got old, that sort of thing.

CHARLES SHAAR MURRAY By 1980, I was majorly burned out. Remember George Orwell's essay on book reviewing, where he said that eventually you end up having to manufacture opinions about stuff in which you have no interest one way or the other? It was getting like that. I was heartily sick of my own opinions. A Bowie book I'd co-written with Roy Carr brought in a little money – and when I say a little money, I mean a *little* money – and it was just enough to make it worthwhile to climb off the treadmill and go freelance. I kept doing stuff for *NME* and *Vogue*, of all things, and a couple of pieces for *Rolling Stone*, plus I blew the dust off my Stratocaster and did a little playing. Basically, I felt adrift in the '80s, musically, politically, socially and creatively. With Thatcherite triumphalism on one side and *Smash Hits* and *The Face* on the other, I felt that the world in which I'd learned to function and carved out a little role for myself was being squeezed out of existence.

CHAS DE WHALLEY Punk enfranchised people to play music, and with them came a whole new bunch of commentators about music, many of whom thought that the attitudes they were striking were more important than the critique they were making. Paul Morley was a great writer, if you can fight your way through his stuff, because of its density. Personally, I haven't got time. Dave McCullough on *Sounds* destroyed everything that was around. The idea was that everything is there to be deconstructed, which is fine, but when the critique is based more or less on prejudice, it can do a lot of damage. That, for a few years between 1979 and 1982, became cutting-edge rock journalism.

VIVIEN GOLDMAN The music I made around that time was pretty out there. I only had two things out of my own, and they weren't necessarily suitable to be played on the radio. I was putting together interesting castes of people – Neneh Cherry; Bubble, the king of the All Saints frontline; and a violinist from a nearby Hungarian restaurant. During the mix, we were wondering what to do with the violin and Johnny Rotten was, like, "Whack it up. Distort it! Who cares?" That's why you hear all those squeals on ['Laundrette'].

JERRY THACKRAY I worked in a newsagents' and used to nick all three – sometimes four (*Record Mirror*, which I didn't like because it was glossy) – titles on a regular weekly basis, as well as cash, in order to finance my vinyl habit. Even in Chelmsford, the singles columns soon became gospel – I never listened to radio, not even Peel – and around that time the writers followed their instincts. Every week, I'd be picking up another armful of wheat and chaff, inspired by writers like Penman and Morley and Bohn and Hoskyns in the *NME* and McCulloch in *Sounds*, not to mention Jane Suck and others not so great at self-publicity and their obvious enthusiasm.

LENNY KAYE Opinions are like assholes, everybody's got one, and I like to read opinions. They have been part of everything I've ever written. But I didn't like to read things like the *NME* headline in 1979 "So You Want To Be

A Rock 'n' Roll Scumbag?" That's name-calling and I don't have time for that, and neither does Patti. But I don't want to be negative, because everybody has their opinion.

CAMERON CROWE By the end of the '70s, I started to burn out on journalism. I was taking on too much and taking too long with stories. I didn't know how much further I could go. I wanted to interview Marvin Gaye, but he wasn't doing any more interviews, and I really wanted to do a Rolling Stones story for *Rolling Stone*. That was when I started on *Fast Times At Ridgmont High*. Having exhausted rock journalism and having kind of hit a wall, I wanted to write this book that would be about high school and the experience I didn't have, because of my mom skipping me all those grades. I took to it immediately, because I thought it was almost more rock than rock to write about the high-school experience. Ironically, I found this entire school year was about the fact that Led Zeppelin was going to come to town and everyone was gearing up for Zeppelin. And then Bonham died and the tour was cancelled, and it really did change lives. The original title of *Fast Times* was *Stairway To Heaven*. I was still writing about rock but from a different perspective.

CHARLES M YOUNG I went into exile from *Rolling Stone* at the end of 1980. I spent the next two years being depressed, unwilling to write, poor and drunk. Timothy White suggested I give the editor of *Musician*, Vic Garbarini, a call. I didn't think anyone even remembered who I was, but Vic had read my stuff in *Rolling Stone* and was eager to have me do what I do in *Musician*. My first assignment was a cover story on Tom Petty in 1983, and it got me back into a groove. Vic has been a great friend ever since. He's one of maybe three people that I can stand discussing music with.

STRENGTH THROUGH OI!
"WHAT THE FUCK WAS THAT ABOUT?"

VIVIEN GOLDMAN One of the differences between the way punk took off in the US and the UK was that they never really went *mano e mano* with fascism as we did in Britain. Punk had a 3D quality which took in economics and politics in the UK, which it never really did in America.

NEIL SPENCER Politics and pop were very closely aligned at that time and I started to address that at the *NME*, which was a change, because Nick was never comfortable covering politics. But pop became a battleground for politics, which is why Rock Against Racism was formed. There were a lot of unsavoury attitudes around – the two-tone movement was ruined by riots at gigs and there was a lot of ambiguity in the politics of people like Jimmy Pursey and The Angelic Upstarts. But I decided when I took over the *NME* that I wasn't going to employ people like Garry Bushell.

VIVIEN GOLDMAN I penetrated the National Front for a report on a Skrewdriver gig. I had to work out what you wore for an NF gig. In the end, I put on this old car coat and went over to Hoxton, in east London. Obviously, the music was really horrendous.

PETE SILVERTON When *Sounds* started to champion the new wave of British heavy metal and the Oi! bands, I left in my head. It was rubbish and boring to write about. They were dull. I was more interested in Sister Sledge and pop music than these people with testosterone problems. At least there was two-tone, which I adored.

SYLVIE SIMMONS I was complementing the NWOBHM with what was going on in America. It was similar to people in London and punk – I was going to clubs, noticing the look and the burgeoning movement in LA. I saw these grass-roots bands springing up and had a finger in their discovery, without sounding too arrogant about it, Mötley Crüe and that glam metal scene, up to and including Guns N' Roses. It was unusual for LA to see all this white make-up and dyed-black hair. They looked odd but were very committed.

NEIL SPENCER The one person who there was always antagonism towards was Garry Bushell. He waged an acerbic war against the *NME*, told a certain amount of lies about us. He came on with these absurd attitudes and competitions about who was more working class. I found this ludicrous. I don't think people like Garry Bushell had ever left Romford. I don't think he had any idea what it meant to be working class in the jute mills of Dundee or the coal fields of Durham or the backwaters of Rotherham.

GARRY BUSHELL The Oi! stuff obviously caused the most repercussions of my time as a music journalist. It would take a book to put the record straight on Oi!. I've just written a 10,000-word prologue to one by George Marshall called *Nation On Fire*.

JOHN PEEL The thing about Garry Bushell was that he was ever such a nice person to go to the pub with. We never talked about politics or whatever. He seemed like a very decent person to have a drink with.

VIVIEN GOLDMAN I just remember the political thing at *Sounds* just got worse and worse 'til I couldn't stand to go in, so I resigned. I will say this about Garry: he is very polite. I'm completely opposed to him, but we never had slanging matches. It was always very civilised. My parents are German–Jewish refugees who escaped Hitler, so I felt very aware of the situation. I dealt with Alan on this, but Garry's was the face that fit rather than the spiritual, peace-and-love, reggae-ghetto vibe I was giving out.

GARRY BUSHELL The Cockney Rejects, who I managed briefly, slapped Pete Silverton around the face once because he cheeked them, and a drunken Blood roadie kicked in the office door, so it was understandable that they resented me, because I brought rowdy bands back from the pub. At the same time, U2 came up a lot to drink with Dave McCullough and I around Covent Garden - well, we drank, they watched - and no one minded them.

PETE SILVERTON The Oi! thing is why I left. I was beaten up at my desk by The Cockney Rejects. I came back from lunch a little drunk. They were sitting all over my desk and I asked them to move. Obviously, I wasn't polite enough, because they beat me up. Not badly - ripped clothes and a little blood. I wasn't backed by Garry, which is fair enough, because it wasn't what I expected, but I didn't get full support from the editor, either. I was probably being a bit precious, but I was bored by that stage and I left pretty soon afterwards.

NEIL SPENCER If you go back and look at *Sounds* from those years, you'll find Garry Bushell writing big pieces about Skrewdriver. Log onto the net now and Skrewdriver are all over the White Power sites. Nicky Crane - who was a big mover and shaker within the British movement - was on the cover of the *Sounds* compilation *Strength Through Oi!*. What the fuck was *that* about?

VIVIEN GOLDMAN At the Skrewdriver gig, I got chatted up by this guy completely in black-leather drag, like a Mussolini thing. He asked me to the pub, so I went along. He was ranting on about the country being over-run "by a race of coffee-coloured bastards" and saying he wanted more women in the movement. At the end, he asked me for another date, and by then I'd had enough already of this toxicity, so I said, "You maybe won't want to do that, because I'm Jewish." So he said, "Oh." Then there was a pause and he said, "Yeah, but you've got to make an exception sometimes." It was like the end of *Some Like It Hot*, you know? "Well, nobody's perfect." So, when the article came out, he sent me this plaintive, angry letter saying I'd betrayed him because he'd been drummed out of the party when his cronies saw the story. That was me striking my little blow against fascism.

PETE SILVERTON I get on fine with Garry now on the phone, but I didn't respect his shtick. If it was a cynical exercise then that's one thing, because I can put up with cynics if what they produce deserves attention, but it wasn't even interesting. There was no irony, no style about him or the music he was writing about. There were none of the things I cherished in pop music in the first place.

NEIL SPENCER Then there was The 4-Skins, who were the ones set up to play in Southall. That became the first riot of the Riotous '80s. They bussed a load of East End hoolies down there, leaning out the window, shouting, "Come on, you fuckin' Pakis," all this bollocks. They were out there picking fights, and all of a sudden they got a shock – the local kids went down and gave them a good hiding. They locked themselves in a pub, the Hanley Arms, because they were so scared, and the place was burned down. That came directly out of Oi!, the championship of these people by Bushell. I wrote an editorial that week about the fact that this is where Oi! had ended up.

INDUSTRIAL ACTION
"AN ABSOLUTE DISASTER"

NEIL SPENCER All the papers benefited from the punk/new wave boom of the late '70s, but what damaged the *NME* was the strike. There was one in 1980 which was an absolute disaster. We were off for ten weeks. The circulation before that was around 260,000, and remember, when I took the paper over from Nick, it had been 180,000 or so.

TOM HIBBERT I got into writing about music by mistake via my friend Mark Williams. He started a magazine called *New Music News*, which was launched by Dennis Publishing during the strike which affected the IPC papers, and asked me to write for it. I was working for Haymarket Publishing, doing stuff on how to improve your home. I'd written off to *Rolling Stone* but never written for the music press. I did my first interview with Alex Chilton on 28 May 1980. I'd never done an interview before, and it was very worrying, so I took loads of drugs in preparation for it, and he'd obviously done the same. Then we did some together and got on very well.

NEIL SPENCER After the strike, [circulation] fell right back. We lost about 40,000 copies. And then *Sounds* very cannily did a good job in cleaning up. They went for the metal kids, which is a bullet I found very hard to bite. And there was the Oi! thing.

TOM HIBBERT *New Music News* was great fun, £100 a week. We thought we were offering something more humorous and scabrous than the others. It was much more *Private Eye* meets *NME*. The atmosphere in the office was barmy, psychotic. It was in a tiny office and everyone was on masses of speed. Then you'd have the most extraordinary people like Brotherhood Of Man dropping by and David Van Day from Dollar and Adam Ant. They used to come in and take loads of drugs with us. But *New Music News* only lasted about a year, because the *NME* and *Melody Maker* came back and finished it off.

MELODY MAKER
"I THREW EVERY TYPEWRITER THROUGH THE WINDOW"

ALLAN JONES It got horribly messy. There had been a great deal of friction between Ray and the staff. We used to make [assistant editor] Mick Watts' life a misery by moaning about the editorial direction every night in the pub. Cunningly, Ray used to keep a low profile. He seemed like my grandad, and it got to a point where you thought, "What the fuck is he doing in charge?" But there was no budging him. But a new publisher, John Reddington, came in and saw that sales were stagnating, so the IPC hierarchy moved Ray to a publishing position – which was a huge mistake, because he kept what they thought was the nominal title of editor-in-chief – and Richard Williams was brought in, and a lot of staff left, like the production editor, Mike Oldfield, who would take his team to the pub for three hours at lunch-time and then come back and slash your copy to ribbons.

RICHARD WILLIAMS After I'd spent a couple of years at *Time Out*, Ray Coleman was going to move out of *Melody Maker*, so that job was going, and I thought that was what I'd always wanted to do. I'm not sure it was, now. Maybe it was just a bad time, or maybe it was just me.

ALLAN JONES Richard Williams was brilliantly refreshing. He made some brave and eccentric decisions – featuring The Pop Group on the cover before they had a record out, having Chris Petit write this strange piece about looking for Kraftwerk in Europe – but it was great to have an editor who was aware of stuff that was happening. But Richard did the same thing with me as Ray – he kept me on the road because he found me an upsetting presence in the office. Fortunately, he liked my writing and said he would keep me on as long as I promised to be out and about as much as possible.

MARY HARRON In 1979, I moved back to England and went to see Richard Williams at *Melody Maker*. I brought him a piece I'd written on The Mekons, who were friends of mine. It was a big office, a little intimidating. I didn't know anyone, although Vivien Goldman had given me a recommendation. A couple of days later, Richard called me to say he loved it, which was a big thrill, and I started writing for them. I became a music writer for the next four or five years. Eventually, I moved to *The Guardian* on Richard Williams' recommendation, but I never felt at home in the British scene the way I did in New York. It was partly because I was always freelance. I remember feeling kind of adrift and isolated during that whole time. I knew that I should be doing something else. I wasn't mean to be a music writer as a real career, because I'm not that musical. I'm not good at analysing the music itself. As a music writer, my talents were for social observation and some kind of cultural analysis, but the older I got, the less connected I felt to the culture, and I knew I had to move on. That was very hard to do, because at that time no one took you seriously if you wrote about pop music. The music press was really ghettoised. A lot of people were trying to break out. And yet there were so many great writers stuck there.

RICHARD WILLIAMS Allan, of course, was great. You'd send him off to interview Squeeze or somebody and he'd write a wonderful piece, really funny.

JON SAVAGE I got burnt out freelancing for *Sounds* after June 1978. One of the reasons was I was doing it part-time, because at the same time I was training to be a solicitor. I qualified and gave it up in April 1979. I didn't want to go to *NME* and Richard Williams was building up an incredible roster of talent at *Melody Maker*.

VIVIEN GOLDMAN I went to *Melody Maker* as a freelance for a while with people like Jon and James Truman. They were in a Nissan hut on the south side of the river, which was a bit strange.

JON SAVAGE I was ploughing the post-punk furrow, really. There was still a lot going on and we all got on. One of the reasons, I think, is that I personally didn't have an urge to be a rock-writer star. I didn't think I was good enough, to be honest.

RICHARD WILLIAMS We had people like Mary Harron, who was excellent, and James Truman, when you could get copy out of him. One of my clearest memories of editing during that period was being woken at about five o'clock on a Monday morning - because I used to set off for the printers' in Colchester at that time - and hearing this *tap, tap, tap* noise from out the window. It was James sitting in his Mini with his typewriter on his lap, and he was still only on page three of 15 or something. And in those days, you couldn't fire it down the line; you had to have the stuff in your hand to take to the printer.

JON SAVAGE Richard had a great team - Michael Watts, who's now commissioning editor at *The Financial Times*; Ian Birch, who's now a senior editor up at Emap; James Truman, now number two at Condé Nast; Paul Tickell, who's a film director; Vivien Goldman; Mary Harron, now a director - so there was an impressive array of people. We always thought it was quite like *Street Life* and thought that had been a lost opportunity.

CHRIS WELCH By the '80s, things had gone a bit sour. People started to get very competitive and aggressive. It's inevitable, having twelve rock journalists in one room. People tended to dismiss each other's tastes in music. There was less tolerance than there had been. There was a gradual deterioration in atmosphere. There were people like Paolo Hewitt, Jon Savage and Chris Bohn. It was like when I joined *Melody Maker*, in 1963 – there were people who had been there in the '30s. There was a huge difference in taste. When I joined, we tended to look back rather fondly at the older chaps, but this time we were perceived as boring old farts.

RICHARD WILLIAMS Punk was already established and the *NME* had a certain amount of rights on it. The *Melody Maker* was struggling to a) catch up with that and b) reconcile it with the rest of its coverage. In other words, it didn't want to drop Led Zeppelin, Genesis and all that. I went back thinking I could improve the *Melody Maker* and make it into a paper that would be better than the *NME*, so I fiddled about with it for a year or so and then we got down to a full-blown redesign.

ALLAN JONES Richard got two designers in and spent nearly a year working on a new dummy, which looked fantastic. They had a massive television campaign ready to go for the full-blown relaunch. It would have been brilliant, absolutely right.

RICHARD WILLIAMS The redesign was great, with a kind of ink-splattered logo and grainy pictures. Pearce Marchbank did it. I'd worked with him at *Time Out*. I was going to have to throw some things away or downplay them a bit, but I was going to try and do it so you'd have Brian Case writing about Tom Waits or Thelonious Monk. But there was going to be a bit less of Radio Jazz, sadly but inevitably. I never really liked redesigns. It's always an admission that something is wrong at the roots.

ALLAN JONES All through this period, Ray had been getting on Richard's case, holding him up and questioning everything at publishers' meetings, and this was against the background of industrial strife at IPC.

The negotiations got bogged down and IPC took the drastic action of sacking everybody.

RICHARD WILLIAMS When we'd completed the dummy for the new look and were ready to go, the strike happened. IPC wanted me to do what we called a "scab issue", without any staff, which I certainly wouldn't have done.

ALLAN JONES We were told by the union to turn up every day for work, which we did, but publication of all titles was suspended. Towards the end of what must have been a six-month lock-out, Mark Williams – who had previously worked for *Melody Maker* – announced he was launching a new weekly called *New Music News*. IPC recoiled at this and Ray Coleman announced he was putting out a strike-busting issue of *Melody Maker*. Richard was charged with putting it out, which was enormously compromising. As I remember it, Richard was given a deadline to put the issue out, he declined it and handed in his resignation. He was given a second deadline of Monday evening at 6pm. That came and went. Richard started to pack his things up.

RICHARD WILLIAMS They certainly settled soon after I resigned. I don't know if it was hours. I was sort of pleased to go. I didn't like them. With the man who was the managing director, it was perfectly cordial, but I felt generally dissatisfied with the management culture.

ALLAN JONES That day, we had been down the pub, so I started to smash the office up. I was so angry, because I knew all the work that Richard had done would count for nothing. I knew that, when he went, Ray Coleman would come back in some form, like the undead. At that time, our offices were in this Nissan hut and I just threw every typewriter I could lay my hands on through the windows, followed by the chairs. It was me alone. Everyone else was a bit stunned. The alarms went off and they smuggled me out before security got there. I was pretty drunk, actually. Funnily enough, word got through to the negotiating team that there was a riot going on, the workers were revolting, and fuck me if that didn't spur them on to settle the dispute. It was settled that night, but too late for Richard to come back.

RICHARD WILLIAMS Allan threw a typewriter though the window that was on the ground floor, rather than the 28th floor. It was sort of a wooden shed. In some ways, it was better being in a shed in the car park than in a corporate high-rise, like the *NME*. We could never work out whether we liked being there or not. It wasn't great, though.

ALLAN JONES I came in the next day and Ray Coleman had already moved back into the editor's office. I thought I was going to be sacked.

JON SAVAGE My last story for "the *Meldo*" involved a trip to New York to write about Ze Records in 1980. By the time I had got back, there had been a *coup d'état* and Richard had gone and Ray Coleman had taken over. He had been very hostile to punk. I remember I walked into the office, saw Ray Coleman and knew it was over. I just turned on my heel and walked out. I did a lot of walking out in those days.

ALLAN JONES I had a thunderous hangover, and walking to the office I could hear the workmen banging hardboard over the broken windows. Ray probably knew what had happened but was considerate enough to overlook the incident and asked me to stay as features editor, because Chris Welch had gone by then.

CHRIS WELCH In 1980, Ray Coleman came up with this brilliant wheeze to launch a magazine called *Musician's Only*. He'd more or less told me there was no chance of my becoming editor of *Melody Maker*, which I was rather hoping would happen. By then, the *Melody Maker* circulation was going down and he was under pressure, so he made me assistant editor of this new magazine, where I worked with Paul Colbert. Then the NUJ called a strike for six or eight weeks and I had no job. It was awful, a nasty, grim time. From travelling the world with superstars, suddenly, overnight, you're made redundant and unemployed. No means of paying the mortgage. Then they settled and we went back to work, and a few weeks later they closed the paper. The circulation had evaporated in the weeks we were off the streets.

PAOLO HEWITT Loads of staff left, so I went in for an interview with Ray Coleman. I'd been freelancing for them for a while by then. I quit college and joined up. *Melody Maker* was painfully aware that the *NME* had kicked their arse over punk, so they were determined to have somebody young and on anything that was coming along. So I got two-tone, with Madness and The Specials, but also fucking horrible things like The Lambrettas. But there was also Dexy's, who I loved, and of course The Jam.

HARVEY KUBERNIK I saw The Dickies at the Whisky and gave them this good review in my *Melody Maker* column, because I thought they were comedic and wacky. The next week, Derek Green [then MD of A&M UK] flies to LA and signs the band. This kind of persuaded me that I had good A&R skills. I knew all of those musicians who became The Knack and went to their rehearsals, went to see them and recognised that whole skinny-tie thing would take off. So in 1981, during the midst of these strikes, I got an offer to work freelance at MCA and asked Ray about it, and he said, "I can't have a conflict." So he cut me a deal not to write about any MCA acts, which was cool with me, because I didn't want to write about Elton John or Lynyrd Skynyrd. I did that for eleven months and gave up the column. Things changed in the '80s. The climate wasn't good for music journalists.

PAOLO HEWITT I wrote this huge thing on The Jam which made loads of references to Woking and small-town life. Then I went to Italy with Madness and all they could talk about was how good it was. So we were starting to improve, but we couldn't really compete with the *NME*. They always got the exclusives.

CHRIS WELCH I went back to Ray Coleman, who told me there was no longer a job for me at the *Melody Maker*. My jaw dropped. I thought, "Ah. After 16 years, that's how they treat you." So I went home and sat and stared at the fire for a few hours, feeling thoroughly depressed. It was just after Christmas. Then the phone rang and it was Ivor Arbiter, who wanted to start a magazine for Fender Guitars. And then I got into freelance and discovered, by dint of hard work, that I was earning more than I had before.

PAOLO HEWITT That paper was dominated by Allan Jones. He had a very domineering personality, very much in that drinking, brawling, Hemingway style. It was OK when I started. You'd go in to the office, work for about an hour on some bloody review and then Jonesy would say, "Do you fancy going down the pub?" You'd be there 'til 2pm, come in pissed up with some cans from the off licence and then go back to the pub again. I was back home at 8pm out of my mind every night.

ALLAN JONES Richard had signed up Simon Frith to be features editor at *Melody Maker* – which I thought was a brilliant idea; his column "Consuming Passions" was just great – so that was another opportunity lost. And then quite a few people left – Ian Birch, Chris Bohn. I went off to the Montreux Festival and had a great weekend with Elvis Costello, Nick Lowe and The Specials and was writing up the cover story on the Monday, and Ian Birch told me they had re-appointed Mike Oldfield as editor. And I thought, "Jesus, this has doom written all over it." When Mick Watts found out, he didn't even bother clearing his desk; he just walked and never came back. The rest of us were filled with trepidation.

PAOLO HEWITT He's a great writer, Allan, but he had such terrible taste in music. He loved that group Any Trouble, on Stiff, and was always proclaiming that Clive Gregson was "the greatest songwriter since Elvis Costello". No! Who remembers them or him now? He was always on at Lynden Barber, this Australian guy, and Ian Pye, who were both seen as effete intellectuals. The thing about him was that he really loved my writing and worked me. I wrote a review of Face Dances and he sent it back to me four times and really had a go at me in front of everybody. If Allan was in a good mood and having a laugh, it was OK, but if he was in a bad mood, everyone knew about it. It all revolved around him. And then Mike Oldfield was brought in, and he was another pisshead.

ALLAN JONES Mike had the most arcane taste in music. He thought we should go back to writing about Genesis and ELP. It was as if punk had never happened for him. He wasn't cut out for the job. Richard's work was ditched and he took it upon himself to redesign. It looked awful, but there was nothing we could do. We had four years of agony under his editorship, basically.

PAOLO HEWITT I really hated the way the new romantic thing had gone, propagated by people like Robert Elms [at *The Face*] and Adrian Thrills [at *NME*], so I wrote a think piece about it which was aimed at them. But we

274

rarely took on the *NME*. We had sales of 60,000 a week, a third of which was probably only interested in the bass-player ads at the back. We were living a great life, so it wasn't worth it. It would have been like Bradford trying to do Man United. We settled for it.

ALLAN JONES I took on Paolo Hewitt and Steve Sutherland, so we still had a good team of writers, but they were hopelessly deployed. And the paper wasn't designed; it was just thrown together.

PAOLO HEWITT Steve Sutherland was my fault. I was on this crusade to make the *Melody Maker* more like the *NME* and I didn't have any allies there. Everyone there was six or seven years older than me – I was 19 or 20. Steve came along as a stringer, and I thought, "Well, he's young," so, without sitting down and talking to him and finding out what awful taste in music he has and what a right-wing shit he is, I invited him into editorial meetings. Suddenly, he was given all this work, writing stuff about Duran Duran and how great pop music was at the time. Then he just toadied up to management and got a full-time job there.

NME
"PRETENTIOUS BILGE OF THE HIGHEST ORDER"

NEIL SPENCER I started to bring in new people. Paul Morley was already working for us and Andy Gill had come in via the "hip young gunslingers" ad. Danny Baker hadn't wanted a job on the paper; he wanted to stay on the front desk, answering the telephone.

PETE SILVERTON Danny was the funniest of all of us, just an excellent writer and hilarious, as he still is.

NEIL SPENCER I coaxed him onto the staff, which meant that Danny had to churn it out like the rest of us. It was always a problem, getting the words out of Baker, because he's a lazy bugger. That's why it was always down to him to write Teasers and review the singles, because it didn't involve doing much work. Monty Smith was involved, having come in from film editing. Angus MacKinnon was writing fantastic analytical but readable prose. I'd also promoted Charles Shaar Murray.

GARRY BUSHELL I didn't really know Danny until a few years later, but I've always admired him. A very witty guy. Very passionate. When Elvis died, some idiots at the Vortex cheered. Danny jumped onstage and told them they were cunts.

PETER YORK With Tony and Julie easing themselves out, the class of '77/78 – the pale boys in macs – came out of the closet in a big way and the critical theories literally flew. There was one I loved called Power Pop which started in *Sounds* in spring 1978 and ran for about two months before it was denounced.

PAUL DU NOYER I went on staff in 1980 and tended to write about anything. I had the Liverpool string to my bow. I did the first feature on Echo And The Bunnymen because I'd been part of that Eric's clique as a weekender. I had a lot of contact with that crowd, people like Pete Wylie and The Teardrop Explodes. I also did news and the production side. So each week I'd schlep up to the printers' in Kettering on an early-morning train with Danny Baker, Ian Penman and Monty Smith.

NEIL SPENCER One thing about the *NME* was that it was incredibly homophobic. There was a real hardcore centred on Monty and Danny. They were always on about it, which was pretty weird, because on the other hand we had Phil McNeill, who used to work for *Gay News*, and showbusiness is, was and ever more shall be full of gay people.

CHARLES SHAAR MURRAY I don't remember Danny being particularly homophobic. He liked disco, for Chrissake. He's got some gay mates, and by temperament he's an equal-opportunity piss-taker. I'm afraid Monty was, though, and Penman, too. Boarding school has an awful lot to answer for.

CHRIS SALEWICZ Along came this lot who were just a bunch of pretentious people. Even though Ian Penman was around, I didn't know him very well, probably because he was so quiet. You wouldn't notice them, apart from the fact that some of their stuff you might not like and be surprised that other people were impressed with it. It was always worrying but also quite funny when people would start a piece with a quote from a French philosopher.

BARNEY HOSKYNS I didn't want to be a music writer *per se*; I just wanted to be a writer. I was a bit overheated, intellectually. At Oxford, I came under the sway of some very bright peers who were into all kinds of shit, like Derrida. When I left, in 1980, I was very impressionable and keen to prove myself but completely unfocused and getting heavily into Class A drugs. Within a month of graduating, I'd had my first experience of heroin.

NEIL SPENCER You've got to give your new writers a go, but I was too indulgent with them, gave them too much space. I remember Paul going off to do The Grateful Dead and he came back and wrote this complete stitch-up of Jerry Garcia, and I swear we lost about 20,000 readers that week. So I shouldn't have allowed things like that. I should have stuck up more for the old guard.

BARNEY HOSKYNS I didn't go knocking on doors, because I was very deficient in self-worth. What happened was that I'd attempted to write a book called *The Cult Of Pop*. I had no idea how to write, and it would be highly embarrassing if I had to look at it today, but I got a copy to Phil McNeill at *NME* and I wrote to him. I'd already written a couple of reviews for Ian Birch at *Melody Maker* and even interviewed Ian Page of Secret Affair. So Phil McNeill said yes, and in late 1980 I started writing for the *NME*.

PETER YORK The more you read this stuff, the more it struck you how far theory had taken over. The little theories seemed to come almost before the bands.

PETE SILVERTON The problem came when people gave up their youthful enthusiasms for cynicism or drugs or, in Paul Morley's case, disappearing into a Julian Kostaba book. Structuralism did for the music press as much as it did for British academia.

BARNEY HOSKYNS I got away with writing pretentious bilge of the highest order because it was the Morley/Penman era. I didn't want to join any club that would have me as a member, so I was very much on the outside of *NME*'s little côteries and factions. I just used to go in there to deliver copy and was extremely intimidated.

CHAS DE WHALLEY The first time I met Paul Morley, we were covering a Be-Bop Deluxe gig in Manchester where he was the stringer for the *NME*. He had long hair, a greatcoat and baseball boots on. This was mid 1976.

RICHARD WILLIAMS I don't have so much of a feeling for the Paul Morley/Ian Penman generation. I thought Morley was good fun, but he was throwing shapes rather than writing anything of substance.

BARNEY HOSKYNS My first feature was Maurice White of Earth, Wind And Fire, and from there I wrote a number, some of which stand up, but some are bloody awful, horrific, quoting from Foucault, all that stuff. I think people like Barthes had a lot to teach us about music and culture, so I wouldn't want to throw the baby out with the bathwater, but whether it belonged in *NME* is another question. A lot of the stuff I and Morley and Penman wrote was completely opaque, but when they thought harder about trying to communicate, they were very good. Paul has this wonderfully playful technique in his interviews, which are brilliant.

NEIL SPENCER I enjoyed some of their copy, but there was a point where I lost my focus on the editorial content of the paper - this would be 1982, I think, allowing the Morley/Penman thing to get so out of hand. Paul just started writing longer and longer articles.

TONY PARSONS We were swept away by them? I thought their stuff moved too slowly to sweep anyone away.

BARNEY HOSKYNS They didn't deign to talk to me. I wrote a big piece on Siouxsie And The Banshees which was quite Morley-esque, and at the *NME* Christmas party Paul took my hand and kissed it. I thought, "I've been accepted!" I did like Paul. Ian was harder going, but he was actually very shy and I think he could only cope with that by being drunk or stoned or belligerent. It was their time. I hate to think what it would have been like with Burchill and Parsons around. I'm glad I missed that!

MICK FARREN I left England for New York because I thought that, if I had to listen to Margaret Thatcher's voice on television for God knows how many years, I would probably strap dynamite over myself and kill the bitch.

Reagan was coming, corporatism was Studio 54-ism. The '80s weren't short of cocaine, but it wasn't Warners doling it out.

BARNEY HOSKYNS I think there had always this intimidatory atmosphere at the *NME* office, dating back to Charles Shaar Murray and Nick Kent. The great irony was that, a little bit later, Kent would come in and no one would talk to him - he'd been rejected as this sad old rockist. In that era, when everyone was wearing baggy trousers, Nick looked like a relic from a museum. It was slightly comical, until The Black Crowes and Primal Scream came along several years later. But everything he had written about was suddenly *passé* and not relevant. There was a little room in the middle of the Carnaby Street office which was supposedly the reviews room. Nick would retreat into there and we'd just gabble for hours with Penny Reel, smoking endless amounts of ganja.

NEIL SPENCER The other thing was that the circulation started shooting up. It was up to 270,000. IPC was the classic indictment of British industry, short-sighted middle management who couldn't see beyond the next balance sheet. They didn't invest and treated it like some flukey golden goose, even though they made enormous amounts of money. We had a dreadful advertising manager who sold adverts inappropriate to the paper, Red Mountain coffee across the centre spread for weeks on end. That'll ruin your appeal when you've got kids picking it up and comparing it to *Sounds*, which always had more pages than us.

SYLVIE SIMMONS *Sounds* was good for me in that they went with what I suggested. I remember saying that Mötley Crüe were going to be huge at a time when they had no deal, nothing - the manager was the guitarist's uncle, who ran a construction company - and *Sounds* put it on the cover. And I was also working for *Kerrang!*, covering everybody. It was an endless series of free trips and jacuzzis. Fantastic, but I never thought about being a woman in a boys' club. I suppose I had a certain novelty value, particularly on the interview circuit. It perked their ideas up, sometimes too much. There were a few who thought that women rock writers weren't necessarily there to write about them.

CHARLES SHAAR MURRAY To me, it all sliced fairly clearly when the world turned

Thatcher/Reaganite. I was on staff until 1980, and it seemed that there were certain sections of the paper who wanted to form cultural, if not specifically political, accommodation with this new consciousness. I was dead agin it. The likes of Morley and Adrian Thrills and Ian Penman were getting very excited about this stuff, which was basically the new glitter. I thought it had been a progressive force in the early '70s, but when it came back in the form of new romantics and so forth it became reactionary.

NEIL SPENCER If you're the editor, it's like being a football manager – every guy on the terraces thinks that they can do the job better than you. None of them know what's going on in terms of dealing with the management, negotiations, all that stuff.

PAUL DU NOYER The trend towards first-person journalism lost something by the early '80s. We lost our ability to connect with a broad readership. The writers were very good, but they were not populist by instinct. Morley and Penman and a couple of others didn't have the popular touch of somebody like Danny Baker, who is also a personality writer. If the *NME* had been full of Danny Bakers, it would have withstood the challenges of the glossies. They had a great grasp of pop culture. Morley was a great A&R writer. He would come in and talk about Culture Club before anybody had heard of them. It was ironic – the *NME* was still very good at spotting these things but not very good at capitalising on them. It also had much more effective rivals – *Smash Hits* took away the pop kids and *The Face* was almost more hurtful because it supplanted the *NME*'s role as the hippest paper.

BARNEY HOSKYNS There was this corner where Monty Smith, Ian Penman and Andy Gill sat. They were very smart and witty, putting each other down and everyone else with these withering remarks, particularly from Penman. It was not a friendly place; it was all about showing off and intimidating. I used to hate it and dreaded going in there. One person who was always very nice was Paul Du Noyer. He never really said very much, so you didn't really know what he was thinking, but he was a terrific writer and very much his own man.

PAUL DU NOYER We were surrendering territory and readers. There was a misguided policy of surrendering things we weren't that keen on: heavy metal, punk at the Cockney Rejects stage and hard rock to *Sounds*; pop to *Smash Hits*; and prog, jazz and folk to the *Melody Maker*. It was painting itself into a corner throughout the early '80s. Editorial meetings had something of the atmosphere of Chinese Red Army cadre get-togethers. There was a fanatical ideological purity about it. Quite admirable in a way, but commercially suicidal. There was a view that, if readers didn't get it, they should just clear off. It was almost as if the readership had to be purged of unsuitable elements. I wasn't keen on this, because I was populist by inclination. To this day, the *NME* never did quite recover the mainstream that it had enjoyed in the '60s and '70s.

CHARLES SHAAR MURRAY *NME* became a battleground. I felt that the kind of attitude and politics and music I liked was entering a downturn and all the stuff I didn't like was coming to the surface and taking the lead. Although I liked him and thought he had some great tunes, Paul and Ian oversold Kid Creole drastically. I hated Duran Duran, Spandau Ballet, all that stuff. To me, the last great groups of that period were The Specials and The Gang Of Four.

PAUL DU NOYER *Rockism* was coined by Pete Wylie in an interview by me, and we hammered it to death. Wylie used it originally as an inversion of Rock Against Racism - the race against rockism. Ironically, he was considered one of the most rockist acts, because he was a straight-down-the-line guitar-heroic, sub-Springsteen character. A very good one. There was a growing feeling around the *NME* that rock - as in the classic guitar/bass/drums line-up - was a spent force. Public Image Ltd, The Gang Of Four and The Pop Group all produced early records which were fundamentally new, but, as it turned out, it didn't lead on to anything fantastically new, and in the end the old patterns reasserted themselves. Rockism survived.

BARNEY HOSKYNS I got very heavily into drugs. It was a horrible time to be writing about music, because there was so little going on. Disco had died. What was happening in rock was so effete and timid. Postcard Records was not enough for me to get excited about. There wasn't anything, apart from The Birthday Party - they were my crusade, but they were regarded as a bit of a joke, just as Nick Kent and Johnny Thunders were. That whole leather-trousers/smack thing was a bit uncool. The new romantics weren't into heroin...'til later! Hard Times was about speed and snakebite. There was a big soulboy thing, and the enemy was rockism.

CHRIS SALEWICZ There were people who came in who didn't seem to get it, basically. There was a certain spirit of "everyone in this together" before that, but all the people who arrived at the end of the '70s seemed '80s people, fucking out for themselves, basically. I certainly wasn't the only one who thought it. All these people writing in the first person about themselves – I thought that was absolute bullshit, and Savage did as well, I know. Both of us deliberately wrote in the third person, because we thought it wasn't the gig, otherwise. It became quite apparent quite quickly that it was very easy to get the cheap laugh by sneering at somebody. Guess what? It wasn't even going to get them anywhere, in the long run.

JON SAVAGE I have enormous respect for Paul Morley's writing, but certainly both he and Ian Penman became personally very obnoxious. But I wasn't interested in what they wrote by that time.

SMASH HITS
"THAT WELL AND TRULY BIT THEM ON THE ARSE"

NICK LOGAN I got the *NME* moved from Kings Reach, then that was it. I didn't want to work for IPC or any company, so I thought about doing a magazine myself and took the decision to leave without anything lined up. I had all these ideas: a reggae magazine with Penny Reel, a British *Rolling Stone* idea I'd discussed with Chris Salewicz and Tony Benyon called *Modern World*.

NEIL SPENCER I seem to remember him saying that I should come along and help him do it. Nick had terrific visual flair, but he didn't know anything that was going on at the ground level, because he was out there in Essex with the wife and kids.

NICK LOGAN I also had a dummy called *The Pop*, and Jack Scott had an idea for a country magazine. Someone at the printers' in Kettering suggested I talk to the people who printed the *NME*, East Midlands Allied Press, who had just set up a magazine division under David Arculus. I didn't want him to see me as somebody who could just reproduce the *NME*, so I talked to him about six or seven ideas, looking for a relationship, but not with me on the payroll. I threw in what became *Smash Hits* to round the ideas out – it was the opposite of an intense newsprint rock weekly – and that was the one they took to. I was a bit thrown by that but decided to work it up for them.

CHARLES SHAAR MURRAY It was actually Nick Logan who did for the hegemony of the inkies, first with *Smash Hits* and then with *The Face*. People wanted something glossy, where the ink wouldn't come off on their hands, and possibly something which didn't ask awkward questions.

NICK LOGAN I was from the hip London weekly and they were from the sticks and didn't have a clue about presentation. There were battles over the title and the content, but I was keeping them at arm's length. In the initial stages, they wanted to call it *Disco Fever* and to fill it with John Travolta and The Bee Gees. That wasn't what I had in mind at all. I said I'd walk, and we compromised on their suggestion of *Smash Hits*. I wanted to call it *The Hit* or *The Pop*.

CHARLIE GILLETT There should never have been a need for *Smash Hits* to exist. It only came into being by default of *NME* and *Melody Maker* abandoning pop music. I was really glad. I thought, "Serves you guys right. You've completely abandoned everything you're meant to be doing."

NICK LOGAN Emap wanted me to go up to Peterborough to develop this idea. I was thinking, "Do I really want to waste my time going up there?" But my mother was living in Lincoln and I thought I should go and see her and drop in on the way back. The wife and kids sat in the car while I went in to see them. They had a plan to test an issue in Middlesbrough but couldn't get the paper they wanted, so they did it on glossy stock. My interest was in getting excellent photography, with the lyrics as the ballast, and bringing these good acts to a young audience, be it The Jam or Elvis Costello. The test issue had Plastic Bertrand on the cover and Sham 69 as the centre spread. The kids loved the glossiness of the paper but hated all the punk stuff. It was, "I hate it. Show me some more." But I told Emap I'd walk if we dropped all that stuff, because I was under no obligation.

DAVID HEPWORTH It survived the unbelievable handicap of having Plastic Bertrand on the cover of the first issue. They put out something like 250,000 copies and sold maybe 200,000, so they were shifting significant numbers, and every time they put out more, they'd sell them. I joined when it had done two or three monthly issues.

NICK LOGAN Finding writers was difficult. I didn't think any writers were going to lower themselves to work for this pop magazine, but that was before David Hepworth popped up out of the blue.

DAVID HEPWORTH In a moment of crisis, I rang up Fred Dellar at the *NME* and said, "Fred. Food on table. I really need some work." He said, "Nick Logan is starting a pop magazine with this company, Emap. I'm doing the crossword and bits and pieces and I know they're looking for people." So I phoned Nick and he said, "Yeah, come along, come along," because they were desperately looking for people to help.

NICK LOGAN Initially, I was the only member of staff, and they paid me a sum to negotiate the song rights, assemble the material and send them the package. I was putting it together on the table in my kitchen and Red Star-ing layouts and pictures up to Peterborough. Then it would be left to a production person at the printers'. They would use holly borders at Christmas time, and I had to beg them not to do that sort of thing. I was prepared to be hugely embarrassed, so I didn't actually put my name in it at first. It was edited by Chris Hall - my son's Christian and my daughter's Hallie - but it became very successful. After three issues, they said they wanted to go weekly, but I wasn't equipped or interested in dealing with that. The compromise was fortnightly, at which point I put my name on it and moved out of my house to an office in two little rooms in an ad agency they were friendly with, just around the corner from where I'd worked at the *NME*. I hired Bev Hillier, my sister-in-law, to check the lyrics; Steve Bush as the art director, who was exceptionally good; and that was the staff, the three of us.

DAVID HEPWORTH By the time I arrived, it was monthly and doing well. In the office was Nick; Nick's sister-in-law, Bev, who was 18 at the time, straight out of school; and Steve Bush, who'd come out of art school and had been running a T-shirt design company. In those days, it was three pages of full-colour colour and the rest was spot colour.

NICK LOGAN Shortly afterward, we moved into offices in Carnaby Street, directly opposite the *NME*, which was very funny. I used to encounter them all the time. Some were very nice. Nick Kent was great. Because I was also co-editing *The Encyclopaedia Of Rock*, I still had some contact with IPC, who really looked down their nose at *Smash Hits*. That well and truly bit them on the arse.

DAVE RIMMER Just after its launch, in January-June 1979, *Smash Hits* boasted a circulation of 166,200, as against 202,000 for the *NME*, 120,000 for *Sounds*, 149,600 for the *Melody Maker* and 107,700 for *Record Mirror*. By July-December 1984, *Smash Hits* was selling just over half a million, while the circulation of all its original competitors had plummeted – 123,192 for the *NME*, 83,398 for *Sounds*, 72,485 for *Record Mirror* and 68,217 for the *Melody Maker*. *Smash Hits* was by now the ninth-biggest-selling magazine in Britain, and while a carbon-copy competitor, *Number One*, had made tremendous strides in circulation since its launch in 1983, overtaking all the other music papers, it was still selling less than half the amount of *Smash Hits*.

DAVID HEPWORTH I was into putting food on the table. The first things I had to do for *Smash Hits* were Elvis Costello. Go and interview The Buzzcocks. Go and interview Dr Feelgood. The idea was, don't talk down; use simple language. You're not here to tell us what you think about Dr Feelgood and your place in the world. Shorter, tighter, more disciplined.

NICK LOGAN I was still a bit sheepish about what I was doing. It was only after the first four or five issues that I thought we were getting towards something.

DAVID HEPWORTH You have to bear in mind – and I think this is the really key point of this whole era – that these barriers between music – this is pop, this is dance, this is hip-hop – didn't exist in those days. When I was at *Smash Hits*, it and the *NME* were putting the same people on the cover –

The Police, The Jam, The Buzzcocks, Blondie, Ian Dury. These were big pop acts liked by 21-year-old Johnny Student and 13-year-old Tracy from Grantham. But then the *NME* made a conscious decision, "We can't be doing the same thing as *Smash Hits*," so they went and covered bands like Rip, Rig And Panic, who nobody gave a toss about.

DAVE RIMMER Its rise mirrored exactly the new pop; the staples of its coverage were – as each came along – Blondie, Police, Jam, Adam, Spandau, Human League, Duran Duran, Culture Club. With Duran, particularly, the relationship was a close one. *Smash Hits* put them on the cover very early in their career and from then on covered every important stage of their career. It boosted both band and magazine, as Duran fans everywhere bought every copy. "You might as well call it *Duran Hits*," Boy George once muttered.

NICK LOGAN I had said to Emap very early on, "This isn't what I want to be doing. I'll set it up and find you an editor." After about a year, I got Ian Cranna in. I remembered him from the "hip young gunslingers" ad and thought his pop sensibility would be perfect.

THE FACE
"I JUST DID WHAT I WANTED"

NICK LOGAN When Ian was appointed at *Smash Hits*, I became managing editor. I'm not the kind of executive who interferes with the editor, so I sat there with very little to do and started to develop the idea for *The Face*. I spoke to Emap about it, and they said, "Maybe. Come back in six months. We've just launched *Match*," the football magazine. I thought, "Well, fuck you. You've only done that with the money I've made you from *Smash Hits*." It wasn't actually that fair of me, because six months isn't a long time, but I'm very impatient, always have been, so I made a few phone calls and found it wasn't as difficult as I thought, using £2,500 Julie and I had in a building society account and a bit of money from co-editing *The Encyclopaedia Of Rock*.

DAVID HEPWORTH Nick launched *The Face* from the same office. The deal was that Nick was still around but they would let him have some office space to do this thing. Everybody pitched in on the first issue. Steve Bush designed the first year's worth, or even longer than that. I wrote stuff for it.

JON SAVAGE It may be difficult to remember, a time before Soho was swinging, but in 1980, when *The Face* and *i-D* appeared, there were very few glossy general-interest magazines.

NICK LOGAN I wasn't into sitting on a committee, having to justify things. I never had to rationalise why it was called *The Face*. Somebody at IPC suggested calling it *Music Week Monthly*, but I just did what I wanted. Obviously, I thought it had to have a degree of commerciality, but the idea was that it was to be a good-looking general-interest magazine which documented its times. Graphically, I had *Paris Match* very much in mind, and there were some Japanese rock magazines with very luscious colour. I'd cut out pictures of Patti Smith from them and they looked great. There was also *Boulevard* and *Ritz*, those rich people's playthings. I thought, "They've got glossy paper and look good. Why shouldn't the common people have glossy paper?" It did feel like a mission, just like the *NME* had. I felt that I had a lot of things to prove.

JON SAVAGE If Nick Logan founded *The Face* on a music base, Terry Jones founded *i-D* on fashion. Through instinct and talent, they both captured a new, socialised pop attitude that seemed refreshing after the extravagant alienation of pop. Central to this was the idea of club culture, of group social activity and of black music used as a metaphor for cool cumunity and that indefinable "soul".

DAVID HEPWORTH *The Face* kind of came out of the same structure, but it was Nick's thing. Then, when *The Face* took off, it was too big a thing for him to maintain any relationship with Emap.

NICK LOGAN When I set out to do *The Face*, I didn't think I'd be doing it on my own for 20 years. I really thought it would be a bit like *Smash Hits* – I'd be more involved, but after 18 months Emap would say, "We'll take it over." But it didn't happen. I produced it from my home and the office. Steve Bush designed the logo and helped me do the layouts and we did the paste-ups ourselves for the first three issues. After a year of doing that, they said, "Maybe you should move out."

JON SAVAGE Nick was a very laid-back, *laissez-faire* editor. You'd go into his little office under Eel Pie Publishing and he'd be the only one there, and there wouldn't be any of the hassle you'd have with the music press, with everyone vying for attention. The first two or three pieces I did were Vivienne Westwood, an interview with Bow Wow Wow and a long piece about David Bowie and sexuality. I was very excited about the way in which all of these were presented.

NICK LOGAN The musical impetus behind *The Face* – and the reason I didn't want to wait for six months at Emap – was two-tone. It reminded me of all those great times of punk, and visually it looked so good. There was energy, fashion and music – everything I could relate to. I was frustrated that I didn't have a vehicle to represent that, which is why I wanted *The Face* out as soon as possible. Ironically, by the time it appeared, that was on the slide. That's why I put Jerry Dammers on the first cover, as a kind of thank you for giving me the inspiration. But I didn't have access to writers at the time. I used people like Adrian Thrills, who could do odd bits for me, but if I tried to get Paul Morley or Charles Shaar Murray, there would have been a block by IPC.

CHRIS SALEWICZ One day, [*NME* assistant editor] Phil McNeill implied that I wasn't allowed to write for *The Face*, which showed that they were threatened. I just said, "Fuck you." I realised I had to get out of there. It was too limiting, just writing about music, so I did quite a lot of stuff for Nick.

NICK LOGAN I had to use what I could and rely heavily on the photos, which I wanted to do anyway. I thought it would be an interesting combination – classy photography with little nuggets of raw and passionate writing, a fanzine with the production values of a glossy. I actually tried out Neville Brody as a writer before I used him as designer. He had come to see me at *Smash Hits*, but I didn't have any work for him then. I used Vaughn Toulouse, Gary Crowley.

JON SAVAGE I was working at Granada TV after I left *Melody Maker* and I met

Gary Crowley on this kids' show, *Fun Factory*. He said, "Why don't you work for *The Face*?" I had an in with Vivienne Westwood, because I was still hanging round with the post-Sex Pistols crowd, so I trotted off and interviewed Vivienne and Nick ran it.

NICK LOGAN Julie had her column and Tony did do a piece in the third issue, but I didn't use him quite as much.

TONY PARSONS When we quit, we realised nobody had heard of us. But Nick Logan was always there to slip us a job. The stuff I did for *The Face* was much more reflective – the first thing I ever wrote for it was about Motown. After leaving the *NME*, I struggled to make a living, because nobody had heard of me. *The Face* stuff would just about cover a gas bill. There was a lot of financial hardship for years and years, when we moved out to Billericay.

NICK LOGAN When Robert Elms turned up, that was the crucial point. I could see that two-tone was going, and then Bob Elms appeared, around the sixth issue, with all this info about this new scene, and I realised there was this pop culture which was alive. The most fantastic thing was that the *NME*, *Sounds* and *Melody Maker* looked down their noses at it.

DAVID HEPWORTH We had this kind of parade through the *Smash Hits* office. In the midst of putting the magazine out, you had this kind of stream of new romantic fops coming in to see Nick.

JON SAVAGE *i-D* had the brilliant idea of snapping the glitterati of this new mood as they stepped blinking into the daylight. Many of these "passers-by" – Boy George, to name one – became pop stars, models, the '80s equivalent of mod "faces". And after a few issues, *The Face* found its cause: the new clubland life and attitude epitomised by groups like Spandau Ballet.

MAREK KOHN It was a means for young, mainly middle-class people living in London to establish a voice. *The Face* was a useful passbook to the young idea for 40-year-old advertising executives.

NICK LOGAN I was lucky that it came along, but I'd done the right thing in creating a vehicle for it. I'd always intended to broaden the scope of the magazine, but I'd accepted the wisdom of people like Ron Phillips, that you couldn't make a general-interest magazine work. When Bob Elms came along and started writing about fashion designers and the pop culture side of things, the sales were getting desperate, so I thought, "I'd better put this stuff in, because we may not last." Even after that, there was still at least a year of absolute desperation, because we could not get this thing to gel. It had been a horrible time spent in a cellar in Broadwick Street with a couple of smelly cats and Steve Taylor as deputy editor. Then Neville arrived and gave us those great design sensibilities. We moved to work alongside Neville's studio and it started to really come together.

LESLEY WHITE It was pre-Yuppie, that dreadful word.

JON SAVAGE One of the things I really liked about *The Face* from 1982 onwards was that it was much more of a mixed-gender arena than the music press proper. I'd point to a long piece I did about androgyny for *The Face* in 1982 as an example. All that boys' club stuff became very wearing, as it still is, if you came at it from a distaff – gay, feminist of any sort – perspective. *The Face* had strong links in that early stage with *Smash Hits* through Nick Logan and many inter-relationships between journalists like Ian Birch, Lesley White, Neil Tennant, Dave Rimmer and myself, and that helped to give it a lightness of touch. Obviously, this mixed-gender effect – prominent when Lesley White was features editor – became flattened out and was overhauled by the ghastly new/old masculinity of lad culture during the '90s.

SMASH HITS
"REVENGE ON THE NME"

DAVID HEPWORTH I was features editor at *Smash Hits*, and when Ian Cranna left, after about a year, I became the editor. I think I probably made it a bit more commercial. Ian had a lot of coverage of indie music, but then all that stuff was swimming around the charts. It was all part of the pop music soup. We started to gather a team together. Mark Ellen was features editor; he had freelanced for *NME* and for us. Steve Bush was the art guy, terribly talented and a very important person. Ian Birch joined initially to launch a new title but became part of the team. Kimberly Leston, was the designer. Bev Hillier was there, too, and Dave Rimmer.

DAVE RIMMER When British groups began to take off around the world, their fans began to pick up on *Smash Hits*, too. Scores of fans I talked to in Japan knew all about it. Likewise in Australia. In January 1984, at the height of the [second] British Invasion, an American cousin, *Star Hits*, began publication under licence. The same year, a *Smash Hits* was launched in Australia.

DAVID HEPWORTH I became managing editor with a view to overseeing that but also launching something else, which proved to be *Just 17*. The company felt, "Hey, this has been a success! Maybe we can do some more of this in a slightly different area." Steve Bush and myself moved over there to develop some new things and Mark Ellen was made editor of *Smash Hits*.

TOM HIBBERT Strangely enough, working on *Smash Hits* could be difficult. You spent all your time flattering people and putting in little jokes to cheer yourself up, and then all these people you never hear of any more – Howard Jones, Nik Kershaw – they were always threatening to sue, and it always turned out to be about getting the name of their wife wrong. We'd have to explain to them that it wasn't actually libellous.

DAVID HEPWORTH *Smash Hits* was put together by a bunch of people who couldn't get anywhere in that *NME* world. It was different in the sense that it was very friendly and the *NME* was not. The *NME* was a horrible place if you weren't part of the charmed circle. A hideous place to be. Very intimidating, snotty, not pleasant at all. Individuals were kind of all right, but together they were just not welcoming people. They were kind of the hipsters and we weren't. It became a little bit of revenge on that whole thing, because we'd say, "All right, we may not be as fashionable as you, but we're more professional. We get up earlier in the morning and we're less snobby."

DAVE RIMMER *Smash Hits* turned into a bit of a pop star itself, a fact that was underlined as the *NME*, desperately trying to work out just what had gone wrong in its fall from the prominence of the punk era, namechecked *Smash Hits* several times in each issue. They were usually slighting references, rather in the manner of the paper looking down from its high horse at, say, Wham!

DAVID HEPWORTH The atmosphere in the office was fantastic. It was a real extended family, and that bunch of people, ridiculous as it may seem, still ring each other up today. There was this bizarre, busy and ironic way of talking. The kind of language that grew out of *Smash Hits*, Mark Ellen and subsequently Tom Hibbert really cultivated that.

DAVE RIMMER At times, there was a sense of real joy in making pop stars jump through metaphorical hoops, dressing them up in absurd outfits or sending them off with a writer and a photographer on some idiotic errand. It was all for their own good, after all. Indeed, some *Smash Hits* features were nothing less than acts of the purest charity, as a writer struggled to gloss over an artist's intellectual failings, hopeless inarticulacy or the fact that they were blind drunk and incoherent throughout the entire interview.

DAVID HEPWORTH It's something that people always underestimate, but I genuinely believe that *Smash Hits* has been the most influential magazine in the last 20 years. There's a huge premium on presentation, and the magazines that have succeeded have been ones that have been really well-thought-out packages; they haven't just been pages with places for writers to fill up with their thoughts.

TOM HIBBERT The *Smash Hits* office was terribly cynical. They were all very young. I was the oldest person there and got them to be very cynical. I was horrible, actually. There was a girl called Maureen Rice who was very enthusiastic about pop, and we were really horrible to her. She'd come in with this fantastically bright and breezy copy and we'd sub it and rewrite it so that, instead of being really nice to Paul Weller, it would appear in the magazine as being quiet nasty. Quite pathetic, really, but good fun.

DAVID HEPWORTH In 1981, maybe earlier, when I was features editor, I sent a circular to press departments of all the record companies saying, "It is my intention to reverse the entire direction of published popular music in favour of entirely trivia. Consequently, we are bringing back The Personal File. We want to know the colour of your artists' socks." That had been totally supplanted by Paul Morley and Charlie Murray and Nick Kent. We got some good responses to it, actually. The likes of Ian Dury said, "Cool. I'll do this. I don't have any problem with this at all."

DAVE RIMMER If an act had an angle of their own – be it Alison Moyet's chickens or Paul Weller's social conscience – Smash Hits would leap on it and sharpen it up. If an act that had to be covered was clearly as boring as a school dinner, we'd rack our brains for some way of brightening them up.

NEIL SPENCER With Smash Hits, and then MTV coming along in the early '80s, there was specialist media of all sorts covering pop and then feeding it into the national press.

DAVID HEPWORTH You had this format that used to apply to David Cassidy now being taken up by Dury, Phil Oakey and Debbie Harry. I'm not claiming that it was the sole reason, but if you look at every magazine in the world, from Vanity Fair to The Spectator, they now have something like that – bitty, capsule-sized pieces of information. We lob the ball to you, you lob it back to us. We're here to play a game. It's got to be entertainment before it's anything else at all.

TOM HIBBERT I had worked at The History Of Rock at Marshall Cavendish, which was awful, and Mark Ellen called me up and offered me work at Smash Hits. I like to think I brought the humour into Smash Hits. Before then, it was the lyrics and very dry interviews. I joined and started making up ridiculous things like the Bits pages, taking the piss out of pop stars. In the Letters pages, we had lots of running jokes about the groups, and the readers picked up on the humour.

DAVID HEPWORTH We didn't look down our noses at the kids, and we were genuinely interested in teen enthusiasm, even if we didn't necessarily share it ourselves. It helped that the stars around then were really interesting people. Debbie Harry, even the likes of Duran Duran and Spandau Ballet, they kind of had lives, you know, which made the magazine have a certain crackle to it. Those people had huge careers without being all over the tabloids. Debbie Harry was terribly well known, but you didn't pick up *The Sun* every day expecting to see something about Debbie Harry. The tabloids weren't desperately focusing on this area of the world like they are now.

DAVE RIMMER While the traditional music press limped off into the sunset of their circulations, *Smash Hits* succeeded by providing everything the new pop fan could ask for every fortnight.

NME EMBATTLED
"THERE WAS A CONSPIRACY"

CHARLES SHAAR MURRAY Nick Logan asked me to do stuff for *The Face*, but I felt that Neil Spencer was going to be really embattled at the *NME* and figured he needed all the support he could get. There was a lot of office infighting over the direction and content of the paper. Paul [Morley], Ian [Penman] and Adrian [Thrills] were on one side with their champion in the hierarchy, Tony Stewart.

NEIL SPENCER There was a point when I lost control of the staff and there was a mutiny on the paper and certain people on the staff – Paul Morley, when he was in his heavy-drinking stage, with the bottle of vodka behind the photo cupboard, Ian Penman, Chris Bohn – were opposed to me, personally. There was a conspiracy. They would bypass me and go through Tony Stewart, the features editor. It was all a bit deranged. I don't know what drugs they were taking. I was in an unhappy phase of my personal life and was overwhelmed by the work. The second strike happened during the Falklands War and was horribly depressing. I was picketed, but because I was a member of management, I could go in. They knew I wouldn't put a paper out. Also, by that time, the music wasn't saying anything to me. Kid Creole was all right, but all those dreadful Haircut 100s... *The Face* was established and there was all this talk among the staff of, "We should be more like *The Face*."

PAOLO HEWITT *Smash Hits* and *The Face* had really challenged the dominance of the *NME*, in particular. In the summer of 1982, I was asked by Paul [Weller] to write the biography of The Jam, so, clever little fucker that I am, I asked

Tony Stewart to edit it. That brought me to his attention, and he said in 1983, "We've got loads of jobs going. Do you fancy one?" So I went there on a free transfer. I was writing about soul and hip-hop at the *Melody Maker*. If it was black, I covered it, and if you write about black music, you get marginalised, so Allan Jones didn't really care about me leaving.

DAVE RIMMER That *NME* critics had spent most of 1981 and 1982 attacking the values of rock and questioning the very practice of criticism only compounded the problem. By 1983, they were in a mess, floundering around in search of a new constituency without even any idea of how to cling onto the old one, which was dwindling anyway.

CHARLES SHAAR MURRAY I felt that a lot of the people on the paper were undermining Neil. He was finding himself increasingly isolated, not through any fault of his own, but I felt there was a coup bubbling. There was this bad vibe. It had occasionally been quite turbulent, like when Parsons punched out Mick Farren, but during the '70s everybody was on the same team, most of the time. In the '80s, that disintegrated.

NEIL SPENCER The management were not receptive to my idea for *NME* to become in format like *Rolling Stone* – slightly smaller, on better paper, heat-set so the ink didn't come off on your hands and stapled together, broad church – music, movies, social stuff, books. A cultural paper centred on music. But there was this schizoid thing which had happened to pop. If you aimed that kind of paper at kids buying Adam Ant, they would not have been interested. Equally, if you put Adam Ant on the cover, people into The Clash wouldn't want to know. The Clash or Simple Minds – who I personally could never stand – were *NME* heartland stuff, because they would sell papers to people interested in rock. And there were plenty of writers on the paper interested in rock; I'd get Dave Dorrell to write up The Southern Death Cult. But the balance at the paper went wrong. It slid out of focus, for which I blame myself.

PAOLO HEWITT I got there and it was one of those things where you realise the dream you've had for ages, and it was horrible. The *NME* was directionless. They'd have Sting on the cover one week, Yoko Ono the next. I was directionless, because I wasn't hearing a lot of good new music. There was a long time between Grandmaster Flash and the emergence of Def Jam, which made the cover in 1985. I fell for the early Wham! like a dick. They were soulboys doing a bit of rap, and I was into that.

DAVE RIMMER The new pop simply didn't make sense, in terms of the only criteria the music press could muster up to with it. It simply didn't look right in artily-unfocused monochrome snaps. And there were few people still interested in reading tortured analytical prose about the even fewer remaining groups that did.

NEIL SPENCER The solution was to pull it back, cut back on the long stuff and toughen up. "If we do a pop band, we do it in a certain way, look at it as a phenomenon, not from the *Smash Hits* point of view." So we got these people who were good writers with a good attitude and the right focus, hard workers not trying to skank around and pull a fast one. Barney Hoskyns was part of the solution.

BARNEY HOSKYNS Apart from the fact that I had no control over it, hanging out with The Birthday Party and doing heroin was for me a revolt against the prevailing mood of the times, which was anti-rockist. Nick Cave represented to me everything that was great – The Stooges, Captain Beefheart, mad, out of control, eccentric, dangerous American avant gardism. I went to New York with them in the fall of 1981 and was out of control. There was a message on a Southern soul e-group the other day about me from some guy who met me then and said I was drunk and virtually unconscious all the time! There was an element of menace and abandon and chaos and splendour at their gigs. You really didn't know what was going to happen. But the drugs got out of hand, and I ended up living in a flat in Paddington with Cave and a bunch of Australian junkies. It all got messy. I became unreliable and unmanageable. I have no idea what people like [assistant editor] Tony Stewart knew. I certainly didn't go flaunting it. I would sometimes inject in the loo at *NME*, and to anyone who knew I would very clearly have been opiated. I wrote less and less. I did an interview with 23 Skidoo and it took me six weeks to deliver it, so I did what we in the recovery business call a "geographical". That's when you go from A to B and, when you get to B, you will miraculously feel different. I thought that, if I left London, my troubles would cease, so I went to San Francisco and got in touch with a photographer to work with on some stuff for the *NME*. Within two weeks, he was a junkie. We were bang at it. I had a dark year in sunny California. I did do some work for the *NME*, but not nearly as much as I could have done, because I was fucked up.

NEIL SPENCER There were also people like Chris Moore. I just said to him, "Go ahead and write about the SWP march for jobs." It was like George Orwell stuff. Chris may have called himself X Moore, and was always a bit too SWP for comfort, but he was a good writer, a bloody good sub-editor and he worked hard. And there was Mat Snow.

MAT SNOW When my friend Barney Hoskyns started writing for the *NME*, I used to accompany him to gigs. I was the plus one. I was working for an oil company in 1982 and attempting to write a novel and took a week off work to get down to it. The first weekend of that week, I broke my arm while attempting a Michael Jackson dance move at a party, and so, feeling sorry for myself, I went along to see a movie with Barney which he was supposed to review. It was an oi/punk/rockular thing called *Rough Cut And Ready Dubbed*. He said he didn't fancy writing about it, so I was thrilled to, clunking away one fingered at the typewriter.

BARNEY HOSKYNS While I was in California, I got into hardcore punk and the stuff which was later an influence on Messrs Cobain and company. It was good to interview Black Flag and other bands who weren't taken seriously here. There was this snobbery that Californians couldn't make punk music. Black Flag's *Damaged* is one of the greatest punk records ever made, certainly one of the most influential. I was there for a year, and in the summer of 1983 I hit rock bottom and then got into recovery and haven't really looked back since.

MAT SNOW I started doing stuff for the reviews editor, Andy Gill, and gave up work on the novel immediately. After a year, I had to give up my job because I was working around the clock. I'd come home to Brixton, change out of my suit and then bugger off to the Ritzy or the Academy, reviewing three gigs a week. Don Watson was giving up being live reviews editor, so Neil Spencer asked me to take over.

NEIL SPENCER I always tried to employ very talented people, because they can supply the content that you need. If you look what has happened to the people I employed, you'll see that there was validity in that approach. A lot of them have gone on to do very good things. Anton Corbjin, Mat Snow, Barney Hoskyns, Stuart Cosgrove, Dave Dorrell, Danny Kelly, Danny Baker, they've all done very well.

MAT SNOW I liked that nexus of Australian bands – The Go-Betweens, The Birthday Party, who I was introduced to by Barney. This was during a cheerful drug phase on my part, which lasted a year or so. Eventually, I wrote a feature on The Go-Betweens, the first version of which was thrown back in my face by [features editor] Tony Stewart. I had another go and they ran it and I *did* get associated with that movement and hung out with them. Rock music then was extremely fragmented.

NEIL SPENCER My personal life improved and I started to enjoy going out more because music was improving. I would go down the Wag Club to see Slim Gaillard. Jazz became hip. Soul became cred again. It was a much better time.

ROLLING STONE AND INTERVIEW
"REALLY UPTIGHT"

GLENN O'BRIEN I became editor of Andy Warhol's *Interview*, and so I gave myself my start in music journalism. After I left *Interview*, I went to *Rolling Stone* and was quickly cured of that. In 1977, I was invited to come back and be the music writer for *Interview* by Andy, and after a while [publisher] Fred Hughes said, "You know, you don't have to just write about music. You can write about whatever you want."

ANTHONY DECURTIS When he was an editor at *Rolling Stone*, Jim Henke – who is now the chief curator of the Rock 'n' Roll Hall Of Fame – gave me my first national assignment. I was an unemployed English professor in Atlanta in 1980 who had written him a note asking if I could review a B-52s concert. One afternoon, to my amazement, the phone rang and there was Jim. He said, "I have no idea who you are or what your writing is like, but go see the show, and if your piece is good, we'll run it." A little over five years later, he hired me to work at *Rolling Stone*, taught me how to be a news reporter and then turned me loose.

GLENN O'BRIEN The atmosphere at *Rolling Stone* was really uptight. I ran the New York office and the women in San Francisco took all the humour out of my stuff. The guy I replaced, who stayed on to work under me, Stu Werbin, was a great guy. Jann Wenner would ask Stu to go get him a sandwich and Stu would get him one and spit in it.

PAUL NELSON I left because Jann was setting rules I did not agree with. The reviews had to be short. I could never write anything short in my life. I told him he was asking us to write sonnets. He wanted 22 lines. That's, like, four sentences. Writers don't want to count words. I did not want to do it any more. During my last years at *Rolling Stone*, I was losing interest in the music.

GLENN O'BRIEN I edited *Interview* because Bob Colacello decided he'd rather spend more time with Andy Warhol and sell art. I only worked as an out-of-the-office editor after 1978. They tried to make me editor of *Spin*, but they couldn't afford it. But I had the best of times – drinking Bloody Marys with Lou Reed very early in the day. Meeting David Johansen and Johnny Thunders at Max's Kansas City. David Bowie coming up to the Factory to meet Andy and being the only person who'd ever heard of him. Meeting Iggy and getting to know him. Hanging out with Alice Cooper and becoming best friends. Getting almost trampled by teenage girls with Alice in Brooklyn after a day of fishing. Lou coming over after the bars closed or calling at an odd hour or visiting him. Drinking champagne with Alice and Marc Bolan. Meeting The Wailers. Smoking pot with Curtis Mayfield. Dating Grace Jones. Interviewing Ted Nugent. Interviewing a really, really sleepy Ronnie Spector. Making friends with Chris Stein and Debbie Harry. Teaching Robert Fripp how to dress. Making friends with Anya Phillips and James Chance. Getting high with George Clinton. Hanging out with Grandmaster Flash at the Police Athletic League in the South Bronx. The Go-Gos being afraid of me because they thought I was a junkie. Sitting with Anita Pallenberg and Marianne Faithfull when they made up. Meeting Tom Waits. Opening for Buster Poindexter as a comedian for a few years. This and that about Madonna.

8 "We Were Phoning It In, Sometimes"

"In those days, writers from the pop papers didn't write for the proper papers, mainly because no one ever asked them to."
   - Julie Burchill

IRA ROBBINS New wave had become new romantic. The class of 1977 was either dead or digging itself into a rut of decreasing quality and originality. The pop stars we could stomach – Adam Ant, The Go-Gos, Culture Club, Cyndi Lauper, Madness, Squeeze, The Stray Cats – were just that, pop stars, which made them less emotionally rewarding to champion. U2, REM, Blondie and others were numerically significant and good, but there weren't enough of them for a monthly. So, yes, in a sense we were phoning it in, sometimes, and that hypocrisy really made us lose enthusiasm for the whole enterprise. Meanwhile, we were somewhat removed from the indie rock stuff that was exciting. The Dead Kennedys, The Neighborhoods, X and Pere Ubu were cool by us, but Black Flag was really not appealing to me musically in 1982. They sounded like the era we'd just come out of, minus the insight and credibility. OK, so I was wrong about that, too.

GINA ARNOLD Being the only woman rock critic in the '80s was a total advantage. First of all, it got me lots of attention, and there were a few wonderful people who actually were concerned about the subject at the time, like Bill Flanagan at *Musician* and my editor at *The San Jose Mercury* and even at *The LA Times*, who were determined to hire women. I know for a fact that Jon Pareles at *The New York Times* hired Ann Powers and Danyel Smith because he wanted to equalise the gender situation. But these days, I don't think it's a topic anyone pays attention to. If anything, things are more sexist now, not less so.

CHARLES M YOUNG For a few years there, *Musician* was the best music magazine in the world, and that was Vic Garbarini's doing. There were a lot of talented writers in that mag, writers who really cared about music, and the artists responded. Mark Rowland, Rafi Zabor, JD Considine and Chip Stern come to mind. I thought Bill Flanagan [Vic's successor] was a sharp reporter and editor whose taste got a little narrow by the late '80s. He and Mark are doing important work at VH-1, now.

THE NATIONALS COME KNOCKING
"NO WONDER THEY ALL HATE ME"

NEIL SPENCER When you think about it, Fleet Street discovered pop pretty late on. It had been in the broadsheets because it had lingered on from Swinging London and they liked good picture stories, but when *The Sun* got hold of it, with people like John Blake, that's when it really took off, and it's been out there ever since.

RICHARD WILLIAMS After I resigned from *Melody Maker*, I went freelance, and then a few months later Harry Evans took over at *The Times*. He wanted to do a weekly listings guide, which I worked on. Gradually, it took over the weekend section, and then I became features editor. I stopped reading *Melody Maker* pretty soon after, because it wasn't exactly painful but I found it uncomfortable to read. I could see what had happened – they were retrenching, and they'd gone in the opposite direction to my redesign, and that made me feel a bit weird.

JULIE BURCHILL In the '80s, I was criticised a great deal by my erstwhile colleagues for "selling out", a charge I found ironic on two counts: one, that the *NME* was owned by Reed International, which had considerable holdings in apartheid-ruled South Africa; and two, that the very people most enthusiastic and energetic about levelling this accusation at me have since then been breaking all known rimjob records trying to get into fascist, racist, imperialist Fleet Street as was. They must be pushing 50 now, and most of them are still not trusted to write about anything but pop. Neil Spencer, hysterically, is the proud author of a weekly horoscope column. No wonder they hate me.

LUCY O'BRIEN In 1987, I contributed an essay on pop music to a book of women writing about various aspects of culture in Britain. Julie reviewed it in *Time Out* and said, "Lucy O'Brien has done her usual impersonation of moi." I felt quite flattered. Much later on, I met her at a do for Elizabeth Wurtzel, who wrote *Prozac Nation*, and Julie said to me, "I like your writing." I said, "I really like yours." And she said, "Yes. It shows."

JON SAVAGE *The Face* had become the big thing in '80s publishing, and suddenly this alchemical process started whereby the people who wrote for *The Face*, who had come out of the music press, started to get taken up by Fleet Street. I worked at *New Society* for Tony Gould and later had a very good editor called Malcolm Imrie.

JOHN PEEL I was *The Observer*'s man in pop for about four or five years. Then they got a new editor, and she was the first person to edit a section of a proper newspaper, and she felt that rock had to be written about seriously and treated as though it was an A-level subject. I'd write about it semi-seriously, in a kind of piss-take way. I mean, any opportunity to have a dig at Eric Clapton...

TONY PARSONS I moved back to London in 1985, after Julie and I split up, and I look back at the stuff I wrote for *Arena*, and it's good, you know? In fact, I wonder whether I can write anything as good now. At the same time, I was also learning my craft at *The Sunday Times*, so things started to improve.

JOHN PEEL I've had death threats from Cliff Richard fans. I went to see him in Hammersmith for *The Observer* and I wrote something in *The Observer* like, "I was one of the very few males there, and one of the very few people who wasn't wearing tracksuit bottoms." I also said that one thing that became very quickly evident is that, much as his fans loved him, there was nobody there who loved Cliff more than Cliff himself.

JON SAVAGE Simon Frith had moved to *The Observer* from the rock critic job at *The Sunday Times* over the Wapping dispute. Incidentally, the person who took the job, and still works there, was Robert Sandall, who is therefore a scab. Anyway, in 1986, Simon got me in to do record reviews at *The Observer*, and then, a couple of years later, I became freelance commissioning editor for their music page.

JOHN PEEL In my defence, at *The Observer* I would deliberately seek out things that I kind of hoped would be crap, like Shirley Bassey at the Albert Hall. I suspect I was the only non-gay male there, but the devotion and dedication of her audience was very moving, despite the fact that they could clearly see no wrong in her at all. I did this thing at the Festival Hall called Meltdown and it coincided with a performance of hers, and she had it in her contract that she was the only person who could use the lift, which made it rather difficult for the rest of us. But you can appreciate that kind of stupidity, and I love hearing stories of the excesses of the stars and their insane demands.

JON SAVAGE I stopped working for *The Face* in 1988, after they printed a 100th issue which included an article saying how wonderful Mrs Thatcher was, and I just resigned.

BARNEY HOSKYNS I was a contributor at *Vogue* for about five years. It's a point that's been made that pop coverage is ubiquitous and you can source it everywhere.

JOHN PEEL I consider myself to be the last of the gentleman critics, because a gentleman doesn't claim expenses. I remember going to review Europe, back when they were playing in Birmingham, and I took my son along, because he was very keen on a record of theirs. We stayed in a hotel in Birmingham, and when I got home I realised that it had actually cost me money. I asked somebody who was a practising journalist how much he thought I got paid and he named a sum six times what I was actually getting. It was at that point that I realised they were taking the piss. The relationship with *The Observer* kind of petered out...

THE DOLDRUMS
"POP MUSIC HAD LOST THE ABILITY TO SURPRISE"

BARNEY HOSKYNS I came back to the UK in 1983 and Tony Stewart offered me a staff job at the *NME*. It was the dawn of the *Smash Hits* era, which by 1984 had turned into another British Invasion – Culture Club, Eurythmics, Duran Duran, all that stuff. I loved the slightly more ambiguous acts, like Soft Cell. The *NME* was accepting these artists, and pop was celebrated between 1983-85, ironically and sincerely. In addition, black music was very big.

PETE SILVERTON By the mid '80s, pop music had lost the ability to surprise, and there didn't seem to be the writers around with a passion for it. The world had changed. Everything became more ordered. Live gigs weren't important events any more. In pop, there was nothing unplanned or exciting, and the *NME* became unreadable.

BARNEY HOSKYNS There were some good writers. Richard Cook is one of the best I have ever read on music. He was writing about jazz but also extremely well about rock and pop. He was an outstanding writer, but because he wasn't an egomaniac or a druggie but grown up and self-effacing, he has never received the dues he should have. Chris Bohn I really respected, although he was very aloof about a lot of music I liked. At least intellectually he was interesting, unlike some people I could mention. Then there were the Adrian Thrills and Paolo Hewitts. Black music was big, from African music, King Sunny Ade and Soca to the early hip-hop to soul. If you think about it, Bobby Womack was on the cover, then.

PAOLO HEWITT I floated around there for about 18 months and then I did Run DMC and started to gather speed. By now, I was convinced that hip-hop was *the* music.

BARNEY HOSKYNS There was a shift in 1984, and we put together four specials on The War On Pop, which Chris [Bohn] and I had thought up. One was about the media, another about soul music, maybe another about politics. I wrote this rant which was anti-*Smash Hits*, anti-dumbed-down teen pop. This was a reaction to a piece Steve Taylor had written in *The Virgin Yearbook* called "The Death Of The Swiftian Function", a rather high-falutin' title for a piece which basically said that, now *Smash Hits* was presenting information efficiently for teen punters, the would-be intellectual, po-faced and serious attitude of the *NME* was irrelevant. I was incensed.

LUCY O'BRIEN One of the most difficult assignments was covering The Pogues while they made that spaghetti Western with Alex Cox in Spain, *Straight To Hell*. They were pissed all the time, and it was difficult to get anything from them. There was Joe Strummer there, Elvis Costello, a really young Courtney Love. I was quite green, but my tactic – which has since proved the best one – was to just hang around with my notebook and chat to people in a light way. When they realise you're not going to come in and grill them, they come to you after a couple of days, and gradually they did. Courtney came over at one point and said, "I've been watching you and decided that you're cool," so then we just hung out together. Then I got lucky, because I was going home, walking past this café, and Shane MacGowan was there having his morning coffee. For once, maybe the first time in his life, he seemed fairly sober, and we actually had an intelligent conversation. I thought, "My God, underneath all that, you're an intelligent, sensitive, literate person."

BARNEY HOSKYNS By the time *NME* moved to Commonwealth House in Holborn, in 1985, there were real factions there which I was on the outside of. I was starting to work on my Southern soul book and bunking off a bit. Neil Spencer called me in and said, "Look, you've got to make up your mind. Are you on staff or not?" So I made up my mind to leave, with no advance. Fuck all. I just wanted to write A Book. It was a very lean year, but I just loved James Carr.

PAUL DU NOYER I left to launch a magazine called *The Hit* for IPC, who pulled the plug on it after nine weeks. It was the brainchild of the *NME*'s deputy editor, Phil McNeill, who had started a pop weekly called *Number One*. His view was that music was no longer central to youth culture, which embraced a wider spread of media – sport, fashion, film, TV. It was a good idea, ahead of its time. It was a lads' magazine before they started, with people like Paul Weller, Depeche Mode, stars of *EastEnders* and the footballer John Barnes on the cover. It wasn't what we'd call laddish now, but it did attempt to cater for the casuals on the football terraces. The targets were very unrealistic, and it was probably selling 30,000 when it needed to sell 150,000. They spent a lot on the launch with cinema ads, but the executive who sponsored it, Jane Reed, left to join Eddie Shah when he launched *Today* newspaper and it was abandoned. The day it closed, I got a call from Mark Ellen to work on the launch of *Q*.

NEIL SPENCER I handed my notice in at the *NME* on the first working day of

1985. I'd had enough. I think I'd restored the paper's good health by that time. There was a new management team at IPC who were sympatico. I finally got a full-time designer on the paper, Joe Ewart, who was very funny and lifted my spirits. Stuart Cosgrove was writing more for us. It was a much happier time. Circulation was on the way up – it had gone down to 180,000 and I got it back to 200,000 by the time I left. I tried really hard to get women writers, and when I left I found out what had been going on – as fast as I'd been recruiting them, certain people on the paper had been getting rid of them, alienating them with chauvinist wind-ups. Vivien I gave work to. Mary Harron. Cynthia Rose we employed, but people didn't like her. Cath Carroll wasn't liked because she was gay. Amanda Root was another one. Lyn Hanna – she didn't last long. Jane Suck. Jaswinder Bancil. There was also Lucy O'Brien, who was really good and writes excellent books now.

LUCY O'BRIEN I always wanted to interview Public Enemy. I put myself forward for it, but it wasn't considered. I think Stuart ended up interviewing them, actually. Then, it was really difficult for female writers to interview big male acts like them, or even Lou Reed or Iggy Pop. It was assumed that they would eat you for breakfast. Actually, as a woman, you can get a lot out of a male artist that a male writer wouldn't otherwise get.

PAOLO HEWITT Let me tell you a funny story, right? Chris Bohn discovered Einstürzende Neubauten fucking drilling the stage of the ICA. He came in raving about them, so they said, "Do the cover story." So he came in on the Wednesday and Tony Stewart asked him where the copy was. He said he couldn't write it because there were some workmen down the road from his flat digging up the road. I said, "You should have gone and interviewed them."

MAT SNOW In 1985, I reviewed a single by Einstürzende Neubauten, whose members included Blixa Bargeld, who was also in The Bad Seeds. I knew Blixa and Nick Cave, who had lived at my flat once for a few weeks, and Blixa had moved in, too, so we were all great chums. I mentioned in my review that the track was more exciting than pretty much anything on the new Nick Cave album. It was a way of me saying to the *NME* readership, "Hey, I've heard this hot new album," just boasting. About a year later, I was interviewing Nick Cave, and he was really weird and cold. I asked him what was up and he said, "To be perfectly honest, I hate you. I was upset by that disloyal thing you wrote. I fact, I've written a song about you called 'Scum'." Sure enough, he had. It's the extra track on the CD of *Your Funeral, My Trial*. It's great, the best thing he ever did, the most virulent, hate-filled record about me and another journalist who had crossed his path, Antonella Black. It's my undying claim to fame in the world of goth.

ALLAN JONES At the *Melody Maker*, we eventually got rid of Ian Pye and he became the editor of *NME*, which was a stroke of luck we couldn't believe!

PAOLO HEWITT It was a ridiculous decision. There was an editor who was very malleable and Stuart Cosgrove, who could talk the fucking collar off your shirt. He's really into his Northern soul. Lucy O'Brien comes along and all the old guard leave, Chris Bohn and Barney Hoskyns.

BARNEY HOSKYNS This whole thing about Cappuccino and Paul Weller and Soho, it was so fucking po-faced. These people took themselves so seriously. I just loathe the man. I think he's very talented and written some good songs, but I can't stand him.

PAOLO HEWITT They used to take the piss out of me a lot. There was a bit of antagonism. They saw me as the lightweight soulboy while they championed The Birthday Party. I read a piece in *Mojo* recently where Barney was saying, "Soho soulboys were all laughing at their lyrics." We weren't laughing at their lyrics. We weren't even listening to them.

CHARLES SHAAR MURRAY During the '80s, I wasn't quite sure whether I was more embarrassed to be there or they were more embarrassed that I was still around.

STUART COSGROVE
"A VERY INFLUENTIAL FORCE"

CHARLES SHAAR MURRAY Stuart Cosgrove was carving out a bigger and bigger empire to the point where Stuart's pages didn't even look like they were part of the same publication. Stuart knew what he was doing, essentially showcasing himself as much as possible as a way to getting a better gig. And, of course, he's had a succession of them.

LUCY O'BRIEN I liked the way Stuart wrote about black music in a really intelligent way. As the media editor, he was a very influential force on the paper when Ian Pye had trouble making his mind up. He was a great one for listening to both sides before deciding, which used to infuriate everyone: "Come on, make a decision. What do you *really* think?"

PAOLO HEWITT What would happen is that we'd sit down at the editorial meeting and Ian Pye would say, "Next week, we have Billy Bragg on the cover of the *NME*." Within half an hour, we'd have Schooly D. That's how good Cosgrove was.

BARNEY HOSKYNS By the time I came back, in the autumn of 1986, I felt I'd been frozen out. Ian Pye was the editor and a lot of people had gone, including Chris Bohn. Stuart Cosgrove had staked out his corner. He was a very charismatic and intimidating presence. We shared a love of Southern soul, but I think he regarded me as a public schoolboy who had no right to write about popular culture. He was a feisty Scottish socialist, and that was what their little gang was all about, soul and socialism.

LUCY O'BRIEN Myself and Paolo often agreed with Stuart, because we were into what he was into. Our attitude was fairly anarchic, and that used to rub people up the wrong way.

PAOLO HEWITT There were the intellectuals – Don Watson, William Leith, Mat Snow – the public schoolboys trying to write like Martin Amis, because he was the big author at the time, and there was Cosgrove, me, Lucy O'Brien and Sean O'Hagan. Then the indie-schmindie merchants – Steve Lamacq, who was the news editor; Danny Kelly; and the Legend – every week we'd end up having an argument down the pub. I once didn't talk to Danny Kelly for two weeks because he wouldn't put this singer, Paul Johnson, on the cover.

CHRIS SALEWICZ At the *NME*, there were parameters that one didn't necessarily understand and seemed to be becoming increasingly constrictive, so for me it was time to go. When people take themselves so seriously, it always goes wrong, and the *NME* seemed to be taking itself awfully seriously.

LUCY O'BRIEN The Youth Suicide cover story I did really stands out in my mind, because it was a really challenging story to write. What I loved about it was that it wasn't just about the music; there were cultural references as well.

CHARLES SHAAR MURRAY I remember I was being steered away from reviewing albums by artists anybody had ever heard of. Instead, it would be, "Here's a box set of an old blues singer," all because I couldn't be arsed to hang around at the office all day sitting on Adrian Thrills' desk to get first grab at new albums. Somebody suggested I should do the new Stones album, and Adrian said, "Well, what's your attitude to this record?" I said, "I dunno, Adrian. I haven't listened to it yet."

MAT SNOW You'll talk to people who characterise 1986 at the *NME* as some kind of hip-hop jihad. That was really Stuart Cosgrove. His mission was that the most exciting music coming through was hip-hop and house and that the *NME* should align itself with that and cut down on rock coverage. My view was that you could have everything, because the people who paid our bills were the New Order and The Fall fans. Whatever he thought of the music and the overcoat brigade, they were the ones buying the paper week in, week out.

PAOLO HEWITT There were independent soul singles coming through and new hip-hop. It seemed to me that this could be the thing for all those people who'd missed punk. It was street music and didn't have anything to do with bags of make-up. With Cosgrove as our leader, we went for it, and we also reacted against the rampant Thatcherism. Miners were losing their jobs and families were being thrown on the scrapheap. For me, that was the most interesting period of the *NME*, when we went for soul, black music and politics. Red Wedge was an element of it.

BARNEY HOSKYNS There was an identity crisis at *NME*. I felt very much on the outside, but by late '86/87 I'd go and do subbing to make a living. I'd sit there in a room with David Swift and Len Brown, who were very nice. At least it meant that I didn't have to be in the other room with people who weren't very nice. I sat in on some editorial meetings and felt alienated by this new guard. Cosgrove was really running the show. I didn't despise Ian

Pye – he's a nice man – but it was very clear that Ian couldn't handle Stuart, and there was a sense of some kind of coup in the making.

PAOLO HEWITT We took over. Danny Kelly and the Legend and all those indie writers were going on about Creation Records, and we just went, "Fuck you. It's Run DMC for us." Look at the paper now and it's completely schizophrenic. If there is a criticism, maybe it's that we shoved it down the throats of the readership. Instead of having Schooly D, Run DMC and Sly And Robbie in one issue, we should have staggered them. Our argument was that rock was dead, so how many more times could you put The Fall on the cover? So we got hate mail from students about slagging Morrissey and The Smiths.

MAT SNOW I quit in April 1987 as the culmination of a long-standing row with Ian Pye. He was, in my view, an extremely weak editor, and effectively his policy was governed by a couple of strong voices, chief of which was Stuart Cosgrove, who I liked and respected. He had a view about what the magazine should be doing.

BARNEY HOSKYNS Stuart was not shy. Very vocal, very bright and ambitious, as his subsequent career has shown. It was just a stepping stone for him. It was obvious he should be in television or on Fleet Street. Fair dos.

MAT SNOW The art editor, Joe Ewart, didn't have any particular music policy but had views on the design which I didn't particular care for. He and I fell out over his treatment of my friend, the photographer Bleddyn Butcher, who he treated in a most dishonest, cavalier and cruel way. He stopped commissioning him but hung him out to dry by persuading him not to go and work for the *Melody Maker*. All of this led to my departure. Ian Pye put Red Wedge on the cover and took a pro-Labour viewpoint but at the same time countenanced this treatment of a freelance contributor, which was extremely dishonest and exploitative.

PAOLO HEWITT There was this disinformation from up above that, if you put a black person on the cover of the *NME*, sales went down. But there was a change in the management view of the *NME*, especially after we put Neil Kinnock on the cover in 1987, the year of the election. IPC came down on us like a ton of bricks. They basically got rid of Ian Pye. He was sent packing after the election.

CHARLES SHAAR MURRAY The *NME* degenerated into a bunch of backbiters, careerists and incompetents. I was delighted to be gone. After I left the *NME*, I continued to read it just to see if my name was still in the contributors list. One week it wasn't, so I stopped buying it.

PAOLO HEWITT Within three months, they brought Alan Lewis in from *Sounds*, the man responsible for the tabloidisation of the music press. Cosgrove was kicked out when we tried to run an issue on censorship but the printers refused to print the cover, which featured the Sonic Youth record sleeve with 21 dicks on it. They used that to get rid of Cosgrove.

LUCY O'BRIEN There was a fight for the identity of the *NME*, and what happened was that IPC grabbed the *NME* back from the writers, who had developed unprecedented power. So the way to do it was to sack the ringleaders, including Stuart [Cosgrove] and Joe [Ewart]. I was freelance, so I couldn't be sacked, but there was a combination of me not wanting to work there any more and I wrote a few pieces which didn't get in, so I left, along with a lot of others who buggered off. The *NME* did change after that into "here's the band, here's the music".

PAOLO HEWITT How do you make the *NME* a tabloid? You say to your staff, "You shall mention Morrissey every week." And that's what Alan Lewis did. He brought James Brown in, all those people.

BARNEY HOSKYNS There was this sense of crisis, and then the Danny Kelly era came in. The next thing I knew, Danny was the editor. The big transition was the *C86* tape. Then the *NME* was saying, "Enough with pop and enough with Bobby Womack on the cover. We need to get back to what the *NME* was when it flew the flag for the early punk bands: an indie aesthetic, championing pale white boys and girls with cheap guitars." Then the whole indie thing came back in with *C86*.

PAOLO HEWITT I always felt that everyone else on the music press felt they'd missed punk and were pissed off about it and trying to get it going again.

That's what the *NME*'s *C86* was about: "We missed out in '77, so let's go now." But it was absolute shit, awful music.

BARNEY HOSKYNS Christ, what a load of junk that was! Primal Scream is the only band from that tape to go on to do anything, and their success has nothing to do with what they were doing then. The fucking Shop Assistants! It was pretty desperate, but the *NME* did dig itself out of that factionalism and, I believe, became more successful. But I was out of there, writing books and for the nationals by that time.

ALLAN JONES After the unfortunate episode with Ian Pye, the *NME* really hit a good streak, putting on circulation through the late '80s with Alan Lewis as editor. He really turned it around and was then instrumental in launching *Vox* with Roy Carr before moving onto a publishing role at IPC and launching *Loaded* in the '90s.

PAOLO HEWITT By April 1988, all my allies had left the *NME*, but of course, being the hip little fucker I am, I went into the office one day and said, "There's this scene developing down a club called Shoom and it's all going off in Ibiza. We should cover it." So I endured a week of jeers about going off on my holidays and then wrote the first piece about acid house. London Records had a group called Beats Working, which Nicky Holloway was in, so I used that as my vehicle. They just thought it was more of Paolo's disco music and wanted to put The Motorcycle Boy or Swervedriver on the cover, so I thought, "Fuck 'em," and just went and enjoyed myself. August comes and it was all over *The Sun*. Front page. Lewis was, like, "What's this?" So I told them, "This is what you've been taking the piss out of for the last six months and it's been right under your nose." Alan Lewis really hated me from then on.

MELODY MAKER
"LIKE A PLANE TAKEN OVER BY TERRORISTS, NONE OF WHOM COULD FLY"

ALLAN JONES Even though we had a good team at *Melody Maker*, there was no sense of direction. They introduced colour on the cover, but the printing was so bad it looked a mess. I was assistant editor to Mike Oldfield and we'd get taken out by young publishers who were given us as a project. One week we were meant to be *Sounds*, the next *Smash Hits*. It veered all over the place, like a plane that had been taken over by terrorists, none of who could fly. It was ghastly. Paolo Hewitt summed it all up after a really long meeting with Mike about who was to be on the cover by saying, "It's like being with Hitler in the Führerbunker in the last days." Mike had lost his bearings completely. Although I got on with him personally, on a professional level it was unsustainable. In late '83, he went on holiday and left me in charge, telling me I had to get at least another Wham! cover, if not a Durannies one as well. I thought, "Over my dead fucking body." Ian Pye was a big fan of The Smiths, and we decided to put them on the cover. Oldfield came back and blew a gasket, saying it would be our worst-selling cover of all time. In fact, it was our best for about two years. So that suggested there was something happening in the margins, not in the charts.

PETER BUCK (REM) Some of the English things were odd. Around 1983, we just came out of nowhere and we got really amazing reviews. Nobody should get reviews like that. One magazine reviewed our album twice because the first guy didn't say it was the best album ever made. The editor went back and said, "I just want people to know how good this really is." And the first guy had given it the highest rating you could get, but that was not quite good enough. I appreciate that, because they were really on a mission to find new things to be excited about, but I had read these magazines, and I always tended to think that the people in them were to some degree not special but somehow validated. This must mean they're famous and big.

ALLAN JONES Everyone breathed a huge sigh of relief when Mike left at the beginning of 1984. I took over as editor and my first tasks were to get rid of several of the people Mike had employed – Helen Fitzgerald, Ian Pye. I wanted to get new people in. We had a brilliant designer in Andy Cowes, who later went on to design *Q*, and he stayed on for the first six months of my editorship and *Melody Maker* never looked as good, in my view. Adam Sweeting was features editor, Colin Irwin was assistant editor and for ages I'd been trying to get Steve Sutherland on staff and I was able to do so by making him reviews editor. And there were new people coming through to write about not just The Smiths but The Cure as well. American music had been in the doldrums with REO Speedwagon and Toto, but David Fricke – who was our American correspondent, who had just started writing for *Rolling Stone* – sent me a tape of this new band whose album wasn't coming out in Britain for six months. It was *Murmur* by REM, which I thought was brilliant. So we ran David's review, and when it came out in the UK I reviewed it again and we put them on the cover straight away.

PETER BUCK Someone sent me the Allan Jones review of *Murmur* in *Melody Maker*, which was really good, but I was driving a van with no air conditioning to be sixth on the bill to The Police in Philadelphia. It was 110 degrees and we were also doing a gig that night somewhere else. I was, like, "God, this doesn't validate us, because we're still poor and starving." I remember we played Philadelphia. It was 110 degrees and there were 90,000 people there. We went on, I think it was one in the afternoon, and it was so hot I threw up afterwards. And then someone gave me the Allan Jones review, and I'm reading it in the van on the way to the next gig and I was, like, "Man, I wish I had an ice-cold beer right now." In a way, it's kind of distancing. Immediately, I thought, "Well, this isn't like the stuff I read when I was a kid," because once you're in that position, unless you're a really shallow person, when you see yourself on the cover of a magazine, you don't feel validated.

ALLAN JONES They came over here in 1985. I think they were recording, so we did a series called State Of The Union about all the new American groups – Los Lobos, The Blasters, The Beat Farmers, Hüsker Dü. It suddenly gave the paper a focus, because nobody else was writing about them. We always figured that, if people wanted to write about music, they'd go to *NME*, which was perceived as the hipper environment, which is what we wanted to be. So I asked Steve to look out for people, and he was shit hot at it. He brought the Stud Brothers on board, looking like they'd just come from two years in the Vietnam jungle, the remnants of a commando crew. I'd never seen anything like them, and they lived up to the name. They were very crude, in terms of the writing, but had great ideas. Very quickly after that, Simon Reynolds joined, then David Stubbs.

From *Sounds*, we got Chris Roberts and Jon Wilde and a whole lot of other people. Sales stabilised at around 80,000 and started to go up, even though for the first six months we didn't get much more advertising. The paper's reputation got better, and through to the late '80s we carved out a niche for ourselves. We had an unspoken relationship with *NME*. What would happen is that I'd see The Stone Roses and say, "Let's put them on the cover tomorrow." They'd be a big hit and we'd have the kudos of doing them first. As their popularity grew, their publicists and managers would move on to the larger circulation that the *NME* could give them, which was fine by us, because by that time we'd found Happy Mondays or Suede or Blur. We were always looking for something new.

By 1989, the *NME* had started to pull away from us relentlessly, but we were covering groups nobody else was paying attention to – The Butthole Surfers, Front 242, Thin White Rope, Skinny Puppy. We also had stalwarts we could fall back on, like The Mission or The Cure, who used to sell a lot for us.

SOUNDS
"SHAPE UP OR SHIP OUT"

SYLVIE SIMMONS I returned to the UK to work at *Sounds* after being their LA correspondent and left pretty quickly because it was a pretty dysfunctional atmosphere. Eric Fuller was editor. I freelanced for about a year and then told them where to stuff it. They were being very sarcastic about the metal stuff. They decided I was the metal writer but at the same time didn't want me to write about it. Around that time, I was sent to write a small piece about Kirsty MacColl, who was pregnant at the time and very jolly, not her usual sardonic self, so the piece was a bit cheery, and Eric took me aside and said he was disappointed because it should have been more scathing. So I told him to roll up his magazine and shove it.

MAT SNOW After 1987, I worked for *Sounds* under Tony Stewart, with whom I had formed a good if sometimes fraught relationship at *NME*. *Sounds* was trying to build on its reputation from the '70s as being the scuzzy, streetwise, aggressive, no-bullshit music title.

DAVID CAVANAGH I wrote a review of The Fortunate Sons at the Bull and Gate and sent it in to *Sounds*. I'd heard that was the way you broke into journalism – you wrote a review, they didn't run it, but they might call back. And that's what happened – they wrote back and said they wanted me to review gigs in London. So I called up the reviews editor, Robin Millar, repeatedly, and I couldn't get hold of him. For four weeks. He would never pick up the phone. But then she took a week's holiday and Shaun Phillips - who was the junior member of the team - rang and said he'd found my letter and got me to review gigs over a year and a half in Harlesden and other places no one else wanted to visit.

MAT SNOW *Sounds* got on board grunge and the other dress-down genres. It was keen on hip-hop as well. It actually had some pretty intellectual writers - Richard Cook had moved there after getting fed up at the *NME* - but its tone was not that.

DAVID CAVANAGH At that age, I was a curious mixture of in-depth knowledge and absolute ignorance of music. For my first two or three years on *Sounds*, I was absolutely bluffing it. Shaun Phillips told me that Tony Stewart sat down and read the magazine and was mortified at how bad it was, so he drew up a list of stringers and freelancers and put it into three groups - those who were definitely staying, those who had to shape up or ship out and group C - bye, see you later - and I was group C. But that week, there was a great gig by Robert Lloyd, ex of The Nightingales, and it was a godsend to anybody who had no experience of writing about new music. Shaun Phillips was there, saw my review and said that it was a fair reflection of what happened, so I stayed. Robert Lloyd gave me a career in music journalism.

TROUSER PRESS AND CREEM
"MUSIC MEDIA HAD CHANGED"

JOHN MENDELSSOHN I did my best writing about rock for *Creem* in the mid '80s, especially after realising that my editors would allow me to do just about anything I wanted. What I wanted mostly was to shame groups like Mötley Crüe, which I regard - along with Kiss - as the worst in the history of music, on the face of the planet. *Creem* had far fewer and less attentive readers, though, and in that sense writing for it was far less satisfying. I'd very much enjoyed being famous, you see.

SYLVIE SIMMONS All the time I was working for *Sounds*, I worked for a lot of magazines in Europe as well as *Creem*, where my editor was Dave DiMartino. It was a wonderful vibe there. That was a family I did want to join. If it hadn't been based in a cold place where it rains a lot, I would have done, though they saw sense and eventually moved to LA.

IRA ROBBINS Finance was only one of the factors that contributed to my decision to end *Trouser Press* in 1984. The music world had changed, music media had changed, the lives of the staff had changed, our audience had changed, all of which conspired to make the original thrill of having a credible forum to do with as we saw fit feel more like a Sisyphean duty to fill up a bunch of damnably empty pages every month.

SYLVIE SIMMONS The downside of *Creem* was the non-existent payments. They would backlog your cheques and go bankrupt frequently. There was this general mismanagement. Nobody cared. And I didn't care, either, because I loved writing for them. In the beginning, I wrote all manner of stuff, talking to Joni Mitchell one day and being sent to Arizona with The J Geils Band.

JOHN MENDELSSOHN There were several wonderful writers, but I always wished that *Creem*'s art direction had been very much better. I've always believed that, for an act to be ultra-deluxe, it need not only sound terrific but look terrific too, as Elvis and The Beatles and the early Who all did. *Creem* always looked woefully amateurish.

SYLVIE SIMMONS At one point, *Creem* set up a spin-off called *Creem Metal* when this new owner came in. I wrote a column from London for that. The owner promised to pay, which he did for a while, until he went bankrupt.

Q
"WE WANTED TO WRITE FOR IT AND WE WANTED TO READ IT"

DAVID HEPWORTH At Emap, we'd launched *Just 17* and then *Looks*, which was a slightly older girls' fashion and beauty magazine. We were looking around at various things and Mark Ellen had finished his time at *Smash Hits*, and that's how Q came along. The self-indulgent explanation for Q: we wanted to write for it and we wanted to read it. The proper publishing reason for *Q*: there is an older demographic who are still interested in music, but they are not going to read inky weeklies any more.

CHRIS SALEWICZ I thought Mark Ellen was good and obviously talented, but basically Mark wasn't perceived as being groovy enough, and I think he knew that. I also think there's a certain motivating factor there in wanting to start *Q*, to say, "Fuck you."

BARNEY HOSKYNS The subtext of *Q* was not only to be anti-Morley/Penman but also anti-people like me or those from the Lester Bangs school. There was no allowing a writer to just...go. There was no room to write about music in a passionate, irreverent, subversive, committed way.

MAT SNOW Working at *Q*, I got to learn at the knee of Mark Ellen, who is by a long distance the best editor I ever had. He is interested in journalistic standards and he saw no reason why we should be exempt from them because we wrote about rock music. He was interested in tone, balance and entertainment. He was not interested in first-person polemic, unlike the *NME*. His vision of *Q* was very clear. He banned what he called "the perpendicular pronoun".

TOM HIBBERT When Mark left *Smash Hits* to start *Q*, I became deputy editor and was getting increasingly fed up with having to talk to press officers about Howard Jones every day. Then Mark rang up and said, "Do you want to do some interviews for us?" I said, "Sure."

DAVID HEPWORTH CD was just coming. That's why the first issue had a giveaway booklet on the best 100 records on CD. Dire Straits certainly pushed it over the hill, because everybody used to get their CDs demonstrated by hearing 'Money For Nothing', but launching magazines is never quite that calculated, is it? You do it partly because you're just interested in it and you fancy doing it yourself and partly because you can see a strong business case for it. I have to say that the business case for *Q* was not as robust as it subsequently turned out to be. The feeling from the advertising department was, "You won't sell ads in a monthly," which proved to be completely wrong. Record companies loved it.

TOM HIBBERT We had several long lunches and worked out what it was going to be. It was always going to be irreverent, but I don't think Mark knew how far it was going to go. When I was writing, I got very cross with people, so I changed the interview style to be more demonstrative.

CHARLES SHAAR MURRAY What turned it around for me was the arrival of *Q*. It eventually became a really ugly magazine, but when it started there was a lot of quirky stuff in there. My first major job wasn't music but a piece on contemporary British horror writing.

BARNEY HOSKYNS I remember Chris Bohn calling *Q* "the rock critic's graveyard". Don't know what the fuck that makes *Mojo*! Obviously, it's very different now from the Ellen/Hepworth baby, but I didn't want to be a part of it then. While it did its job very well I found it rather smarmy. It took away the danger, glamour and mystery of music for me, because its tone was always not to take anything seriously.

MAT SNOW *Q*, with *Smash Hits* and *The Face* before it, broke the stranglehold of the three-party music press. Obviously, they were all staffed by refugees from *Sounds*, *Melody Maker* and *NME*. That they got the best writers from those papers shows how out of touch they were.

DAVID HEPWORTH It was going to be called *Red*. We said, "It can't be called *Music Review*. It's got to be something with a bit of mystique to it." We also deliberately put several images on the cover, because we wanted to give an idea of the range. We also didn't like the idea of just Bryan Ferry being on the cover, because if you didn't like Bryan Ferry you might not buy it, so we thought we'd do a cover that was slightly more like a contents page, someone zany over here, someone a bit wacky over there. You could put over your attitude more, which was very successful for a long, long time.

CHRIS SALEWICZ *Q* was interesting because it was quite clear that there was a market for it, no question. I think it says something about my interests that the first issue has the big McCartney interview, and I had Strummer and Jones next to each other because they were in the studio together. I didn't see any contradiction. That wouldn't have been allowed at the *NME*. And, because I'd done a positive book about him, McCartney gave an incredible interview.

DAVID HEPWORTH [McCartney] had a record out and we sent a load of dummy layouts down to MPL and he looked at it. We just basically said, "It's this kind of magazine," and he said, "All right." Chris Salewicz did this interview with him which was like his riposte to *Lennon Remembers* – it was his chance to say, "I'm not just the bloke who wrote 'Yesterday'; I'm a bit serious, and if anything John was the one going home and in bed with his cocoa at half past nine." He really went off on one, and it was fantastically quotable stuff. We were just very fortunate.

CHRIS SALEWICZ When *Q* celebrated its tenth anniversary, Hepworth was speaking in this very self-congratulatory way about the first issue, saying, "We knew we were going somewhere. We got a McCartney interview, so we had a great interview to put on the cover," and I thought, "You didn't get the fucking interview at all. You didn't work on the fucking interview. I got it." So that kind of annoyed me.

DAVID HEPWORTH I had a disastrous interview with Bob Dylan in the first issue. It was my worst nightmare. He wouldn't talk to me. And when Bob Dylan doesn't talk to you, ohhhhhh...it's something to tell the grandchildren. I sat in Bob Dylan's dressing room at Madison Square Garden while he played the guitar and studiously ignored me. And there was only me and him in the room. He did talk occasionally, but, you know, it was not easy. Anyway, so basically we wrote the story in *Q* saying, "Fuck, how rude is this? Would you like to be here?" Mark's feeling was that you can always make a yarn out of anything, which is absolutely right.

TOM HIBBERT The interview at the front, "Who The Hell Do They Think They Are?", was Mark's idea, but he didn't realise how demonstrative it would become, and he got really pissed off at the end because no one would talk to him. I didn't get any trouble from record companies, because I worked from home. Mark got it all. They'd ring up and complain about "this disgraceful article" and he'd have to deal with it.

BARNEY HOSKYNS I did think Tom Hibbert's "Who The Hell...?" pieces were hysterical. There has been a long tradition of very funny stuff in the magazine, and the photo captions are still hilarious, but it's what it has come to represent which is antithetical to the kind of music writing which set me on fire.

JOHN PEEL *Q* stitched me up with that "Who The Hell...?" section. They came down to talk to me and we were hospitable. I even asked them to wait until my kids came home from school so they could meet them. Then they wrote this piss-taking piece where they took the piss out of my dad, who's dead. I can't remember who wrote it, but he's a complete cunt. It's rather old fashioned, but I thought it was a betrayal of our hospitality. We hadn't been nice to them in the hope that they'd write us a nice piece, but it was totally distorted and unfair.

DAVID HEPWORTH I've always believed that people work best when they're happy. I don't want to work with arseholes. I don't mind working with people who are difficult. We all have a few of those. There's enough people who write about music – there always have been and always will be – who are miserable, introverted inadequates. It's a fact. They don't tell jokes, they're not extroverts. I know many of them who can write fantastically argued prose but wouldn't know how to introduce themselves to a granny. *Q* is not serious at all; it is deeply personal. It really is interested in the ups and downs of your love life, problems, whatever, alongside everything else. But I don't think it's vindictive. It should be a thumping good read. That's what it's there for.

BARNEY HOSKYNS *Q* was part of the Spiñal Tapping of rock 'n' roll, all that "Sir Bonzo of DogBandshire". There is this *Q* prose which came from the congruence of Mark Ellen's public school persona – as the deacon of rock 'n' roll, ha ha ha – and David Hepworth's rather-pleased-with-himself grammar-school take.

LUCY O'BRIEN I respect *Q* because, despite the fact that it's a corporate brand, there is an appreciation of musical knowledge and an irreverence and sense of humour. It doesn't presuppose ignorance on the part of the reader.

SYLVIE SIMMONS I failed miserably to get regular freelance work from *Q*. It was as if they thought, "We've already got our woman writer," who would have been Lucy O'Brien, I guess.

LUCY O'BRIEN I went to Sydney for five days on one of those gruelling music business trips to write about Alanis Morissette for *Q*. This was in the first flush of her success, around the time of *Jagged Little Pill*. What was interesting was that she was the calm buddah at the centre of this maelstrom and around her was this hierarchy, the music biz writ large – the band, the roadies, the crew, the management, the after-show liggers, like Claudia Schiffer and David Copperfield. It was surreal.

TOM HIBBERT It sounds pathetic now, but Bananarama were the ones who were most annoyed about "Who The Hell...?". They got really snotty and then they tried to defend their position by saying I hadn't asked them enough horrible questions. David Crosby and Cliff Richard were brilliant, as was Johnny Rotten. We became friends with him after that. We used to live within two streets of each other and he used to come around and listen to old Neil Young records and drink lots of beer.

DAVID HEPWORTH We had some kind of very woolly criteria of trying to find who the readers would be, and after a while it proved that it was almost immeasurable, but the view was, "This ain't going to cost a lot of money. You wouldn't be able to launch it on the telly or anything like that. Just give it a go." The first issue sold 39,000, or something like that. Second issue was slightly less, third issue up a bit, you know. It kind of grew like that. As it started to grow, we started to put a bit more money behind promoting it and it grew steadily for years and years and years. It was one of those classic magazines that, whenever you sampled new readers, a really high proportion stayed with it, which is really unusual, because you usually have sample, drop-off, sample, drop-off. This was steadier.

TOM HIBBERT At *The History Of Rock* and *Smash Hits*, I was really fed up with what I was writing about, so I invented sarcasm as a way of dealing with it. That came out in *Q*. I didn't start writing until I was 28. I was a truck driver and all sorts of things. I wasted ten years of my life trying to be a pop star, among other things. I was in a band called One For My Baby, I was in The Sneaks with Jane Kennaway and I was in Elvis Costello's first band, Flip City, for two gigs. I was asked to interview him later, but I thought that would be too close to home. I'd like to do it now, because he's gone completely mad.

DAVID HEPWORTH There were some key decisions on *Q*. For an early issue, Steve Rapport went off to take some pictures of a band and he came back with this kind of moody, strangely-lit picture where you kind of couldn't see what was going on, and Mark and I looked at it and said, "What's this all about?" And he said, "That's the way they want to be seen." You've got to remember, that's the way people were presenting themselves in those days, which had been invented by *The Face*. They were there to project a mood. But we said to photographers, "We don't give a fuck what they want to project. We want to see the story." So the classic *Q* photographic style was always an artist in context – things like shooting the band from behind onstage so you can see the audience, so you can see the can of coke next to the amp, so you can see the set list – and really informative captions. It was a kind of a documentary approach which became widely adopted.

ANDY PEMBERTON *Q*'s voice is based on PG Wodehouse. That's why it sometimes is accused of being tweedy.

DAVID HEPWORTH Mark, in his moment, will decide to do a story and will sit the freelance down and say, "Right, here's my headline. This is what the picture's going to look like. This is what the story's going to be. Now go off and do it." That was completely the other way around from what was being done at that time.

BARNEY HOSKYNS Mark Ellen was such a clever, charismatic, seductive, manipulative man. He wanted everyone to write like he wrote. There was no room in *Q*-speak for individual voices. There is a house style and you write like that. It's all very chortlesome. For me, there was this awful sense of self-congratulation.

DAVID CAVANAGH *Q* was for those people who watched Live Aid and went, "You know what? Queen and these other bands may not be hip, but they're really good." The *NME* characterised *Q* as a magazine for people who didn't buy records but maybe went to two gigs a year, both of them at Wembley Stadium, but they were wrong. It was actually for people who bought a lot of records, replacing their vinyl with CDs. So they were grown-up music fans who had grown up reading Nick Kent and Charles Shaar Murray and, hey, here was this magazine where they could read Charles Shaar Murray again.

CHARLES SHAAR MURRAY Every time they did another reader survey, something else I liked about the magazine vanished.

TOM HIBBERT The real old farts – Neil Young, David Crosby – are great, people like Alex Chilton and Arthur Lee. I'm talking brain damage, basically. Meeting Roky Erikson at his mother's house was really sad. I took him out for a meal, took him to a charity shop. There was no communication. He'd point at cuddly bears and ask, "What is that?" But I enjoy that weird situation more than a straightforward sit-down interview, because you can write about it and put colour into it. Or meeting Arthur Lee, who was as mad as a meat axe. I met him in a hotel on Ladbroke Grove watching that bloke with the sideboards who does the racing, John McCririck, and he spent the whole interview saying, "What is that guy on?" I loved that. Roger McGuinn invented my life, basically, because I think The Byrds were the best group ever, but when I met him he was a completely boring arsehole.

DAVID HEPWORTH Another key thing happened when Dave Rimmer produced a review of a David Sylvian album. We'd told writers that the star-rating system meant they had to stand aside from the music, because the review was not purely their opinion. Dave Rimmer's review came back with five stars and Mark and I said, "No, sorry, David Sylvian does not rate five stars." He said, "But...but...but..." And I said, "You're wrong. David Sylvian has not made a five-star album." It caused a bit of a to-do, but I think we were actually right, because we put ourselves on the side of the readers rather than the writers. That's a big difference. Most writers you meet don't think they're in media; they think they're in the music business. It's a fundamental mistake. You're not. You're in the media, and if you're in the media, you work for the public. You're producing something that they like and are excited about. So we docked a star. They got the hang of it. There's a kind of anti-gravity thing that takes place with reviews, star ratings or whatever, because writers are always trying to get attention, so they take a load of space in the magazine going, "Oh, this is great! No, this is great!" But it can't all be great. The truth is probably only one of them is right, so the editors are the ones pressing down against that, with the view that the truly sensational stuff will make itself known.

TOM HIBBERT When you interview young pop stars, there's always the press officer sitting there saying, "No, you can't ask that." That became so irritating. Then you get the old farts who were lovely, wanted to take you for a drink and stuff. A good interview is when they stop talking about their music. You bang on about personal stuff to try and get something interesting and they just go on about the third track on the second album.

COPYCATS
"WE'VE GOT ONE OF THOSE"

DAVID HEPWORTH It's one of those classic things, isn't it? You launch something and the competition go, "It'll never work," and then, when it works, they go, "Oh, we've got one of those," which is how *Select* and *Vox* came into being. When IPC launched *Vox*, it was a very serious competitor for a while, but it then kind of fell away. I think *Vox* only prospered when *Q* was slightly off its game. When *Q* got back on its game, *Vox* went off its game a bit. They kind of couldn't sustain it. Even when it was off the boil, *Q* it always had the reviews section, which was valued by readers. You *had* to buy it. If you were interested in music and not buying *Q*, it was a bit of a contrary thing to do.

DAVID CAVANAGH By the end of 1988, I and *Sounds* art guy were working with Tony Stewart on what became *Select*. Tony would never admit it was a response to *Q*. He phoned me up – and this is typical of his sense of humour – and said, "Hi, Dave. It's Tony. I'm sacking all the freelancers. You're out." Then he said, "Only joking." He'd phoned me to get in on Project X because he'd read a Van Morrison review which showed that maybe I had sufficient musical knowledge and the appropriate writing style. He described it as mature and not at all emotional, without the dogmatic style you'd read in the weeklies. I said, "What, like *Q*?", and he said it was to be more like the kind of magazine you'd get with *The Sunday Telegraph*. *Q* was a *verboten* letter in the *Select* office.

DAVID HEPWORTH Spotlight – who published *Sounds, Record Mirror, Kerrang!* – decided they were going to launch *Select* with Tony Stewart as editor.

DAVID CAVANAGH The dummy had David Byrne on the cover, talking about his interest in Brazilian music. It was so painfully *The Guardian/The Late*

Show/WOMAD, it was just untrue. I did something about John Lennon. We didn't hear anything about Project X for a year, and suddenly it was on again and I was reviews editor. Tony has always had younger people to bounce ideas off. At *Sounds*, it was James Brown, then Billy Mann, then it was me, and at various times it was Shaun Phillips. My job description was basically "the guy that Tony Stewart bounces ideas off".

LUCY O'BRIEN I had a year on *Select* when Tony Stewart was editor, who was as sweet as pie and no longer as daunting as when I first met him, when I was young and starting out. I was film editor for a while. It was an interesting magazine, because it was the first of the glossy monthlies to cover film and be more broadly based than *Q*.

DAVID CAVANAGH I was then made deputy editor simply because there wasn't one. Tony got some of his older people in from his days on the *NME* – Paolo Hewitt, Richard Cook – and I got in Graham Linehan and Andrew Perry, who was a student at the time. We were now allowed to mention *Q*, so the thing was to outdo them every month in the number and diversity of reviews. Richard was good enough not to show up my deficiencies as a reviews editor and Paolo was really good – he wrote a fantastic interview with Prince – but my favourite was Graham, because he was so spot on and funny. But it was a difficult time. We certainly weren't a threat to *Q* in any way. The first issue was 100,000. The next two did 50,000 and 30,000, respectively. Tony didn't tell me was what was going on and I wasn't really there. My idea of a working day was to get there at eleven o'clock, go to lunch with Duncan Holland and my friends from *Music Week* at 12.45pm, come back at 3.30pm and get into the bar – Poppins, which was downstairs in the *Express* building, – at 5.30pm. I would smoke and drink at my desk. I was always drunk and Tony was getting into champagne, so we were off our heads while we were running this extraordinarily unpopular magazine.

We launched in April 1990, and by the autumn we were in trouble. In the first weeks of 1991, I was sent on a management training course in Bournemouth. I came back fired up only to hear the latest circulation figures were dreadful. One issue, with The Dream Warriors on the cover, did 28,000.

DAVID HEPWORTH I don't think *Select* ever did particularly well for them. It had been going about a year and they decided they were going to get out of the business.

DAVID CAVANAGH There was a real laughter-in-the-dark atmosphere, because we were in the *Express* building with *Sounds*, which was also seriously ailing at the time. Their cover stories were things about bootlegging or upcoming festivals, simply because they couldn't get a respectable artist to put on the cover. The record companies didn't want to know. By this time, *Melody Maker* was on 60,000 and *Sounds* was struggling to get 40,000, while *Select* was also sinking, and in April I arrived for work to be told there was a meeting in the famous *Punch* boardroom. Mike Sharman, who was the MD, announced that *Select* had been sold to Emap and that we should gather up everything we needed, because we were being bussed to their headquarters. We came out and *Sounds* went in, and they were told it was being closed down and they were all out of their jobs.

DAVID HEPWORTH They sold us *Kerrang!*, which is what we wanted, because we had *Raw* by then, having bought it from an indie publisher. *Raw* was a *Kerrang!*-alike. We saw *Raw* as our way of getting into the metal market, and what happened was that we made it nearly impossible for Spotlight to publish *Kerrang!* profitably, because we promoted *Raw* and they had to promote back, and it ate into their margins.

DAVID CAVANAGH We got on the bus – I had a little bottle of vodka and a carrier bag of records – and were greeted by the Emap MD, Tom Moloney, who gave us a little pep talk. There was us down one side of the office and *Kerrang!* down the other. None of us were happy, but Crusher was livid. He threw a massive fit and threw things around, because he wasn't used to working in these conditions. Tony [Stewart] was on holiday in Dublin, so I had to ring him and tell him it was all over. He resigned and then got a job with *Rage*, which was Robert Maxwell's magazine, nominally run by Gary Crowley. There were tears and much gnashing of teeth, and Mark Ellen stepped in as the man in charge. I got on well with him 'til he found out I liked to turn up to work pissed and leave early. There was more than one occasion when I turned up on acid. The behaviour was a little bizarre, and I was supposed to be the guy in charge, but I was down the pub with Leo

Finlay, God bless him. I got bollocked a few times, and it was politely suggested that I might be more useful as chief feature writer.

DAVID HEPWORTH We bought *Kerrang!*, closed *Raw* and Mark and various parties overhauled *Select* – with some success – as a younger indie cousin to *Q*. Somehow in the deal, we obtained the name *Sounds*, and those at IPC inclined to conspiracy theories confidently expect that we were just waiting for our opportunity to launch an *NME* competitor.

DAVID CAVANAGH Mark suggested we concentrate on one style of music, because *Select* was all over the place at that point. He'd been paying close attention to the *NME*, where Andrew Collins, Stuart Maconie and James Brown had been championing baggy music. Madchester had gone commercial by this time – Happy Mondays were in the charts and The Stone Roses were hidden away making what everyone assumed would be their great return masterpiece. I didn't like it – I thought it was childish – but Mark thought it was hilarious, so he said we should cover it and use the glossiness and colour quality of the magazine to our advantage. There were also bands like Ride, Lush, The Pixies and Primal Scream to do once every four or five months, waiting until the weeklies had made their minds up and then coming in with a more considered viewpoint. It all made terrific sense. I remember, the day *Select* was going to survive was when the projected cover star was going to be Electronic (the collaboration between New Order's Bernard Sumner and The Smiths' Johnny Marr). By three o'clock it had moved to The Farm, slightly up the commercial ladder, and by the end of the day it had moved to The Cure. Mark's approach to press officers was, "This may be *Select*, but I'm Mark Ellen." He'd come from *Q*, assimilated a lot of knowledge of this music and was word perfect on it. He was very on the case, but he did squeeze some people out, like Lucy O'Brien, because he wasn't very good at dealing with women. Very public school. Wasn't comfortable in the company of women journalists. Couldn't deal with them. But he was a good sport, and he transformed that magazine almost single handedly.

CHRIS SALEWICZ I'm just trying to remember when I first came across the term and the concept of copy approval. It would have been the '80s. I'm quite proud because I once did a piece on Van Morrison for *Q* and he insisted on copy approval after that and did things like insisting that the only person who could interview him was Spike Milligan.

DAVID CAVANAGH Within a year, *Select* was very healthy, from 28,000 to more than 80,000. It was the publication that all the hip labels - the Creations and the Factorys - wanted to be in, and by the end of 1992 Andrew Harrison had come back from *Rage* and was in charge. Andrew is fantastically bright and, as he wrote in his application letter, knew "when to buy a story and when to sell it". He brought in a lot of people he'd known from Leeds University - Adam Higginbotham; Clark Collis; Steve Hicks; Andy Pemberton, who later edited *Q*. It was an endless supply of Leeds students who were all really on the ball, who finally brought some humour to post-dance culture. Meanwhile, Mark had brought in Miranda Sawyer, Richard Lowe and William Shaw, all from *Smash Hits*, but Graham Linehan was doing less and less, because Mark just didn't think he was funny. I thought he was the future of comedy, because I'd seen the early scripts for *Father Ted*. Anyway, this all gave *Select* a slightly younger Tom Hibbert sense of humour. For some reason, Mark never had a problem with "Bunny" Sawyer. She had a roving brief, so she did things like Happy Mondays' disastrous recording sessions in a haze of smack and crack for *Yes Please!* in Barbados and was winning awards and getting us noticed. Eventually, there was one magical day when the sales went over 100,000. That was the summer of 1993. By then, I'd also been freelancing for *Q* for some time, after being approached by Paul Du Noyer. They were very insular, very difficult to get to know, would keep you waiting in reception for a slightly unnecessary length of time, but obviously successful. There were awards all over the *Q* offices.

TOM HIBBERT I made the leap from *Q* to *The Observer* in 1996 because Jocelyn Targett - who was a big fan of the "Who The Hell..?" pieces - rang me up and offered a column. I swore, when I went there, that I'd never interview a pop star again. Emap Metro were paying no money, and I fancied writing for a national newspaper. They'd just cancelled "Who The Hell...?" and Lynn Barber had stolen the idea. By the end, they were getting me to interview third-rate actors from television that no one cared about. Robson And Jerome. What could you say about them apart from, two crap actors who make dreadful records? I've been told that *Q* had changed by then, but I wasn't a big *Q* reader. I just read my pieces to see whether they had cut my jokes out.

DAVID CAVANAGH When Danny Kelly became editor of *Q*, at the end of 1992, I started to do a lot more work for them. I wrote a piece about Suede, which was Danny's big gesture because he'd come from *NME* and was putting a band who'd never had an album out on the cover. And the magazine became hilarious. He had a very bullish attitude to editing. He had an orange coal miner's helmet which he would put on if he had to talk to a press officer and lie to them. What he would usually be lying about was "Who The Hell...?". He would tell them that the artist concerned was absolutely not going into "Who The Hell...?". There was a guy called Graeme Hill at EMI who called Danny five times in three days to get assurances that Adrian Deevoy's interview with Cilla Black wouldn't appear there. When it did, Graeme Hill called him up and said, "You lied to me." And Danny said, "I know. But I was wearing the orange hat."

CHARLES SHAAR MURRAY In the '80s, I seem to have made a career out of leaving publications when Danny Kelly came in to edit them. Not that I dislike him or didn't get on with him socially – though that whole sport-boy thing misses me by a mile – but it's a matter of sensibility. When he was about to take over *NME*, we were talking and he said, "Don't get me wrong, I like black music as much as anybody, but it doesn't work in the *NME*. We've got to get back to our roots, white boys with leather jackets." I thought, "Is that all it is?" and didn't write for them again. When he arrived in the Big Chair at *Q*, I think I did one more piece for them, which was an interview with BB King, but by then *Q* had moved from what someone once disparagingly referred to as a "dad's rock mag" to a "lad's rock mag". *Mojo* was about to launch, so jumping ship was a relatively painless and straightforward matter. So I guess *Mojo* is the dad's rock mag now.

9 "Pop Coverage Was Ubiquitous"

"At Arena, I remember big arguments with Nick Logan about a piece I did on the construction of the New Lad in 1988. He was extremely keen not to threaten the world of masculinity he was attempting to construct, even though half the models and stylists on the mag were gay, and delving into this construction was almost as bad as having Arena racked next to the gay mags in the newsagent's. This inability to face reality became one of the reasons why I couldn't work for Arena."

– Jon Savage

'ZINE CULTURE
"I USED TO READ **YOUR FLESH** TO MY MOTHER"

JOHN PEEL I used to really like *Your Flesh*, a wonderful American publication. There was one bloke who used to write for it and he used to make records himself. His reviews were fantastic. I wrote them a fan letter and I used to read the issues to my mother, who was a great appreciator of literature. Of course, she had no idea what they were about, but she used to relish it. The reviews were just gorgeous, so beautifully written, and I liked the idea of expanding the language. I'm not one of those people who wants the language to remain the same, although I do regret the fact that, as new words come out, old words disappear. Their use of language on *Your Flesh* was just terrific.

MICK FARREN There are publications, websites, fanzines. Hundreds of them. I'm always pleased when *Ptolemaic Terrascope* drops into the letterbox and look down the contents and see a retrospective on Viv Stanshall. Fucking great.

RICHARD REIGEL There's that weird dichotomy now in which the independent mags and labels, etc, can publish pretty much anything they want but not expect any widespread distribution of their stuff, not like *Creem*, which was somehow underground and mainstream simultaneously. When I look through *Punk Planet* now and see all the hundreds of indie bands and 'zines listed, it almost scares me to think how many of the great ones will probably end up being known only by very tiny cults.

MOJO
"SUBCONSCIOUSLY ATONING FOR Q"

PAUL DU NOYER While I was editing *Q*, there was this sense that it had become the mainstream music publication, and being big and mainstream is nice but it limits you to covering only mainstream music, as you try and reach the biggest possible audience. It struck me that there was a generation of writers who weren't being given the outlet they deserved. I thought of *Mojo* as being a place I could bring in Jon Savage, who never had much of a place within the mainstream music press, as well as Charlie Murray, Nick Kent and a newer breed as well.

BARNEY HOSKYNS In a funny way, when Mark Ellen and Paul Du Noyer came to do *Mojo*, it was Mark subconsciously atoning for what *Q* had done, which was snuffing out the real spirit of rock 'n' roll and packaging it as this chortlesome subject. I think *Mojo* represented for Mark a deep commitment to music and to writing about it, and I know it did for Paul as well.

PAUL DU NOYER There was this tendency among 18-year-olds to develop a fascination with music made before they were born and a generation of middle-aged music fans who were not nostalgic and MOR in outlook but were curious about new music, so I had this romantic notion of generation speaking unto generation. It happened. It succeeded.

DAVID HEPWORTH The acts at the centre of the *Q* universe were Eric Clapton, Paul McCartney and Bruce Springsteen, with U2 at the young end of it. By the mid '90s, they had got too old for *Q*, but nonetheless there are still people really interested in reading about them. That was the idea for *Mojo*, a magazine that you can write and read in depth about classic rock acts. There are fans who will always want to read more. If you put out a special issue of *Mojo* that was, like, four times as thick and cost £15, I think there's

10,000 people who'd buy it. Well, *I* would. It's one of those things that some people can never get enough of.

BARNEY HOSKYNS For me – and I was involved from day one – *Mojo* was much more than cosy nostalgia. Not that there wasn't going to be room for humour, but we decided we would allow writers to write quite impassioned and great big pieces about obscure acts.

SYLVIE SIMMONS When I found out it was being launched, I called Paul Du Noyer right away, and he was so open about what I could do. I tended to get commissions on women – a Tori Amos interview, Chrissie Hynde, and Shirley Manson from Garbage – but it's changing now. [Current editor] Paul Trynka seems to be less gender biased.

DAVID HEPWORTH There was this really great thing about CDs which nobody predicted. Everybody thought that all you would get was super marketing of very obvious albums, but we didn't; we got more music available than there has ever been in the history of the world. Ancient Mississippi Fred McDowell records, German industrial techno, dance music, whatever. It was all there. So there was just this incredible richness that *Mojo* could cover.

PAUL DU NOYER Circulation quickly hit pleasing levels. We were hoping to get to 30,000 in a year and we got above that, and advertisers were attracted to it because the readership is high quality. They're also very demanding and won't let you get away with anything sloppy, which is why writers are usually working at the top of their game at *Mojo*.

JOHN PEEL I wrote something for the second issue of *Mojo* about a box set of the worst period of Elvis and gave it a terrible savaging, I must admit, rather in the hope that I'd get more death threats! But there was no response at all. Quite a disappointment.

PAUL DU NOYER It was never conceived as mass market, but I always fancied *Mojo* as a global magazine. That's why I picked the name – it had a sense of the magic at the core at music and looked like the kind of word that French and Japanese people might get their tongues around. I dream of the day that it sells big in those countries. When I was developing it, I first came across the Internet, which seemed to have been invented by a mixture of Pentagon military and dope-smoking Deadheads in California. I thought, "Yes, these are our people. If we could get in on this Internet lark, *Mojo* could reach these people." Ironically, that's where I am seven years later, developing the *Mojo* website to reach the worldwide audience of *Mojo* people.

RICHARD REIGEL The one current rock mag I read regularly is the Brits' own *Mojo*. I like the flashy, colourful format and the extensive coverage of '60s artists, even when I know they're catering to my old-guyness by reliving the '60s on a monthly basis. *Mojo* has a good quotient of dry British humour, too, so, while it's not quite *Creem*, it comes closer than any other current mag to that Boy Howdy ambience I miss so acutely.

SYLVIE SIMMONS When it started, *Mojo* did have this grey image, but it's much younger now. The new regime - people like Paul Trynka and Andrew Male - exude an *NME* sort of age, and there are a lot more females working there. But there was a reason for it. When Mat Snow was there, they did a survey and found that 90 per cent of the readership was male, so they are very wary of scaring off their core readership.

LOADED
"CUTTING THROUGH THE PRETENSIONS"

JAMES BROWN Alan Lewis built *Sounds* up to be the biggest-selling music weekly of the '70s, and he did the same for the ailing *NME* in the late '80s. It was there that I met him, and it was immediately obvious he had seen it all. In my first week of work at the *NME*, I inadvertently threw up all over his office after a particularly heavy interview with Zodiac Mindwarp. Alan merely tutted and said, "Someone get his girlfriend to take him home..."

To appropriate the words of Spinal Tap's Nigel Tufnell, Alan Lewis is the man who turned music publishing up to eleven. That's one louder. Imagine a cross between John Peel and Captain Mainwearing and you're there. In his time, Lewis launched *Black Music*, *Kerrang!*, *Musik*, *Uncut*, *Later*, *Vox*, *Punk Lives* and *Noise*. Some were more successful than others.

JON SAVAGE I'm sorry, but pop should be giving pride of place to the outcasts, not yer average good bloke. Let them stick with sport!

JAMES BROWN Alan Lewis knew how to create magazines that young men and music enthusiasts would lap up, cutting through the pretension musicians like to project and creating titles that were exciting, noisy and very readable. In 1997, he won the prestigious British Society of Magazine Editors' Lifetime Achievement award. This was in recognition both of his music magazines and of his being responsible for getting the straight-laced ministry of magazines, IPC, to launch *Loaded*.

BRUCE SANDELL Alan Lewis has just got an unerring knack for putting the simple things in. He knows what's going on, more so than the writers. Even when he was 50, he could tell you what the best new dance records were.

JAMES BROWN Significantly, it was Lewis who came up to me three days before launch and said, "James, you have everything young men like: music, football, clubs, humour. But you haven't got women." Then he promptly ripped out a page about Rod Stewart and stuck in a picture of Liz Hurley in La Perla underwear.

BRITPOP
"COVERED FROM ANGLERS WEEKLY TO MOTORBIKE RIDER"

STEVE LAMACQ During the *NME*'s celebrations for its 40th anniversary, former writer-turned-TV-and-radio-personality Danny Baker was asked to comment on his stint at the paper in the '70s. I can't remember the quote word for word, but the gist was, "Everybody thinks their time at the *NME* is the best. We all think it goes downhill after we leave." Danny, you are spot on, except you can forget Baker and the '70s; the team at the *NME* at the start of the '90s was one of the all-time greats. OK, we disagreed at length, at least once every week, and I and the LPs editor, Stuart Bailie, tried unwisely to launch a ska revival at one point, but we were good, honest. I swear on U2's life (ha!). Alan Lewis had moved on to become publisher, so Danny Kelly took over as editor with the whizz-kid James Brown on features. When Brown took off to pursue other projects, Andrew Collins replaced him... It was a precariously balanced but determined team.

So, when the paper was good, it was genuinely good, and when it was bad – when you saw another two-bit band being handed a feature on the basis of one crap single or you saw press-office hype triumphing over common sense – well, then...then...oh, it made you want to scream.

PETER BUCK (REM) I get a kick out of the English mags, because they're always hiring a new generation of kids to write. They always have 23-year-olds who've never heard of The Beatles. It changes the way the music business is, over there. Here, people still can remember Talking Heads when they were a brand-new band. I mean, forget The Beatles and Talking Heads; over there, they'll review things that are in every conceivable way not all that important or exciting, but they're brand new, and the writer is 21 years old and going nuts, so The Manic Street Preachers are the best band ever, which is kind of good – you get people excited. But there is a lack of critical background. You read these things – "This performance by The Manic Street Preachers was the best performance ever." You read a real lot of those. Guys who are third on the bill get that. And then you buy the records and go, "This is second-rate Clash." In a way, it's nice to have the press have an adversarial relationship to the bands, because it keeps you on your toes. You can't get away with doing the same old. The criticism you could make about American criticism is that established favourites get more latitude in making not-good records.

CHARLES SHAAR MURRAY It's funny. I felt too old in the '80s, but in the '90s, when Britpop replaced the last dregs of the new romantic movement, and in the States, when grunge saw off big-hair stadium metal, suddenly I didn't feel too old. I realised then I *wasn't* too old. It's just that the music was shit.

ALLAN JONES The *Melody Maker* benefited from grunge. Everett True picked up on Nirvana very, very early. I went to see a showcase by Pearl Jam at the Borderline and couldn't believe how good they were, so we put them on the cover immediately. That went all right for us, because we had championed bands like Screaming Trees and Tad.

PETER BUCK The English press, especially, is focused completely on the personal. With the English magazines, it seems that, if you sit in a room and you just want to talk about the music, they'll find a way to make it not about the music. Maybe it's because the magazines come out every week and you have to appeal on a flash level. I mean, a lot of the English press are closer to *The Enquirer* than to *The New York Times*, so every three years you get this generation of English bands who make absolutely great copy and maybe not necessarily such great records.

DAVID CAVANAGH Everything was fine until the release of *(What's The Story) Morning Glory?*. It completely changed the music press in this country forever. By the summer of 1995, Blur were a *Q* band. The readers loved them and they had commercial appeal. Their albums had depth and personality and lots of '60s references. Perfect. Oasis were regarded as a band for the lads down the corridor at *Select*. *Q* had given *Definitely Maybe* a 140-word review with no picture because reviews editor John Aizlewood regarded Creation as "a fuckin' indie label". Also, nobody liked dealing with Johnny Hopkins, Creation's press officer, because he was a bit flaky and never did what he said he was going to do.

ALLAN JONES When Britpop came along, we really suffered quite badly. If we'd maybe stuck to the more maverick acts, we might have seen it out in much healthier fashion. You may think that the music weeklies thrived during that period, but *Melody Maker* certainly didn't. We started to lose readers even though we were right in the thick of it, famously doing the Suede cover before their first single came out. Steve Sutherland kept saying how brilliant they were and was going to do a double page spread. [Photographer] Tom Sheehan came to the pub with these shots and Steve was blathering about them so much I thought, "If they're this good, why not say, 'They're the best new band in Britain,' and put them on the cover?" We did something not dissimilar with Blur later on. But the problem was that the coverage of Britpop was ubiquitous – the Gallagher brothers were all over *The Mirror* and you couldn't pick up a magazine of any kind, from *Anglers Weekly* to *Motorbike Rider*, without seeing coverage of Blur, Oasis or Pulp.

DAVID CAVANAGH: When Oasis exploded, Stuart Maconie had written a two-page report in *Q* without interviewing the band. They were interested, but Blur was still *Q*'s main band. When *The Great Escape* came out, Paul Du

Noyer gave it a five-star review and said it was a work of genius. A month later, I reviewed *Morning Glory*, which indicates there was not much interest from anyone on the staff. I'd heard about it from John Harris, who joined *Select* from the *NME*, and he'd slated it, saying it was hilarious, that it was shit and that they would get sued for every song. I heard it, liked half of it and wrote what has gone down in history as a slag-off – three out of five stars.

DAVID HEPWORTH The interesting thing about pop music is that it's at its healthiest when everybody is looking at the same page, like Oasis and Blur. The rivalry between them – whatever you think of the groups involved – was really exciting, and it was exciting if you were reading *Smash Hits*, *NME* or *Q*.

DAVID CAVANAGH The general verdict on *Morning Glory* from the journalists I talked to was fairly to very negative. So the review came out, no problem. Suddenly, it went to Number One and stayed there. There was a pro-Oasis buzz at *Q*, with the inkling of an anti-Blur buzz, and the most important thing is that the readers went for it, well ahead of the journalists, and voted them for the *Q* Awards. At that point, *Q* phoned Creation and the band's management and got the response, "Oh, OK. We see. You want Liam and Noel to come and get an award for an album which you said was no good." They were told, "Aaah! One of our freelancers said it was no good. We love it." And then you had all these people who'd slagged it off saying it was great. I didn't get any work for three months. People like John Harris – who's from a very middle-class home in Cheshire – was suddenly talking like Terry Christian. A lot of people saw the bus leaving and wanted to get on it. I preferred walking.

DAVID HEPWORTH When The Spice Girls were really happening, they'd be on the cover of every magazine in a way that Boyzone will never be, in a way that Travis will never be. When the media gets too specialist, you start to get acts who design themselves for that media – a whole generation of acts were invented to be on the John Peel show, not for anything else – and I think you get a narrowing of horizons, which is rather sad.

DAVID CAVANAGH So Oasis and a lot of other bands became *Q* property. Pulp and the kings of Britpop - Supergrass, Black Grape and everybody else - were on the *Q* cover, which left *Select* with slim pickings - The Foo Fighters and The Seahorses. They were in the same position as the *Melody Maker* in regard to the *NME*, angling for the same groups but not getting them because the sales didn't justify it. *Select* was fucked, and they weren't alone - it hit *Vox* and *Melody Maker*. Here was a band, a genre, which appealed to the readers of all the magazines, from *Smash Hits* to *Mojo*, and how it was decided was that those with the biggest circulations won out. It sowed the seeds for the destruction of *Select*, *Melody Maker* and *Vox*, which were all shut within a couple of years.

ALLAN JONES Maybe *NME* came out of Britpop better than we did, but Britpop never did us any favours. We probably lost some of our heartland readers who were used to writing which was a little more considered. As Britpop was brash, so the writing assumed this rather shrill quality. The Stud Brothers were still writing good stuff, but Chris Roberts had moved on and so had Simon Reynolds. The newer generation were less composed, less cool. Something was missing, and our readers spotted it before some of us did. They had been buying us for our eulogies on Mark Eitzel and American Music Club, but now we were saying, "Menswe@r. What a super group." If I had to put Menswe@r on the cover one more time I would have shot myself or somebody was going to suffer.

DAVID CAVANAGH When the *Select* logo changed in 1999, I suspected that something was up. It looked like a sports magazine. It had people on the cover who couldn't get 40,000 sales, let alone 100,000, but it was the best they could do. The research showed it had poor recognition and retailers didn't know where to put it because it didn't look like a music magazine any more, so it was no surprise to hear about it closing at the beginning of 2001. I went along to the Emap leaving-do pub and bumped into John Harris, who had been editor of *Select*. I asked, "Who are all these people?" He said, "God knows." Andrew Harrison - who had made the decision to chop it - was networking furiously.

ALEXIS PETRIDIS The research told us [at *Select*] that, no matter how many features we did on Destiny's Child, people still thought we were a magazine about Oasis. We were forever associated with a music in decline.

10 "The Juice Went Elsewhere"

"Corporate capitalism has a dreadful, homogenising effect. Most editors edit like a dog pisses – not to improve the fire hydrant but to mark their territory."
　　　　– Mick Farren

MUSIC JOURNALISM NOW
"THINGS RUN THEIR COURSE"

IRA ROBBINS　There's an astonishing amount of mediocrity in music journalism nowadays, a shocking lack of history and context combined with a congenital audience-pleasing inability to express an independent critical view. I think bad editors have, for good reasons, encouraged a lot of weak writers, who have become even worse editors, propagating a downward cycle of incompetence. That said, the worst editor I have ever worked with was a grizzled old veteran who insisted that everyone should write as incompetently as he did. I tried that for a while but couldn't hack it and left a very lucrative freelance set-up.

JOHN PEEL　The record industry is more in control now than it has probably ever been. I've stopped reading about it. You always know who's going to be covered and the music press just became too predictable.

PETE SILVERTON　Pop's gone back to what it was like before The Beatles: showbiz. Look at the tabloids of the 1950s and you'll find pop music and TV stars all over them, just like now. When The Beatles arrived, people looked to pop music for something more than just entertainment, and that stopped at some point. Things run their course, I guess.

JOHN PEEL　The things I was interested in weren't, generally speaking, written about. We already know all that is possible to know about

Eminem. I just want to pick up the possibility of reading something I don't already know about. I want to read them and go, "Actually, I want to listen to that."

ROBERT CHRISTGAU Space limitations, as well as the usually cited commercial constraints, have taken a serious toll, as has careerism among young journalists. There aren't as many as there used to be in it for love, although it still happens, which – given the economic prospects for the average crit – it had better.

GREG SHAW That whole tradition of extended essays about music has just gone. The whole point of the music press now is to get ads on the releases that the labels are promoting. And the music isn't important enough. It doesn't have the cultural significance that you can sink your teeth into. What could you say on Oasis? There may be 20 books out on them, but they all say the same thing.

JOHN PEEL I like things like *Jockey Slut* and some of the dance stuff. In a way, they're similar to the things I read in the late '50s, like *Jazz Journal* and *Jazz Monthly*, in that they're written by fanatics. I play a lot of dance stuff on the programme and I've listened to an amazing number of dance records, and I look at their charts and don't recognise a single name. I quite enjoy *Sleaze Nation*, but I don't know what it is they're talking about. I kind of like the exuberance of it all.

RICHARD COOK: There are a few creative outposts, but mostly it's useless now. The weeklies are little more than abusive personality pushers and the monthlies are dominated by Emap styling, which means cretinous fifth-form humour and jollity in place of tough critical thinking.

PAUL DU NOYER A couple of things happened. Competition for the music press arrived in the form of new, highly professional, exquisitely designed magazines and music lost its place in the imagination of youth, at least in Britain. It became one more competing leisure pursuit for all but a few die-hards. It was no longer the be-all and end-all of what it was to be young here. And the discovery of music by the national press robbed the music papers of their news function. Beyond the bread-and-butter stuff of tour dates, if there is anything significant happening in pop, you'll find it in your morning newspaper.

JON SAVAGE The thing about pop is that it has penetrated all parts of life and become this huge industry, too large to be run in the old chaotic way that it did. In 1977, it was chaos, really. They were flinging money at it, drugs were everywhere and it was a glorious mess. It was a great time to be a music writer, because you could exploit the gaps. Now, everything is niched and market research runs everything, not like when Nick Logan started *The Face*. He had an idea, a vision, and just went with it.

IAN MACDONALD The music press lives by the music. Anything that's happened to the music press in terms of decline or fragmentation has happened to the music first. The music's no longer a vibrant force – not compared to what it once was, anyway – so neither is the music journalism that goes with it. You can't carry on for long writing about boring artists without your readers noticing that it's all becoming a bit forced and depressing. That's why the monthlies like *Q*, *Mojo* and *Uncut* are still thriving – they can draw on almost the entire rock era for their subject matter. Plus, they have more time to get it right and make it look good. In the end, though, they too will run out of source material.

DAVID CAVANAGH By putting The Spice Girls on the cover [in late 2000], *Q* is really in a bad place. In the '80s, and under Danny Kelly in the early '90s, it did cover mainstream pop, but they'd send Tom Hibbert, who would rip the fucking piss out of them in these incredibly funny pieces full of vitriol and bile. Now, if you read about a pop act in *Q*, it's completely uncritical. It's even positive. The magazine is interviewing those at Number One in the charts as celebrities, forgetting, of course, that we read about this everywhere else. It is not putting enough critical distance between itself and these silly crap disposable muppets who'll be replaced by another set of silly crap disposable muppets in two years' time.

IRA ROBBINS The careerism that emerged once mainstream magazines began covering rock in the '70s has been a boon and disaster for the field, making it a field one can earn a living in – as opposed to the $10 *Creem* used to pay, forcing the first wave of writers to live on label largesse and free T-shirts – but encouraging the shallowest of efficient lame-brains who can pitch well and write smoothly but have no original ideas. Considering how many magazines are written largely by freelancers, there's a major lack of critical depth and strength in a lot of what I read.

CHARLES SHAAR MURRAY: Most of what you read about pop stars now is simply gossip-column stuff. The stars are almost interchangeable with cast members of *EastEnders* or *Big Brother*. They're just celebrities. Who was the last performer to have a genuine cultural significance? Maybe Eminem. Certainly Madonna, but she's now fucking 42 years old and has spawned a bunch of brainless spiritual daughters. Most of the white boys with guitars are so tedious. When I heard Coldplay, I thought, "Come back, Travis, all is forgiven," and I thought they were about as wet as it could get.

DYLAN JONES Music journalism has become so commonplace, so everyday, that true opinion, true experience and true style have become difficult to find, not to mention difficult to trust. Reading a lot of rock writing nowadays, you start to wonder why the people involved picked up a pen in the first place.

GINA ARNOLD You know, 99 per cent of the hate mail I receive is from men, and it's all about me, not about my opinion or what I said in the article. A woman will write me, "I disagree with your opinion about Sonic Youth because..." A guy will write, "You are a horrible person who is probably a big fat ugly cow!" And I know they wouldn't write that to a man. For some reason, my opinions are read as threatening, and I don't know if that's because they are uttered by a girl or because they actually *are* threatening – although, if it's the latter, people sure are easily cowed – but I sometimes wish I had used a non-gender-specific byline. But then, maybe I wouldn't be as well known as I am, and for doing as little.

JOHN MENDELSSOHN I don't pay much attention. It's far easier to tell you a rock writer I rather enjoy detesting – Ms Gina Arnold, whose work has always struck me as a remarkable meeting of completely unfounded self-assurance and glaring incompetence. I believe her to be the worst critic of anything in the English language.

GINA ARNOLD I have never had a lot of success writing for the regular music magazines - *Rolling Stone*, *Spin*, etc. I think my point of view irks them; it's a little too radical. Also, that game is all about who you know, and the editors are all a lot younger than me now. Admittedly, I don't actually read those magazines, so it's not like I probably should write for them.

IRA ROBBINS The old values of rock journalism - which, to my mind, are no different to the current values of good journalism in general, like what you see practised in *The New Yorker* under David Remnick - have been set aside in favour of a comfortable and profitable collusion between stars, audience and publication. At *Trouser Press*, we always saw ourselves as beholden to no one, and I think that's largely been lost.

MARC WEINGARTEN The music press is as good as the writer's moral code. So many writers have been completely compromised by music industry largesse - junkets, free meals, etc - that they no longer maintain any critical distance from the subjects they write about. It's a major problem. When I see the byline of a writer whom I know is cosy with publicists, I can't possibly take the work seriously. What has been forgotten is that this is journalism, not PR work. That separation has been lost.

JAAN UHELSZKI Daily newspapers and mags like *InStyle*, *US* and *People* get the best access now, because publicists perceived they reach many more people, albeit a more mainstream fan base. We were a small, outspoken ghetto faction in the early '70s and had so much access to the stars and weren't penalised for actually telling the truth, which we did. When music became more corporate, our access was curtailed - big bucks were perceived to be at risk, and you were barred if you wrote an unflattering profile.

JON SAVAGE There are a lot of confused motives in this field. You've only got to look at what a lot of music journalists do. Some go into PR, some want to be in A&R, there are those that want to be writers and those that want to be rock stars and groupies.

RICHARD MELTZER It was never a vibrant force...but at least it once gave minimal support to some wild and nutty people not interested in following style sheets... All that was over forever by the mid '70s.

MILES The music papers are published for one reason only: to get record company ads. Look what's happened to *Rolling Stone*, a once-great paper. I think rock 'n' roll has been co-opted, but the papers probably led the way.

PAUL NELSON I don't read *Rolling Stone* any more. A lot of us that worked there used to pose the question to one another, if we didn't work there, would we buy the magazine? And my answer turned out to be no. Everything is *People* magazine now. It's all celebrity driven now. You can't say anything bad any more.

LINDSAY HUTTON There are no illusions about how the machine works and not enough people who really give a shit willing to kick against it. *Mojo* is still great and goes from strength to strength, but *NME* has morphed into *Sounds* circa the NWOBHM. Their attempt to embrace the pop and so-called rap/R&B culture really reaches new depths.

LENNY KAYE I'm always wary of this thing where people say, "Things have closed down a lot more. It was different in the golden era." Why the golden era is always 20 years ago beats me. Was it a golden age then? It was a lot smaller scale. A lot less people read the music press. It was a lot more for the cognoscenti, for real music fans who had records which never got to be platinum. I mean, how many people bought *Nuggets*? I know what my royalty statements were like. I got $750 advance, and after ten years – by which time I hadn't even made back the advance – they said, "We're not going to even bother sending you royalty statements. The figures are too low." But who cares? I'd rather have 3,000 people buy the record who were passionate about it than 30,000 people who regarded it as some Indian takeaway and they're looking for the next meal.

TONY PARSONS I was looking at the *NME* the other day and some of them are still there. I think it's sad when you see names there now who were there in 1982. That's a shame, because Julie and I showed you can take it anywhere – a column in *The Daily Mail*, write books, on television.

DAVID DALTON I occasionally flip through my son's magazines – *XXL*, *Vibe*, *Murder Dog*, etc – but I don't think I'm competent enough to judge. The writing is probably better, hipper, even kind of psycho-telegraphic and code-lingo saturated, and I'm always glad to see that, to watch words morphing. I'll sometimes see a review in *Mojo*, for instance, and it reads like a Japanese cyber-punk haiku.

LINDSAY HUTTON *Kerrang!* is particularly awful, the single review for Wheatus' 'Teenage Dirtbag' being a big case in point. Most of their writers wouldn't know a decent rawk band if it teased off their nipple rings. Them and their nu-metal is turning kids into bigger ginks than they are already. The big but here, though, is that this is the music that actually sells. Kids are buying this tripe. The nu-lifestyle is doing serious business and breathing life into record sales. There's a lot more stuff in general out there vying for the limited person-to-person attention span. The column inches attributed to Radiohead in hard print and via electronic media is wasted on me, but even people who I consider to have taste have been duped. Tell you what, I'll stop whining if Thom Yorke does.

JOHN PEEL The music papers no longer dare to take a chance of delighting their audience, by which I mean you have to be able to take them by surprise. What I want is for people to be sitting at home or driving or whatever and to think, "What the fuck is *that?*" But the music press has got to put JJ72 on the cover, or whatever this week's craze is. I don't have anything against these people, other than a lofty indifference, but you feel as though they're a part of a kind of Masonic thing. It's not something I lie awake at night thinking about, and I'm sure if I try and detail it further it'll sound like some kind of conspiracy...

LENNY KAYE Rock writing is now a very specific thing – your personality piece, your political review, your journalist-as-star piece. To me, that means that somewhere there's a new thing happening that doesn't have a name, just like rock writing didn't have a name when it was somewhere between "My Dream Date With Wayne Fontana" and pieces on chordal progressions in Mahler's fifth.

IRA ROBBINS Oddly, a lot of the best music journalism is now in daily papers – which once treated pop music like a problem – rather than the music magazines that are devoted to it. I am always happy to read Jon Pareles (by far the finest working critic in America), Greg Kot, Jim DeRogatis, Steve

Hochman and Tom Moon, among others. Dave Fricke of *Rolling Stone* is just as enthusiastic and compelling a writer as he was two decades ago. Tom Sinclair and David Brown both do great work in *Entertainment Weekly*. I've enjoyed Steven Daly's features in *Rolling Stone* and Douglas Wolk in *The Voice*. And, while I hasten to note that they are both close friends of mine, I am a big fan of Dave Sprague and Michael Azerrad.

TOM HIBBERT That's what's boring about rock now. I sound like such an old fart, but it is everywhere. When your father knows more about Echobelly than you do, because he's read about it in *The Times*, you know something's up.

TONY PARSONS *The Mirror* wanted me to go up to Birmingham with my son and review Eminem, but I've kind of drawn a line under that stuff. One of my old colleagues from the *NME*, Gavin Martin, kept calling me up and leaving message about doing something about The Sex Pistols in *Uncut*. I was Number Two in the UK bestseller list at the time, selling 20,000 copies a week of *Man And Boy*, probably the biggest thing of my career, and there's this guy - who I know and like, by the way - wants to talk to me about old news. There was something happening that day which was far more interesting, know what I mean? I didn't want to get into, "And then Sid got out his bike chain. I remember it like it was yesterday..." I just feel it's passed.

MARC WEINGARTEN The three critics at *The New York Times* - Neil Strauss, Ann Powers and Jon Pareles - are, in my opinion, just about the best critics in the country. As someone who has newspaper experience, I know how hard it is to file something that's trenchant, cogent and smart on deadline, and they really do it better than anyone else I can think of. Powers, in particular, blows me away. She's a terrific writer, and her insights into popular music and popular culture are razor sharp.

CAMERON CROWE Celebrity journalism is different now. The story the kid files at the end of *Almost Famous* - he's been the mediator a little bit and left some of the warts out, but left quite a few of them in, and made his moral judgment on the band and wrote about what he saw. Now, though, pieces don't get as long. The access is way different and way cut down. All this stuff happens in a hotel room on a junket for 30 minutes. It's a different environment. There are a number of times where the bands or musicians I was writing about back in the '70s – Neil Young, for example – would say, "Write about what you see." Part of that is that they wanted to see their life mirrored back to them. It's therapy, in a way. They want to get your perspective on what's going on. "How do I appear to the outside world?" Of course, you never appear the way you think you do, so whenever you hold up a mirror to somebody, they're going to see things that bother them.

ALMOST FAMOUS
"DON'T GET ME STARTED..."

JAAN UHELSZKI *Almost Famous* was the Jimmy Stewart version of rock writing in the '70s – sweet, touching and sanitised. But how else would the general public accept if it wasn't served up that way? Cameron Crowe knew the limitations of his audience and played to them. I'm glad that it was covered at all.

JON SAVAGE Don't get me started on *Almost Famous*! One of the things that I hate about contempo/retro culture is the way that it turns something that was always edgy and uncertain into a hazy feelgood fest. See also Nick Hornby. People did actually go mad and overdose, a part of the story which, like sexual and gender diversity, all those accounts of suburban punk and last trains missed entirely overlook or, worse, attempt to censor out of history.

MILES The movie certainly brought back memories. There was, of course, no way that *Rolling Stone* would have commissioned anything other than a record review without first meeting the writer. For a Hollywood film, I thought it was pretty good. But then, I never watch Hollywood films, except on TV or on planes. I saw this on a Virgin flight to New York City.

MARY HARRON I was a friend of Lester's, and I believe he does deserve the mythic status. I'm very glad that Cameron Crowe wanted to portray him and give him credit, but I thought the portrait was too neat and tidy. Literally, as my friend Frances Pelzman – Lester's good friend and my co-screenwriter on *Please Kill Me* – says, Lester always had a blob of mustard on his T-shirt, and the apartment in the movie was way too neat and tidy. And the lectures Lester gave in the movie were too professorial. They didn't quite capture the flavour of Lester's brilliant, hilarious rants. But I did love the moment where the kid asks Lester why he's at home on a Saturday night and he says something about how it's because he's a loser, all writers are... That sounded very like Lester to me.

BEN FONG-TORRES Aside from the Hollywoodening of my character and the *Rolling Stone* editorial process, I loved the film and its capturing of the passion a young person can have for music and for the chance to get close to it by writing about it. I don't think Cameron Crowe mythologised Lester; he clearly played an important role in young Cameron's life, and this was his way of acknowledging him.

RICHARD MELTZER The film did not grant Lester Bangs mythic status or grant him anything... It simply dropped his name.

BEN FONG-TORRES For all the huffing and puffing the movie Lester does about the evil empire out of San Francisco, he had about 150 bylines in that very magazine. However he may have felt about us, we obviously loved him.

LISA ROBINSON Lester certainly never wore a clean T-shirt in his life, so they definitely got that wrong in the movie. When I saw Cameron at the *Vanity Fair* party at the Oscars, I'd been drinking champagne all night and went up to him and grabbed the Oscar, shouting, "This belongs to me!" I was, of course, joking.

TONY PARSONS Cameron Crowe is an interesting character because he was always one of the more boring, anodyne writers at *Rolling Stone*, not a great music writer. But he was young and looked just right. Now he makes great films and is apparently a nice guy, and he's shown that it doesn't have to be the end, working on the music press. It shouldn't be the great shining moment in your life and then it's all over.

RICHARD MELTZER I'm probably not the person to judge his *oeuvre*, but *Almost Famous* strikes me as insufferable dogmeat, coming from the same never-never land - with the briefest shot of nipples thrown in - as a bad week's episode of *Happy Days*. A first-string ditz based on the auteur's mother provides plot annoyance throughout (hey, she's a player). Has there been such parental non-exclusion in an alleged rock film since *Bye Bye Birdie*? All-age sentimental slop, the sort of film that, if it wasn't nominally a rock film, you'd bring in violins to ensure and intensify audience submission at every emotional checkpoint. The scene towards the end where the William kid wags a finger at the guitarist (whose music he so-o-o respects) for mistreating the groupie (who respects and loves the bloke), thus triggering plot resolutions that culminate in fame and fortune for both (and vicarious gratification for the groupie), is something Ron fucking Howard wouldn't put in one of his dogmeat films. And the actual "rock" soundtrack? Well, the first two tunes are the Chipmunks' Christmas single and Simon And Garfunkel's 'America'. Ye gods.

MELODY MAKER CLOSING
"HOW IT HUNG ON FOR SO LONG, I DON'T KNOW"

ALLAN JONES Alan Lewis, who had been a successful editor of the *NME*, was promoted to publisher of both *NME* and *Melody Maker*, and then he became editor-in-chief of the two titles. From the day he joined, he admitted he never understood *Melody Maker* and had never heard of half the people we put on the covers. It was his strategy to make *Melody Maker* much younger to differentiate it from *NME*. I could feel in my bones disaster looming. I could see what they wanted to do and didn't feel capable of delivering that. They had their way when I left in 1997, and now there is no *Melody Maker*.

IAN MACDONALD I wasn't very surprised. To be frank, there isn't enough contemporary music worth writing about to keep a weekly going any more.

ALLAN JONES They changed the format and inherently changed the direction. When it relaunched in 1999, the editor, Mark Sutherland, made no bones about chasing the *Smash Hits* market. Look back on the first covers – Gillian Anderson from *The X-Files*, a string of Spice Girls, All Saints. Of course the readers started drifting away again, much as I'd lost readers when we had to cover Britpop. The readers weren't getting the thoughtful pieces by the likes of Simon Reynolds or David Stubbs.

RICHARD WILLIAMS I felt glad, really, when it closed. Not because it put anyone out of work, but the paper bore no resemblance to what it had been at its height. I thought Allan [Jones] was a terrific writer, a very, very clever man and a good editor, but I thought there was something missing. Things don't have the right to exist forever, so I was quite glad that there wasn't going to be a paper called *Melody Maker* around any more. I think there should be publications for people who want to read about that kind of stuff, but it seemed weird having it called that. I mean, if you were starting a paper now, you wouldn't call it *Melody Maker*. I suppose I was happy that it championed new bands and that kind of stuff up until its last incarnation, but the last couple that I saw were more like *Smash Hits*.

CHRIS WELCH When it changed to magazine format [in 1999], I was interviewed on Radio 5 with the new editor, Mark Sutherland. I said that it looked like the *Melody Maker* in 1926, which was this tiny thing about dance bands. He looked quite miffed. I apologised to him afterwards. Within a year, it had folded. They weren't selling enough copies to justify the print costs. When I joined in 1964, they said it was closing because it was only selling 40,000 a week. At its height, it was up to 300,000. In the end, it was brought down to 20,000.

CAROLINE COON I was expecting it four or five years ago. The music papers weren't at the vanguard of culture; they were sexist, homophobic and didn't like dance culture. They weren't relevant. So how it hung on for so long, I don't know.

CHRIS SALEWICZ It confirms that my kids aren't only interested in music. My ten-year-old is probably upstairs watching a WWF video, which is rock 'n' roll dressed up, and he's probably playing The Offspring at the same time. They're into other stuff. It isn't just rock 'n' roll any more, and I think that's probably the mistake that was being made at *Melody Maker*.

CHRIS WELCH It looked dreadful, like *Bunty*. It lost all its roots and threw away the best things about it. That's the thing I couldn't understand. What's so terrible about being a musicians' paper? They form the bands which sell records. It did pretty well in the '80s and '90s. People like Carol Clerk were very good, and they covered Britpop well, but the sneering tone was too much, a mistake which narrowed the readership. You can't be cynical and use in-jokes all the time, because it corrupts and degrades the relationship with the readers. It's a bit like running a magazine for brain surgeons and saying, "We hate brain surgery." What a load of crap.

TONY PARSONS As a journalist, I don't like to see people losing their jobs and titles closing, but they were the opposition when I was on the *NME*. It was a bit like Rangers and Celtic – we loathed each other. Twenty-five years on, it seems ridiculous playground stuff, but there was a lot of bitterness between the papers, and part of me felt that the *NME* had won, because I still feel some loyalty toward my *alma mater*. But at the same time, it's all a very long time ago, and the nature of the music press has changed. When I was there, it was like national service – you did it for a few years and got out.

CHARLES SHAAR MURRAY I admit to having felt a pang of regret, mainly because I remember when it was a crowded field with five rock weeklies: us, *Sounds*, *Melody Maker*, *Disc* and *Record Mirror*. Now, *NME* is the last man standing, and I guess that, if there has to be a last man standing, then at least it's my old home. But it's only a victory by default, and I take no pleasure in it.

RICHARD COOK I was wistful, really. Not so much because of its recent history – it's been rubbish for years – but because it was the first real British music paper, stretching back to before the war.

JOHN PEEL It was sad to see *Record Mirror* go, because it literally ran everything, even if it was just a couple of lines. *Sounds* I was particularly sad to see go, because I'd been an old *Sounds* man myself, but I was sorry to see what happened to *Melody Maker*, not because I read it but in the same way I was sorry to see *Punch* go. You felt it was something an enlightened government should sustain because of the good it had done in the past.

MAT SNOW The closure was an inevitable consequence of IPC's very bad stewardship, not only of *Melody Maker* but of the whole music market. I haven't read the *NME* for many years, but just looking at it on the stands, it appears at least to be vibrant and punchy under [current editor] Ben

Knowles. Its principal problem would seem to be the website, which gives you for free something which the paper should be selling – an updated gig guide and news pages. As a strategy, it's typical of IPC's mismanagement.

BLENDER
"LESS AL GORE"

DAVID WEIR These days, Jann Wenner oversees three successful magazines [*Rolling Stone*, *US* and *Men's Journal*], and if that doesn't provide enough fodder for Wenner-watchers, there are plenty of other angles for the wags to whisper about – his much younger boyfriend, designer Matt Nye; his many Hollywood buddies, including David Geffen, Barry Diller and Richard Gere; his long-time business partner and now ex-wife, Jane, and their three sons; and the accoutrements of his success – the Hamptons mansion, the driver and car, the jet and the private Idaho retreat for summers.

THE WALL STREET JOURNAL Is Felix Dennis mad?

JOHN STRAUSBAUGH British magazine publisher Felix Dennis clearly has a genius for identifying a gap in the news-stand and throwing a title at it. His US version of *Maxim*, launched in 1997, has been a spectacular commercial success, quickly racking up circulation figures and reported ad revenues that crush those of every competing men's magazine. *Maxim* spin-off *Stuff* is also doing very well. In March 2001, Dennis launched *Maxim Fashion*, a quarterly, and in April introduced a US version of his popular UK title *The Week*. Hardly pausing for breath, Dennis premièred a new music magazine, *Blender*, on Tuesday 8 May. There was a CD-ROM music magazine called *Blender*, but the title is the only similarity. Four issues will appear in 2001, with the idea that it will go monthly.

NINA MUNK Just as *Maxim* made the older men's magazines look and feel stodgy and snooty, so does *Blender* promise to be younger and more inclusive than its competitors.

SIMON DUMENICO How breathtakingly depressing it must have been for the gang at *Blender* to spot the June *Redbook* on news-stands. Alas, *Blender* (subtitled "The Ultimate Music Magazine") shares its cover subject, Janet

Jackson, with the 98-year-old women's magazine. Granted, *Redbook* (subtitled "Balancing Family * Work * Love * Time For You") is relatively demure about its "get" – "Exclusive: Janet Jackson on her private battle with depression, the painful betrayal of her second (secret) marriage and her inspiring search for self-confidence and happiness" – while *Blender* blares, "BOOTYLICIOUS! JANET, THE QUEEN OF POP, IS BACK!" But still, if you're trying to make a go of it as a fresh alternative to *Rolling Stone* and *Spin*, you probably don't want to be sharing your cover girl with one of the Seven Sisters.

CRAIG MARKS (BLENDER EDITOR) *Blender* is less Al Gore [than *Rolling Stone*]. Much less. It's an all-music magazine, essentially, with a few detours into TV and movie reviewing and some hardware coverage, audio crap, but basically it's a music magazine, so it differs from *Rolling Stone* greatly in that respect.

FELIX DENNIS *Rolling Stone* is so boring, so corporate...so depressing.

JANN WENNER *Blender* has no frequency, no circulation and no strong editorial point of view. It's like a mini-*Maxim*, a *Maxim* junior.

SIMON DUMENICO That dis would sting a lot more, save for the fact that *Maxim* is hyper-successful, having gained 2.5 million paying readers in the mere three years since its launch. You can expect Dennis to trade off of *Maxim*'s subscriber database to help fix that "no circulation" problem – *Maxim*, like every new magazine, started at zero, too – and while *Blender*'s a quarterly, its frequency will be quickly ramped up if the title takes off. Besides, *Blender* has a strong point of view, or at least an entirely consistent editorial voice. Like *Maxim*, it's basically a comedy magazine. *Blender* is all about applying the Dennis house style – bawdy wit – to the world of music.

NINA MUNK Unlike *Rolling Stone*, *Blender* will not write about political or cultural trends. And rather than focus on one style of music, as *Spin* and *The Source* do, *Blender* will cover whatever kids are listening to on their MP3 players. Above all, *Blender* intends to be as irreverent as *Maxim*. It will not be self-important.

CRAIG MARKS I remember when you could like pop songs and R&B songs and metal songs and not feel quite so divisive about "I only like this" and "I only like that." We're hoping to get a slightly older audience than, say, *Spin* has or *Vibe* and *The Source* has. My guess is that, as you get a little older, or into your late 20s, say, you get a little less provincial about what you know, less "I only listen to bands that sound like the Dead," or whatever your stringent tastes are, and you broaden them a little bit, and you're, like, "It's OK to like Destiny's Child, even though my little sister does. I like that song." It's all just songs. The culture's become more of a song culture and less of an album culture, partly because of Napster and partly because people have sort of smartened up and realised that that's the best way to enjoy music.

SIMON DUMENICO *Blender*, like *Maxim*, is not a serious magazine, and it has no intentions of becoming one. It is simply yet another Dennis-produced form of Short Attention Span Theatre, and it succeeds quite nicely at that. And it helps that the magazine's got a killer app, too: The Guide, a burly, back-of-book section which reviews 206 CDs (as proudly noted on the cover) in the debut issue. This innovation is, of course, cribbed from *Q*, the stellar British music magazine which *Blender* editor-in-chief, Andy Pemberton, used to edit.

JOHN STRAUSBAUGH Clearly, the time is right for a new general-interest music magazine. *Rolling Stone* is stumbling in its dotage, *Spin* is floundering and *Vibe* is adrift. *The Source* is doing better than those three, but it's too narrowly focused. Given that competition, there's every reason to suspect that *Blender* will be a commercial success. Editorially, however, it doesn't strike one as a magazine with much of a vision; like other Dennis publications, its only sense of purpose seems to be to sell a lot of copies. That blithe approach is probably a large part of what makes Dennis magazines such fabulous sales machines but questionable editorial vehicles.

ANDY PEMBERTON Felix has an interest in the covers. The man is worth half a billion. He tells you what he thinks about the cover, you're gonna listen. He has really valuable advice. He's often right.

CRAIG MARKS He said to me, "I'm useless about music." He's not interested in the music as a thing that he wants to listen to; he believes that there's a gap in the market and that he can fill the gap.

RUSS SMITH *Rolling Stone* has to be worried. It's the first major challenge since *Spin*, which they didn't take seriously when Bob [Guccione] started it. Second, it's a down time for magazines. Third, Wenner's up against the Dennis machine, and the Dennis machine is an abominable snowman. His stable is one of the few positive forces in publishing.

CRAIG MARKS I think Felix Dennis is a definite heavyweight and can duke it out with Jann, and he has resources that Bob didn't have.

SIMON DUMENICO In 1999, I worked for Jann Wenner. I spent a few months at Wenner Media developing an ill-fated magazine prototype. Coincidentally, while I was there, I briefly sat right next to *Blender* editor Craig Marks, who at the time was doing some guest editing for *Rolling Stone*. Marks is also a former *Spin* editor and, before joining *Blender*, was an Inside.com editor, though I never worked with him at Inside. Now I suppose they're both mad at me.

RUSS SMITH When Bob launched *Spin*, he was underfunded, and it was the mid '80s and economic times were good. This is a down time for *Rolling Stone*. I read something in *Ad Age* that they're down 29 per cent in ad pages for the first quarter of 2001, so they've gotta be shitting bricks, especially with Dennis with his various tie-ins that can be exploited. It seems pretty exciting to me.

SIMON DUMENICO Editorial cohesion is simply impossible for any music magazine in an era when there's no prevailing genre, but by yukking it up with snarky captions and silly charticles, *Blender* might be able to charm its way into the hearts of a sizeable audience of teenage and college-age dudes.

AND IN THE END...
"POP WILL EXCRETE ITSELF"

TONY PARSONS When Dylan Jones at *GQ* offered an interview with Oasis, I was interested. Noel Gallagher was great. I liked him a lot. He would have been very much at home in the late '70s. He always seems quite unguarded and honest, not watching what he says, speaking from his heart. Oasis are the only band I've seen at Wembley Stadium, and that's about as far from the Roxy as you can get. I once saw The Jam at the Roxy, and there were more people onstage than there were in the audience. Oasis I liked, though I regretted going to Wembley, because it was such a hideous experience. But I think the last great British band was The Stone Roses. There hasn't been a band to touch them since. So it's like me and Nick Kent with Noel Gallagher and John Squire – the other one's cleaned up while the talented one is scraping a living, which hardly seems fair!

RICHARD WILLIAMS Reading about pop music isn't quite as significant an event as it was 30 years ago, so I was not surprised by what happened to the music papers.

TONY PARSONS The good thing about the time on the music press was that I was there, on the road with The Sex Pistols, on the boat on Jubilee Day. It's like a bad photograph of Kennedy being shot – it's still a photograph of Kennedy being shot. My stuff had power and validity because at least I was in exactly the right place. It was great, a real education. I can't imagine what my life would have been like if I hadn't worked at the *NME*, not just because I met Julie there but also because it allowed me to do what I wanted to: write for a living. That's the big difference between me and a lot of people in the music press. I didn't go to university, didn't even get A-levels. Writing for a living was not an option, in my world. When I said I wanted to write, people didn't get it. It was like *Billy Elliot!*

MICK FARREN It will obviously go on functioning. *Rolling Stone* will put Britney Spears on the cover and then they'll put somebody else on after she has gone. There is still the fight between, do you try and inform and connect people who are united by music and tell them everything they want to know about everything, or do you talk about music? That very largely depends on the state of music, and at the moment it's parlous.

TONY PARSONS When the Pistols reformed, I got inundated with people inviting me to the press launch or the concerts, but I saw them at the

Screen On The Green and on Jubilee Day and went on the Anarchy Tour. That's just so different from a bunch of 40-year-olds investing in their pension plan. It was all about a moment in time, and the moment has gone.

LUCY O'BRIEN In the '70s and the '80s, the music press felt like an exciting place to be. You felt you were forging new ground and there was continually this sense of getting away with it. But, come the late '80s, the bottom line really was sales and shareholders and marketing and branding. That crept in and swallowed up the anarchy and creativity, so people interested in those things have shifted into other areas. They may go into small record labels or small publishers, Internet company and fanzine culture. It's still there, but it's gone back to the margins.

CHARLES M YOUNG The problem is music itself. I suspect that rock 'n' roll is now where jazz was in the early '70s – its cultural resonance is spent. The last great, important band was Nirvana. The forms will remain, the fans will gradually dwindle. The history is important, the juice went elsewhere. Maybe I'm wrong. Rock has demonstrated great powers of renewal in the past.

MARY HARRON Paul Morley and I didn't get on at the time, when I was writing for *The Guardian*. The first time I met him, he came up to me and said, "I thought your article on so and so was crap!" And I used to dis him for writing such endless articles, even though I thought he was talented. Anyway, we didn't really know each other until I was directing for the BBC's *The Late Show* and he joined as a presenter. Meeting again, ten years later, we found that our music journalism background gave us so much in common, in terms of influences and sensibility. We started working together, and I did a whole series of films with him as the writer/presenter. They were short films for the BBC and Channel 4 and they really allowed me to experiment a lot and explore different techniques. So I'd have to say Paul influenced me the most, but as a film-maker rather than a writer. Paul always said I was a better director than a music journalist, and I have to agree. The last thing we did was really wild. It was an hour-long surreal variety show for this Channel 4 series *The Thing Is...* I think it's the most interesting and experimental thing I did for TV. The critics really, really hated it at the time, but some day I'm going to make sure it gets shown again.

ALLAN JONES In 1996, I went to Nashville to cover Lambchop, whose first album I loved. I was sitting there, writing it up, and it suddenly occurred to me that the readers the *Melody Maker* were supposed to be aiming at wouldn't get it, so I gave up. Soon after that, Alan Lewis said he'd noticed I hadn't been writing much, apart from for the only section I cared about then, Media, which covered films, books and other stuff. This had become a burgeoning part of the magazine. We found we were getting access to people we'd never have expected, like Don DeLillo, who we covered the first time he came to the UK, mainly because nobody on the broadsheets had heard of him. I did Elmore Leonard, John Carpenter, a whole bunch of people, and that's how *Uncut* came about – we decided that there was more than enough content, and enough interest in it from readers, for an entire monthly magazine, which has proved correct.

MAT SNOW The music press is everywhere, diffuse. If you did a count of the readers of all the specialist music press, from the pop end to *Mojo*, there are probably the same number of readers as 20 years ago, but back then it was divided between three papers – in the UK, at least.

MICK FARREN The craft of writing that kind of criticism doesn't seem to be in terribly good shape, because the 'zine writers don't have enough pressure or competition. They ain't pros, so they're not in the combat zone. On the other hand, chickenshit magazine publishers aren't going to hire the new Lester Bangs.

JOHN PEEL What I find depressing these days is the predictability of it. You always know what records they're going to review in *The Guardian* every Friday. My favourite record of the last ten years and possibly of my life is an LP by a New York woman born in Nashville called Laura Cantrell. It's country, and I don't know why I like it, but it has the same sort of effect on me as Roy Orbison had in the '60s, and you think, "Instead of yet another review of Eminem, or whoever, why doesn't somebody review Laura Cantrell?" But in our area, a good writer is someone who agrees with you. If they say, "Laura Cantrell is the best thing I've heard in a decade," you think, "There's someone who really knows their stuff." If they say that JJ72 are the future of popular music, you think, "Oh, fuck off."

MICK FARREN The difference is in the quality of the artists. Pete Townshend would be ranting about the Vietnam war or something. J-Lo is not going to be talking about executions in Texas because she's just read the paper. The only way out is to sink into an enormously fragmented and very healthy, loosely artistic scene, but there's very little money in it. There are some good 'zine writers, but the problem is they are reaching a limited audience. The *NME* scenario that we enjoyed is probably unrepeatable in print. But that's doomed, anyway. We can't afford the trees.

CHARLES SHAAR MURRAY The best band name of the last 15 years was Pop Will Eat Itself. What we're seeing now is not that pop is no longer eating itself; it's in the process of excreting itself. While there is still good music being made, I can't see pop ever mattering again the way it did then. Pop is now another part of the entertainment industry. Maybe it always was, but there was a time when it seemed to mean much more, and that was the time in which I was fortunate to be part of the circus.

Bibliography

BANGS, LESTER and NELSON, PAUL: *Rod Stewart* (Delilah, 1981)

BANGS, LESTER: *Blondie* (Fireside, 1980)

BURCHILL, JULIE: *I Knew I Was Right – An Autobiography* (William Heinemann, 1998)

CHRISTGAU, ROBERT: *Grown Up All Wrong: 75 Great Rock And Pop Artists, From Vaudeville To Techno* (Harvard University Press, 1998)

COHN, NIK: *Awopbopaloobopalopbamboom* (Paladin, 1970)

DeCURTIS, ANTHONY: *Rocking My Life Away* (Duke, 1999)

DeROGATIS, JIM: *Let It Blurt: The Life And Times Of Lester Bangs* (Bloomsbury, 2000)

DRAPER, ROBERT: *Rolling Stone Magazine: The Uncensored History* (New York, 1990)

FIELDS, DANNY and REISFELD, RANDI: *What's Your Fave Rave? 16 Magazine – Teen Idols As You Knew Them...AND As They Really Were!* (Boulevard, 1997)

FONG-TORRES, BEN: *Not Fade Away* (Miller Freeman, 1999)

FOUNTAIN, NIGEL: *Underground* (Comedia/Routledge, 1988)

GREEN, JONATHON: *Days In the Life: Voices From The English Underground, 1961-71* (Pimlico, 1998)

HOLMSTROM, JOHN (editor): *Punk: The Original* (Trans-High, 1996)

JONES, DYLAN (editor): *Meaty Beaty Big And Bouncy – Classic Rock And Pop Writing, From Elvis To Oasis* (Hodder & Stoughton, 1996)

KENT, NICK: *The Dark Stuff: Selected Writings On Rock Music, 1972-95* (Da Capo, 1995)

LAMACQ, STEVE: *Going Deaf For A Living* (BBC, 2000)

MARCUS, GREIL (editor): *Psychotic Reaction And Carburetor Dung: The Work Of A Legendary Critic – Rock 'n' Roll As Literature And Literature As Rock 'n' Roll* (Alfred A Knopf, 1987)

MARSH, DAVE: *Fortunate Son: The Best Of Dave Marsh* (Random House, 1985)

McDONNELL, EVELYN and POWERS, ANN: *Rock, She Wrote: Women Write About Rock, Pop And Rap* (Delta, 1995)

McNEILL, LEGS and McCAIN, GILLIAN: *Please Kill Me* (Abacus, 1997)

MELTZER, RICHARD: *A Whore Like All The Rest* (Da Capo, 2000); *The Aesthetics Of Rock* (Da Capo, 1987)

MURRAY, CHARLES SHAAR: *Shots From The Hip* (Penguin, 1991)

NEEDS, KRIS: *Needs Must* (Virgin, 1999)

PERRY, MARK: *Sniffin' Glue: The Essential Punk Accessory* (Sanctuary, 2000)

RIMMER, DAVE: *Like Punk Never Happened* (Faber, 1985)

SAVAGE, JON: *Time Travel* (Vintage, 1996)

SMITH, PATTI: *Complete Patti Smith* (Doubleday, 1998)

TAYLOR, DEREK: *As Time Goes By* (Abacus, 1973)

VARIOUS: *The Rolling Stone Rock 'n' Roll Reader* (Bantam, 1974)

YORK, PETER: *Style Wars* (Sidgwick & Jackson, 1983)

Interview Sources

ALTHAM, KEITH: author interview (January 2001)

ARNOLD, GINA: "Gina Arnold In The Present Tense" by Steven Ward (© rockcritics.com)

BAKER, DANNY: from *Sniffin' Glue: The Essential Punk Accessory* (Sanctuary, 2000)

BANGS, LESTER: from *Everyone's A Rock Critic: The Lost Interview* (© rockcritics.com); from *Rod Stewart* (Delilah, 1981)

BELL, PAT: from *Days In The Life* by Jonathon Green (Pimlico, 1998)

BESSY, CLAUDE: from "Cocktails With Claude" by Richard Meltzer (*LA Weekly*, 1979)

BETROCK, ALAN: from "Rockin' Around In NYC" by Andy Schwartz (*Village Voice*, April 2000)

BROVEN, JOHN: author interview (April 2001)

BUCK, PETER: from *Rocking My Life Away* by Anthony DeCurtis (Duke, 1999)

BURCHILL, JULIE: from *I Knew I Was Right - An Autobiography* (William Heinemann, 1998)

BUSHELL, GARRY: author interview (June 2001)

CAVANAGH, DAVID: author interview (February 2001)

CHRISTGAU, ROBERT: author interview (May 2001); from "A Conversation With..." by Barbara O'Dair (© salon.com)

CLAPTON, ERIC: from *The Rolling Stone Rock And Roll Reader* (Bantam, 1974)

CLARKE, DICK: from *The Best Of 16 Magazine* (1999)

COHN, NICK: from *Meaty Beaty Big And Bouncy*, edited by Dylan Jones (Hodder & Stoughton, 1996)

COOK, RICHARD: author interview (May 2001)

COON, CAROLINE: author interview (February 2001)

COOPER, CAROL: author interview (April 2001)

CONGAR, WALLY: review of *Time Between* (*LA Free Press*, March 1973)

CROWE, CAMERON: from *Portrait Of The Director As A Young Rock Critic* by Dave McCoy (© salon.com); from *Guardian, Unlimited* (November 2000)

DALTON, DAVID: "El David: Saint Dalton Shoots His Mouth Off" by Steven Ward (© rockcritics.com)

DeCURTIS, ANTHONY: author interview (May 2001); from *Rocking My Life Away* (Duke, 1999)

DeROGATIS, JIM: from *Let It Blurt: The Life And Times Of Lester Bangs* (Bloomsbury, 2000)

DE WHALLEY, CHAS: author interview (November 2001)

DELLAR, FRED: author interview (June 2001)

DEXTER, JEFF: from *Days In The Life* by Jonathon Green (Pimlico, 1998)

DOANE, REX: from an interview with Nick Tosches (November 1999, © salon.com)

DU NOYER, PAUL: author interview (August 2001)

DUMENCO, SIMON: from "Felix Dennis Takes On...*Redbook*" (May 2001, © salon.com)

FIELDS, DANNY: author interview (April 2001)

FILIPELLO, CONNIE: from *Like Punk Never Happened* by Dave Rimmer (Faber, 1985)

FARREN, MICK: author interview (April 2001)

FONG-TORRES, BEN: author interview (May 2001); from *Not Fade Away* (Miller Freeman, 1999)

FOUNTAIN, NIGEL: from *Underground* (Comedia/Routledge, 1988)

FRAME, PETE: author mini-interview (June 2001)

FRITH, SIMON: author interview (April 2001)

GILBERT, JERRY: author interview (February 2001)

GILLETT, CHARLIE: author interview (February 2001)

GOLDMAN, VIVIEN: author interview (April 2001)

GOODCHILD, JOHN: from *Days In The Life* by Jonathon Green (Pimlico, 1998)

GREEN, JONATHON: author interview (June 2001)

HARRON, MARY: author interview (July 2001)

HELL, RICHARD: from *Please Kill Me* by Legs McNeill and Gillian McCain (Abacus, 1997)

HEPWORTH, DAVID: author interview (November 2000)

HEWITT, PAOLO: author interview (November 2000)

HIBBERT, TOM: author interview (March 2001)

HOLMSTROM, JOHN: from *Please Kill Me* by Legs McNeill and Gillian McCain (Abacus 1997)

HORNBY, NICK: from "Litchat" by Cynthia Joyce (© salon.com)

HOSKYNS, BARNEY: author interview (February 2001)

HUTTON, LINDSAY: author interview (May 2001)

JONES, ALLAN: author interview (March 2001)

JONES, DYLAN: author interview (March 2001); from *Meaty Beaty Big And Bouncy – Classic Rock And Pop Writing, From Elvis To Oasis* (Hodder & Stoughton, 1996)

KAYE, LENNY: author interview (April 2001)

KENT, NICK: from *Let It Blurt* by Jim DeRogatis; from *Meaty Beaty Big And Bouncy – Classic Rock And Pop Writing, From Elvis To Oasis*, edited by Dylan Jones (Hodder & Stoughton, 1996); from *NME* (1973)

KINN, BERENICE: author interview (January 2000)

KINN, MAURICE: author interview (January 2000)

KOHN, MAREK: from *Like Punk Never Happened* by Dave Rimmer (Faber, 1985)

KUBERNIK, HARVEY: author interview (April 2001)

LAMACQ, STEVE: from *Going Deaf For A Living* (BBC, 2000)

LODER, KURT: from "Whatever Happened To Rock Critic Paul Nelson?" by Steven Ward (© rockcritics.com)

LOGAN, NICK: author interview (March 2001)

MacDONALD, IAN: author interview (April 2001)

MAHON, GENE: from *Days In The Life* by Jonathon Green (Pimlico, 1998)

MARCHBANK, PEARCE: from *Days In The Life* by Jonathon Green (Pimlico, 1998)

MARCUSON, ALAN: from *Days In The Life* by Jonathon Green (Pimlico, 1998)

MARKS, CRAIG: from "Q&A With *Blender* Editors" by Russ Smith and John Strausbaugh (© salon.com)

MARSH, DAVE: from *The Best Of 16 Magazine* (1999)

McNEILL, LEGS: from *Please Kill Me* by Legs McNeill and Gillian McCain (Abacus, 1997)

MELTZER, RICHARD: author interview (May 2001); certain quotes from "Cameron In Hell, Erm, Heck" (*San Diego Reader*, November 2000); certain quotes from *A Whore Like All The Rest* (Da Capo, 2000)

MENDELSSOHN, JOHN: from "A Rousing Interview Of Self-Affirmation" by Steven Ward (© rockcritics.com)

MILES, BARRY: author interview (May 2001)

MORRISSEY: from *Meaty Beaty Big And Bouncy – Classic Rock And Pop Writing, From Elvis To Oasis*, edited by Dylan Jones (Hodder & Stoughton, 1996)

MUNK, NINA: from "Q&A With *Blender* Editors" by Russ Smith and John Strausbaugh (© salon.com)

MURRAY, CHARLES SHAAR: author interview (January 2001); from *Guardian, Unlimited* (November 2000)

NEEDS, KRIS: from *Needs Must* (Virgin, 1999)

NELSON, PAUL: "Whatever Happened To Rock Critic Paul Nelson?" by Steven Ward (© rockcritics.com)

O'BRIEN, GLENN: author interview (June 2001)

O'BRIEN, LUCY: author interview (November 2000)

O'DAIR, BARBARA: from "A Conversation With Robert Christgau" by Barbara O'Dair (© salon.com)

PARELES, JON: from "Whatever Happened To Rock Critic Paul Nelson?" by Steven Ward (© rockcritics.com)

PARSONS, TONY: author interview (March 2001)

PEEL, JOHN: author interview (March 2001)

PEMBERTON, ANDY: from "Q&A With *Blender* Editors" by Russ Smith and John Strausbaugh (© salon.com)

PETRIDIS, ALEXIS: from "Quick, Smash Up A Hotel Room (*The Guardian*, February 2001)

PERRY, MARK: from *Sniffin' Glue: The Essential Punk Accessory* (Sanctuary, 2000)

POP, IGGY: from *The Dark Stuff* by Nick Kent (Da Capo, 1995)

REISFELD, RANDI and FIELDS, DANNY: from *What's Your Fave Rave?* (Boulevard, 1999)

REIGEL, RICHARD: from "From Jester To Lester" by Steven Ward (© rockcritics.com)

REYNOLDS, SIMON: author interview (April 2001)

RIMMER, DAVE: from *Like Punk Never Happened* (Faber, 1985)

ROBBINS, IRA: from an interview with Steven Ward (© rockcritics.com); author interview (June 2001)

ROBINSON, LISA: author interview (April 2001)

SALEWICZ, CHRIS: author interview (January 2001)

SAUNDERS, "METAL" MIKE: from "Metal Guru" by Scott Woods (© rockcritics.com)

SAVAGE, JON: author interview (March 2001); from *Time Travel* (Vintage, 1996)

SCHWARTZ, ANDY: from "Rockin' Around In NYC" (*Village Voice*, April 2000)

STRAUSBAUGH, JOHN: from "Q&A With *Blender* Editors" by Russ Smith and John Strausbaugh (© salon.com)

SHAW, GREG: author interview (April 2001)

SILVERTON, PETE: author interview (November 2000)

SIMMONS, SYLVIE: author interview (February 2001)

SMITH, PATTI: from the Buffalo Rock Symposium (1974)

SMITH, RUSS: from "Q&A With *Blender* Editors" by Russ Smith and John Strausbaugh (© salon.com)

SNOW, MAT: author interview (June 2001)

SPENCER, NEIL: author interview (January 2001)

SUGERMAN, DANNY: author interview (April 2001)

TAYLOR, DEREK: from *As Time Goes By* (Abacus, 1973)

THACKRAY, JERRY: author interview (July 2001)

TOSCHES, NICK: from an interview with Rex Doane (November 1999, © salon.com)

TOOP, DAVID: author interview (May 2001)

TURNER, STEVE: author interview (November 2000)

TYLER, TONY: author interview (April 2001)

UHELSKI, JAAN: author interview (June 2001)

WALLER, GEORGE: from *What's Your Fave Rave?* (Boulevard, 1999)

WARD, STEPHEN: from various articles (© rockcritics.com)

WELCH, CHRIS: author interview (February 2001)

WEIR, DAVID: from "How The Ultimate '60s Rock Groupie Built His Fantasy Into A Media Empire" (© salon.com 2000)

WEINGARTEN, MARC: author interview (May 2001)

WENNER, JANN: from *The Rolling Stone Rock And Roll Reader* (Bantam 1974)

WHITE, LESLEY: from *Like Punk Never Happened* by Dave Rimmer (Faber, 1985)

WILLIAMS, MARK: from *Days In The Life* by Jonathon Green (Pimlico, 1998)

WILLIAMS, PAUL: from *Time Between* review by Wally Congar (*LA Free Press*, March 1973); author interview (June 2001)

WILLIAMS, RICHARD: author interview (2001)

WOOLCOTT, JAMES: from "Q&A" by Russ Smith and John Strausbaugh (*New York Press*, April 2001)

YORK, PETER: from *Style Wars* (Sidgwick & Jackson, 1983)

YOUNG, CHARLES M: from "The Rev Charles M Young Calms Down, Grows Up And Sings The Joys Of Middle Age" by Steven Ward (© rockcritics.com)

The Principal Players

KEITH ALTHAM Teen press writer in the early '60s before joining *NME*, when he also became a broadcaster. Departed in 1972 to embark on a career as a publicist representing the likes of The Rolling Stones, Paul McCartney and The Who.

DANNY BAKER Worked in One Stop Records in London's Soho before joining friend Mark Perry at punk fanzine *Sniffin' Glue* in 1976. Wrote for *Zigzag* and was receptionist at *NME* before becoming their star writer, specialising in disco, soul and funk acts. Later a national paper columnist, TV presenter, radio DJ and scriptwriter.

LESTER BANGS Started his journalist career as a contributor to *Rolling Stone*, *Creem* and *The San Diego Reader*. Moved to Detroit in 1971 to become assistant editor at *Creem*. Freelanced for *The Village Voice*, *NME*, *Circus* and many other titles. Died in 1983. His collection *Psychotic Reactions And Carburettor Dung* was published posthumously. Was portrayed in Cameron Crowe's film *Almost Famous*.

CLAUDE BESSY Founded *Slash* in LA in 1977, nurturing local talent. Also helped found Slash Records. Died in Spain in 2000.

ALAN BETROCK Record collector/historian and New York scenester. Founded the mail-order auction ad business Rock Marketplace, which was folded into the seminal mag *New York Rocker*. Died in New York in 1999.

JOHN BROVEN Helped launch *Blues Unlimited* in 1962 with Mike Leadbitter. Blues historian/consultant on compilations and catalogue reissues.

JULIE BURCHILL Recruited to *NME* via their notorious "hip young gunslinger" ad in the summer of 1976. Left in 1979 to freelance for *The Face*. Became a columnist for various Fleet Street papers, including *The Mail On Sunday*. Books include the novel *Ambition* and *I Knew I Was Right – An Autobiography*. Currently columnist for *The Guardian*'s Weekend section.

GARRY BUSHELL Fanzine writer drafted in at *Sounds* in 1977. Championed street-level pop movements, including the skinhead-based Oi! movement. Fronted his own band (The Gonads), compiled albums and managed The Cockney Rejects. Joined *The Sun* newspaper and became a TV pundit and author. Left *The Sun* acrimoniously in the summer of 2001.

ROY CARR Grand Old Man of the *NME*. Was a member of a beat group in the mid '60s before turning to journalism. Became a record historian and author, often in tandem with Fred Dellar. Launched *Vox* magazine within IPC in the late '80s and is currently a consultant at *Uncut*.

BRIAN CASE Jazzer noted for his cool wit. Contributed to the *NME* in '70s, where his style was also deployed to cover such acts as Ian Dury And The Blockheads and to review movies. Moved to be the jazz specialist at *Melody Maker* and later became a regular at London listings magazine *Time Out*.

DAVID CAVANAGH Cut his teeth reviewing indie acts for *Sounds* in the late '80s, then worked on the launch of *Select* magazine and subsequently contributed to monthly magazines *Q* and *Mojo*. Author of *The Creation Records Story – My Magpie Eyes Are Hungry For The Prize* in 2000.

BARBARA CHARONE *Sounds* features editor allied with giant groups of the mid '70s, particularly The Rolling Stones. Wrote a biography of Keith Richards. For many years was a senior publicist at WEA UK, representing a raft of artists including Rod Stewart, Cher, Enya, Chrissie Hynde and Madonna. Left in 2000 to form an independent PR company representing many of these artists with fellow ex-Warner employee Moira Bellas.

ROBERT CHRISTGAU The so-called dean of US rock criticism. Started his career as a for *Esquire*, then joined *The Village Voice*, where he was responsible for the Consumer Guide and became music editor in 1974. Former partner of fellow New York music critic Ellen Willis.

NIK COHN A teen chronicler of '60s pop culture, the stylish Cohn wrote three books between the ages of 16 and 21, including the epochal music study *Awopbopaloobopalopbamboom*. These and other superb writings are collected in his *Ball The Wall*. His journalism also acted as inspiration for The Who's *Tommy* and the film *Saturday Night Fever*.

RAY COLEMAN Ebullient *Melody Maker* editor of the 70s who cut his teeth in Fleet Street and at *Disc And Music Echo*. Responsible for the recruitment of a raft of writers including Caroline Coon, Chris Welch and Richard Williams, who chronicled rock as it moved through prog to glam and punk.

CAROLINE COON Dropped out of the Central School of Art in 1967 to found the youth drug agency Release and was a prominent member of London's underground. Modelled and wrote for women's press before joining *Melody Maker* in 1974. Was the first music press writer to champion punk. Left in 1978 to manage The Clash. Artist and writer.

CAMERON CROWE Almost famously won a place as a *Rolling Stone* writer at the age of 15. Interviewed and championed leading '70s bands before writing *Fast Times At Ridgmont High*, which became a successful teen movie. Subsequently directed *Singles*, *Jerry Maguire*, *Almost Famous* and *Vanilla Sky*.

DAVID DALTON *Rolling Stone* photographer turned writer who won the prestigious Columbia School of Journalism Award with David Felton for their interview with Charles Manson in 1970. His books include *Faithfull: An Autobiography*, *James Dean: The Mutant King* and the highly peculiar *El Sid - Saint Vicious*.

ANTHONY DECURTIS Staff member at *Rolling Stone* from 1986-95, interviewing subjects from U2 to Martin Scorsese. Presenter on VH1 and GetMusic.com, executive editor at CDNow and author of *Rocking My Life Away* in 1999.

JIM DEROGATIS Pop music critic for *The Chicago Sun-Times* and contributor to *Guitar World* and *Penthouse*. Books include *Kaleidoscope Eyes: Psychedelic Rock From The '60s To The '90s* and *Let It Blurt: The Life And*

Times Of Lester Bangs.

CHAS DE WHALLEY Contributor and pub rock champion at *NME* in 1975, then a staff member *Sounds* from 1976-78. A&R man at CBS Records and music publishing executive at various companies. Also worked at *Vox*. Currently information director at CMP Information, whose titles include *Music Week*.

FRED DELLAR Record collector/historian. Was import and catalogue specialist at *NME* for many years before joining Roy Carr at *Vox*. Currently contributes to *Mojo*.

PAUL DU NOYER Contributor and then staff member at *NME* from 1976-85. Became launch editor of *The Hit*, reviews editor and then editor of *Q* from 1985-93 and launch editor of *Mojo* from 1993-5. Currently oversees Emap Digital's online activities.

DANNY FIELDS Editor of *Datebook, Hullaballoo* and *16* magazines. Became publicist at Elektra Records, then manager of The Stooges and The Ramones. Chronicler, archivist and participant in the US punk scene. Sworn enemy of Jim Morrison and author of *Linda McCartney: The Biography*.

MICK FARREN Doorman at UFO, editor of *IT*, frontman of The Deviants and solo singer. Contributed to *NME* between 1975 and 1978. In the '80s, contributed to *The Village Voice* and many other titles based in New York. Author of *The Black Leather Jacket*. Resides in Los Angeles, where he continues to write a variety of books, many with a science fiction theme. His memoirs, *Give The Anarchist A Cigarette*, were published in late 2001.

BEN FONG-TORRES Hired by Jann Wenner from college to work at then-new *Rolling Stone*. Star writer for the magazine for eleven years. Books include *The Hits Just Keep On Coming: The History Of Top 40 Radio, Hickory Wind*, his memoir *The Rice Room* and the collection *Not Fade Away*.

PETE FRAME Rock historian. Founded *Zigzag* magazine in 1969. Progenitor of the Rock Family Trees, which spawned a series of books and a BBC television series.

SIMON FRITH Academic who was a prime mover at *Let It Rock* magazine in the early '70s before moving on to become music editor of *The Sunday Times*. Left there during the industrial action of the early '80s and switched to *The Observer*. Currently based at Stirling University.

JERRY GILBERT Folk fanatic who worked at *Melody Maker* and *Sounds* in the late '60s and early '70s. Left for a short-lived sojourn at the dubious WorldWide Artists before taking up an A&R position at Charisma Records and running Disco International. Now a respected PR for pro-audio companies.

CHARLIE GILLETT Wrote the defining pop overview *The Sound Of The City* and established name for himself as a writer at *Let It Rock* and as a broadcaster at the BBC. Throughout the '70s in London, his *Honky Tonk Show* on Capital FM became mandatory listening, where he helped discover the likes of Elvis Costello, Dire Straits and Kilburn And The High Roads, whom he also managed. Continues to be a pioneer of non-mainstream music via his Oval Records label and broadcasts on BBC Radio 2 and Radio London Live.

VIVIEN GOLDMAN Publicist at Transatlantic and Island Records. Features editor at *Sounds* during the punk era, when he evangelised on behalf of rising reggae acts and recorded a single with John Lydon. Wrote the first biography of Bob Marley. Contributed to *Melody Maker* and *NME* before moving to *Actuelle* in France. Now based in New York.

JONATHON GREEN News editor of the ill-fated UK *Rolling Stone*, which became *Friends* and then *Frendz*. Author of arguably the best pop culture oral history, *Days In The Life*, and *All Dressed Up*, both about the underground movement of the '60s. As England's leading lexicographer of slang and jargon, his books also include *Cassell's Dictionary Of Contemporary Slang*.

MARY HARRON Canadian-born contributor to *Punk* magazine in 1975 before moving to England to cover the new wave scene for *Melody Maker* and *NME*. Then moved into television, working on such programmes as *The South Bank Show*. Now a New York-based director, her films include *I Shot Andy Warhol* and *American Psycho*.

DAVID HEPWORTH Contributor to *NME* who became features editor and then editor of *Smash Hits*. Often works in tandem with Mark Ellen. Is also a launch executive behind teen mag *Looks* as well as *Q*, *Mojo* and *Heat*, all within the Emap stable.

PAOLO HEWITT School acquaintance of The Jam's leader, Paul Weller. Hired by *Melody Maker* to cover the two-tone movement in the late '70s. Then switched to the *NME*, where he proselytised on behalf of nascent hip-hop, new soul and house scenes. Books include biographies of Oasis, The Small Faces and The Jam, as well as *This Ecstasy Romance Cannot Last: Alan McGee And The Story Of Creation Records*.

TOM HIBBERT Trade journalist and failed pop star whose entrée into the music press came via the short-lived *New Music News*. Successively worked at *Smash Hits*, where he was features editor, and *Q*, where his caustic wit was best exemplified by the column "Who They Hell Do They Think They Are?" Subsequently contributed to the national press.

JOHN HOLMSTROM Launched the highly influential *Punk* magazine with Legs McNeill in New York in 1975.

NICK HORNBY Best-selling novelist and music obsessive whose application for the "hip young gunslinger" post at the *NME* was ignored. Author of *Fever Pitch*, *High Fidelity* and *About A Boy*, among others.

BARNEY HOSKYNS Contributor and then staffer at the *NME* in the early to mid '80s recognised for his championing of Nick Cave's early group The Birthday Party, as well as his interest in Southern soul. Subsequently the author of books across a wide range of subjects, from glam to a history of the LA music scene to Southern soul, The Band and the unpleasantly styled haircut known as the mullet. Contributor to *Vogue*, *The Guardian*, *Mojo* and a host of other publications. Editorial director of rocksbackpages.com.

LINDSAY HUTTON Trash-culture enthusiast and contributor to *Sounds* in the late '70s/early '80s. Founder of fanzines such as *Rockin' Bones* and *The Next Big Thing*, which continues to this day.

CHRISSIE HYNDE Ohio-born ex-pat whose association with Nick Kent led to freelance work at the *NME*, where she wrote about many of the leading pop bands of the day, as well as her '60s heroes such as The Kinks. Left for a brief spell as an assistant in Malcolm McLaren and Vivienne Westwood's King's Road boutique Sex before forming a number of music ventures culminating in The Pretenders.

ALLAN JONES *Melody Maker* stalwart from the mid '70s who was appointed editor in 1985. Left to launch *Uncut* magazine within the IPC stable in the late '90s.

DYLAN JONES Contributor and leading light at style magazine *i-D* in the mid '80s. Editor of *Arena* between 1989 and 1992, then group editor of *Arena* and *Arena Homme* before taking up the same post at *GQ*. Books include a biography of Jim Morrison, a history of lounge music, a biography of the designer Paul Smith and the collection of rock and pop writing *Meaty Beaty Big And Bouncy*.

LENNY KAYE Historian and record collector who wrote for a range of magazines in the '60s and '70s, including *Creem, Cavalier, Jazz & Pop, Rock Scene* and *Disc And Music Echo*. Compiled the groundbreaking garage rock retrospective *Nuggets* 1972. Around this time, Kaye teamed up with Patti Smith, providing musical backing for her poetry. Continues to be her leading collaborator today.

NICK KENT Cambridge University dropout whose work at *Frendz* magazine aligned him with the decadent glam scene of David Bowie, Iggy Pop and Lou Reed. Recruited as part of the so-called "Class of '72" at the *NME*, he flowered as a chronicler of wayward acts from The Beach Boys to The New York Dolls, was the boyfriend of future Pretenders leader Chrissie Hynde and jammed with the nascent Sex Pistols. Drug and health problems – as well as the failure of his band, The Subterraneans – kept him off the scene for the first part of the '80s, although he re-emerged with superb writing about newer acts such as The Smiths for *The Face* and *Arena*. He now lives in Paris, where he works in television.

BERENICE KINN Wife of the late Maurice Kinn, owner of the *NME*. Friend and confidante of a showbusiness circle that included Brian Epstein.
MAURICE KINN Big-band agent who acquired the ailing *NME* for £1,000 in

1953. Having established the charts and spotted the potential in following the progress of rock 'n' roll, he sold the paper to IPC in 1963 for £500,000. Remained as editor-in-chief for another ten years. Famed for his celebrity-packed parties and his hard-hitting "Alley Cat" column.

BARRY KRAMER Record/headshop owner who launched *Creem* in Detroit in 1968 with partner Tony Reay with an investment of $1,200. Took sole control on Reay's departure and recruited a stellar staff, including the likes of Dave Marsh and Lester Bangs. Became the manager of Mitch Ryder And The Detroit Wheels and moved the magazine to a farm 30 miles outside the city. A target for FBI scrutiny, his relations with staff were often strained. Died in 1981. Coroner's verdict: accidental suicide.

HARVEY KUBERNIK Los Angeles-based writer and pop culture fiend, *Melody Maker* correspondent from 1975-82 and acquaintance of Phil Spector and Brian Wilson, Kubernik acts as a consultant and historian on such projects as Rhino's Beat Generation box set and contributes to a variety of magazines, including *Mojo*.

STEVE LAMACQ *NME* news editor in the late '80s whose championing of indie rock acts led to a career as a broadcaster, notably as presenter of BBC Radio 1's *The Evening Session*.

KURT LODER Experienced reporter and feature writer at *Rolling Stone* who joined MTV soon after its inception and continues as the familiar and heavyweight face of the music channel's news coverage.

NICK LOGAN Former mod who overhauled the *NME* with Alan Smith in the early '70s, launched *Smash Hits* in 1978 and then successively *The Face* and *Arena*. Sold his remaining interests in the latter two magazines to Emap in 2000.

IAN MACDONALD *NME* staffer responsible for memorable and humorous headlines but also a deeply cerebral reviewer and critic. Books include *Revolution In The Head*, a painstakingly detailed history of The Beatles' recording sessions.

PEARCE MARCHBANK Justly celebrated magazine designer and graphic artist whose career started at *Friends* magazine before moving onto *Time Out* and a variety of other leading publications.

GREIL MARCUS Contributor to Bay Area magazines. Appointed reviews editor at *Rolling Stone* in 1969 and later contributed to such titles as *Creem*. His deeply intellectual approach to pop and rock is evinced in such books as *Lipstick Traces*, which is about The Sex Pistols and situationism. Compiled a collection of Lester Bangs' writing in *Psychotic Reactions And Carburettor Dung*.

CRAIG MARKS Co-editor of *Blender* magazine with Andy Pemberton.

DAVE MARSH Editor of *Creem* and leading light at *Rolling Stone* in the '70s and '80s. Author of several titles, including the Who biography *Hope I Die Before I Get Old*, *Louie Louie: The History And Mythology Of The World's Most Famous Rock 'n' Roll Song* and the collection *Fortunate Son*. Credited with coining the term "punk rock" in his "Looney Tunes" column in *Creem* in 1971.

LEGS MCNEILL Resident punk at *Punk* magazine and author of *Please Kill Me* with Gillian McCain.

RICHARD MELTZER Iconoclast of US rock criticism who launched career on the back of his 1970 book *The Aesthetics Of Rock*. Author of a dozen books, including the recent collection *A Whore Just Like The Rest*, he has contributed to *The Village Voice*, *The LA Weekly*, *Spin* and *Rolling Stone*. Now lives in Portland, Oregon, and is vocalist for the band Smegma.

JOHN MENDELSSOHN Prominent stylist of the US rock-crit scene and contributor to range of magazines. Frontman of proto-glam/punk band Christopher Milk. Wrote *I Carumba: Confessions Of An Antkiller* in 1995.

BARRY MILES UK underground mover and shaker who organised the groundbreaking Poets' Conference at the Royal Albert Hall in 1965, was a founder of the Indica Gallery, established *IT* magazine and later contributed to such titles as *Crawdaddy!* and *NME*. Now a resident in France, his recent books include a collaboration with Paul McCartney.
PAUL MORLEY: An NME staffer from 1978-83, Morley's application of then-

fashionable structuralist theories to pop criticism set the tone for the post-punk music press. Along with fellow traveller Ian Penman, he championed certain new romantic acts as well as the out-and-out pop of the likes of Dollar. Subsequently handled the marketing and promotion for such ZTT Records acts as Frankie Goes To Hollywood, was a member of The Art Of Noise and is an accomplished broadcaster and novelist.

CHARLES SHAAR MURRAY Started his career as contributor to the notorious *Schoolkids* edition of *Oz*, moved through the underground press to *Ink* and then *Cream* before making his name at the *NME*, combining enthusiasms for blues, glitter rock and Zappa to street-level music from The Sensational Alex Harvey Band to The Sex Pistols. Author of several titles, including definitive biographies of Jimi Hendrix (*Crosstown Traffic*, which won the Ralph J Gleason Book Award in 1989) and John Lee Hooker. Contributor to a range of publications, from *Guitar World* to *Mojo* to *The Guardian*.

KRIS NEEDS Trained local paper journalist who ran the Mott The Hoople's UK fan club before pitching up at *Zigzag*, which he transformed into a punk fanzine. Dance music enthusiast and DJ, he has written for a number of specialist publications, lived in new York and Aylesbury, been the brains behind dance act Secret Knowledge and written a book of memoirs, *Needs Must*.

PAUL NELSON Founded pioneering folk fanzine *The Little Sandy Review* in the early '60s. Very early champion of his friend Bob Dylan. Later publicist at Mercury Records, where he worked with such acts as Rod Stewart and signed The New York Dolls. In 1978, was appointed reviews editor of *Rolling Stone*.

GLENN O'BRIEN New York scenester, staffer at *Rolling Stone* and editor of Andy Warhol's *Interview*. Champion of New York bands, paramour of Grace Jones and sometime stand-up comedian.

LUCY O'BRIEN Contributor to the *NME* in the mid '80s, during which time she brought a broader perspective to the paper's coverage of youth and social issues. Subsequently published a number of books, including a celebrated biography of Dusty Springfield, and contributed to *Q* and *The Guardian*.

TONY PARSONS Cut a swathe through UK music journalism in partnership with Julie Burchill in the late '70s during his period as a staffer on the *NME*. After a hiatus in Essex, he returned to contribute to publications including *Arena* and *The Sunday Times* before becoming a Fleet Street columnist, most recently at *The Mirror*. Scored a best-seller with his novel *Man And Boy*, the follow up to which was 2001's *One For My Baby*.

JOHN PEEL Broadcaster and leading figure of UK underground in the '60s, first with his pirate radio activities and then with his show *The Perfumed Garden*. Operated independent label Dandelion, championed punk via his late-night BBC Radio 1 show in the '70s and '80s, contributed absurd column to *Sounds* and is now a familiar face and voice on TV and radio, where he presents BBC Radio 4s weekly show *Home Truths*.

ANDY PEMBERTON Co-editor (with Craig Marks) of *Blender*, the music/lads' magazine launched by Felix Dennis in 2001. Former editor of *Q* magazine.

IAN PENMAN Fellow traveller of Paul Morley's as *NME* post-punk writer. Contributor of regular and excellent pieces to *The Wire* and *The Guardian*.

MARK PERRY Bank clerk who founded the fanzine *Sniffin Glue & Other Rock 'n' Roll Habits* in 1976, closing it after twelve issues to launch his own band, Alternative TV. Still pursuing a career in music. Sanctuary Publishing recently published a collection of his original *Sniffin Glue*s.

SIMON REYNOLDS Recruited to *Melody Maker* in the mid '80s, where he adopted a deliberately academic approach to pop writing. Resident of New York. Author of such books as *The Sex Revolts*.

DAVE RIMMER Wrote the classic '80s text *Like Punk Never Happened*, having established a solid reputation as a contributor to *Smash Hits*. Continues to write about music and other youth subjects for a range of publications.

IRA ROBBINS Launched *Trans-Oceanic Trouser Press* with Dave Schulps in New York in 1974, championing post-glam acts, many from Britain, such as

Mott The Hoople, Cheap Trick, Todd Rundgren, Sparks and Roy Wood. Renamed *Trouser Press*, the magazine also featured new wave acts from Elvis Costello to The Clash and went on to cover the rise of Culture Club, Adam Ant and The Cure before closing in 1984. Robbins also ran Trouser Press Books between 1983 and 1999.

LISA ROBINSON Wife of Richard Robinson, with whom she became the focal point of the New York scene throughout the '70s. Columnist to *Disc And Music Echo* and *NME* and editor of *Hit Parader*, she was appointed by Mick Jagger to run press liaison for The Rolling Stones' 1975 tour of the US. Also plugged into the CBGB scene, which she championed with *Rock Scene*. Subsequently became a syndicated columnist and broadcaster and is now music editor of *Vanity Fair*.

LILLIAN ROXON Australian-born rock critic who served as New York editor for *The Sydney Morning Herald* and published *Lillian Roxon's Encyclopedia Of Rock*. Died in 1973.

CHRIS SALEWICZ Contributor to *Let It Rock* who became part of the mid '70s *NME* Mafia. Became assistant director of punk documentary *DOA*, contributing editor at *Time Out* and contributor to *Q*, *The Sunday Times*, *The Face* and *The Sydney Morning Herald*. Founder member of MTV Europe. Books include *McCartney: The Definitive Biography* and (with Adrian Boot) *Midnights In Moscow*, *Bob Marley: Songs Of Freedom* and *Jimi Hendrix: The Ultimate Experience*.

"METAL" MIKE SAUNDERS Reviewed for many titles, including *Rolling Stone* from 1968-73. Formed Vom with rock critics Richard Meltzer and Gregg Turner. Also founder of The Angry Samoans. Regular contributor to *The Village Voice* since 1999.

JON SAVAGE Plucked from the fanzine *London's Outrage* to write for *Sounds* in 1977, where he championed "new musick" and post-punk acts from Cabaret Voltaire to Devo. Regular contributor to *Melody Maker* in the late '70s and early '80s and then to *The Face*, *New Society* and *The Observer*. Author of *England's Dreaming: The Sex Pistols And Punk Rock* and co-editor, with Hanif Kureishi, of *The Faber Book Of Pop: Collected Writings In*

Time Travel.

GREG SHAW Record historian and collector who edited pioneering 'zine *Mojo Navigator* in San Francisco in the mid '60s before founding *Who Put The Bomp?* to detail accurately artist biographies and discographies. Contributed to a number of music press titles, advised on record company reissue programmes and also helped steer *Phonograph Record Magazine* before managing The Flamin' Groovies and forming Bomp Records.

PETE SILVERTON Freelance contributions to *Trouser Press* and friendship with Joe Strummer scored Silverton a place on *Sounds* in 1976. Covered the punk and new wave scenes for the paper before departing in 1979 for a career in national newspapers after an in-office altercation with Oi! band The Cockney Rejects, managed by fellow *Sounds* staffer Garry Bushell.

SYLVIE SIMMONS *Teen* magazine contributor who relocated to Los Angeles and became area correspondent for *Sounds* in the late 1970s. Coverage of the rise of big-hair metal resulted in regular work for such magazines as *Kerrang!* on her return to the UK, in the 1980s. Subsequently broadened her coverage to include an acclaimed biography of Serge Gainsbourg and regular contributions to *Mojo*.

ALAN SMITH *NME* staffer plucked by IPC management in sink-or-swim maneouevre in 1972. Oversaw recruitment of staff from underground press, including Nick Kent and Charles Shaar Murray, before handing over the reins after 18 months to deputy Nick Logan. Returned from Spanish sojourn to launch the ill-fated *National Rockstar* in the mid '70s.

PATTI SMITH While working in New York bookstore, she was a regular contributor of poems and reviews to several magazines, including *Creem*, for whom she wrote a memorable piece about The Rolling Stones in 1972. Went on to form The Patti Smith Group with fellow rock scribe Lenny Kaye.

MAT SNOW An acquaintance with Barney Hoskyns landed Snow regular reviewing and feature work at the *NME* in the early '80s. Associated with darkest post-punk sounds emitting from the likes of The Birthday Party.

Left the *NME* after a disagreement with editor Ian Pye to work at *Sounds*. Subsequently became editor of *Q*, *Mojo* and *Mondo* magazines.

NEIL SPENCER Started his career at *Beat Instrumental* before spending a brief spell as a school teacher. Freelanced at the *NME*, where he wrote about reggae and soul, before a staff job took him to the editorship of the newspaper in 1978. Left in 1985 to become assistant editor at *Arena* and founding editor of *Straight No Chaser*. Currently at *The Observer*, where, among other things, he writes the weekly astrology chart.

DANNY SUGERMAN Teenage associate of Jim Morrison and The Doors, publicist at Elektra Records and associate of Iggy Pop. Co-author of The Doors biography *No One Gets Out Of Here Alive* and *Wonderland Avenue*, a biographical and chilling account of growing up in LA in the '70s.

DEREK TAYLOR Started his journalistic career at *The Hoylake And West Kirby Advertiser* before a move to national newspapers brought him into contact with The Beatles. Became a leading publicist of West Coast bands in Los Angeles in the mid to late '60s and was one of the organisers of the Monterey Pop Festival. Moved back to the UK in the '70s to work with The Beatles and the Apple organisation, where he was instrumental in the creation of the *Anthology* box sets. Died in 1997.

JAMES TRUMAN Contributor to *Melody Maker*, New York correspondent to *The Face*, editor of *Details* and mover and shaker within Condé Nast US.

NICK TOSCHES Prominent chronicler of the forgotten byways of '50s and '60s rock and pop culture. Contributor to *Fusion* and *Creem* as one of the three Noise Boys, along with Lester Bangs and Richard Meltzer, as well as to *Vanity Fair*. Books include *Dino*, *Hellfire* and *Night Train: The Devil And Sonny Liston*, which is now being developed into a major movie. His own celebrity profile on biography.com includes the deathdate of 2022.

TONY TYLER *Beat Instrumental* editor and Emerson, Lake And Palmer publicist recruited by Nick Logan at the *NME*, where he became assistant editor. Responsible for much of the editorial style of the paper, he left in 1976 but returned to handle the appointments of Julie Burchill and Tony

Parsons and also the move from Kings Reach Tower.

JAAN UHELSKI Recruited by Barry Kramer to *Creem* while selling sodas at Detroit's Grande Ballroom, Uhelski started as "subscription kid" and became an editor, feature writer and confidant of Lester Bangs.

PENNY VALENTINE One of the few female pop journalists of the '60s, she cut her teeth on teen titles before joining *Disc And Music Echo* in the late '60s. Then moved to *Sounds*, when it was launched, and later *Street Life* before working for Elton John and Dusty Springfield. Now a contributor to *The Guardian*.

STEVEN WARD Writer and music press expert. Author of several interviews with leading music critics (available on rockcritics.com).

MICHAEL WATTS Leading light of the *Melody Maker* staff of the early to mid '70s whose pieces include the celebrated cover story in which David Bowie declared his bisexuality. Later assistant editor and now senior editor at *The Financial Times*.

CHRIS WELCH Joined *Melody Maker* in 1973 as a reporter. Having established links with beta boom groups, he championed the Marquee acts who sprung up in its wake, particularly Led Zeppelin. He is linked to progressive rock artists including ELP and Genesis. Left *Melody Maker* in the early '80s to pursue a freelance career.

JANN WENNER Founder of *Rolling Stone* magazine and media magnate whose empire includes *Men's Journal* and *Us* magazine.

MARK WILLIAMS News editor of UK *Rolling Stone* and underground magazine mover and shaker. A candidate for successor to Nick Logan as *NME* editor, he launched *New Music News* when other inkies were hit by industrial action.

PAUL WILLIAMS Founder of *Crawdaddy!* magazine who went on to sing on 'Give Peace A Chance' and become an editor at *Rolling Stone*.

RICHARD WILLIAMS Cerebral features editor at *Melody Maker* in the early '70s. His skill in spotting the talents of then-unsigned Roxy Music scored him an

A&R job at Island Records. Returned as editor of *Melody Maker* in the late '70s before departure over the breaking industrial dispute. Worked at national newspapers, including *The Sunday Times*. Now prominent a sports writer at *The Guardian*.

CHARLES M YOUNG Known as "the Rev Charles M Young", started working for *Rolling Stone* covering the CBGB scene but went on to interview the likes of John Belushi before departing for *Musician*. Returned to *Rolling Stone* in the '80s to write features on such subjects as Noam Chomsky and Ralph Nader. Currently a contributor to sister magazine *Men's Journal*.

Index

THE LOOK
Adventures In Pop & Rock Fashion
Paul Gorman
Foreword by Malcolm McLaren

A refreshing new account of fashion and style and their relationship with the music scene over the last 50 years on both sides of the Atlantic.

Featuring interviews and unseen artwork from the designers who clothed Elvis, The Beatles, Bowie, Madonna, The Spice Girls, The Sex Pistols and many more, **The Look** tells how a post-War generation of music fans were no longer content to just buy their heroes' records – they wanted to dress like them as well. The results are captured in this stunning, lavishly illustrated coffee-table book.

1 86074 302 1 $30 | £20

THE STRANGLERS
Song By Song (1974-1990)
Hugh Cornwell with Jim Drury
Foreword by Paul Theroux

The Stranglers have outlasted and outsold virtually every other band of their era, recording ten hit albums and scoring 21 Top 40 singles. Their catalogue of hits – including 'Golden Brown', 'No More Heroes' and 'Always The Sun' – was written against a background of spectacular success, dismal failure, drug dependency, financial ruin, infighting and misfortune, with a story behind every song.

As a response to David Buckley's one-sided biography of The Stranglers (*No Mercy*, Hodder & Stoughton, 1997) and the band's reticence in revealing the true meaning behind their songs, Hugh Cornwell, founding member and songwriter, sets the record straight in **The Stranglers: Song By Song**, dispelling the myths and for the first time explaining the real stories behind the band, his departure and the origins of their songs.

1 86074 362 5 $18.95 | £12.99